Invisible Masters

Other books by George Weinberg:

Self Creation
The Action Approach
The Heart of Psychotherapy
The Taboo Scarf
Nearer to the Heart's Desire

Invisible

Compulsions and the Fear That Drives Them

Masters

George Weinberg

Grove Press

NEW YORK

Published simultaneously in Canada
Printed in the United States of America

Library of Congress Cataloging-in-Publication Data

Weinberg, George H.
    Invisible masters: compulsions and the fear that drives them / George Weinberg.
    ISBN 0-8021-1472-5
    1. Compulsive behavior.   I. Title.
  RC533.W443   1994   616.85′227—dc20   93-5047

First edition

Design by Laura Hough

Grove Press
841 Broadway
New York, NY 10003

FIRST PRINTING

I saw a man pursuing the horizon

Round and round they sped.

I was disturbed at this;

I accosted the man.

"It is futile," I said,

"You can never—"

"You lie," he cried,

And ran on.

—Stephen Crane

Contents

Preface

A sophisticated woman of very high
intelligence can't resist stealing
items from stores. She has shoplifted all her life, though after each theft she
despises herself and feels "less than human." To her horror she discovers
that her young daughter also steals. The daughter is not copying her
mother—at least not consciously; she has no way of knowing that her
mother has a long history of unpremeditated theft. Yet somehow the trait
has been passed along unconsciously.

A man, who had imagined his long marriage to be successful and
happy, finds himself in uncontrollable pursuit of a young woman for sex and
soon afterward he feels a desperate need to spy on her. He becomes
distraught when he can't spend hours in surveillance of her house; he needs
to know if she has another lover. It seems to him that he will go insane if
she does. He spends so much time spying on her that he jeopardizes his
family life, his job, and even his physical safety. But still he can't stop.

These people suffer from compulsions. We will soon be meeting them, among others.

People with compulsions live as if under the control of invisible masters. They must engage in their compulsive activities again and again in order to keep those masters at bay.

Nearly all of us know people with at least one of the widely shared compulsions—compulsive gamblers or drinkers or so-called workaholics. It's not simply that those people engage in these activities; they suffer from a feeling of necessity to engage in them. There are of course worldwide organizations for helping people cope with certain compulsions, Alcoholics Anonymous being the largest and best known. But for every widely shared compulsion there are hundreds of others, many idiosyncratic and carried out in private but very costly to the persons afflicted with them.

This book is about compulsions in general. It is a descriptive anatomy of what they are, how they evolve, and what a person can do to break the grip of a compulsion.

My stories about people with compulsions have, of course, been altered to protect the anonymity of my patients. Anything I thought might be identifiable—such as physical descriptions, places, times of occurrence, and of course the people's names—has been changed. However, I have been as true as I could to the compulsions themselves, describing them in detail as they were and presenting without alteration how they started and what we did to free the person of them. To the best of my ability I have been true to the outcomes of these cases.

I would like to thank Dianne Rowe for her careful reading of the manuscript at every stage and her many contributions, and also those who volunteered ideas along the way: My editor, Jim Moser, Drs. David Balderston, Jean Balderston, Henry Katz, Helen McDermott, Cindy Mermin, Louis Ormont, Joan Ormont, and Hank Schenker.

And special thanks to Olivia Katz for her insight and encouragement.

...1...

The Urgent Ritual

*E*very compulsion is an act of terror. It is an attempt to regulate something concrete and controllable because the person cannot identify and control some real psychological problem.

The victim of a compulsion is performing a symbolic ritual as a way of subduing ideas or feelings that seem too hideous to be accepted. Although he or she seemingly is engaging only in some simple and circumscribed activity, such as filling in the *o*'s and *e*'s in a newspaper before going to sleep or washing his hands over and over again, the victim is actually combating unseen inner forces. The compulsive is stilling fear, symbolically removing something that is experienced as a dire threat.

By performing a compulsive activity, the person is in effect singing a lullaby to himself, as if to say, "There is no danger. I have removed it. This act [of filling in letters or washing my hands] will protect me and put me at ease."

In this respect, we now alive are as primitive as our ancestors. True, we believe in modern science and reap its benefits. But even the least superstitious of us engage in covert magic rituals to subdue irrational fears. We obey invisible masters.

The fear that prompts compulsive behaviors—and, to repeat, compulsions are always motivated by fear—is some broad, irrational unknown; it is a conflict within the psyche that is merely symbolized or represented by the particulars. For instance, a person compulsively arranges all the bills in his billfold so that the pictures are facing forward. The real fear is of being confused and incompetent, and the person has a long history of this dread. It is an unconscious dread, and the orderliness of the bills symbolizes to the person that there is nothing to fear, that he is quite sane and capable.

As another example, take the person who keeps looking at his bankbook to verify his holdings. He does this dozens of times in a day. He is elderly, and his real fear is that now that he is no longer capable of making money, he will lose all his friends and his self-respect.

Nearly always, compulsions regarding money have less to do with money itself than with unconscious doubts that the person harbors about his own competence.

Or consider the person who checks the gas jets many times an hour to be sure they really are turned off. He remembers having gone into the kitchen to verify this only minutes ago but fears that he or she has mistakenly turned them *on* during the last verification. The person's real fear is surely of something else entirely—it is a fear of acting on some unacknowledged impulse.

In the case of one woman I worked with, her real fear was of dying because she felt she deserved to die. She had always been self-sacrificial. She had recently married quite happily but felt that she didn't deserve her husband, or this joy, and had real though unconscious urges to expiate what seemed like a crime. In repeatedly making sure that the gas jets were off, she was countering her unconscious impulse to turn them on.

Guilt, the desire to atone, and the *impulse* to atone—all are unconscious. The compulsive is aware only of the need to engage in the compulsive activity, because unless he does, the result could be dire.

In the compulsive person vague, irrational fears come to the surface in concrete form. The process is akin to what occurs in dreams, where, for instance, guilt over wrongdoing, real or imagined, may take the form of being in an actual prison. Or the sense of being lost in a work project may turn, in a dream, into the scenario of being lost in a forest where trees block the view on all sides. The compulsive person, like the dreamer, tries to cope with the particulars but is really struggling to deal with something deep and psychological.

Although, strictly speaking, only about 2 percent of people would be diagnosed psychiatrically as suffering from "obsessive-compulsive disorder," estimates are that 80 percent of us have at some time been afflicted by compulsions. And even this seems to me an underestimate. I doubt that anyone goes for long without engaging in some compulsive activities, activities whose real purpose is to cope with an unknown fear by means of carrying out very specific routinized activities.

Freud, who wrote extensively about compulsions and made the study of them virtually the starting place for psychoanalysis, was fond of likening compulsive activities to primal religious rituals. The person is attempting to exert control over something in his life that feels utterly out of control. By the compulsive activity the person is doing something concrete, material, orderly in an effort to regulate what feels like chaos; he deludes himself with a sense of potency, much as our ancestors imagined that by their magic rituals they could control the climate or stock their rivers with fish.

Because the problem is deep-rooted, a person's engaging in any compulsive activity can bring at most momentary peace. The real underlying problem remains, and before long the person feels the need to engage in the compulsive behavior again. The compulsive activity is no more than a sop, a form of self-delusion.

On the other hand, simply refraining from the compulsive activity will not bring permanent peace. Even if someone heroically resists impulses— say, to binge on food or to gamble—that resistance is not enough to annihilate the underlying dread. And this is true even if the person holds out for a very long time. People who resist compulsions often report that their anxiety does not go away even after months or years.

Still, resistance does help to an extent and it is worthwhile. But so long as the problem remains, it subjects the person even years later to blistering assaults of impulse to resume the compulsive activity.

Only after an unblinking investigation of oneself and identification of the real underlying problem can a person become truly free of his compulsion.

Everyone knows how destructive certain compulsions can be. Some compulsions overwhelm the person's whole life. One man I worked with had so many stipulations and conditions for getting ready in the morning—such as beginning each dressing activity with a particular hand, picking up his clothes only from a certain side, performing every function, from turning on the coffee to buffing his shoes, in exactly the same order all the time—that he took many hours to dress.

His rituals kept increasing in number and complexity. Eventually he found himself having to go back countless times to redo each feature of the ritual. He would start again until he deemed the activity perfectly completed and could finally consider himself adequately cleaned and coiffed.

By the time he became aware of the problem, his toilette was taking him two hours and he was constantly being reprimanded for lateness at work. At the end of a year it was taking him twelve hours to get dressed, and obviously he had lost his job. Finally, the very idea of starting the rituals became so forbidding that he gave up cleaning and dressing entirely, and condemned himself to remaining housebound.

The mental and physical disintegration of billionaire Howard Hughes is well documented. Hughes began with a cleanliness compulsion, and his rituals multiplied until they became impossible to maintain. In the end, Hughes broke down entirely and died malnourished and in filth.

Great publicity has been given to certain widely shared compulsions. Their tragic destructiveness has been etched into our minds by essayists, playwrights, celebrities, and by the mass media in general. These sources have dramatized the course that such compulsions can take and have encouraged people at all stages of succumbing to these compulsions to seek help.

We've all heard stories of compulsive gamblers who plunged themselves into decades of debt, shredded their reputations, and forfeited the trust and companionship of their loved ones. We're also familiar with the tragedy of alcoholics who fare even worse than gamblers and in bigger numbers. Most people afflicted by these obviously harmful compulsions know at some level that their behavior is senseless and irrational. Some spend a lifetime kicking their activity by dint of horrible suffering and then returning to it as if the compulsive behavior were the one true comfort possible for them.

However, in an even larger category are those whose compulsions pass as successful endeavors in society. The workaholic who acquires capital but never "has time" for intimacy, which he wants but fears, was not even recognized as a compulsive until the term "workaholic" came into use about twenty years ago. We now have some understanding of what may motivate such a person beyond the simple desire to succeed. The person may dread what he wants most. Suffering from an incapacity to love or to accept love, he settles for a big bank account or business success.

Most people with compulsions treat them as a private matter and manage to conceal them for many years or for good. Perhaps only a lover knows, or the family, that they have the insistent need to engage in certain rituals that delay their lives and limit their freedom. Or perhaps no one else knows, and even they themselves cling to some rationale that seems to explain what they do.

Meanwhile, their compulsions elaborate, becoming huge embarrassments and requiring the sufferer to take increasingly radical measures to rationalize them and conceal them.

Any emergency or special time pressure becomes a particular form of hell for a compulsive. The person simply cannot dispense with his particular ritual, and if he has to when under duress he experiences great discomfort.

Most compulsions are private rituals, and people characteristically keep them that way. It takes a rare event to bring the compulsion into public view, and such events may cause havoc in their life.

Guy de Maupassant, in his story "The Piece of String," describes Maître Hauchecorne, a thrifty Norman farmer with a compulsion to pick up anything he sees that might conceivably be useful. So driven is Hauchecorne to do this that he bends down for stray worthless items despite severe rheumatism. (One can only conjecture what Hauchecorne truly feared losing or being deprived of.)

On one particular day, when Hauchecorne snatches a useless strip of thin cord from the ground and pockets it, another farmer coincidentally loses a wallet bulging with francs. As bad luck would have it, several people have seen Hauchecorne surreptitiously pick something up. Word reaches the mayor, who accuses Hauchecorne of keeping the money. People don't believe his denials, even after the wallet is found in the fields the next day. The townsfolk assume that Hauchecorne returned it merely to escape stigma.

For the rest of his days, Hauchecorne pleads his innocence, but many continue to doubt it. The poor man dies repeating over and over again, "A bit of string . . . a little bit of string . . . look, Mayor, here it is."

And sometimes an "indispensable" ritual itself results in an injury that could not have been anticipated. A baseball player on the old New York Giants had the compulsion never to allow a baseball cap to touch a bed or something tragic would happen. When a teammate threw his cap down, the player lunged to rescue it, broke his shoulder, and missed playing in the World Series.

Apart from whatever impact a compulsion might have on a person's intimates or on society at large, all compulsions have certain deeply personal inner costs that vary only with the magnitude of the compulsion. Every compulsion, from the least to the most pervasive, represents a form of servitude. Were a stranger to demand of us that we repeat some action by rote not once but over months or years, we would doubtless rebel. But in the case of a compulsion, the demand comes from within, and any refusal to comply only heightens the sufferer's sense of dividedness. Refusing to do the thing brings instant anxiety, which even a hundred refusals do not eradicate. The enemy is within. The costs of every compulsion include a loss of freedom and the degraded feeling that goes with it.

Challenge even the smallest compulsion and there is a sense of indecision, a feeling of helplessness. Hesitate even a moment and there is predictable self-doubt. On the other hand, giving in to the compulsion is a kind of enslavement. Even compulsions that no one else becomes aware of separate the person from others. To some extent they interfere with intimacy and creativity and they puncture tranquillity. Instead of pursuing discovery and expansion, the person with a compulsion is forced to do the same thing thousands of times. His life is repeatedly interrupted by commands to act in some pointless and meaningless way.

A woman reports that she gave a dinner party that her guests greatly enjoyed. But twenty times during the evening she had to leave them to be sure that her phone receiver was properly resting on its cradle. For years she had harbored a powerful, unconscious desire to escape her highly demanding mother. Fear of her mother's wrath had always prevented her from doing the things she wanted to do. The better her life was at any time, the more she feared her mother's scathing criticisms, and in particular the jibe, "The only person you care about is yourself."

Recently she had experienced a particular surge of desperation to escape her mother. The desire was unconscious, but she felt prodded by it and sought to compensate for it by staying in close touch with her mother. Her impulse to remain available and not leave home psychologically was behind her compulsion about the telephone.

Being out of touch with her true motives—the dread caused by her mother's mixed influence on her—the woman had access only to the sense of her mother's not being able to reach her. As she continued to engage in her compulsive activity, she widened her concern by experiencing repeated thoughts that a critical call, perhaps even from someone other than her mother, would come and she would miss it.

The woman had suffered from her compulsion on occasion for years, but it had never been so demanding as during an evening when she felt that she was drawing closer to people than ever before. This night, for the first time since her divorce, she had assembled real friends in her home. It was as if a demon were saying to her, "So you want intimacy and happiness and seek it this way. Well, I will keep interrupting you with this thought of the telephone and make sure that you don't have it."

Compulsive urges come to many people during their happiest moments or at times when they are venturing something new. This is because the person's real fear is of being undeserving. The timing seems diabolical, almost calculated to induce a sense of hopelessness about changing. Disobeyed, the compulsion seems angry; obeyed it becomes punitive. Either way, the compulsion seems to take hold and mere resistance isn't enough.

This is how the experience of a compulsion differs from that of a mere habit. Habits may be broken by prolonged resistance of the urge. But with a compulsion, even prolonged resistance does not set the person free; the secret fear remains. A compulsion is a habit—and more. It is also a learned, automated behavior, but the special cover-up function of a compulsion differentiates it from an ordinary habit.

An addiction is a particular kind of compulsion—one that entails reliance on a substance, such as a narcotic or pills or even cigarettes. The addict adapts to the substance physiologically, with the result that stronger doses usually become needed over time. Refraining from an addiction brings not only psychological desire to resume but a bodily craving for the substance itself.

Every addiction, just like an ordinary compulsion, starts with an underlying dread. The choice to drink or resort to drugs has usually been a form of flight from some psychological problem. People in emotional pain are much more prone to turn to hard drugs than those who aren't. And even where flight was not an original motive, the person who toys with drugs and gets hooked soon suffers psychological problems and continues partly to escape them.

An addict turns to his or her particular substance, which might be drugs or sleeping pills or alcohol, just as any other compulsive turns to his own special ritualized activity. An addict might take heavy doses of pills each night in order to sleep. An ordinary compulsive might instead line up the items on his night table for hours for the same purpose: to go to sleep. The added factor in the case of the addict is the physiological dependence on what the person imbibes.

★   ★   ★

Many compulsives also report having *obsessions*—fixed ideas that repeatedly assault the person's mind. These haunting obsessions seem impossible to shake off. A man is obsessed that his wife will fall out of love with him and will leave him imminently. He compulsively refuses to look at movies or books in which divorces are central. His is a form of sympathetic magic, which says, "If I read about divorced people or hear about them, I will end up divorced." Finally, as his compulsion grows, he crosses out the word "divorce" in reading material whenever he comes across it.

Another man, who unconsciously despises his teenage sons for their youth and potential, becomes obsessed with thoughts of how he might accidentally kill them. He has visual images of them getting cut by knives or falling out of the window. Whenever these thoughts come, the man recites a bland little poem to himself, the same five lines over and over again.

Reciting the poem takes on a life of its own after a while, and he recites it repeatedly during the day whenever he feels tense about anything. The ritual relieves him but only briefly. The poem was something he recited to his sons years ago, when they were still very young and he hadn't conceived of resenting them yet. Reciting it is an incantation to make them young and nonthreatening.

Some obsessions appear so sensible that the sufferer feels delinquent not paying attention to them. The mind offers up the false logic that the cost of doing the thing, even if it was just done, is trivial, whereas the downside of not doing it may be quite serious, possibly disastrous. And so the compulsive engages in the ritual, just to be on the safe side.

"You left your door open. Turn the car around, go back home and lock it, or someone will come in and ransack your house."

"Open that envelope and look inside. You forgot to sign the check. Your insurance will be canceled."

The sufferer may have gone back to his door and bolted it minutes ago, and perhaps has carried out the ritual two or three times this morning already. But being late for work seems far less hazardous than having his house broken into and wrecked.

As for the person who keeps prying open the envelope he has already sealed, the downside of having his insurance canceled because of a missed payment outweighs any harm that one more repetition might incur.

But it is the nature of compulsions that the memory plays tricks. The person questions whether he really did the thing: "How can I be sure I checked the door that last time? Now it seems to me that I may have unlocked it by mistake."

Obsessive thoughts can become so terrifyingly vivid that they eclipse not only memory but all other considerations. One writer on the subject described a physician who called his laboratory fifteen times in an afternoon because he obsessively imagined that he had misheard the report of a patient's white cell count. Conceivably, doubts about his own competence might have expressed themselves in this physician's need to keep reassuring himself. Or perhaps it was an unacknowledged hostile wish or resentment.

It is impossible to know, but almost surely there was more to the case than the physician's natural concern over his patient's health. And one can bet that the physician was obsessional and compulsive not just in this instance but in many others as well, since such an underlying conflict would manifest itself repeatedly.

Obsessional thoughts can appear to explain why a person engages in the compulsive behavior, as if they furnish the motive. But not all compulsives are obsessive too, and obsessions, even when present, do not truly cause compulsive behavior. The deeper psychic conflict that urges the compulsive behavior also commands the obsession. Obsessional thoughts merely belong to the urge, which is generated from deep inside. They are excuses for the impulse to engage in the compulsive behavior, mental correlates of the urge. The person would feel the same compulsive urge without any thoughts at all.

For instance, Lady Macbeth's obsession that her hands were bloody, and her washing them repeatedly, were both products of her guilt over murdering the king. Her preoccupation with the imagined blood on her hands was not why she wanted to wash them, but rather it was the language of her guilt. Obsessions are the conscious verbal descriptions of the compulsive urge and tell us no more about causation than the urge itself. Obsessions are never the true motives for compulsive behavior.

Not surprisingly, people with compulsions are often also quite depressed. In many cases the depression came first. The person sought refuge from it in some way—through gambling or working around the clock—and in the process became compulsive.

But even if they weren't especially depressed to start with, once a compulsion becomes full-blown it leads to depression. What could be worse than feeling helpless to quit some activity! Having resolved to stop doing anything evidently pointless and repetitious, only to discover that one can't stop, this is ample reason to be depressed.

Finally, people who become compulsive often expect too much of themselves, and the inability to meet those standards (no compulsive person is ever truly satisfied with his or her own performance) can itself lead to depression.

For the same reasons, anxiety is also a frequent concomitant of compulsions. To the compulsive it seems impossible to banish whatever is feared unconsciously, to find lasting solace or safety.

Because depression is so often a contributing factor, many people in very severe compulsive states have been helped greatly by antidepressant drugs. In some very acute cases, it is believed that the brain lacks the ability to utilize the naturally occurring chemical serotonin. Medications, especially clomipramine, given in conjunction with ongoing psychotherapy, have produced radical improvements.

Of course, medications are only for acute sufferers and not for the vast majority of us who get caught in compulsive patterns. No one would insist that a shortage of serotonin would be the problem for most of the people mentioned so far in this book—at least not without knowing considerably more about them. And even where there is a physical breakdown, the cause may be psychological. As one expert on compulsions put it:

Since the brain is both a biological organ and the recipient of sensory and psychological inputs, it is only to be expected that strictly psychological causes can have biological effects.[1]

A number of treatment methods for compulsives that ignore the underlying unconscious dread at the heart of the problem have been tried and discarded. For years, psychosurgery was done on acute sufferers. Such surgery had no rationale, except that it stifled the sufferer, whose incessant musings and repetitive behavior got on everyone's nerves. Psychosurgery killed some of its victims and induced lifelong epileptic seizures in many more before it was discontinued as inhumane and pointless. Its replacement by medications represents major progress for the few.

Another whole class of treatment, which also takes no stock of the compulsive's underlying dread and does not differentiate a compulsion from a habit, is categorized as behaviorist methods.

A popular behaviorist method is to punish the compulsive behavior by administering electrical shocks when the person engages in it. A second is to literally prevent the person from engaging in the behavior. A third, called "flooding," treats compulsions to overeat or to smoke by forcing the person to overdose ad nauseam, while in yet a fourth treatment behaviorists expose the patient to gradually increasing stimuli for the activity to help the person develop immunity to the compulsive urge. New behavioral methods are constantly being put forth, and by the time you read this there will doubtless be brand-new ones.

The shortcoming is that behaviorists seem to equalize all activities, as if none sprang from deeper personal roots than others. To consider the naïveté of their work not only helps highlight what compulsions really are but reminds us once more of the almost bottomless human complexity that may be manifested in small acts.

The complexity of the psyche is especially manifest in compulsions, and this means that it takes some subtlety to deal with them—on the part of a therapist or of a person fighting a compulsion alone. Becoming com-

[1]Judith Rapoport, *Scientific American,* March 1989, p. 87.

pulsive is itself an intricate process. In fact, when the intricacy of the compulsive condition was recognized in the nineteenth century, it was thought that compulsives were superior people who had degenerated. A term for such people was *dégénerés supérieurs*. However, as we now know, even the least intelligent people may have highly complex motivations. Nor should this be surprising when we realize that the relative simplicity of the conscious self is accomplished by billions of working parts.

The compulsive person is acting in a meaningful and consistent way, coping with an underlying psychic fear by doing something highly specific and circumscribed that symbolizes a solution. The person is engaging in a ritual to handle the chaos within, and our method must be to decode the ritual and bring to the surface the conflict that gives rise to it.

Such is what the psychoanalyst Carl Jung called "the antiseptic power of consciousness" that even before the psychic problem is resolved, the person's discovery of it deprives the compulsion of at least part of its function, which is concealment, and thus weakens the grip of the compulsion.

Though people often rationalize their own compulsions, trying to make them seem defensible or even logical, the serious sufferer nearly always comes to see his or her own behavior as grotesque. Second only to the person's worry about the compulsion is the worry over its being found out by others. In terror, the person may take extended precautions to conceal his secret, avoiding a wide range of situations in which it might rear up and cause him to be branded as a laughingstock. The poor sufferer is in the position of hiding a compulsion, which is itself a complex way of subduing and concealing a psychic problem.

In the case that I am going to present in the next chapter the person took such precautions. In this case may be seen the classic elements of compulsions that I've mentioned. The rigid and implacable quality of the compulsion made it absolutely bewildering to this man, who was otherwise methodical and highly rational. His compulsion looked as mortifying to him as it would to others and he knew how it would be regarded.

Certainly the setting and the single event that gave rise to this compulsion were in some respects chance occurrences. But we may conjecture that the man's underlying problem would have surfaced before long anyhow, and only the symbolic solution he found, the compulsive activity, would have differed. The conditions were set.

The case illustrates how with compulsions, the person's unconscious, forbidden wishes have given rise to a fear. There has been an attempt to cope with that unconscious fear without facing it squarely. The person has arrived at a symbolic solution, his attempt to squelch the fear by the artificial act that becomes compulsive. The person's fierce but hopeless attempt to subdue that fear becomes a compulsive activity.

Therapy, as always with compulsive patients, proceeds in part like a detective's investigation. The difference is that the aim of therapy is to untangle a web of *self-deceit;* the deceit of others has played at most a very secondary function. My method was to study the compulsion by examining both its external circumstances and the internal processes that gave rise to it. My purpose was to decipher the compulsion, to see how it served the person and what unconscious conflict it ministered to.

There is some releasing power in the person's simply understanding what the compulsion means. The rational mind refuses to accept the kinds of illogicality that the unconscious has long been utterly comfortable with. But, of course, the person's own willpower must also play a part.

Observe in this upcoming case the person's perfectionism, a usual component of compulsive behaviors. It is this perfectionism that makes the unconscious wish or fear so deadly that the person will do nearly anything not to have to deal with it. Here the person's ritualistic removal of self-doubt became unmistakable. This case illustrates how the compulsion looks from the outside and how it feels, as therapy progresses through layers of repression to the real conflict.

...2...

The Boarding School

"How all occasions do inform against me."

—Hamlet

Near the quietly busy town of Gloucester, Vermont, is the Gloucester Prep School for Boys, situated on a large parcel of land, with a panoramic view of the countryside. On its manicured campus are three buildings of Flemish bond and a fieldstone house that became a library in 1953. There is also a theater building, a learning center (which receives constant infusions of the latest audiovisual and computer materials), and a chapel attended regularly by most of the 280 boys. The two dormitory buildings overlook the lawn, beyond which lie the tennis courts and other playing fields.

Proud of its emphasis on the arts, the Gloucester School comports itself as if insulated, like Dostoevsky's Palace of Crystal, against the harshness of the outside world. It is truly a world unto itself, and the boys' parents, 10 percent of whom attended the Gloucester School themselves, pay dearly to ensconce their sons in this world, or rather to insulate them from the outside world as long as possible. The ratio of faculty to students has always hovered around one to seven, and Gloucester even boasts of a gourmet cooking club.

For their tuition fees and generous gifts, the families of the students want only that the school remain a small, attentive, extended family and that it maintain its standards of academic excellence and a kind of unspoken cleanliness. They wish no more for their sons than that they go on to an Ivy League college, that they get the right job, that they prosper and marry well.

Though 30-odd percent of these parents are themselves divorced, this presents no contradiction. They choose the Gloucester School for its very insulation from the stresses that they imagine have beset them and resulted in their own later mistakes. When the school opted for a sex education course, it was partly to teach safety from physical disease, but also to immunize the young scions against falling in love with the wrong woman.

Every June, when the landscape glimmers and the roads are edged with wildflowers, the parents come to remove their children for the summer. Not long after the boys come back for the fall semester, it turns bitter cold in northern Vermont, the winds howl and the days darken. Good fellowship and serious study become a way of life with little alternative—at least that is what the parents envision occurring in the Gloucester citadel of learning.

Somehow, however, even in this tightly lidded container of democratic youth, there occur yearly without fail examples of the worst worldly values. Certain of the younger, smaller boys get beaten up or are forced to run the gauntlet of having their clothes hidden, or their schoolbooks or even a computer disappear under their noses. True, the bigger crimes, which would amount to larceny in the real world, are usually only temporary—items of value return mysteriously. But word spreads through the school community of how the victim took his loss. Did he whimper or make false accusations, or go to one of the masters for justice? If so, new indignities are surely in the offing for him.

One can only speculate as to how such cynicism manages to insinuate itself into such a sealed-off environment. Can it be that certain traits of villainy are inborn and reach maturation at a particular time even in a vacuum? That would be the so-called "spontaneous generation of evil" theory. It would mean that the dream of a hermetically sealed container of virtue is just that—only a dream—and every block of human beings is more or less a miniature of the wide world, with all its foibles and its evils, as well as its virtues. If this is true, no one has actually failed, certainly not the Gloucester School.

In any event, on an early November day in 1983, the postulate that "boys will be boys" found close to its supreme expression. Two days of constant snow had already buried the landscape, leveling the terrace with the lawn, and a new storm was spending its fury over Vermont.

Over the previous three weeks a handful of second-year students had been making life hell for little Robert Finch, a newcomer to the school and barely thirteen years old. The clique, led by fifteen-year-old Glen Lindstrom, tall and lean, with black hair slicked back, and Josh, "the Bull," had locked little Bobbie in a closet, threatened him with bodily mayhem, and would have inflicted it had he not eluded several traps they set for him. Bobbie, tall though not yet at puberty, was almost grotesquely angular and yet full of a strange grace that troubled them.

Only a few days before the snowstorm, when another newcomer sent to collar him and bring him to the gang had asked Bobbie if he was "Bobbie Finch," the boy had lied outright and then disappeared from view. On that and other occasions Bobbie had stowed himself in the apartment of the master on duty for the evening. Masters were on call two nights a week, which meant that they ate with the kids on those nights, and their apartments remained open to any boy who cared to visit them and talk, for whatever reason.

Bobbie's biweekly visits were to a reserved man in his thirties, whom the boys respected for his objectivity and feared for his subject matter, which was mathematics. The teacher, Jonathan, showed a special liking for Bobbie and seemed particularly available to him. Bobbie was very good at mechanics, and would often discuss with Jonathan plans for some new invention. If Bobbie had ever complained to him about the boys' tyranny there was no sign. Jonathan's wainscoted apartment on the second floor of the dormitory building was a sanctuary that the ill-intentioned boys could not penetrate.

The pranksters wondered what Jonathan and Bobbie spoke about.

Perhaps they were even aware of a curious physical resemblance between the youth and the teacher. Jonathan resembled a young Henry Fonda, elongated not by Modigliani but by Procrustes, who made him jug-eared as well as too tall.

By the third day of snow, when the violent storm was brewing, the natural restlessness of the boys was high. Doubtless it had been roiled further by Bobbie's evasion of them with his audacious lie. Thus it was that at seven-thirty in the evening, after the boys had already changed out of the jackets and ties worn to dinner into T-shirts and jeans, they took their revenge.

Jonathan had just returned from the dining hall when he heard a terrible clamor in the yard below his apartment. At first he thought it was a school cheer, but the cacophony of it was almost eerie, and after a few moments he rushed to his window. Looking down into the yard, he saw that the kids had pushed little Bobbie outside, naked. There he was in eddies of snow, banging on the school's oak door, sobbing and freezing. To Jonathan the boy must have looked heartbreakingly fragile, with nothing on except for his silver medallion, his hands clutching his crotch as he begged them to let him go back inside.

In an instant, the lanky Jonathan, still in his blue cloth overcoat, had descended the staircase and was with Bobbie in the yard. Piles of garbage lay uncollected in drifts of dappled gray snow. The boy was fighting tears but had stopped banging on the door. Jonathan bundled him in the overcoat, which reached the boy's ankles, and tugged him inside, but the boy must have been in shock and hardly moved.

As Jonathan carried Bobbie toward the door, he could see a half-dozen faces behind the window above. The conspirators were there, looking out and chortling with glee, with obscene delight. He was aware of Glen Lindstrom and Josh "the Bull," his crooked teeth showing, and a few other boys, sporting incipient mustaches. Then, in an instant, they all disappeared.

Jonathan deposited Bobbie in a stuffy, carpeted room on the first floor, heavy with carved-oak furniture—the recreation-library room. He sat with Bobbie for a few minutes and waited with him while the boy collected himself. Then they walked up to the infirmary through a building as silent as if it had been vacant for a century. Jonathan filled a warm tub and told Bobbie to get in, which he did, speechlessly. He was careful not to make the tub too hot, since that would be dangerous.

He rubbed the boy's back and marveled that Bobbie was not crying; he was quite intrepid. He wondered what Bobbie was thinking but waited patiently in silence. "Are you feeling okay?" he asked the boy several times, for want of anything more precise. "Fine," the boy answered. "Come into my room if you want to," Jonathan said.

The boy didn't respond, and remained alone that evening. Nor did anyone trouble Bobbie again, not even the authorities for his account of what had happened; they had enough other witnesses. The ringleaders of the incident were suspended, and soon afterward Glen Lindstrom transferred to another school. Rumor had it that it was his third prep school.

Josh "the Bull," who apologized personally and also in a dictated note, was allowed to stay on. The note specified, "I will be a big brother to you from now on." Not that Bobbie wanted him in that capacity, but it was deemed that undirected by anyone else's nefarious brain, Josh would be harmless and deserved a second chance.

There was no further harassment of Bobbie. The boys, all chastened and fearful, took pains to be kind to him. But he had withdrawn sharply. That he never thanked Jonathan was no surprise; gratitude is hardly a teenage trait. But as part of his subsequent reserve, he never again knocked on any master's door, or sought Jonathan for companionship or to discuss an idea or one of his mechanical inventions.

It was late in January. The young man sitting in front of me in my office was tall and gangly, with dark hair. His face was narrow and rather pale and, but for his wide ears, he had a handsome, aristocratic look. When he told me that he was a schoolteacher, I immediately thought of Washington Irving's description of Ichabod Crane.

He wasted no time getting to the point. "I'm becoming incredibly anxious; I have nightmares. I have this feeling that something terrible is going to happen to me."

"Do you know what it is?"

"No, that's what's so strange. I can't say exactly, but it's driving me crazy, and it's getting worse . . . as if there's some terrible outcome . . . a disease. I've been afraid to have a medical test, because I'm afraid that I have some fatal disease that will suddenly show symptoms and then kill me.

"It's getting sharper and sharper in my mind. I don't know what I'm afraid of, but it's driving me crazy. I used to put this out of my mind, but now these attacks come and I can't bear them. When they come, I can't stop shaking."

"You've had nightmares?" I asked him, hoping to get a lead.

"Yes. Terrible ones. But I can never remember them."

"When did all this start?" I asked him.

"Start? I can't really tell you that exactly either. I think I've been nervous ever since I came to this school, but nothing like this."

He said that before taking his present teaching position, he had taught in a public school for four years, in Boston. But that proved a great disappointment—there was too much pushing and jostling and inattention, too much record keeping. The job was more custodial than anything else; he really couldn't teach the wonders of mathematics to more than a few of his many students.

"You really do love the subject, don't you?" I said.

"Yes. There is a great beauty to it, and I want to give that to the kids. The important thing isn't exactly how much they learn, but whether they want to learn more."

He quoted a line from a poem by Edna St. Vincent Millay: "Euclid alone has looked on beauty bare."

I commented that I wished I'd had more teachers who felt that way. "And where are you teaching now?" I asked him.

"I'm at the Gloucester School. You probably never heard of it, it's in Vermont," he said.

"No, I haven't."

"I've been there for almost two years. I got the job in mid year, when the teacher, a woman, left to go across the country with her husband. Two years ago February."

"Is the school what you thought it would be?" I asked him.

"Well, yes. Small classes. It's a boarding school for boys only. The teachers are mostly very caring, except for maybe one or two. Our campus is a whole community, though we do take the kids on trips, to plays, concerts, the opera—that's how I got your name."

"What do you mean?"

"We were in New York City, and a friend of mine, Anne Brody—I guess she was a patient of yours, she didn't say—anyhow, she mentioned you. That was two months ago, and I thought these terrible anxiety attacks would pass. But they're getting worse. I sometimes feel that I'm splitting apart."

He had waited till his semester break, and then had come all the way back to New York City to see me.

"What did you mean about the medical tests, that maybe it's something physical?" I asked. "Why do you think that?"

"Well, that was the first thing that occurred to me. I have no reason to feel this way. I have a good job. I'm the advisor to six kids who are really nice. The headmaster seems to like me—at least I thought he did. He lets me teach the way I want—"

"What do you mean 'thought he did'?"

"Well, once or twice I had to stay in my room because I was too anxious to go downstairs."

"You missed classes?"

"No. Never. I'm okay when I teach. But I've already had to miss a faculty meeting. I told Mr. Phelps later that I wasn't feeling well. He said, 'Fine,' and then later on he asked me how I was feeling. But I wondered if he was really disappointed in me. I didn't like shirking a responsibility like that."

"You've missed other meetings?" I asked him.

"That's the only one I missed in almost two years," he said proudly.

It crossed my mind that he was pretty fierce on himself, and a perfectionist. It certainly seemed unlikely that the headmaster would alter his opinion because of one missed meeting. And then I became concerned about Jonathan's hypothesis that his anxiety might have a physical basis. The very fact that such an idea had come to him was significant. I would need to have him follow it up, go for a medical checkup, no matter how scary the prospect felt to him. People with physical problems often do receive subsensible cues, indications of trouble that they can't pinpoint. The story is well known in our profession of how George Gershwin died of a brain tumor while going to a prominent psychiatrist who hadn't bothered to check out his symptoms because he was so sure that they were psychosomatic.

But though I knew I would have to ask Jonathan to go for a physical, I didn't want to do it just then. I didn't yet have his confidence and he could too easily reject both the exam and me. Besides, the overwhelming probability was that it was psychological.

Then, almost as if he knew what I had been thinking, he returned to the topic. "At first I thought these terrible attacks were physical. But I don't really think so. It feels as if I sort of *knew* this trouble was coming . . . that it's something I've been expecting for years."

"What is that?"

"I don't know. 'The end.' " He puts his hands in the air, as if framing the quotes around that expression. He smiled wanly. "Maybe that I would be destroyed. No, that's not really it. But that's part of it. That I would *destroy myself.*"

"Destroy yourself? How? For what?"

"I don't know. But I feel there's something destructive inside of me."

"Do you mean self-destructive?" I asked him.

"I told you, I don't know," he said to me sharply, for the first time losing his composure. But as quickly he caught himself. "I'm sorry," he said. "I didn't mean to snap at you. It's like there's a demon loose in the world. Sometimes I feel as if I'm going crazy, do you know what I mean?"

I could say only that I realized how horrible his experience must be.

I thought of asking if it was a demon loose in the world or a demon loose inside of him. But I decided that the question might be too threatening, so I let it go. It was enough that I made the translation for myself.

In the latter half of the session, Jonathan told me a little about his childhood. He and his older brother, James, had been brought up by his mother; their father had walked out when Jonathan was about nine. James was now making big money in the stock market in New York City; Jonathan was staying with him on this trip, which was during the semester break of the Gloucester School.

Because he had only a week in New York City and would have to take long trips to see me on weekends once classes resumed, we decided to set up four sessions in that one week.

I began the next day by asking him if he'd had any thoughts about what we had discussed in our first meeting, or about me.

"Well, there is something," he said.

I waited for him to tell me what it was, but he stopped sharply. Either he had decided that it would discredit him or he didn't trust me enough. In any event, he said no more about it then.

In spite of my curiosity, I decided not to pursue my question. I hoped that when he trusted himself, or me, more he would tell me.

Somehow, we got onto the subject of the Gloucester School and the emphasis on the student's attendance at chapel. Jonathan told me that when he was young, his mother would take him and his brother to church regularly. At eight he was playing the piano "not all that well," but he had learned to read music and dreamed of becoming a composer "like Bach, and have my music heard every week in churches all over the world, especially at Christmas time."

"Christmas was important to you?" I said.

"It always was. For years I kept thinking Daddy might come back at Christmas time. That would be the big present. But he never did."

In junior high Jonathan emerged as the math prodigy of the school. He loved hard problems, not just for the recognition he won, but for the pleasure of doing them. Math never let him down. "It has a kind of precision and perfection that nothing else can match," he said. "The answers are invariant; they don't change from day to day."

The way people, especially your father, did, I thought but didn't say.

He had blazed his way into Dartmouth as a math major with a full scholarship. But he couldn't envision a whole life of sitting alone at a desk and solving problems; that life loomed as too lonely. And so he switched to education as a major, got a master's degree easily, and became a high school teacher.

Both he and James began giving money to their mother for her support. James, who was also excellent at math, had come to New York

City, married, had two children, and was now giving their mother most of that support "because my job doesn't pay all that well."

"I guess you really like what you do, though," I said.

"I love teaching kids. It's what I've always wanted to do, I guess, though I didn't know it years ago."

Looking at him, I got the impression that he himself was a kid, and not the thirty-two he said he was. His face was curiously untouched, as if life had not yet engraved it with appropriate lines.

He said that James offered him well-paying opportunities with his own firm, and assured him that he could become a top-notch securities analyst. "But it's not what I want to do. Problems with dollar signs in front of them aren't necessarily that interesting." And so he had turned down his brother's repeated offers with no regret.

"But when I saw the difficulties of teaching math, of *really* teaching math, in the public school where I was, I knew this wasn't what I wanted either. I began to dream of teaching at a place like the Gloucester School. I applied for a couple of years, but couldn't get such a job. But finally I did. The Gloucester School offered me an apartment, food, and more than enough money."

"Do you live at the school?"

"I didn't until Julia and I broke up."

"When was that?" I had wanted to ask about his romantic life and was pleased that he had bridged the way to it.

"This semester. We had an apartment in Taylor, Vermont—that's a farm town halfway between Gloucester and the school. She's a real estate agent in that area."

"How long were you two together?"

"Two years."

They had been very attached to each other initially, but according to Jonathan they had quarreled a lot about "values."

"She thought I had no ambition. I told her that teaching *was* my ambition, it's very fulfilling—you know, Doctor, fifty years ago our whole society respected teachers in a way that they don't anymore—"

"You don't have to convince me," I said. "Anyhow, it was what you wanted to do, and it still is," I said, half asking.

His face changed, and I had the impression that he suddenly looked serious. I asked him why.

"I'm thinking that I do what I want. I have the perfect job, and yet I'm in such bad shape. It doesn't make any sense."

"Do you miss Julia?"

"I do. Sometimes a lot. But that's over. She's going with a real estate guy. He can buy and sell me." He uttered this last sentence with both irony and wistfulness.

"I see what you mean by 'values,' " I said. "Did you enjoy sex with her?"

"It was great at first," he said. "Then that went too. The last six months we weren't having sex. I think she was already having an affair with someone. I used to call from the school late at night, when I was on duty, and she wasn't there. Once I called at two in the morning."

"Do you sometimes want to be back with her?" I asked.

"Never. Best of luck to her," he said.

"Are you going with anyone else?"

"No. I moved into the school full-time in October. No women for a while; I'm not up to it. Too many complications."

Before the hour was up I invited him, if not to divulge his "secret," at least to talk about it.

"This 'something else' you mentioned. Could it possibly give us a clue as to what you're worried about—I mean these terrible anxiety—"

"Oh no. Absolutely not," he said at once.

But then he fell silent and, obviously, he was mulling over his "secret," whatever it was.

Then he said mysteriously, "I'm afraid I'm a lot more disturbed than you imagine."

His demeanor was quite calm, even placid, when he said this. His very composure gave it a more ominous Jekyll and Hyde cast, I thought, than if he'd blurted out that self-appraisal in desperation.

I asked him, "By 'disturbed,' are you saying 'agitated and anxious,' or are you telling me that you think you're more mentally unbalanced than I might think?"

"Both," he said.

Right after he left I had a kind of revelation that felt almost uncanny. When Jonathan had called himself more disturbed than I suspected, he had meant it quite literally. His saying that there is "something else you should know" suddenly felt quite ominous. His own composure and my desire to diminish tension by putting him at ease had conspired to mask what I now took to be a frank declaration of insanity.

During his next visit I brought up that medical checkup early in the session so as to give us plenty of time to discuss it if he resisted. I reminded him of his concern that something was wrong with him physically.

"I don't think it's that. I'm not worried."

But he looked worried.

"Well, I'd feel better if you had a checkup. As you say, it's almost surely psychological, but I just want to clear out the possibility—"

"The possibility of what?"

"We don't know. Anxiety can come from a lot of sources. It could be a vitamin deficiency, or something else quickly correctable."

He agreed to see a physician, but then very quickly specified that it would have to be someone in New York City instead of up in Vermont. He also brought up the matter of scheduling subsequent visits to my office.

"I was thinking, I could come to see you on late Friday afternoons, and I guess I could see the doctor on a Friday, too."

I had wondered why he had opted to journey so far to see me rather than pick someone closer, and here he was doing it again with a physician.

"Why not someone up there?" I asked.

"I don't want to. I don't mind traveling." He spoke with a finality that verged on overkill.

At that moment he seemed almost disjointed. Sprawling on my couch, he looked especially thin and bony, and less a master of his arms and legs than he should have been.

"Oh," I said. "I was wondering because there surely are good physicians up in Vermont." His very adamancy had led me to push, just to see what might be behind it.

"I don't want one up there. I definitely don't want someone who knows me, or could know one of the people I work with."

"Okay." I backed off.

That was my first real sense of Jonathan's intense, almost fanatical, premium on secrecy. It made me all the more curious about whatever deep truth was gnawing at him. Obviously, even as we were in pursuit of it, he dreaded its emergence.

Jonathan struck me as more immature than I had originally thought. I think this was because he tended to manifest his conflict in a scattered physical appearance in a way that most adults learn not to.

He began the next session by talking about the Gloucester School and its headmaster, Mr. Phelps, who had given his all to it for his twenty-two years as headmaster. "Oh, he's a very decent guy, a dapper little man with a close-shaven, round head. He was born in Glasgow. The kids call him 'baldie' behind his back. He doesn't care, but if they said it to his face, he'd be very tough. He would say that they should learn discretion. But, of course, he hears them anyway, sometimes. He told us at a meeting once that if no one ever called him 'baldie,' he'd think something was wrong with them.

"Mr. Phelps can be tough when he wants to be, but he's always fair. His wife is nice, too. She teaches English."

"Uh huh." I had no idea where Jonathan was heading.

Nowhere, apparently, because he suddenly stopped and I could see he was coming to another subject.

"Look, Doctor," he began, "I'm going back there in a couple of days, and I'd hate myself if I didn't tell you. I've got to tell you."

"What's that?" I asked, as casually as I could, readying myself not to seem jarred, whatever it turned out to be.

"Well, it's very embarrassing, actually," he said. "I have a habit. Something I do every day. I used to do it in the evenings, but now I've moved it up to earlier in the day."

I could see him getting tense.

"I told you about these terrible anxiety attacks, the sense of doom that comes over me, that makes me shake so much I sometimes wish I was dead."

"Yes, you did. I guess they're the main reason you're here."

"Okay. Well, every day I go to the gym. Sometimes when the anxiety is unbelievable, I go there. But even if it isn't. I have to go there every day. I get a basketball and bring it to the foul line and look at the hoop. I get ready to shoot a shot. I say to myself, 'If this ball goes in, nothing terrible will happen to me. This shot will decide.' "

"Uh huh."

"No, you can't understand. How could you? I *have* to do it. I'm incredibly anxious when I shoot the shot. If the ball goes in, suddenly I feel better, all better. But if it doesn't, I feel like I'm going to pass out. If it doesn't go in at least once, I'm in hell."

"At least once?"

"Yes. I give myself two chances. Two shots. I have got to make one of them. That's the rule."

"I think I follow you—"

He seemed annoyed. "Maybe. But not really. You can't possibly understand the way I feel, how important it is, how urgent. If I miss, everything is ruined, my whole life. I might as well be dead.

"Doctor, I don't mean to yell. But what you can't follow is that I think about that shot *hours* beforehand. I worry about it. When I pick up the ball and aim it, I'm a nervous wreck. It's everything to me. Especially if I miss the first one.

"Listen to me, please. One day, about two weeks ago, the gym was locked. I couldn't get in. I couldn't make the test. The gym was locked, and I almost passed out, because I wouldn't know.

"I went to the janitor to get a key. Tommie knows I'm no athlete, so I said I left something there. Doctor, what you don't follow, what you can't *possibly* follow, is how important that verdict is every day.

"So, you see, I'm much sicker than you think. I guess you can understand why I didn't want to tell you. I know it's ridiculous. That is, intellectually, I know it's ridiculous, but in some other part of me, I just can't help it. You're talking to a *madman*."

I waited, trying to assuage him by my very nonreaction. Very likely, feeling the way he did about this compulsion, he anticipated a very acute, judgmental response from me.

Just then, the adage of Kinsey's researchers in those early days of interviewing in uncharted territory came to me: "Never lean forward and never lean back."

I asked Jonathan, "How long have you been doing this?"

"A few months."

"Can you remember when you started?"

"No. Only that if I don't do it, I feel like I'm going to die. In the beginning, when the ball went in, I thought, I actually thought I would stop. But now I feel safe only for a few hours, maybe a day. Now I know I can't stop.

"In the beginning, I used to give myself one shot. Everything on one shot. But then I decided that one shot wasn't fair. It wasn't a real test."

"Test of what?"

"Of whatever! I don't know." He looked puzzled.

"What about when you come to New York City?" I asked him.

"No. For some reason, I don't have any need when I'm not at the school. I don't get those attacks either. But just because I'm discussing the school now, I'm beginning to get nervous. It's terrifying just to tell you. I'm sweating even talking about it."

I could see that he was tense. I asked him if he'd played basketball much as a kid.

"Not at all. That's the strange thing. I thought about that. My brother played a lot with the older boys. I tried, but I could never get any good, so I quit." He smiled ironically. "Why, do I look like a basketball player to you?"

"Well, you're tall," I said.

But, admittedly, he looked far from being an athlete. His body was lean but soft, and he kept his hands almost unnaturally close to his sides, as if afraid to offend with them.

I asked him if he had any fantasies connected with taking those shots.

"No."

"Or memories?"

"No," he retorted, as if mildly annoyed. "Why do you ask that?"

"Just to understand it better," I said.

"Honestly, tell me. Have you ever seen anything like this before?" he asked me.

"It's a compulsion," I said. "Compulsions differ in the activity. One thing they have in common, though, is that they're very hard to stop. "They seem to have a life of their own."

I don't think he heard me. He said, as if freshly incredulous, "It's really ridiculous, isn't it, that I should be this way? I don't believe in magic of any kind whatsoever, and look at me. *Look* at me. Would you believe that I'm basically a rational person?"

"And you're a very bright person," I added. "But everyone—including you and me—we have what might be called pockets of irrationality. Obviously, you're doing this stands for something very important in your life . . ."

Again he seemed preoccupied, and this time I paused for a thought of my own. It was that nowhere do people seem more divided than when afflicted by a compulsion. A person can, figuratively, watch himself from the outside, even evaluate himself as off-the-mark, while doing the thing. Jonathan was like a man observing himself being caught in a tide. But the "tide" was inside of him.

"If you ask me, it's humorous," he said, shaking his head.

But it was hardly a comedy to him, or to me, despite the undeniably comic element, that this nonathletic man would every day shoot a foul shot on which his very life seemed to depend.

"A comedy? Not at all," I said. I quoted the eighteenth-century writer Horace Walpole's line: "The world is a comedy to those who think and a tragedy to those who feel."

He said that I was the first person he had ever told about this, and he begged me not to tell another soul.

Of course, I promised him I wouldn't.

He was fighting tears.

I did not recommend that he try to quit his compulsion. Failing outright could frighten him even more than he was now and leave him feeling even more helpless and demoralized.

However, I did ask him to try to remember any thoughts he might have while shooting at the basket or just afterward, whether the shot went in or not. He said that he would.

He immediately went back to talking about his classes at the Gloucester School. He loved the place, and I was glad for him to find refuge in this far less thorny subject matter.

Toward the end of the session he told me that he had devised an excuse for his trips to New York City to prevent the school administrators from finding out that he was coming to see a therapist. The school had recently asked Jonathan to help them put their data on computers and had offered to pay for special computer training for him. He had planned to wait until the summer, but now he'd decided instead to find such a course in New York and come here for classes on Fridays.

He said that he would call as soon as he could make this arrangement, and he was sure that he would be given permission.

He did call, on Wednesday, saying that he had found a Saturday computer course and could see me late Friday afternoons. We agreed on a time.

He arrived on the dot, with a fresh concern. "By the way, you didn't tell anyone about me, I mean what my problem is or that I was coming to see you?"

I assured him that I hadn't, and inquired why he had asked.

"I wouldn't want anyone up there to think that there's anything wrong with me. I know you professionals talk among each other, about patients and about their problems. I just thought you might have said something."

"What made you think so?"

"Well, they were so quick to give me the time for that computer course. They weren't even surprised. I thought that maybe they knew that since I was making this long trip to New York, it would be for therapy, to see you."

"Did you mention therapy to them?" I asked him.

"Not at all. But it's really such an expensive round-trip every weekend. Who can make that? My brother's paying for it, and I'm staying with him. Of course, I told Jimmie."

"What did you tell him?"

"Oh, nothing about basketball shooting, but about how anxious I get and how concerned I am. I told him I was seeing you, that you were good, and how important this is, and he said he would be glad to pay."

He'd had several blitzing attacks of anxiety during the week, one after he'd missed both shots. The other came when a boy had visited him unexpectedly at his apartment on campus, to talk. That had been in the afternoon, and Jonathan had worried that he would miss the gym before it closed.

Saying that he had to make a phone call and that his phone was broken, Jonathan had excused himself and hurried across the street to the gym. There he had feigned making a call, after which he had grabbed a basketball and rushed to the foul line. He had sunk his first shot and felt utterly relieved. When he had gotten back to his apartment, the boy had gone.

"I thought Eric might be mad at me, because he had come over to talk about a grade. Eric's parents are getting divorced, and he likes to talk to me. He got very upset over the vacation because they were arguing violently about money. He's worried that his schooling is costing too much and that they're going to pull him out of Gloucester. I told him he had nothing to worry about—I happen to know that they're super-rich. But I hated to run out on Eric like that. When I saw him at dinner, I apologized, and told him it was a very important call, and he said, 'No problem.' Eric is a very good kid. I feel sorry for him."

Jonathan explained to me that during his two nights on duty he is expected to be in his apartment until midnight.

"The kids know I'm there, and anyone who has a problem or is just lonely can knock on my door. A kid can come in and talk if he wants, or I'll look at his homework with him, as long as he does it himself, or we just watch TV. Naturally, some of them are lonely. They want to just hang out."

Jonathan said that sometimes a boy would talk about a problem he had with a teacher or with another kid. Or a problem at home. "Like Eric,

whose parents are in the middle of this divorce. I counsel them. I guess I am to Eric what you are to me."

"Do you like that part of the job?" I asked him.

"I love it. The kids are so open and eager. It's a wonderful age. If it wasn't for these terrible anxiety attacks." He fidgeted with his red tie, straightening it and pushing it inside his jacket.

"The school is wonderful," he said. "The kids are wonderful. The problem is me. I'm making it a nightmare. That's what my brother says, and he's right. 'You've got what you've always wanted. So enjoy it.'"

Then Jonathan moved on to the subject of mathematics, and rhapsodized about its beauty. Geometry because of its pure form, and algebra with its orderliness and power. What could be nobler than imbuing in these kids a love of those subjects, with a sense of their stark elegance! "Do you realize?" he said, leaning forward, "that most kids judge themselves as smart or stupid over a *lifetime* by whether they're good or bad at math—at basic math!"

As he said this, his lanky, loose-jointed frame seemed to collect itself, as if a force surged through it, and he was for the only time I'd seen him a master of himself, a leader. "And whether a boy feels smart or dumb depends in large part on how good his early math teachers are."

"So it's a major opportunity, teaching at a school like the Gloucester School."

"Major!" he echoed my word. "I've got to get over this."

As he spoke, somehow the purity of the school, of Jonathan's simple ambition, of mathematics, of geometry, of algebra, swam together in my mind. *Purity*—it was an ideal, a Platonic entity that seemed to course through Jonathan's presentation. But I didn't regard it as an ideal. Straining to see the experience through Jonathan's eyes, I saw it as a reality, as his reality. And then I remembered the assignment I'd given him—to try to recall any thoughts that had come to mind while experiencing his attacks or while shooting the basketball.

"Gee, I forgot completely that you asked me to do that," he said, with seeming unconcern.

But he promised to do his assignment in the future, and I stressed that it could be important.

He talked a little more about his life. His mother was devoted, "pure"; his father hadn't liked to work, and had had women on the side. "My mother said he tried to seduce every woman he saw."

When I asked Jonathan why his father had finally left, the answer had nothing to do with women: "I guess he just couldn't take it. We were all too much for him."

At the door he thanked me, and said he felt a lot more relaxed. I didn't especially believe him, and even if he truly felt better, we surely hadn't accomplished anything real.

Jonathan was my last patient of the week, and that session stayed with me for the next few days. He had seemed driven by a desire to serve as the loving, indulgent father to these boys, as instructor par excellence—the father that he himself had never had.

His father, at least to Jonathan, had been a scurrilous, motley man, who had found every impulse compelling and who had succumbed to a myriad of them. Very likely, Jonathan had waited a lifetime to relive his own uncertain childhood, with the roles reversed. And here he was, unsteady, hammered at by inner strife, and, it occurred to me, a miniature of his father, who had run out on the boy who needed uninterrupted time with him—and doubtless on others.

He was disturbed by his own constant uneasiness. But that very reaction bespoke something deeper and far more hideous within him that he could not accept even long enough to face what it was.

During the next week, Jonathan had several more bouts of panic, including one when he went to the gym and found it set up as an auditorium, with chairs everywhere. He was told that the Gloucester School was lending that room to a local women voters group. It was the only place in the area capacious enough for the three hundred participants.

Jonathan pushed aside some chairs and sank his foul shot. Though he felt relieved, it struck home to him how utterly dependent he was on his ritual.

When he recounted this to me, I asked him, "What do you think your success or failure at sinking a shot might mean?"

He had no answer.

"And nothing comes to mind during those anxiety attacks either?" I asked, half skeptically.

"Only that I'm going to be destroyed, ruined somehow—nothing else comes to me."

"Okay," I said. "Right now, make something up, *anything,* as if you were writing a story. What do you see? What's going to happen to you?"

"I don't know. I just don't see anything."

I told Jonathan that we'd let it go, but entreated him to try to manufacture any ideas, no matter how farfetched or fictional they might seem to him, the next time he was in the gym. I asked him to recall any fantasy, no matter how fleeting, that came to him while he was there, or at any other time, especially during his attacks.

He promised that he would.

Next I asked if there was anything he could remember about how the compulsion started, and when.

"I told you I don't know," he said sharply. "You asked me that before. All I remember is that it was a couple of months ago." He hesitated, as if drawing a blank; then, in surprise, he said, "Oh, that's funny, there is something, I remember now. I'd forgotten all about it.

"It was a few months ago. I had this terrible, inexplicable anxiety attack—one of the boys, Rick, was in my room. We were watching a basketball game on TV, a college game. Duke was playing. Rick's father went to Duke. Rick was wearing his Duke T-shirt and he was cheering. It was a close game, and I thought I was going to pass out, I couldn't explain it. I said to myself, if this guy makes this foul shot, I'll be all right. I know how crazy it sounds. Anyway, once the guy made the shot, I felt okay.

"It's funny I haven't thought of that until now. The whole habit started with my watching basketball games on TV. Several times I prayed for people to make shots, always foul shots. Then, one day I was passing through the gym and I took a shot. Two shots—and then it switched over to me. I had to be the one shooting. Because the demon is inside of *me,* no one else can save me."

So now he, too, was considering that the demon was within him, and not outside.

It seemed important that his habit of shooting baskets had begun quite recently.

I could see that the whole subject made him tremble, but I had to push ahead.

I asked him if there were any other such practices, anything that might also be a compulsion. He couldn't think of any. "Except that I do math very methodically."

"And in the past, when you were a child?"

Again he drew a blank.

"We're not getting anywhere, are we?" he said nervously.

"Maybe we are," I reassured him. "We've got to collect our data. It's you and I trying to identify the problem."

I took that opportunity to remind Jonathan of the necessity to check himself out medically also, "to leave no stone unturned." Though he had agreed to do this, he had obviously put off finding a physician.

This time he asked me for the name of one, which I gave him.

Later it crossed my mind that now he seemed to be actually hoping that the problem was physical, though by then I felt quite sure that it wasn't.

Once again, he talked about how wonderful his job was. It was a beautiful school, and Mr. Phelps was an ideal headmaster, "always thinking of the boys." Jonathan boasted that Mr. Phelps continually sought to erase as many distinctions as he could between rich kids and poor kids, and usually succeeded.

I concurred that this was ideal, but this time as Jonathan extolled the school, I thought I picked up an unreal sound, a hollow sound, though I didn't know what to make of it.

Though much of the session had been about disturbing issues, Jonathan thanked me politely at the door, and repeated the empty phrase, that I had been "helpful."

Moments later he was gone, and in retrospect I could hear the same false note in his complimenting me that I'd heard in his encomium of the Gloucester School. Though so far I'd done nothing for him, he might well have seen some value in me. He had trusted me somewhat, but his complimenting me at the door each session smacked more of desperate dependence than of real appreciation. Did he feel that he had to curry favor with me so that I would do my best; that is, compliment me so that I wouldn't let him down?

As for the school, fearing as he did that it would become the scene of his destruction, if not the actual agent, could he possibly be as uncritical in his approval of it, as in love with it, as he let on? The answer rang out: No.

For the first time I pictured him as possessing some mammoth misgiving about the school, or at least about his work there. And paralleling that must be a misgiving about me, whether he was conscious of it or not.

Of course, I thought, how could he not? My being privy to his anxiety attacks, my very knowing the nature of his "secret insanity," made me potentially dangerous to his security, and not an undiluted ally. In his anxious state, he would very likely feel that my very knowledge was power over him, if I chose to misuse it. I recognized how appallingly alone he was—afraid to confide in anyone without increasing his danger.

Then I realized that his real secret, something almost surely still secret from himself, was an even greater source of conflict and reason for him to fear me than anything I already knew. By the very nature of my assigned task, I was drawing closer to that demon, which he feared could demolish him. Was that not my very function—to pull it out by the hair and hold it up, with all its horror? Whatever it turned out to be, it was as yet a gorgon to him. His terror would very likely increase as we drew closer—and as we reached it—if we did. Not until we held it up to the light, that gorgon, for a long enough time to deprive it of its horror could he truly accept it, and accept me.

Meanwhile, his complimenting me, those thank you's at the door that had felt syrupy and unreal, must have, as at least part of their motive, that of persuading me that everything was fine. He was trying to keep me away from the gorgon, and in doing so was, in effect, trying to sabotage his own expressed aim in coming to me and my efforts to help him.

Over the month that followed I could make no progress solidifying my relationship with Jonathan. At my request, he excavated some interesting memories, but his very doing so kept his guardedness high. The more he revealed to me, the more threatening I became to him. It was as though our relationship paid a price in intimacy for every shard of information about himself that he unearthed.

I prodded him to muster any mental associations he could to his shooting those baskets, and for ideas, even wisps of thought, that accompanied his bouts of anxiety. But all he could tell me was that he felt impending doom at such times—nothing more. Doom from what direction? In what form? I knew that my repeating these questions was bothersome to him, but I couldn't honestly put them aside.

Because compulsions, especially one so dominant in a person's life, seldom occur in isolation, I was surprised when Jonathan insisted that he had no others. In fact, when I asked him if he could recall any compulsive behavior in childhood, he couldn't.

He had been a very nervous child, and for good reason. He and his brother would cower in their room while their parents fought, always praying that they would reconcile. Though the household had become quiet suddenly after his father moved out, he had felt great sadness and a sense of failure. Their mother had been warm, but she had been busy working, and his own devotion to his studies had become the spine of his life in his early years, and remained so.

But the week after Jonathan told me that he could recall no other compulsions, he came in and volunteered the memory of one. "I guess it's in the same category. When I was in school, I could never stand handing in a paper that was less than perfect."

"You mean you had to get an A in everything?" I asked incredulously.

"Oh, no. I don't mean it that way. If I didn't know something, I could live with that. But I could never hand in a paper with smudges on it. It was just that any . . . any, uh, *blemish* on the paper, like an ink spot or even an erasure mark that I couldn't see, I wanted to fix up."

"And if you turned in a paper that wasn't a hundred percent neat?"

"I never did. Oh yes, once I did, against my will. Mister Winston, my fourth-grade teacher, was asking for papers once after a test in class. It was a history test. I had ripped my paper erasing an answer, and I was copying it over frantically, when Mr. Winston said it didn't matter and snatched the paper right out of my hands."

"How did you feel?"

"Miserable. I remember feeling like hell. I must have, because I can still remember it. I guess back then I had a strong perfectionistic streak in me. I still do."

I wondered if Jonathan took that streak out on the kids up at the Gloucester School. I was tempted to ask him, but this didn't seem the time.

"Do you think that is related to what's happening to me now?" he asked.

"Well, you were pretty fierce on yourself back then," I said, "and you still are."

I told him that I was interested in the fact that the penalty for failure, for imperfection, for even *near success* was so great back then.

The next session brought two interesting revelations. Finally, Jonathan had been able to capture a thought that had accompanied his shooting those foul shots.

"Right after the ball went in, I had the fantasy of Mr. Phelps watching me. He saw the shot go in, and he smiled, and said, 'You'll be all right.' It lasted just an instant, but I remembered it and I wanted to report it."

"That's great," I said.

"Is it?" he replied flippantly. "What does it mean?"

"Tell me what you think about it, that's more important," I said.

"I don't know," Jonathan snapped back at once.

"Well, it might imply that his approval means something to you," I suggested.

"Doctor, I really don't think I care whether Mr. Phelps thinks I'm a good foul shooter or not," he said sourly.

"In that moment you did, for some reason," I said, and we let it go.

Our second discovery was prompted by the visit to the Gloucester School of a sex education team. "A man and his wife—they call themselves Bert and Gloria, to be informal. They showed films and answered questions."

I asked Jonathan about the films.

"I didn't see them, but I hear they were very explicit. Birth control devices and how to use them. How to have sex. They talked about masturbation. Everything, I guess."

I remarked that it sounded pretty comprehensive.

"No, it wasn't. That's just the point. Not at all. Mr. Phelps doesn't want them back. He announced at our meeting that he was very disappointed with their presentation."

"Really! Why?"

He said they were okay on sex acts, but they didn't say anything about love or feeling. They presented sex in a kind of void. He said they made all sex sound like masturbation, like some isolated 'get it on,' without any caring. He thought it was terrible, 'much too mechanical'—those were the words he used. Anyhow, they're gone."

"I see!"

"Oh, my God. I just remembered another ritual of mine that I forgot to tell you. When I was thirteen and fourteen, maybe even fifteen—"

"What was that?"

"I was trying not to masturbate. I thought it was really bad. But it was hard not to. I had a ritual. It used to drive me crazy when I couldn't get there, just as it does these days with the basketball shots. Oh, my God. So that's what was so familiar."

"What do you mean?"

"I was trying to stop, and I couldn't. I vowed to stop. I was sure it was bad for me. So I started keeping a notebook with a record of when I masturbated—how often, at what time. I remember, I used a special symbol in case someone, mostly Jimmie, saw the book. I also had in the book reasons why it was wrong to jerk off, they were in code too. They actually helped me, they gave me more willpower—at least I thought they did.

"I used to go to look at the book, just to prove I was doing better, to help me fight the battle. Sometimes it was very embarrassing. Like when I got anxious. I guess I thought jerking off would ruin my brain. I didn't know very much, did I? I would get terrified when I was away from home and couldn't rush to look at that black book. That's funny. It is very much like this, isn't it?"

"It is," I said. "The ritual, and your desire to be pure—"

"But the ritual didn't really help, did it?"

"What do you mean?"

"Well, I forgot the book after a while, after a year or two, and I kept jerking off. My God, that's terrible!"

"Does that mean you're impure?"

He didn't hear me. He looked very flustered.

"Why is it terrible?" I asked him.

This time he chose not to answer me.

At the door that session, instead of his usual comment that I had been helpful, Jonathan said, "I guess we're not really getting anywhere, are we?"

"I think we're doing okay," I said. "I wish we could go faster too. I know those attacks are awful."

He looked at me as if I were kidding. I had the flash impression that he thought I was insincere, perhaps that I didn't actually care how much he suffered. Then he left.

During the week he called me and said that he had gone to see the physician I had recommended, and that his tests had come out fine.

"That's great," I said. "Thanks for telling me."

"Yeah, it just means that I'm mentally ill, that's all," he said dourly. Then he hung up.

In every session since the first he'd said one way or another that he was mentally ill. His very compulsion served to announce this to him, and the memory of an earlier compulsion, his rushing to that black book and hating himself for masturbating, perhaps confirmed his conception of himself as strange.

I mulled over Jonathan's fantasy of Mr. Phelps smiling and saying that Jonathan would be all right since he had sunk the basket. Jonathan seemed quite upset at the idea that he cared so much about Mr. Phelps's opinion, and he was also upset at my being in possession of that momentary image of his.

In other cases I had worked extensively with the illusions that accompany people's compulsions. Fragmentary as these illusory pictures are, they hold precious information. Their seeming irrelevance to what the person truly thinks and believes is consistent with their being glimpses into his deeper world. Fears and desires, suppressed from consciousness but fueling the compulsion, sometimes escape in these images.

I had entreated many patients to stop their compulsive activity, if only for a few days, because without the activity the accompanying illusions often burst into consciousness. But stopping his activity was next to impossible for Jonathan. I would have to keep pressing him for whatever he could think of while continuing with it.

One thing had emerged: Jonathan's sinking those baskets was almost surely aimed at demonstrating something to himself. He was trying to allay some profound worry by engaging in that compulsion, much as some people who pursue money compulsively or tally up their holdings are really trying to reassure themselves of their intelligence or their self-worth.

But, I kept asking myself, exactly what was Jonathan seeking to assuage? He seemed out to demonstrate his innocence on some score and his worthiness to carry on. But for what crime—for what impurity—did Jonathan imagine he needed absolution? What was there about him that he felt Mr. Phelps would so strongly disapprove of?

By that time I had a sense that Jonathan could almost put into words what terrified him about himself. I half expected him to come in and tell me what it was.

But instead, the next time he came in, he surprised me by accusing me of betraying him. "You've been talking to them up at the school," he said menacingly. "I know you have."

He glowered at me so hard that I thought he might have it in mind to try to punch me.

I insisted that I hadn't, making clear that this was a very serious charge he was making against me, and that he had no warrant for it.

Then he went on to say that people weren't as friendly as usual to him around the school. He had thought I'd called them and said something about him.

For instance, some of the other teachers weren't saying hello in the halls. And the other night a few had gone out for a drink and hadn't invited him. These were people who had always called him.

"Can you think of any reason why they'd exclude you?" I asked him.

Some questioning led me to realize that he'd been on duty that night, which was more than sufficient reason for them not to invite him. But that answer didn't satisfy him.

The next week he surprised me by talking about the Gloucester School unfavorably for the first time: "There are too many in groups." "The kids are too obsessed with money and status. They don't want to learn." "There are too many boys, like one boy, Josh, who doesn't give a damn about anyone. I'm not even sure I want to stay."

When I asked Jonathan what had led him to see the school so differently, he didn't acknowledge that it was a new appraisal. "This is how I've always felt," he said.

Then he explained that a lot of people there were acting strangely toward him. He said that even Mr. Phelps wasn't as friendly anymore.

"And the other day a couple of the kids asked me to play basketball with them. They know I don't play. I think they're on to me. I could see them smiling."

That had brought on a terrible anxiety attack. He had stayed alone in his room, had lain on his bed for hours.

"What were they smiling about?" I asked him.

"I don't know. I was trying to figure it out. I'll bet they know something about me, though. I'm sure Josh does."

"Why Josh?"

"By the way he smiles."

But that was as far as he could go.

Thinking about it later, I realized that Jonathan was becoming *paranoid*. And in a sense, I—or, more exactly, my work with him—was the cause. As we closed in on whatever it was that we were to discover, Jonathan had begun to imagine that others were already discerning his secret. Our peeling away of layers was terrifying him—making him feel *transparent*.

Within weeks he had begun to manifest not just feelings of transparency, the sense that others could discern his wants and fears, but other classic signs of paranoia. I could see signs he was feeling persecuted and grandiose.

His imagining that people were laughing at him and shunning him was evidently paranoid. To Jonathan this was real persecution, and his pain was certainly real.

The grandiosity was subtler but also unmistakable; it lay in his notion that so many people were devoting such considerable time to watching him and discussing him. With this view, Jonathan mistakenly attributed to himself a central role in people's lives that he surely did not have. People were far too busy with their own lives to give him anything like the attention he imagined they gave him.

So paranoia, caused by his anxiety over the imminent surfacing of his secret, was to be our last obstacle. Curiously, in this case such a fear was an indicator of progress toward our discovery. We were already so close that he imagined others had arrived at it before us.

For a few days I felt convinced that he could control those illusions, that they wouldn't get the better of him.

Then I began to worry that he might do something at the Gloucester School, act in some way that would ultimately harm him. I imagined him accusing some other teacher, or even Mr. Phelps of betraying him, of doing him in—much as he had accused me. Or who knew what else he might do? In a day, in an hour, he could earn himself a reputation that might be hard to erase. He might jeopardize his job. And though right now he didn't seem enamored of the job, I felt sure that he would be again, once this thing was figured out and resolved.

I had an impulse to call him in Vermont and warn him, "Don't do anything offbeat or defensive. Above all, don't accuse anyone of anything."

But then I recalled how even mildly paranoid people react to unsolicited advice, especially from an unexpected source. They almost always become more paranoid. Jonathan might hear me out, consider what I'd said, even thank me. But not long after hanging up, he could too easily misconstrue what I'd said or reinterpret it in his own way. It would be preferable to wait and tell him in my office.

I was gambling that Jonathan was still able to entertain the idea that he was experiencing an illusion. People with true paranoid psychoses cannot look at themselves this way. They become enveloped by the illusion; it is all that they see, which is why they are sometimes very dangerous. But nonpsychotic paranoid states, such as Jonathan's, are common. Perhaps most people have suffered at least one such experience, either in the office, or with friends, or in irrational jealousy. When in these states people can understand that they may be misguided and that it's advisable for them not to act on what they think they see.

When Friday came Jonathan lost no time in telling me more anecdotes of persecution. I couldn't tell for sure how much of it was imagined and how much was real. Of late his reactions to people had become wooden, and he had taken to asking fearful questions. Perhaps people were backing away from him.

I could see why they might. The following week the parents were to visit the Gloucester School; Jonathan had repeatedly asked other faculty members not just how he came across, but whether they thought the parents would like him. Such questions apparently took people by surprise. He reported that some teachers would tell him, "Don't worry. Just be yourself."

This was exactly the kind of thing I was afraid of—overt and pointless displays of self-doubt and intense anxiety. Jonathan didn't want people to see something about him, and he was checking his camouflage.

I told him that in reality people couldn't see a hundredth of what he presently thought they could. And I spelled out for him that he was suffering from an illusion of transparency and explained what that meant.

"There's something you don't like about yourself," I told him. "As we get closer to finding out what it is, you may feel more transparent. But that's an illusion. No one can possibly think that there's anything wrong with you—*unless* . . ."

Then I filled in the "unless."

"Unless you accuse people of excluding you or of laughing at you, the way you accused me of calling up the school. With me it was okay, but if people don't know you well, accusations like that can really turn them against you."

Then I told him that he also stood to harm himself by asking for too much reassurance.

"Those other teachers have no real answers for you. When you keep asking them how you look and how you're doing, you only alert them to the fact that you're in trouble. Then when they treat you differently, you'll only become more upset. No one can tell that anything's wrong with you unless you announce it by varying sharply from your usual style."

He thanked me at the end of the session, and I got the impression that he had truly heard me, and that what I'd said had made sense.

After he'd gone I wondered if Jonathan had done any real damage already. I hoped that if he had, it was slight, and that he could repair it.

Finally the truth emerged—Jonathan's secret—although the sluices didn't open all at once.

On a bright April day Jonathan came in looking flustered. For the first time his hair was uncombed, and he obviously hadn't shaved. Once in my office he sank into my couch as if all strength had deserted him.

"I'm ruined," he began. "It's too late."

"What happened?" I inquired. "Did you do something you're sorry about?"

He looked at me as if surprised. "No. Not at all. Your warning last week was very helpful. I just don't think teaching is for me, that's all. It's too hard. It's too much of a strain. People don't appreciate anything. The kids are spoiled, so they torture each other."

"Jonathan, I'm aware that kids can be pretty mean sometimes. But it sounds as if you have something very specific in mind."

"One thing? No. I've got a lot of different kids in mind. Maybe this kid Josh is the worst. He's supposed to be turning over a new leaf. Meanwhile he pushes the little kids around, and he threatens to brutalize them if they say anything about it."

Jonathan fidgeted and scanned the room, his eyes pausing briefly when he saw the leafy trees across the avenue in Central Park. "Josh has a little gang that follows him around. They do what he tells them. They sell little green caps to the freshmen—they demand ten dollars a cap. A kid has to take one. They just seize the money and give him a cap."

"Look, Doctor," he said. "Unless you're connected with one of these schools, you can't imagine—"

"Jonathan, why are you particularly talking about this *now?* You never mentioned this kind of cruelty before. I'm sure you're not seeing it for the first time."

"Why now? Because the parents came up this week, and you have to figure out what to say. What do you tell a parent? 'They're extorting money from your kid'? Or, 'Your little boy was beaten up, and if you say anything about it, he'll be in worse trouble?' "

By then Jonathan was talking loud and fast.

"So you're saying that dealing with the parents presented a real dilemma?" I said.

"Dilemma?" He looked at me as if my word were woefully insufficient.

"There's this other kid," he said, "Bobbie—Bobbie Finch. I practically saved his life. He went into a state of shock. His parents know the whole story, and now they blame me."

This was obviously very painful for him.

"Bobbie's father was at the school. He didn't even talk to me. Why should he? He seems to *hate* me."

"Hate you? Why?"

"Let's put it this way. Mr. Finch spent an hour in Mr. Phelps's office on Thursday, and I'm certain they were talking about me. When they came out they were smiling, and Mr. Phelps had his arm around Mr. Finch's shoulder. Later that day Finch walked right past me, and we didn't say a word to each other."

"Does this Mr. Finch have any reason to hate you?"

"I told you I don't know, but I feel that he must have."

"You mean you had some problem with his son?"

"Yes." He nodded. "I must have."

"Maybe you better tell me what it was," I said, as warmly as I could.

"I can't tell you. I don't know."

"All right," I said. "Tell me what you do know."

When he looked blank I said, "Why don't you start off by telling me a little bit about Bobbie."

Jonathan described the boy as soft-spoken and intelligent. Bobbie would drop in on him a few nights a week. Jonathan, feeling very alone after he had broken up with Julia, welcomed Bobbie's visits.

"Bobbie liked his classes, but he found most of the other kids immature and silly. He didn't actually complain about them very much, he just stayed by himself. He was always inventing something. For his history class he made a beautiful model of a water mill, the kind they had centuries ago, and it worked perfectly.

"I would tell Bobbie about famous people, what their lives were like. I told him that a lot of them were loners like him, and not all of them were even good students, the way he was. He loved hearing real-life stories about major figures. The more time he spent with me, the more I came to realize that the other kids were mostly very mean to him."

"Why was that?"

"Because he was so studious, I guess, and quiet. Maybe because he was physically small. And he never joined in with their nonsense. They tried to bully him a lot, but they couldn't make him cry. I once asked Bobbie, 'Don't you feel like crying sometimes, like when Glen Lindstrom'—he was the lead bully—'punched you in the arm?' He just said, 'Nope.' I believed him. He didn't want to talk about it, and we didn't."

Jonathan stopped at that, as if waiting for my next question.

"So far," I said, "I have no idea what went wrong between you and Bobbie. What took place that anyone could react badly to?"

"Well, one night this weird thing happened. I had just gotten back to my apartment after dinner, and I heard this terrible clamor. I looked out of my window, and there Bobbie was, standing alone in the snow, stark naked and banging on the door.

"At first I thought it was a girl down there. Bobbie had the figure of a woman, and I couldn't tell. I went out into the yard as fast as I could, I don't even remember going down the stairs."

Jonathan filled in a lot of details. He said that even though Bobbie was freezing, he was trying not to cry.

"I could hardly put the overcoat around him, because he threw his arms around me when he saw me. He had such a tiny waist and narrow hips. I think that at one point Glen tried to lock us both out in the yard, but I thrust the door open with my foot, and it knocked him down. He ran away.

"I glanced up at a lighted window above me, and I saw that the rest of Glen's gang was already upstairs viewing the spectacle and laughing. I figured the kids would lurk on the first floor landing to hear what was going on. So I brought Bobbie into a big room downstairs and I closed the oak doors and sat with him there to calm him down for a few minutes.

"By the time Bobbie and I started up the stairs to his room, the others had all disappeared. When I got him upstairs, I gave him a hot bath. The incredible thing was that he was calm.

"I often think about those vicious kids up in the window—laughing. At the time I swore to myself that Glen Lindstrom wouldn't be in the Gloucester School for long if I had anything to do with it. Can you believe his trying to lock us both in that yard? Bobbie could have frozen to death."

"That was pretty awful," I said.

"I made my report to Mr. Phelps immediately. He asked me not to mention the incident to anyone else and, of course, I didn't—I guess you don't count."

"No. Of course not. This is a special situation. Nothing you say will ever leave this room, so far as I'm concerned."

"The next day I guess a few of the kids must have been scared. They stepped forward and admitted that they'd taken part in the plot. They apologized and begged Mr. Phelps not to tell their parents.

"Mr. Phelps confronted the rest of the boys whom I had seen. They all said that Glen was behind the whole thing. When Phelps spoke to me about it, I told him some other ways Glen had intimidated Bobbie and the other kids. Secretly I said to myself, 'If this kid stays, I look for another job.'

"Phelps didn't tell me how he was planning to handle it. But the following month, Glen was gone. The other kids who were involved got off with punishments proportional to what they did. That kid Josh, who I mentioned, and a few others were put on probation. They were told that if they didn't shape up, they were out, too."

"Jonathan, I can certainly see why this shook you up," I said, "but—"

Jonathan wasn't with me. He seemed to be calculating something in his mind. I heard him say to himself, barely audibly, "Two months, three months, I guess it was just before Thanksgiving . . ."

"What was?" I asked him.

"God, I'm just figuring," he said. "This night I just told you about. That was when my anxiety attacks started."

"Are you sure?"

"Definitely. Because I remember having a picture of those kids leering down at us from the window."

"Is that when that basketball compulsion of yours started too?"

"Yeah. That's astonishing. Maybe a little after that. And I used to have this terrible vision of the kids looking down through the window and laughing at me—"

"At you?"

"Yes, that's funny, isn't it? And I swear Josh still laughs at me when he sees me, as if he knows something."

"What could he possibly know?"

Jonathan ignored my question and went on. "You know what kills me, Doctor? Bobbie is a different kid. After that night he never came to my room again, except once—to borrow a dictionary. I think he blames me for something."

"For what?" I asked.

"I don't know. I have no idea what's on his mind. He hardly even talks to me. Other kids still seek me out, of course, like Rick, the boy who was in my room watching the Duke game when I had to go to the gym.

"God, I hate it when that happens, when I feel almost commanded to go to the gym—and a kid's in the room with me. Of all times! Once or twice I had gotten through the day without going there, and then suddenly, bam!, when a boy was with me, I got this terrible urge to find out if I could sink a basket. I couldn't bear it—"

"Couldn't bear what?"

"That sense that I had to go to the gym. Like a calling. As for Bobbie, it's too bad, but our friendship is over."

"I hope not. I know you like him a lot."

"I do. I really identified with him out there in the snow. The way the kids laughed at him. I went through that sort of thing as a kid. Let's face it, I'm still going through it."

"I can see why it was so painful," I said. "Because you identified so closely with Bobbie, as you say. But it sounds as if you did everything you could."

"Did I? Maybe you think so. But maybe I could have done a lot more."

Astonished by that comment, I asked him, half rhetorically, "Jonathan, what else could you possibly have done?"

Once again he didn't seem to hear me. He wrinkled up his face in self-reproach and seemed engrossed in his own sequence of thoughts.

A full thirty seconds elapsed before he surfaced his next idea in words, with the thunder of a train suddenly emerging into the open from the underground.

"You know what kills me about the Gloucester School," he said. "On the outside it looks so honest and clean—and special. To the world it looks just great. People aren't aware of all the violence and ugliness."

"Well, it does sound as if it can be pretty bad at times," I said, not knowing where he was going.

"But it's a fake. It's *rotten*," he cut in, and I knew that he hadn't changed the subject at all, that he was still talking about himself.

"And you know who *knows* it's a fake," he went on. "Mr. Finch, and Bobbie, Mr. Phelps, and even Josh the bully—they call him 'Josh the bull.' It's not really a school. It's a mockery of a school."

"Are you saying that's what you feel like—a mockery?"

"I am. That's right. I look good on the outside but not on the inside. Well put. Just like the Gloucester School."

"Please explain that," I virtually implored him. "I think I know what you mean, but I need to know more how it applies to you."

But Jonathan ignored that and kept talking about how he thought other people viewed him.

He said, "Bobbie and, of course, his father, and Mr. Phelps, and even Josh—I should say especially Josh, with that smug smile—they know, and they hate me."

"Hate you? Why? For what?"

"I don't know. I'm not sure what they know. Or rather, what they think. They know I look good on the outside. And so do a lot of the masters and the other kids. They know. It's like they're saying, 'Come on. You're not fooling us.' "

" 'Fooling us'? I don't follow you. What did you do wrong that day? You did everything you could to protect Bobbie. You said a month ago that you practically saved his life. Jonathan, I simply don't know what you're talking about."

"Doctor, I don't know. I just feel that way."

He was voicing his self-hate through the medium of those who were "on to him," who supposedly saw through him. He was poised on the brink of a dire self-discovery. However, for him to make it, I felt I had to return to the primary source of his mortification, which was his scathing judgment of himself.

"Don't you see," I said, "that other people have nothing to do with this. You're obviously very worried about yourself, and you're putting them in the picture, where they don't belong."

"Maybe that's true."

I thought I saw him clamp his lips, as if to stifle his next words, and then he waited.

His compulsion came to my mind just then, and I thought it would serve as a good example.

"Jonathan," I said. "When you go to the gym to shoot those foul shots, it can't be to convince other people that you're okay. Somehow, it must be to convince yourself."

"I guess so," he said reluctantly.

When our session ended I had an enormous urge to keep going. I felt sure that we had reached a critical moment without squeezing its real value out of it. I couldn't legitimately lengthen the time, however, because my next patient, a prim and critical man, was entitled to begin his hour.

That evening, when I called my answering service, the only message was from Jonathan.

"Doctor, he wants you to call him back tonight, if at all possible," the operator said.

Jonathan picked up on the first ring. "Is there any way I could possibly see you tomorrow? I know it's Saturday, but I've had a lot of thoughts. I almost can't wait until next week. I want to tell you what I feel guilty about."

We settled on 10:30 the next morning.

It was a sunny April day, and Jonathan was standing outside the building when I got there, looking slim and debonair in denims and a red cable-knit sweater.

Inside my office, he began at once. "I want to tell you, I finally realized what everyone's accusing me of. People think that *I* put him out in the snow."

"Who? Bobbie? They think that *you* put him out in the yard?" Of course, I was astonished.

But Jonathan seemed strangely composed.

"Yes. That I put him out there. Naked. I know it sounds ridiculous, but that's what they think."

"Who thinks?"

"All of them." A smile touched his lips. "And I think you think so, too."

He expounded on this notion, so groundless as to defy belief, as calmly as if he couldn't even imagine that I might doubt it. He could hardly have seemed more pleased if he had been the one to isolate DNA or to solve some mathematical problem that had stood unsolved since antiquity.

As it dawned on me what he was saying, I felt frightened for him. I experienced a momentary urge to tell him that I had no such picture that he had done that to Bobbie—and even that his thesis sounded outlandish. But, obviously, he would not be convinced of my denial; he would conclude either that I was lying or that I was very naive. I decided that it would be better if he simply spoke on without my intervention.

I looked at him across from me, appearing so haunted, and this time I automatically construed his mysterious "they" as really a metaphor for himself. In talking about others, Jonathan was telling me only what he believed regarding himself—he was projecting. And so I switched from his vernacular to the more immediate universe centered on him.

"Why would you put Bobbie out there?" I asked.

"That's what I asked myself last night," Jonathan said. "And when I couldn't think of anything, I imagined I heard you saying, 'Then make up an answer and say it out loud, no matter how farfetched it sounds.' So I did.

"Then suddenly I knew. I decided that I did it, that I put him out there, to see his naked body."

So that was the demon that had haunted Jonathan—he was desperately afraid of whatever sexual desires he had for the boys at the school.

"You mean you had sexual feelings for Bobbie," I said, I felt, quite matter-of-factly.

"Yes, I did," Jonathan answered.

I asked him if he had been sexually attracted to any of the other boys, and he said yes, that at times he had.

Jonathan took his sweater off, and I noticed great blotches of sweat under the arms of his blue shirt.

"Yes," he repeated. "And I'm sure that's what Josh and the boys, and Mr. Finch, and probably everyone was talking about.

"Damn it," he said. "I thought I had gotten over all those sexual feelings. I hadn't had any for months. I suppose you knew all the time that I used to be attracted to young boys, didn't you?"

"How on earth would I know?" I asked him, more to make a point than to raise a question.

"How could you not? I get so anxious. Like now."

It didn't take much to see that he was very alarmed and, of course, I had seen him that way before. But that I could infer anything more intimate about him than what he had told me in words was a purely imaginative leap.

Again I resisted an impulse to reassure him that he wasn't transparent. Instead, I asked him, "Jonathan, exactly why did you think I knew how you felt?"

"Well, last night, among other things, I remembered your reaction when I told you about the incident. The way you smiled. I'm sure you knew."

"Jonathan, at the time you were telling me the story, right then while you were talking, did you think I knew then?" I asked him.

"No, at that point I didn't know myself. I didn't realize that I put him out there, or why. I just hadn't put it all together yet."

"But what exactly do you think you put together? You told me that Glen and his crowd had been responsible. You said they even confessed. Do you still remember that?" I asked him.

"Yes, I know," Jonathan said. "I know they actually did it and they confessed. But what worries me is that maybe I let them do it. Or maybe I suggested it to them some way. I don't know."

"But Jonathan, you were in the dining hall when it happened, and you certainly didn't tell them to do it in advance."

Jonathan didn't answer. He didn't seem to want to talk about logistics or reality. All he did was to repeat, "Somehow I was responsible. It must have been me."

I didn't press him further, not wanting him to manufacture a greater, more detailed explanation that he would then believe. One of the first things I had learned to do with paranoid people was not to fight them logically, which would only encourage them to build a superstructure that becomes ever so much harder to tear down.

Because Jonathan took delight in seeing the boy's naked body, he had unconsciously assumed responsibility for denuding him. The case bore a resemblance to that in which a boy-child feels responsible for a father's death because the child feels relieved by that death and can repossess his mother. As I had already seen, Jonathan's paranoia was related to a sense of infantile omnipotence.

So Jonathan had fused the literal with the figurative, resulting in desire. I wondered how far he had carried this confusion.

"What other thoughts have you had about all this, since I last saw you?" I asked him.

"What thoughts can I have? It's over. I'm *destroyed.*"

At that moment, I wondered: Although Jonathan had not actually put Bobbie out in the yard, did so catastrophic a reaction of his indicate that he might have done something else? Might he, on some other occasion, have gone further—fondled a boy, perhaps Bobbie, or actually engaged in mutual sex play, and be suffering these feelings of transparency as a form of guilt for what he had actually done.

I asked him, "Jonathan, is there more that I should know?"

"More?" He seemed furious. "What more does there have to be?"

"Did you molest Bobbie, Jonathan?"

"No. I didn't actually molest him. No. Of course not. I wouldn't do that."

"Or any of the other boys? I mean, did you fondle them? Or proposition them? Did you do anything that would make you a child molester?"

"Doctor." He smiled. "I don't think you quite understand. I think you're very behind the times. I'm actually surprised at you." He said this last with sardonic relish. "You really don't know much about the status of child molesters. I mean, of even an accused child molester."

"Okay. Tell me what you mean."

"What I mean is that all you have to do is be *accused*. Have one person think you fondled one kid, or wanted to, and you're ruined—a pederast, undesirable near any school. Anywhere near kids."

"Even if you didn't do anything?"

"Oh, that's not the point. Nobody asks for proof, like in geometry. You're not indispensable. This is the modern witch-hunt. Once the idea gets out, it doesn't matter what you are—guilty or innocent. You're marked. You're labeled. And I'm labeled."

My immediate impulse was to rush in and comfort him by saying that having homosexual feelings certainly doesn't make someone a child molester. In fact, the great majority of child molesters are heterosexual. But, apparently, Jonathan equated having his feelings with being utterly unworthy of his job.

Once again I decided not to interpose my own opinion. Any reassurance from me would necessarily fall flat. The most I could do was to address his transparency as it related to me.

"Jonathan, I give you my word I had no idea of this. I guess you've had a lot of these feelings," I said.

He hesitated. "Some."

"About Bobbie?"

"Not just him. It got pretty bad sometimes when a boy came into my apartment. They would come in just in their shorts without a top. They'd sit around and talk."

"And you had these sexual feelings?"

"I used to. But recently, no. Afterward, when I was alone, I would think about a boy. But I was always afraid that it would happen, and I would give myself away.

"Then a few months ago all those sexual feelings went away—just like that. I thought they were gone forever. Lately I've been so worried about shooting those baskets that I didn't think about anything else."

"I guess you wished that those boys would stop knocking on your door," I said.

"No. Definitely not. I like it when they come in. That's the funny part. I like them as people. I'm lonely, and so are they, and I love to talk to them. It's just that this anxiety comes over me, like a sense of doom."

I felt almost certain that Jonathan had done nothing overt—nothing, except to mentally savor the bodies of boys and perhaps picture himself engaging in sexual acts with them. And even that, only in their absence. His dread was that the impulse would come at a time when it was hard to deal with, not that it *had* come at such a time. But even having these fleeting thoughts felt to Jonathan like a crime for which he could not expect forgiveness.

Before he left I hastened to reassure him: "Jonathan, I can see why this shook you up. But nothing you told me is so terrible. Nearly everyone has all kinds of feelings and impulses in a lifetime . . ."

Possibly he believed me in the moment, but I knew that I couldn't bolster him for long this way.

On Tuesday he called apologetically. He was in his room, tremulous after a hard day, during which he had stuttered several times while teaching classes. He hadn't had sexual feelings, but rather a sense of physically crumbling. He told me that he was contemplating handing in his resignation. It was all too much.

I begged him not to, but to wait. I promised that if he did, he would very likely see things differently.

I said, "It's like a dream in which you feel you did something evil.

You certainly shouldn't be punished for that. And it makes no sense to punish yourself, Jonathan. You haven't actually done anything amiss."

He thanked me profusely, as if he thought himself a dangerous leper and me the only living human ready to spend time with him on the lonely island to which he was relegated. Because both his leper status and his consignment to some small plot of land were his own creations, I felt like telling him not to be so appreciative.

But I merely accepted his thanks. Relying on his newfound belief in me as his last friend, I once again asked him simply to lie low until we could speak further. If his blasts of anxiety became great, I told him, I would be quite open to his calling me as often as he needed to for a while.

He didn't call again before I saw him.

The next time we talked a little more about his compulsion, which he thought might have lost a bit of its urgency, but which still gripped him.

"Apparently, it still has some significant implication for you," I said.

"What implication?" he asked.

"You tell me that."

He smiled for the first time in months. "I hate that therapy trick of yours of turning things around."

I told him that it wasn't a trick, and that I really didn't know nearly as much as he did about himself. I said that whatever words came to his mind were worth a lot more than anything I could surmise, since they proceeded from the source.

"Well, if the ball goes in, I won't suffer disaster," he said.

"Why not?"

"I guess it means that I'm a man. I'm okay. I'm not some effeminate pervert."

It was a harsh judgment of himself and the world, but that was nothing new for Jonathan. It crossed my mind that it was also a horribly narrow view of masculinity, and Jonathan was paying a terrible price for it.

"Isn't it crazy," he said, "that I would leave it up to a basketball to decide my fate?"

The phrase "magical extrapolation" came to me, and in that instant

I saw Jonathan in a larger perspective. Virtually all societies, from prehistoric ones to the most advanced modern ones, have used rituals to cleanse and purge themselves, just as Jonathan was doing now. I recalled having read about ritual sacrifices: the ancient practice of killing a chicken to examine its entrails for augury; the study of heavenly constellations to measure chances of survival, not just that of individuals, but of whole societies. And what about me? Could I honestly say that after hitting a tennis ball hard and well, I myself had never felt even a glimmer: "Hey, I'm really okay. I'm a great guy, and I've got what it takes."

"But why basketball?" I asked Jonathan.

"I guess because my brother played it, and I never could. And because I watched it on TV with the kids. And they look up to it."

"You mean foul shooting is the measure of the man?" I said.

Again he smiled, and I had a solid sense that Jonathan had granted me a measure of trust. My discovery of his secret and seeming acceptance of it were welcome to him. But I knew, too, that his trust in me was fragile. It might break without my doing anything, merely as a result of his reconsidering our session and remembering—or, rather, misremembering—some comment of mine that could look treacherous to him suddenly.

Those weeks in early May were long for Jonathan, as he existed alone with his discovery, not at peace with his "imperfection" and unable to confide in anyone.

I had Jonathan go through all the details of his rescue of Bobbie Finch again. I asked him to speculate about why the boy had drawn back from him afterward, and also why, in Jonathan's opinion, Bobbie's father had not spoken to him. It had been Mr. Finch's not stopping by to say hello that mostly troubled Jonathan and had triggered the worst of his paranoia.

Jonathan was sure that Bobbie had accused him to his father.

"But of what? What did you do? What could he actually know or guess?"

Jonathan couldn't say.

That night, while rescuing Bobbie, had he done anything that could be interpreted as undue?

"Well, Bobbie held on to me desperately, and then he clutched me again in that big room when he let himself cry."

"That was him, not you."

Jonathan nodded.

"And when you gave him a bath?"

"No. I just rubbed his back to calm him down. I swear I didn't do anything else."

"So why should anyone think you did?"

"I don't know, Doctor. You tell me. Why did Mr. Finch avoid me? What did he have to say for so long to Mr. Phelps?"

Jonathan again said that while actually with Bobbie he didn't have sexual desires. Curiously, it was only later, while thinking over those scenes, that he feared he would.

As we continued going over the same ground, Jonathan began to accept that perhaps he wasn't quite so transparent. "But then," he said to me, "Doctor, you explain why Bobbie is so different with me lately, why he's avoiding me."

"Well, it was pretty humiliating for him, Jonathan. I have a theory that he just doesn't feel ready to associate with anyone, even a friend, who saw him go through that nightmare."

As I was speaking, I recalled Jonathan's line of poetry about mathematics, not exactly but vaguely, and I asked him to recite it again.

" 'Euclid alone has looked on beauty bare,' " he said. We both laughed.

I wondered if he'd had it in mind all along, months before he actually told me about the incident, the way people sometimes sing songs that reflect their deepest thoughts even before they "know" they have those thoughts.

It was the middle of May, and the school year was coming to a close when Jonathan came in and said that he'd had a fierce confrontation with Josh.

Jonathan was teaching a math class in the computer room in the audiovisual center. He said that he'd seen Josh standing over a computer and shaking his fist at a much smaller boy, who was sitting at the computer trying to solve a problem. The smaller boy was a member of what Jonathan referred to as "Josh's team."

When I asked Jonathan what he'd meant by a "team," he told me that encouraging group effort was a whole new trend in math teaching.

"We assign teams to solve problems. Everyone does his own calculations, and then the captain puts the results together. We're trying to get away from the competition in math that used to put kids under so much pressure."

Jonathan said that he had gotten furious at Josh. He had shouted instantly, "If you ever threaten another boy again, you'll be out of this room, and maybe out of the school."

After Josh smirked, as he often did, Jonathan demanded to know what was so funny.

Jonathan told me, "You know, I didn't realize until later that Josh looked startled when I said that. I went right on. I told him, 'I will not tolerate bullies in this class.' "

Apparently, at that point Josh for the first time looked like the frightened kid that he really was.

For Jonathan that confrontation had been no small victory. For months he had ruminated fitfully about Josh grinning at him, at times imbuing the boy with the superhuman power of being able to see into Jonathan's own heart. At worst, he had actually imagined that the boy had discerned some dark truth about him that he himself didn't know.

Almost surely Josh, who was a poor student and had no genuine friends, hectored people simply to camouflage his own deep feelings of inferiority. His smug grin was for want of any real ability to articulate himself. But such meaningless grins have a way of deeply puncturing the exteriors of people who are also unsure of themselves, and Jonathan had needed little more than Josh's grin as a stimulus to torture himself.

Confronting Josh head-on had restored the boy, at least temporarily, to his proper magnitude, and had made Jonathan himself more certain of his right to run his own classroom. He had struck a blow against the tyranny of his own paranoia and morbid self-doubt.

Later that session Jonathan realized why he had so feared this particular boy. Josh had been a primary figure among those peering down from the window on that fateful day when Jonathan had rescued Bobbie. Josh had grinned down at them in the alley between the buildings, as if he had put the two of them into a cage.

As the unsettling aspects of the incident had subsided into the depths of Jonathan's unconscious he had "forgotten" the exact role that Josh had played. However, a shadowy sense of Josh as sinister remained. In time, Josh had become for him a repository of the unnerving implications of that incident.

It had become clear that Jonathan's compulsion was an aid to repressing what troubled him. It had replaced his anxiety over having illicit sexual feelings for boys by a much more tolerable anxiety over whether he could get to the gym and could succeed there.

However, despite Jonathan's facing his true fear, and realizing the uselessness of his compulsion, he continued to be troubled by strong urges to go to shoot foul shots in the gym.

I wondered why, since the device had lost its function as a camouflage, Jonathan was still addicted to it? I began to suspect that the compulsion had some secondary function, some payoff that I had overlooked, that was locking it in place and making it harder to give up than necessary.

I set about to determine what that payoff might be.

During the next few sessions I asked Jonathan to recall for me as much as he could about how the compulsion had started.

He again placed the beginning of the compulsion in one of those periods when he had watched basketball in his apartment with one or more of the boys present. Jonathan had felt terribly anxious and played the game with himself of deciding that if a player's foul shot went in, he was safe.

Of course, Jonathan's conscious mind would never have settled for the kind of evidence he was accepting here—especially not Jonathan's, he so emphasized rationality in all things. But the unconscious of even the most rational people is capricious, impressionable; it is animal, in the sense that it devours whatever satisfies it. And so Jonathan became addicted to a kind of proof that his unconscious accepted as valid.

This was what I came to regard as the first stage of his compulsion, the stage in which it was merely a lighthearted game for him.

Using his system of watching players shoot fouls, Jonathan sometimes had turned out to be okay, and sometimes not. But even on those days when Jonathan's system had told him he was fine, the proof could not reassure him for long. Inevitably, he had become anxious again. Jonathan's own inner life was not frozen but fluid, and those feelings he had for boys, those yearnings, had always returned and terrified him.

The second stage of the compulsion had occurred when Jonathan's conscious mind had had its momentary say, and the idea had come to him: "I shouldn't be depending on *someone else* to decide my status." With this the venue had switched from the TV set in his own apartment to the gym. Jonathan had hurried there to attempt his proof, as the ancients had run to their oracles, and as many of us moderns run to seers of various kinds for assurances about ourselves.

As with Jonathan, those who seek external signs to learn about themselves should logically need to find them only once. However, people who rely on such signs never trust them for long because they are, in effect, asking about themselves, and nothing outside a person can truly assuage self-doubt. This is why they keep going back. And why Jonathan had.

So, before long, Jonathan's compulsion had intensified. It had become hard for him not to go to the gym, and then virtually impossible not to go.

Suddenly, while I was reflecting on the second stage of the compulsion—Jonathan's running from his room to the gym—I came to see an immense payoff in the activity. It was a payoff still present and contributing mightily to Jonathan's compulsive need.

Jonathan had told me that his urges to go to the gym would typically visit him precisely when a boy was alone with him in his room. I now realized that by excusing himself hastily for another activity that had such urgency for him, Jonathan could escape the ordeal of being alone in his apartment with the boy. His compulsion, apart from its meaning as a test of himself and a measure of his safety, was still serving him by extricating him from the ordeal of being alone with a boy.

This was the lurking payoff: that the compulsion got him out of the room, and fast. The compulsion enabled him to escape a tight situation. On his way to the gym, and certainly once he was there, with his thoughts obsessively given over to shooting baskets, Jonathan could avoid sexual feelings, turmoil, and even the idea that he might be running away from his experience.

With this knowledge I classified Jonathan's compulsion with other compulsions whose function is largely avoidance. The alcoholic, beyond the lure of drinking itself, is "drowning his sorrows." And most gamblers become driven after a time not just by the urge for money but by a need to escape having to think about how much harm they have already done to their lives. The gambling itself so absorbs both their time and their passion that they have little left for remorse, this way.

My new understanding revealed the land ahead that Jonathan would have to cross to earn his freedom. My next step would be to help him recognize his "hoop compulsion" as a tactic of escape. After that, when the urge actually came, Jonathan would need to resist it and translate it in his mind back to its more fundamental form: "I'm anxious. I want to hurry out of this room. I want to run to the gym to prove myself. But I won't, it wouldn't work. The real problem is that I feel . . ."

Jonathan himself would have to supply the details, after resisting his usual conversion into the more acceptable language of basketball. He would have to cure himself of his fears by standing fast against whatever thoughts or urges beset him. If it turned out that Jonathan had sexual ideas about boys when alone with them, he would have to acknowledge these thoughts. Then, after appreciating that he could control his actions, he could come to see that such thoughts alone were not truly dangerous to him. After that, each time he acknowledged his own sexual imagery for what it was, he could grow stronger, until eventually his sexual thoughts would lose their power even to disturb him.

Where could such an acknowledgment lead Jonathan? Certainly not toward actually molesting children. Unacknowledged wishes or impulses exert far more force on us than those that we recognize and that we resolve not to express in action. It would be in no way dangerous for Jonathan to have a sexual thought about a boy once he clearly recognized those thoughts and saw that he could control them. In this respect, the truth—Jonathan's acknowledging his own fantasy life—would set him free.

★ ★ ★

But as I was discovering what Jonathan had to do, another reality was emerging in my mind. I should not be the one to go on this journey with Jonathan, much as I wanted to. Jonathan's visits to me, usually once a week, had been at great cost of time and money to him. Until then they had been his only alternative. My very geographical distance had squared with Jonathan's need for distance from himself. Seeing me had been simultaneously Jonathan's attempt at allowing the sunlight in and keeping it out.

However, with his enlarged self-acceptance I thought Jonathan could now face telling his story to a therapist geographically nearer to him. He could more profitably use both the money and the transit time he would save by seeing a local therapist two or perhaps three times a week over the coming year.

That way, if Jonathan felt anxious while alone with a young boy, he could know that the very next day he could see his therapist and recount his experience. That option would make his suffering a lot more endurable. Jonathan could progress a lot faster than he would in the more occasional relationship he had with me.

It was May and Jonathan was already busy with finals. Soon the parents would come to collect their kids for the summer. The boys would hug their instructors and say fond good-byes. The parents would drop by to wish them a good summer and thank them. Then the masters would meet individually with Mr. Phelps, who would renew their appointments for the next year. They would each have an hour or so with him to discuss their strengths and weaknesses. Mr. Phelps, who was a kind man and who was utterly identified with the Gloucester School, appreciated the masters' efforts. He nearly always addressed them in a constructive vein and with a communal spirit.

Jonathan told me that he was nervous about his evaluation. Mr. Phelps had been talking warmly to him again, but still seemed quite preoccupied, especially with the graduation ceremony coming up.

It struck me as egocentric of Jonathan to expect much more than he was getting, but I recognized that this grandiosity was a residue of his paranoia.

I told Jonathan that in thinking about his compulsion I had seen an important extra role that it had played—namely, that of bailing him out of anxiety-evoking situations. When he asked me what I meant, I reminded him that the urge to rush out and go to the gym often came to him when a boy was in his apartment visiting. Jonathan and I spent much of the session on that topic. Jonathan agreed; he had been dimly aware of using the compulsion that way, and he resolved to try not to in the future.

Over the following week a number of boys would be dropping by Jonathan's apartment to discuss their final math projects. A few who especially liked him would even come over to discuss their work in other courses. Many boys were already starting to miss him, and their topics were a pretext. Only a few would openly say that they were visiting just to talk, since the boys were at an age when to say that might seem an admission of weakness.

Jonathan would have a good chance to observe himself and to begin accepting his feelings. He resolved that when with these boys, even if his basketball urge grew intense, he would do his best to stay with them and to brave it out. He would study the thoughts and feelings and impulses that came to him.

Though I wanted to give him the longest possible lead time to consider going off to another therapist, so that he could mull the idea over and reject it if he wished, this didn't seem the session to bring it up. Jonathan was deliberately allowing himself to be off balance, willingly subjecting himself to anxiety in order to conquer it, and I didn't want to tip that imbalance any further.

That week a number of boys did come by, including Bobbie. To Jonathan's astonishment, Bobbie thanked him.

"For what?" Jonathan had asked.

"For everything."

Jonathan would have let it drop, but Bobbie added. "For not telling my father about that time the boys put me out in the yard."

"No, I didn't tell him. That's true," Jonathan had answered.

"Neither did Mr. Phelps, because I really begged him not to," Bobbie had said. "I just knew *you* wouldn't. You won't mention it when my father comes to pick me up, will you?"

"I promise I won't," Jonathan had said.

He was unutterably relieved.

I voiced the obvious, reminding Jonathan of how sure he was that Mr. Finch had avoided him because Bobbie had accused him of some unpardonable sin. And I took time to compare that misconception of Jonathan's to his suspicion that I had called the school.

"The moral," I said, "is that you are prone to feeling done in by people, and your mind plays tricks on you. The next time you have such an impression, don't trust it too fast. You're probably imagining enemies where there aren't any."

Jonathan had spent a half hour with Bobbie without an impulse to leave; he had felt only occasional anxiety, which had seemed unaccompanied by distinctly troublesome thoughts.

But then a boy, Kevin, whom Jonathan had mentioned only once or twice, had induced great anxiety in him. Jonathan told me excitedly, "I had this terrific urge to run out and go to the gym. But I didn't."

"That's great."

"I stayed with him. Kevin is the best math student in the place. He loves math, especially hard problems. We do some great ones together.

"Kevin told me he loved me and that he missed me already. He said he didn't want to see his mother, that he hated her. He said she was a phony. She was going to pick him up, spend the night with him in Boston, and then send him off to some horrible camp. She was going to Europe. He loves his father, but his father lives in California with a second wife. Kevin is a terrific kid."

"So what happened?" I asked.

"I said, 'I'll miss you too, Kevin—a lot!' He reminds me of myself when my father was gone. I wanted to run out. I wanted to leave, right then. Maybe go to the gym. Anywhere, just to get out of there.

"But I didn't. And I realized it's not just sex I'm running away from. I love this kid. I feel like he's me. I want to take care of him, and a lot of them. I know I can't, but I want to."

"You mean you're afraid of your warm feelings, your intimate feelings, for these boys?"

"Yeah?"

"Why?"

"I don't know. I've never really been close to a man. I don't know if I can handle it. I guess I hate to see myself so lonely. I just want to hold those kids, Bobbie and Kevin."

"Can you live with that, Jonathan?"

"I don't know. That the sexual part should be there upsets me." He smiled, as if his answer were silly.

"I was thinking, Jonathan," I said. "You know you would do well, I think, to see a therapist more often than you can get to me."

"I don't think so. We have a nice relationship. And I don't think I'd want to talk about all this to someone else."

We said no more about it that day. I realized that Jonathan was undergoing plenty of separation as it was. Later I thought about how reliant Jonathan was on those boys. He had suffered a loneliness that only they could assuage. And what had touched off his sexual yearnings most, more even than a boy's nakedness or partially clad body, was a boy's unrestrained expression of warmth toward him. Those expressions had threatened to evoke his own responses—reciprocal warmth and whatever other desires might accompany it.

It wasn't that Jonathan's sexual yearnings were so tumultuous. It was that to Jonathan any yearning to embrace a boy was like the roar of planes to someone who grew up in a city that was bombed. Jonathan had never been willing to wait around long enough to see what the "roaring" really signified. By his very flight from the imagined danger, he had escalated his own dread of what lay inside of him and what he himself might do.

A number of parents dropped in to wish Jonathan a good summer. Mr. Finch came by with his wife, whom Jonathan had never met, to thank him for his hard work. It seemed a miracle to Jonathan that no one suspected anything of his inner life.

The following week Mr. Phelps told Jonathan that his dedication to the school and his abilities were "a pleasant surprise." Jonathan's strength, Mr. Phelps said, was the rare ability to glorify math and to make problem solving a game that the kids could like.

"And next year I'd like to see you more aggressive," Mr. Phelps told him. "The kids wouldn't mind it if you were a little tougher with your assignments and with your grading." He observed that Jonathan was perhaps "too forgiving" and "that's no great service to them in the long run."

Jonathan felt sure that the headmaster knew that he had been quite withdrawn for a few months and come out of it. Perhaps Mr. Phelps had surmised more about Jonathan than he had let on, recognizing that some things are best left unsaid. If Mr. Phelps did sense anything more, his decision was charitable. I realized that the reticence that Mr. Phelps had observed in Jonathan derived from Jonathan's fear that any open display of emotion would betray his sexual feelings and ruin him.

Jonathan and I had only a few weeks left before I was to take my own summer vacation. We again spoke about his continuing his treatment with another therapist. He appreciated the logic in this plan, but he hesitated hard. He dreaded telling another soul, even a professional committed to confidentiality, that he had sexual feelings for boys.

I asked him, didn't he think that many young teachers cope with similar feelings, "including many who do their jobs well."

He looked at me blankly.

"What makes or breaks you," I went on, "is whether you can surmount your feelings and not be shattered by them yourself or act on them. The measure of your merit is not what you think or feel. It's what you do."

"Well, maybe," Jonathan granted.

I conjectured that if every teacher, every physician who examines patients, and every therapist with sexual feelings for those in their charge were dismissed at once, few would remain in these professions. "And those left would probably be among the poorer practitioners, because they would include the more robotlike members."

Jonathan allowed that this might be so, but my saying it didn't affect him much. Nor could anything I said change him basically. A therapist could only point the way, after which Jonathan would have to build his own self-esteem by choices that he made for himself. However, as I put it, his very talking about his feelings, sexual and otherwise, to this new therapist would help him see that he had a right to those feelings and was no less a person because of them.

Already his compulsion was much weaker; it had lost much of its function. Exposing his secret fear to another therapist would further reduce his need for camouflage activities. The more openly he acknowledged his secret the less he would dread it.

I predicted as much. I told him that his gamble of confiding in me had in itself been heroic, and now it was time for a new incursion against his personal shame, a final attack that would free him of it entirely.

Jonathan understood but expressed sadness about ending therapy with me. My very suggestion, though he could see its advisability, made it seem to him as if I were abandoning him.

I told him that I could understand that feeling, but that it shouldn't stop him from doing what was best for him. Naturally, he could still contact me in a pinch, and even if he had no special need of me, I would be eager to hear from him and to find out how his life was going.

Toward the end of the session, Jonathan volunteered that he would actively try to find someone else.

It was late in June. I was to see Jonathan twice more. He and several of the other masters who lived at the school year-round along with the caretakers, were the only staff left. Mr. Phelps and his wife were preparing to travel across the United States, and stop at the homes of a few former students who were now grown up with families of their own.

In the penultimate session Jonathan talked about his future as he rarely had. He mentioned some fantasies he'd had recently about being married. I could sense that he longed for intimacy, but also that he felt hobbled and unsure of himself after his relationship with Julia. Still, I construed it as favorable that Jonathan was looking ahead at all. His gaze was no longer riveted on what he had experienced as daily threats to his well-being, and he could now pause, if only in moments, to consider what he might want for himself in the years to come.

In my work with Jonathan I had been forced to dwell more than I usually do on day-to-day emergencies, as opposed to discussing with him what he aspired to in the long run. But with Jonathan perceiving his very survival as at stake almost every week, I'd had little choice. I had been without the luxury of addressing his life on a grander scale.

All the while, I'd had questions about Jonathan's past, as much as about his future. I had often wondered, for instance, about the origin of his diffuse anxiety and of his compulsive nature. How had he arrived at his inordinate demand for purity and his sense that almost any deviation, even in his thoughts, might prove calamitous?

Now these questions obtruded on me. I become conscious of them clamoring for my attention, perhaps because I knew that I would never discover the answers. They were not to come within my compass, I realized, but within that of Jonathan's next therapist, who would join him back in the past as well as accompany him into the future.

Still, from what I already knew, I could say one thing with authority. Not just Jonathan's very early years, but the period around his parents' divorce, must have been crucial in his life. As I thought about this, the evidence for it seemed incontrovertible.

After all, I realized, many young children become overly scrupulous, as Jonathan did. And many of them adopt magical rituals to protect themselves. Apparently, Jonathan's catastrophic response to his own imperfections, even to his having imperfect thoughts, had begun as such reactions usually do. He had assimilated the idea—or more precisely, the requirement—from a mother who was fearful, highly anxious, and a perfectionist herself.

But most such children outgrow that anxiety-ritual stage by the age of nine, and certainly, by puberty. Jonathan had not managed to free himself from that stage. If anything, the grip of anxiety on Jonathan, and his inclination to rituals, had grown more fierce with age, and the question was why.

Exactly what force had driven Jonathan toward rituals, especially in that era of strife between his parents? I asked Jonathan to talk about this period of his life one final time, hoping that I could confirm a hypothesis already evolving in my mind.

He could remember his mother becoming very agitated the year before her husband left, and she had remained that way. She would often mutter that her husband was "filthy," which the boys knew referred to his affairs with other women. Jonathan would always cry when his mother had said that. It had been unbearable to think that his father was never coming home, and that it was folly even to picture his return.

I wondered if Jonathan had imagined for a time that if he himself behaved flawlessly his father might be allowed to return. Such infantile omnipotence is not unusual in children of divorce, who commonly blame themselves for their parents' breakup. Jonathan's having imagined that would explain the catastrophic significance to him of his own departing in any way from perfection.

I asked Jonathan about the rituals he had engaged in back then. I reminded him of the notebook he had once kept, in which, he'd said, he had recorded the number of times he had masturbated, in his vain effort to stop. He had been thirteen. What had he really been afraid of? What had he feared would happen if he continued?

At first, Jonathan could reply only that to him in those days, masturbation had seemed a disgusting act. I asked him what he had imagined its consequences could be?

He thought a while, and then said he assumed that if his mother had found out, she would be so horrified that things would never again be the same between them. But there he stopped.

My hypothesis—that Jonathan had tightened his demand for inner purity while using it as a kind of charm to bring his father back—received no real support. Nor was it disproven. It would have to remain what it was—merely a hypothesis.

To my successor would be left the task of learning how Jonathan had become so ritualistic. But even in those last few weeks, Jonathan's compulsion continued to lessen. During the week before Jonathan and I parted for the summer, he said, he hadn't gone to the gym to shoot baskets at all. He said that he was pleasantly surprised that the few urges he'd had were not very strong.

Understandably, he added, he was afraid that those urges could again rear up without notice, as if his compulsion were a monster who had simply gone to sleep.

I sympathized with both his delight at its disappearance and his concern that it still dwelt inside of him and was only dormant.

"But you put the 'monster' to sleep," I reminded Jonathan, "by your greatly improved acceptance of yourself.

"And the way you're going, as you keep looking squarely at your own impulses, I have no doubt that you'll put it out of its misery altogether before long."

We shook hands good-bye, agreeing to see each other again. As for finding another therapist, unfortunately I didn't know anyone in his area whom I could recommend, but I suggested that he call the University of Vermont for leads.

In the fall I got a letter from him, saying that he was working with a woman he liked very much. Catherine, he said, was the second psychologist he had seen; the first had been a man who appeared so formal and remote that Jonathan couldn't conceive of confiding in him.

Three months later Jonathan called me and said he was coming to New York City to see his brother. I invited him to drop by. He told me a little about his therapy with Catherine. He called her a wonderful antidote for Julia—"very gentle and forgiving."

An antidote to your own worst self, I thought but didn't say.

Then Jonathan told me that shortly after the boys had come back to the school, he'd begun to anticipate his problems returning. He hadn't shot a basketball all summer. Catherine had suggested that he go to the gym and shoot a hundred foul shots, deliberately missing the hoop every time.

Jonathan had, and he said that he felt it had helped.

"But there was no way I could have done that six months ago," he hastened to add, perhaps worrying that I might feel bad because it had been her idea and not mine.

Shades of being caught in a parental duel and torn between loyalties, I thought. But once again I didn't say anything. It was no longer my province to interpret or even to ask him what lay behind his comments.

After that, I heard nothing from Jonathan for nearly three years. Then

I got an announcement of his wedding, which was to take place in Chicago, where the bride's family lived. That was the last I ever heard from him.

I actually saw the Gloucester School only once, and that was two years after I had stopped working with Jonathan. I was visiting a friend who had rented a summer cottage in the area, and I was eager to see the place that meant so much to Jonathan.

I could easily picture it as his ideal school, with its manicured lawns, its modern centers, and its mission-style dining room, noisy with boys devoted only to the moment, while their future lives quaver before them. But of course not even this ideal can be composed solely of goodness and eagerness to excel. There must also be, even in the ideal school, misdirected efforts, sometimes dishonesty, and the occasional taint of brutality.

And I imagine that Jonathan has by now discovered that the same holds for him. His universe is not so fragile that an imperfect thought or a single foul deed will shatter it. I also imagine that having learned these things, he needs no further rituals or incantations to cleanse his inner world. Nothing will suffice except self-acceptance.

...3...

The Classical View

*F*reud's view of personality, that a person's childhood memories reside in a "timeless unconscious" and still influence the adult, did more justice to the complexity of our makeup than any psychological theory before or since. We are indeed creatures who keep dark secrets even from ourselves, and nowhere is our layered complexity more evident than with compulsions. Voices from deep within us seem to command our observance of their dictates, and when we resist they boom and cause our whole foundation to shake.

Even though we have progressed well beyond Freud in many realms of psychology, our starting place for examining compulsions must be with him. I for one am not a strict Freudian, but all psychologists, whether Freudians or not, owe a debt to him in understanding the nature of compulsions. Without Freud's work we could hardly distinguish compulsions, in all their intricacy and depth, from ordinary, simple habits.

We psychologists—whether by profession or interest—are virtually all post-Freudians in the sense that we believe in a psyche with unconscious layers, and we believe that unconscious forces affect people's thoughts and actions.

Above all, we believe in the complexity of personality and in the influence of a person's past, of long ago experiences, on people's contemporary lives. And Freud's own view was the first great argument for this.

Early in this century Western society was thunderstruck by the writings and claims of Freud and his followers. Only when those theories were not borne out by massive cures did there come articles and books by the truckload attacking Freud's premises and promises. Many failures of practicing psychoanalysts (the term used to denote Freud and his followers) were there for all to see, and the master himself acknowledged disillusionment.

Slowly the cadre of orthodox psychoanalysts dwindled. Today, though virtually all therapists accept some of Freud's main ideas, his original writings have been scrupulously dissected and found wanting in many respects.

Still, Freud removed the curtain from human complexity. He taught us to picture the existence of psychic events that have deep roots and multiple layers, though the events themselves may appear to be simple and insignificant. In applying this approach to compulsions he gave us invaluable insights. He identified the critical elements of compulsions and of personality in general, though time has proven that he sometimes misunderstood their relationship.

Therefore, it is worth pausing to review certain of Freud's ideas in order to distill the elements necessary to our post-Freudian understanding of compulsions.

To utilize the relevant portions of Freud's work, to amend his original concepts and add to them what the half century since his death has revealed, it is important first to examine certain of his main ideas.

Freud had two distinct sets of premises. One had to do with the *milestones of development* in a person's life that he regarded as common throughout all humanity. He saw the same particular events as the critical stages of every life. These include his well-known Oedipal stage, his belief in an anal period, and his theory of childhood penis envy.

Today relatively few people believe in any such universal stages of all human existence. Virtually all the milestones that Freud identified as decisive in every human development have been downgraded as certainly not universal—and some as not operative at all. The paramount importance of sex, with its underlying every problem, the Oedipal syndrome, the little girl's so-called penis envy—and the list could go on and on—the majority of students of psychology have come to disbelieve in the universality of any of these.

Moreover, it has been noted, if these milestones do seem to be important for certain individuals, it is for reasons very different from those Freud suggested. For instance, as Simone de Beauvoir observed, if indeed little girls sometimes do envy a boy's penis, it is because the girl has already learned that those who have penises—boys—seem to be privileged, so that possession of a penis is merely a symbol of power. Not sexuality but social prestige is fundamental.

Freud's milestone concerning compulsions was the toilet-training phase. He claimed that all compulsions begin then. In particular, he maintained that compulsions begin with the child holding back feces to control the parents, and often as a form of sadism, especially when the parents are overly demanding regarding the child's bowel movements. He repeatedly used the term *anal-sadistic* in connection with compulsives.

Freud believed that it is after controlling his parents in the only way he could that the child develops the controlling personality that even today we agree is so often found in the compulsive.

In Freud's view, holding back feces translates into a triad of personality traits: cleanliness, orderliness, and thriftiness. The character structure forms and sustains after that, and *anality* becomes a motif throughout the person's life.

Over time, according to Freud, what was once an option—to withhold something—becomes the adult's only way of doing things. The adult's fear of losing control, as he did or nearly did in childhood, assumes a variety of forms and gives rise to a variety of rituals. Some, like compulsive hand washing, seem more clearly related to perfectionism and a need for control than others. But even seemingly unrelated compulsions, like touching lampposts or avoiding cracks in the sidewalk, Freud related to the perfectionism of the toilet-training stage and the fear of chaos.

Freud regarded all compulsions as coming out of this desire for rigid perfectionism and excessive dread of losing control. According to him the compulsive, once his character structure is formed, has no choice but to continue the pattern and is driven to do so throughout his life.

Seeing this toilet-training milestone, along with others, as part of the formation of the compulsive personality has lost favor, even with psychoanalysts. As one, Aaron Esman, wrote regarding compulsions a few years ago:

> We have, of course, long ago given up the id-psychological connection associated with toilet training traumas.[1]

Today we dismiss as an early guess Freud's connection of compulsions with the toilet-training period. Few believe that all compulsions are the continual replaying in different guises of an anal urge for control.

However, it is true that compulsive people are seeking symbolic control and are trying to stem unconscious fears, just as Freud said. Moreover, as he observed, compulsives are often controlling people; as their fear constricts them, they constrict others.

But what drives the compulsive is a fear more general than any connected with the bathroom. The compulsive adult may have evolved his unconscious fear in any context. All that matters is that he has the fear and is attempting to minister to it. The control sought by the compulsive is that of a person terrified of what he or she sees as chaos and imminent danger all around him. Such a person feels that he has no hope but to regulate everything that can be regulated.

Perhaps Freud imagined that the dread that gives rise to compulsions is imprinted in the toilet-training period because that is a time when harsh and exacting parents are often at their worst. Such parents, who undoubtedly make more of a fuss over toilet training than other, more lenient, parents, would create a context of scrupulosity and fear generally, not just in the bathroom. We might expect such demanding parents to raise children who develop more compulsions than those of other parents. Doubtless

---

[1]Aaron Esman, *Journal of the American Psychoanalytic Association,* vol. 37, 1989, p. 330.

Freud observed this, and as with his other milestone theories, he overgeneralized from the specifics of his own patients.

In most cases, and not just with compulsions, subsequent study has not borne out the universality of Freud's milestone theories.

However, his second set of premises—those that compose what we may refer to as his *dynamic theory*—still remain useful and are indeed our best starting place for the study of compulsions. Freud's dynamic theory refers to his work describing how personality operates, about the forces and counterforces that make the psyche function.

Included in it are Freud's notions of repression and of the denial of unconscious problems by the use of defense mechanisms. Freud taught the Western world to think in terms of a layered psyche in which people use defense mechanisms to repress old conflicts and relegate them to the realm of the unconscious. He taught us that these repressed fears, still operating from their underworld, continue to wreak havoc on people. This idea—that there are levels to the psyche and that a person represses fearful ideas to lower levels—is indispensable to understanding what a compulsion is.

This concept of the mind was new. Freud and his followers presented it in thousands of pages and made it so well known that by now even most ardent anti-Freudians automatically think in terms of these levels.

As with many great theories, Freud's dynamic description struck an immediate chord in people. Presumably, many had already sensed the existence of some deeper undiscovered layer of the psyche. From time immemorial geniuses had here and there talked about unconscious motivations. They had alluded to unconscious phenomena somehow reaching upward, motivating us and planting ideas in our minds,

By the mid-eighteenth century, for instance, historians speculated that certain kings had possessed unconscious desires that had governed them.

Shakespeare, the great observer of human nature, sometimes has characters talk about these subterranean levels of their own psyches. Brutus talks about a council going on inside himself, and then about an "insurrection" when on the verge of killing Caesar. And even the thug Tybalt, in the household of Juliet, explains his nervousness as the result of a clash between his rage and his need to control it. With astounding self-perception he names these two forces, which would ordinarily be unconscious. In the real world we might expect him to notice only his conscious symptom, his trembling. Tybalt says:

> *Patience . . . with willful choler meeting*
> *Makes my flesh tremble in their different greeting.*

In another instance, the poet Horace, in 50 B.C., talks about tears involuntarily gliding down his cheeks. He attributes them to certain thoughts so deep within him that he cannot identify them.

And my favorite reference to unconscious motivation was found on a fragment of stone inscribed around 700 B.C. by the Greek poet Alkaois:

> *War*
> *Speaks*
> *For that murderer,*
> *Fear.*[2]

But the notion of layers of the psyche, though old, had before Freud surfaced only in fragments. Freud alone sought to explain how ideas become unconscious and described the whole personality as one integrated, layered system. He codified the notion of the unconscious, he collected the ideas about it and incorporated them, and he gave us our picture of the psyche as a dynamic field of forces, only some of which are conscious.

Freud's view was that the subterranean level of this multilayered psyche was its core and that this core was eternal—a *timeless unconscious*.

He wrote that this core evolves in childhood, when all the basic

---

[2]*Lyrics from the Greek*, translated and edited by Burton Raffel (Writers Workshop, 1978).

repressions in a person's life occur. Once childhood is over, these repressed early memories, mostly fears, remain bound up in the unconscious realm. The psyche congeals. After that these memories, locked in their congealed psychic core, are no longer subject to change by anything the person does.

They go on governing the person's life, however, in some few cases blessing the person with self-esteem, but more likely wreaking havoc from the underworld—in either case, determining the person's actions and giving rise to thoughts and impulses over a lifetime.

It was fundamental to Freud that what he called *character structure* congeals. He believed that nothing can basically change a person, except, that is, for psychoanalytic treatment, which he was fond of likening to surgery on the psyche itself. He tried different methods of tapping the unconscious as he went along. He never revised his basic belief, however, that the psyche congeals after childhood. In fact, over time he came to believe even more strongly that this fixed psyche determines personality and the whole course of the individual's life.

Armed with Freud's explanation of the psyche as layered, and of compulsions as attempts to deal with unconscious dread, we are now led to ask, What causes this fear to keep erupting in the compulsive person?

Freud specified that what prompts the memories are the person's own impulses. The compulsive person has impulses in the present that are tinged with a sense of danger from the past. He is afraid of doing something, or thinking something, or imagining something that, owing to a past experience, seems loaded with danger. The very prospect strikes fear in him.

Freud wrote that in order for a childhood event to cause this, to transmit a signal of danger into the future, the child must have been a player in some threatening scene—perhaps a player only in desire or fantasy, but an active participant nevertheless. In maintaining that the child must play some role, even in the case of a tragedy, for a compulsion to develop, Freud was abiding by a corollary of his dynamic model that stipulated that all the vying forces are within the person, and not outside.

Freud maintained that for a memory to become and remain unconscious, and to influence the adult, it is necessary for the child himself to do something. This "doing something" includes any kind of natural reaction—for instance, hating a brutal parent, or forgiving a loved parent who has molested the child, or remaining silent while a sibling is beaten.

In each case, the child's act or fantasy or wish or impulse is what causes the trouble later on. That kind of wish or impulse, now connected with trauma, becomes contaminated for them. If forgiveness was a problem—if the child forgave the offending adult and suffered—then in later life any impulse of forgiveness might cause dread in the person and lead to compulsions.

If hating a parent for brutality was itself terrifying to the child, then the child might afterward fear his own aggression. In later life he or she might forgive too many people automatically, rather than hate them or even indict them in his or her own mind. Many adults adopt compulsions so as not to feel angry because they were so afraid to be angry when they were children.

Indeed, it is hard to imagine that a child subjected to sharp conditions would not react in some way. But it is the reaction of the child that becomes the problem later on and not the brutality in itself.

Theoretically, a child might even be hospitalized, perhaps after a serious car accident, for a few days or longer with no trauma. However, if the child had some wish or fantasy connected with the mishap, the danger of long-term dread and compulsive behavior would be great.

For instance, if a child had secretly wished that his mother "leave him alone" and she then died or was incapacitated in the car accident, then ever afterward when the child wanted things there might be a sense of doom and wrongdoing about desiring them. The adult might conceivably become limited by a fear of wishing for ideal outcomes—even for a good marriage or for happiness.

Freud believed that this occurred in Dostoyevski's case. He maintained that it was not the early death of Dostoyevski's father, but the young Fyodor Dostoyevski's *wish* for his father's death, the boy's "fantasy parricide," that created long-standing implications in the psyche of the great author.

The evidence—and certainly my own study of compulsive people—has borne out this highly dramatic insight of Freud's. People with compulsions are responding to themselves, to impulses, fantasies, urges that they cannot identify; they are responding to their own impending action that carries with it a sense of past danger. By the compulsive activity they are trying to stifle an impulse that has been tainted by unconscious memories. "Within himself the danger lies/ Yet lies within his power," wrote John Milton in *Paradise Lost*.

This theory, properly understood, points up even more sharply than we had realized how hideous it is for parents to molest children sexually. That such abuse does not merely impart bad memories but contaminates the child's basic impulses, such as the sexual impulse or the desire to forgive or the ability to trust, shows that the mischief is even worse than we had thought. With this understanding of the real injury, we may indict those adult aggressors even more strongly than we did in the past.

A highly dramatic case of mine points out that when people feel haunted by the past, more than a mere memory of being mistreated is apt to be involved. Mere memories are passive. But the real danger is that even when people have been brutally mistreated and had no options, they often imagine subsequently that they had some option, that they played a determining role in what was done to them. For instance, they unconsciously blame themselves for an impulse or wish they had at the time. Later, the terror they feel is a reaction to that impulse or wish returning in a new context.

A Jewish man spent four years, from ages eight to twelve, in a German concentration camp. He was there without his parents, who had both been put to death in another camp.

In my office the man spoke slowly and in a tedious monotone. He seemed pathologically orderly and low-key, more dead than alive. He had left his previous therapist because the man fell asleep repeatedly during sessions, and as my patient spoke I could see why my predecessor had become somnolent.

My patient worked as a draftsman, and did his drawings in a room with forty others. He told me that he had lost one job after another after his bosses had accused him of being "too rigid."

We had been working together for a few months when an order came down in his company that henceforth all drawings were to have the corners crossed—that is, the lines were to extend a little past the corners to make the drawings look artistic. The man balked at the order, protesting that doing this was technically wrong, since the lines should by rights stop at the corners. He compulsively *had* to complete the corners properly, so as not to violate the physical reality of those corners.

After repeatedly refusing to comply with the new order, because he could not, he was fired once again.

Discussion revealed that my patient was totally possessed by the company's original demand for pinpoint accuracy and was absolutely terrified to go against it.

In my office he recounted one story after another in which anyone who violated a rule in the camp where he "grew up" was put to death. For instance, every morning at 5:00 A.M. the inmates were made to stand in the freezing cold for two and a half hours, and anyone who fell to one knee was shot at once. To steal a piece of bread could mean death.

Not surprisingly my patient had spent his early days with fantasies of breaking the rules, of killing the guards and rejoining his parents, whom he assumed were still alive. But those fantasies of what we today might consider healthy aggression were at the time loaded with terror for the young boy. He would sometimes awaken from dreams imagining that he had just broken a camp rule and had only seconds to live.

As an adult my patient thought that he had left the camps behind him, except for the memories, of course. But in fact he could not discard his unconscious associations to them—in particular, his terror of doing anything aggressive, of breaking any rule, of doing anything that might silhouette him against others for the instant it took to be seen.

His dread of breaking rules, even invented ones or those he inferred mistakenly, had riddled him with rituals. Nor could he change his own rules even when his "camp" or his company asked him to. In the end, he was silhouetted against the others and shot, over and over again.

Although the culprits were obviously those who had put him in a concentration camp, the man's continued terror was a response, not directly to the camp experience, but to the piece of himself, programmed in his unconscious, that had mentally defied the guards. Who could have guessed that horrible experiences in a concentration camp would translate into a compulsion about perfect corners? The unseen intermediary phase was that the camp had induced a dread of even the slightest urge for personal expression.

Freud's formulation that the person "repeats his behavior rather than remembering" captures the idea that the activity keeps blinding the person to his real fear while allaying that fear, though only temporarily. The compulsive is engaging in a symbolic ritual to deal with an unconscious dread. This is why the compulsive person can never find lasting solace in doing what seems so urgent. The activity is not removing the real source of dread, which is unconscious.

Keep in mind this phrase, which Freud used quite often: *repeat rather than remember*. We are going to make extensive use of it later on.

Fortunately for people with compulsions, the twentieth century has taught us that character structure does not congeal. The timeless unconscious is not completely resistant to the best efforts that people can make to change it.

Freud was too quick to conclude that people who suffer from unconscious fears didn't change because they couldn't change. His perception of people as victims of their own congealed nature was unwarranted.

Freud believed that there was no point to a compulsive's deliberately refraining from the compulsion—refusing to say the little poem hundreds of times a day or fill in the *e*'s and *o*'s in the newspaper before going to sleep, for instance. Whatever the person unconsciously feared would remain unaltered, even after such a prolonged heroic effort. The drive for the compulsive act would still be there undiminished, even if the compulsive activity was not carried out for years.

And of the compulsive gambler Freud contended that it doesn't matter if he gambles or stops gambling. Freud believed, by the way, that many compulsive gamblers are driven by an urge to self-destruct. He believed that because the compulsive gambler secretly wants to destroy himself, not gambling would make no real difference. The gambler's unconscious need to self-destruct would be the same, which would mean that even if he stopped gambling for a while, he would only seek to destroy himself in other ways. In fact, referring to the gambler, the eminent Freudian psycho-analyst Edmund Bergler did say just that.

Or take the draftsman I mentioned. His association of any noncon-formity with punishment by death, Freud would aver, would persist whether he obeyed or disobeyed rules—no matter what he did.

Freud concluded that the deep, unconscious motives that prompt people to act as they do—in many cases consistently and neurotically over a lifetime—simply exist like motors that the person cannot touch. Or to put it another way, Freud saw a one-way cause-and-effect relationship: The unconscious motives (in the compulsive's case, the dread) cause the person to act.

In this one-sided view, nothing the person does, no series of decisions made even over a period of time, can exert any effect on the unconscious forces below the surface.

However, my view is that people can influence their own motives—even their deep unconscious ones. To insist that our character structure hardens after childhood, much the way our skull hardens in its shape, is to trivialize all our personal endeavors. I believe that the relationship between one's motives and behavior *goes both ways*. People can change whole constella-tions of attitudes, their whole outlook, by how they act.

The compulsive gambler, for instance, will affect his subjective need to gamble by stopping. Consider, for example, a man who harbors an unconscious picture of himself as weak and a sissy alongside his brother and father. He gambles compulsively because he is in dread of perceiving himself as such a weakling. To him, his big bets at the track are symbolic of masculinity, and when worrying about the horses he is saved from having to think about himself. He acts compulsively rather than remembering how lowly he is—or, rather, how wretched he feels he is.

Refraining from gambling *will* bolster this man's sense of worth some-what. And if he revises his behavior in other ways, he can further strengthen himself psychologically. No matter that the man felt weak and like a loser in life for many years. As long as he lives, he retains the power to revise his self-image and to eradicate his dread of self-scrutiny. He always remains able to develop the genuine pride afforded by breaking any compulsion.

Granted, the man cannot do this by giving up gambling alone. If he tries to do so without making other revisions in his behavior, he may find the going almost impossible. It seems to him that everything in his life depends upon his gambling, that he is defined by the activity and by his skill at it.

In order for him to raise his self-esteem permanently—that is, to confront his dread of being a weakling and to overcome it—he must discard other behaviors that are part of his gambling persona. Among these might be boasting about his abilities and his wealth, name dropping about important horse players whom he knows, expressing contempt for people who work hard in daily jobs, lying, and exaggerating to get attention. In short, he has to face who he really is, which he has never allowed himself to do.

But the point is that these action changes would change his outlook. They would in time do away with the unconscious dread and the feeling of fraud that seems to allow the man no choice but to defraud himself further by gambling. Instead of seeing himself as a weakling he could feel like a hero in facing his reality, and his reality itself would not seem so bad. Almost surely, after making these changes, he would form new perceptions of gamblers and braggarts; he would see them and not himself as shallow. He would not need to gamble as he did.

People remain forever able to alter their natures, including even their deeply unconscious motives. True, the psyche is layered with unconscious motives at the subterranean level. But changes at the top—surface changes if you prefer—penetrate deeply into the core. The field of forces is there, but we construct and reconstruct that field. We do this in any case, and we might as well know exactly how so that we can construct the field that we want.

Indeed, the reason that unconscious fears perpetuate is that people unwittingly renew them. Nothing is frozen. Rather, people continually refashion themselves in their own image without realizing that they are doing so.

★ ★ ★

Many organizations who work with compulsives, like Alcoholics Anonymous, know this. They insist that compulsives refrain—from overeating or
alcohol or gambling or whatever. These groups have come to describe
compulsions as "progressive," meaning that the activity feeds the very need
to engage in it. Giving in to the compulsion sends the worst possible
message to the mind. If one overeats because of despair over a marriage, the
marriage will seem worse as one overeats more. Whatever hopelessness gave
rise to the compulsion, that hopelessness will only deepen.

These self-help groups also recognize that the compulsive must
change more about his behavior than the single compulsive activity.

For the compulsive, the challenge is to identify precisely which of his
other regular behaviors are keeping him or her dependent on the compulsion. Which of the person's many routine activities are restoring the unconscious dread?

As the boasting makes it hard for the gambler to stop gambling, an
overeater might discover that he or she has been avoiding mirrors, belittling
his or her appearance, using self-derisive humor, rebuffing other people's
genuine attempts at intimacy—in short, giving up on even the potential of
being stylish and confident. Such acts induce pessimism and dispose the
person to go on overeating.

Many people who compulsively overeat are giving too much emotionally and not getting enough back. The person might, say, be pouring
out emotion to a lover or friends who do not reciprocate. The person
doesn't see this clearly, but dimly senses it and feels starved, then unconsciously translates the hunger for love into hunger for food and feeds
himself.

Breaking the overeating compulsion requires identifying where one is
giving too much and then curtailing those behaviors that induced a sense
of deprivation. Of course, this is easier said than done, but many people
find, quite unexpectedly, that after a failed love affair, when they are on
their own and no longer giving too much to the wrong person, they can
diet almost effortlessly, whereas previously they felt like hopeless food
junkies. The point is that every compulsive need is reinforced not just by

the compulsion itself but by other behaviors that undermine the person. Identifying and stopping these subtle actions that induce pessimism and hopelessness is absolutely necessary in order to break the grip of compulsions.

It is possible for a person to identify the acts that are maintaining his or her own dread or self-loathing. Since acts affect a person's underlying motives, even unconscious motives, there are in every case critical acts reinfecting the person with his dread. The compulsive needs to find those actions in his particular case and eliminate them in order to annihilate any urge for the compulsion.

There is a two-way relationship between act and motive. Psychology in its first century as a profession has been far too busy thinking of motives as causes, and of acts as outcomes, to appreciate the degree to which acts create motives. And yet this last truth is the vital one for anyone with a compulsion to understand.

We may certainly welcome Freud's conception of a layered personality, and in large measure his explanation of compulsions. But what the compulsive does now, in adult life, will either renew his set of motivations and, in particular, his dread, or will eradicate whatever unconscious fear motivates the compulsion.

For now, just keep this idea in mind: The persistence of compulsions attests not to a congealed psyche but to the person's unknowingly replenishing his character in exactly the same form year after year. To grasp this reverse causality between motive and act rounds out an understanding of their relationship.

Whereas Jonathan's compulsive ritual was so urgently driven that I was forced to study him while he continued it, the man I am going to discuss next was able to stop his pattern for a while. When he did, the results stunned both of us, bringing forth especially dramatic revelations, as I think you will agree.

Unlike Jonathan, Martin quite enjoyed his compulsion. He never felt ridiculous the way Jonathan did. Nor would Martin have described himself as a victim of inner forces or as self-defeating.

However, Martin was deeply unhappy. He had lost the relationships most precious to him, and he lacked even the emotional language to describe his tragedy. In a sense, Martin seemed more preposterous to the world; he was every bit as much a victim of inner forces and far more self-defeating than Jonathan ever was.

Martin was in the vast category of those who suffer from a whole network of compulsions that the sufferer construes as reasonable and appropriate. He experienced none of the panic that others might over the loss of volition that compulsions entail. Though he had sacrificed virtually everything worth living for in deference to his compulsive patterns, he would readily have maintained that he was doing only what he wanted to do. In fact, he prided himself on how he lived. He saw himself as only coping with a hostile world—and coping quite successfully at that.

...4...

The Landlord

*In 1848 John Jacob Astor was eighty-four years old, and the fat
of his body drooped like tallow drippings on a guttering candle. The last
few weeks of his life the only nourishment he could take was milk from
a woman's breast. For exercise his servants gently tossed him up and
down on a blanket. One of Astor's rent collectors was present one day
as this went on, and from the blanket Astor asked in a feeble voice if a
certain woman had paid her rent.*

—Edward Ellis, *The Epic of New York City*

*A*t first I didn't realize that Martin
Roth's obsessional thoughts about
a stray cat were a direct result of his doing what I had asked him to do. I
had been staggered by how moved Martin had been by what he, and
presumably millions of others, had seen on television.

"Right in the middle of the game, it was maybe the sixth inning, the
announcer, Tim McCarver, said, 'Oops, the batter is stepping out of the
box, there's a cat loose in the outfield.'

"Then they showed this black cat running as fast as it could, it was lost
out there on the field, in front of all those people. Some of the players and
the ground keepers chased it, but they couldn't catch it. It was a pretty black
thing. They couldn't catch it.

"The cat was terrified. Finally it ran into the dugout, and the Oakland manager, Tony La Russa, picked it up. The announcer said he had a lot of cats, and that he was a big animal-rights person. And I figured he took care of it. But I wasn't sure."

Martin hadn't thought about the cat anymore right after that night; he imagined that he had forgotten about it. But a few days later the cat had started coming back into his mind. At odd moments during the day, and sometimes when he woke up at night, he would think about that cat, worrying about it.

While Martin was going over his receipt book with his secretary or actually engaged in a business dealing—sometimes ten or twenty times a day—he would see that cat, frightened almost to death, running around that outfield in Oakland. The vision seemed almost to have a will of its own, the way obsessional images do, as if it broke through the pales and barriers of his head demanding his attention.

Once or twice when he mentioned it, I thought about the creature in Edgar Allan Poe's story "The Black Cat," the one that couldn't be silenced by the murderer and that finally drove him half insane and whose muffled cry caused him to give away his near-perfect crime to the authorities.

The whole memory was remarkable for Martin for several reasons. One was that it entailed so much sympathy for another mortal—and an animal at that. I had never heard Martin express genuine sympathy for anyone, man or woman or beast; that is, for anyone other than himself.

Secondly, it was remarkable because Martin, who ordinarily was utterly unobservant, remembered so many details. He seemed almost to cherish the image of that lost cat on television, of the stadium, and of the announcer's words—even though the total memory tortured him. Martin was a man who ordinarily paid attention to almost nothing, who remembered nothing, who walked through almost all of his life in a trance.

Martin had come to me for one reason: He wanted his wife back. He swore that he would give anything if she would agree to his moving back in with her. Now, six years after their separation, he had suddenly decided that he had nothing to live for without her. And yet when I had asked him what she looked like, Martin had seemed puzzled, as if he had never thought to look at her. "Well, is she tall or short?" I had asked, testing the limits of his unconcern.

"Tall, I guess." He nodded, as if pleased that he could acquit himself well on that one. He could also recall that her hair was dark. "But she kept changing its color," he added with annoyance. Change of any kind bothered Martin.

Her height, and the fact that his wife had been a little overweight when he had lived with her, were about as far as he could go by way of description.

On a whim, because money and buying things were so central in Martin's life, and because he had so often substituted money for human caring in the equations he expressed to me, I asked him that day when he told me about the image, "If you could pay a thousand dollars to make this memory of that black cat go out of your mind, I mean so that you never thought about that cat again in your whole life, would you do it?"

"No," he said. "I don't want to just put it out of my mind. I want to know the cat will be okay. I'd pay a thousand in a minute if I could be sure the cat was going to be all right. I have to know that."

It had actually crossed Martin's mind to investigate, and perhaps to offer some money for protection of the cat, but he had demurred, fearing that he would uncover the worst, that it had been put to death.

So much caring for one of the most seemingly uncaring men I ever knew caught me up short, sent me back to the drawing board.

From the moment I had met Martin Roth six months before that session, he struck me as exactly the kind of man whom women are warned against by friends who know the type. He was unemotional, unexpressive, uncaring, un-everything that a woman should want in a man.

So why would any woman want Martin enough to become involved with him—and hurt by him? Why did Martin not simply exist alone for his life span (if one could call his a "life"), in as harmless a fashion as the edge of a cliff that no one approaches, or at best as a serrated knife blade in the kitchen, which a person might look at but employ only guardedly if at all?

Some reasons why women succumb may be posited: the woman's yearning for the inaccessible; incomplete relations with her own father; the lure of power (Martin had plenty of money); the desire to pry humanity out of an oyster; the curiosity that will some day send us to other galaxies.

In any case, few women had actually tried to get through to Martin, and that was probably a good thing, because those who did had failed miserably. Martin was a losing proposition for every woman who knew him, and the closer a woman got to him, the more damaged she was when the relationship ended.

Money was Martin's compulsion: earning it, investing it, bargaining for it, lying for it, squeezing it out of strangers—even in small amounts—counting it, evaluating his net worth compared to other people's.

Moreover, Martin's perception of the world was that everyone shared his monomania for money. The first time I saw him, I had asked him to sit in my waiting room while I finished a phone call. When I finally admitted him into my office, apologizing for my few minutes' lateness, he had asked, "Were you talking to your stockbroker?"

From that very first session, Martin had struck me as a colorless man; he had gray hair, a white shirt, gray eyes behind ultrathick lenses, and usually a gray suit to match. Even his eyeglasses were colorless. He was of average height, and apparently about fifty.

He had come to me because, after their six-year separation, his wife, Lila, wanted to put through a legal divorce. He had no idea why Lila had thrown him out in the first place, and he described her wanting this divorce as "stupid on her part" because she would get a lot less money than he was giving her now.

Martin conceptualized nearly everything in life by its efficiency, meaning whether it made money. His reasons why Lila should take him back were all items that she had received: "She has four good fur coats." "She has her own car." "I pay all the insurance for her and the kids—anything they come to me for, they get."

He seemed bewildered that anyone could feel discontent in such a nirvana, and yet over the years Lila had reduced their conversations to necessities.

"And my daughters talk to me only when they want something," he said, and imitated them: "Daddy, I want to go to Europe with my friends over Easter." "Daddy, I dented the car."

"Why do you want to go back into that household?" I asked him.

He just shrugged.

"Do you love Lila?"

"Believe me, Doctor, I give all of them a great deal. I'm not Donald Trump, but I have done well. But they're always complaining. Nothing I ever give them is enough." He smiled, oddly, I thought.

Then he asked, "What do you think of that?" as if I must surely appreciate the irony and injustice in his situation.

I could understand his family's wanting him out of their lives a lot more readily than why he wanted them back.

Toward the end of that first session, he finally distinguished between his daughters, whom he had characterized up to then as an abusive unit. There were two of them: Anne, who was nineteen and in college, and Joan, who was twenty-three and worked in some office.

"What kind of office?"

He wasn't sure. "Something to do with movie leases. Her boss travels a lot."

When I asked Martin to talk about his eighteen-year marriage, he made it sound remarkably uneventful. Near the end of that span, Lila had gone back to school and made plenty of friends. At the very end, she and Martin had absolutely nothing to say to each other. She had accused him of not being interested in anything. Lila would schedule their social life and would lug him along.

I extracted from Martin that he had no friends of his own, only business associates, and when out with Lila's friends he seldom joined in conversations. "But I took her friends out to good restaurants. Some of them were artists and very poor, and they accepted me. Lila was the one who didn't."

He told me that Lila had gone into therapy a year before their breakup, and that he had gone to see her therapist a few times.

"That woman therapist of hers didn't like me," Martin said. "Do you know what I paid for Lila's therapy, and then the therapist told her to leave me? Fifteen thousand dollars." He smiled again.

I asked him a few general questions about his life since being separated. He had lived alone for the six years in one of the buildings he owned, in a small, one-bedroom apartment. He could well afford more space in a better building, but he told me, "Why occupy an apartment that can yield two thousand dollars a month when this one will do as well?"

It was rather easy to see that Martin Roth was a brutally punishing person whose most consistent victim since he left his family was himself. He alluded to having dated for a while after Lila broke up with him, but that had stopped. His solitary daily routine was waking up at six, riding his exercise bike for a half hour (not watching television while he did), dressing, and going out to a local breakfast spot. He usually ate alone (the same breakfast of poached eggs on toast), though a few men who also owned buildings in the area sometimes dropped by. They would talk about property values or complain about how unfair the law courts were becoming in favor of tenants who were late with payments or delinquent altogether.

Then to the office. He had a secretary. "She's all right, I guess. But not too much up here"—he pointed to his head. He refused to trust any managing agent, preferring to do all the bookkeeping, billing, and collecting himself. He even went with his lawyer to the courts regularly, since there was constant trouble with one tenant or another.

In recent years, he would go a few times a week to the office of a neighbor, a mostly retired man, very rich, and would play gin rummy with three or four others in his own stark, lonely category. That had been Martin's social life, but he had just given it up after deciding that they smoked too much. Nowadays Martin would pick up a light dinner, heat it up, watch some television, and go to sleep.

Martin Roth's was the most constricted and boring life I had ever heard described, not simply because it was one note, but because it seemed unrelieved even by imagination or hope. I found myself depressed even contemplating it. Whistler's mother seemed a better candidate for therapy, so little differential was there between the life Martin actually led and the one he wanted. His whole existence seemed a testimony to the insufficiency of money.

At least that was how it appeared when I saw Martin in the early days. Whatever fascination he held for me derived from my sense that I was at last getting the chance to meet the quintessential stingy property owner whom the world complains about. I would not just encounter him, but possibly delve into his psyche to have him reveal himself as he never would to the world. Something must have made Martin turn out the way he had, and perhaps I could discover what it was.

Such strong reactions beset all therapists. We cannot shun them. They help us understand how others see our patient, how he may hurt himself with people—and even how he sees himself. Indeed we are often most effective with people who evoke discomfort in us because it becomes so clear, and remains so clear to us, what we must deal with. Idealizing patients may by the same token sometimes blind us.

But Martin hadn't come to see me, I realized, in order to improve himself. He was merely putting up with my questions before coming to what he considered the real point.

"Doctor, I'll tell you why I'm here. I want you to talk to my wife. She won't listen to me. But she'll do what you say. She believes in therapists."

"I don't follow you, Martin."

"Tell her to take me back. How much do you want?"

"Martin, 1 can't possibly tell another person what to do with their life."

From anyone else the offer might have shocked me—it was so unethical and manipulative. But it didn't surprise me after what I had seen so far of Martin.

"Why not?" he asked, making a sour face.

"First of all, I don't know what's right for someone else. And second, the person wouldn't listen to me."

"She'll listen to you. Lila will."

"Martin, she has to decide on her own."

"Look, I'll pay you whatever you want. I certainly give Lila enough money. There's nothing she or my daughters want that I don't give them."

"Apparently, money isn't the only issue."

"Then what is?" he asked me.

Perhaps because of this dialogue, I realized how poor Martin's actual eyesight was. I also noticed that his eyes seemed pallid, nearly inanimate, as in a painting.

He leaned forward, possibly to discern any reaction of mine that he might capitalize on, and for a moment I felt sorry for him. He was quite alone.

Then it came to me that I was virtually the only person Martin knew, along with a few judges in the courts, who were not dependent on him or in any way in his power. He was entreating me to give him a verdict, as if I were in flowing robes. But Martin had no genuine respect for me or my work; it was only that he believed that Lila did. She was the one he wanted, and so he had decided to present his case to me.

"Why, apart from money, would Lila and your kids be better off if you were back with them?" I asked, utilizing the power he had invested in me.

He looked perplexed.

"I mean, could I tell Lila that you love her, or that you miss her, or that you'll work very hard to be more caring? I mean, as I'm trying to tell you, obviously, the money isn't enough."

He looked surprised. "Then you've talked to her," he exclaimed.

"No. Of course not," I said.

"Well, will you?"

"No. Not at this point. The only hope is for you to change. Then, if she can see that you're different, and if it's not already too late, maybe Lila will gamble on you, little by little. Then maybe, conceivably, things could be different—"

"And I could go back."

"Conceivably," I warned him.

"Would you talk to her then?" he asked. "If you could tell her that I changed."

"Maybe," I said, "if she wants to come in with you."

"And you believe that if I change, she'll want me," he pressed.

I repeated, "Maybe, I don't know."

"But suppose I change, and I do all these things, and I'm caring in the ways you say, and Lila still doesn't want me?"

"That could happen, Martin."

"Well, that wouldn't do me much good, would it?" He sneered.

I started to say that I thought he'd be a lot better off anyhow, but he broke in.

"Who are you kidding?" He simply didn't want to volunteer anything, to feed himself even a spoonful of life, if it wasn't guaranteed.

"Martin," I said peremptorily. "Our time is almost up. Let me explain something to you. I'm not a deal maker. All I can do is to try to help people understand themselves, soften, improve relationships. I sometimes help people open themselves up to intimacy—not always, but often, if they try. But whether Lila or any particular woman will want you, that's not up to me. It's up to the woman."

I went on to tell him what I saw: that he seemed isolated, and certainly not happy or fulfilled. He could improve his chances for intimacy, that was all. But he had every right not to undertake such a project.

"How much time would this take?" he asked, with, I felt, a note of skepticism.

I suggested seeing him at least once, or maybe twice, a week for a couple of months, and then we could stop if either of us thought we weren't getting anywhere.

Just then the doorbell rang, and I left to admit my next person into my waiting room.

When I returned, Martin said, "Okay. I'm going to tell Lila that I started in therapy and to wait before the divorce."

I should have guessed that he wouldn't commit himself even to therapy without squeezing some immediate profit out of the deal; in this case, a bit of extra bargaining power with Lila. I felt dismayed, but then I realized that of course this was his nature. If I were to work with Martin, I had better brace myself for cynicism and for the shallowest kind of practicality at every turn. Otherwise, I would be dismayed repeatedly.

He made a sour face when I mentioned my fee, and I felt momentarily guilty, as if I had crushed him. I obviously wasn't fully ready for him yet.

We set up a twice-a-week schedule.

At the door he extended his hand, as he must have after signing deals with tenants. But this wasn't a business deal, and I didn't grasp his hand. I just said good-bye.

Especially in those early sessions, I was sometimes aghast as Martin told me about maneuvers that only revealed his penury and hostility toward the world. Although Martin was worth perhaps ten million dollars, he would exult over a few items a tenant might leave behind in his eagerness to clear out of his apartment in time to recover his month's security. Whenever a tenant left, Martin would make sure to come in before the plasterers and painters so that he could personally capture any such items—a bookcase or a second telephone—and perhaps throw them into a future deal to clinch an advantage.

He specialized in semilegal tricks for ousting people who, for whatever reason, fell a few months behind in their rent. And let the relative of someone who died in one of Martin's apartments try to establish residence there: Martin would take delight in working with his lawyer to banish the relative and wrest his legal increase from a new tenant. For Martin, owning buildings was one long war, and he seldom lost even a skirmish.

At our second meeting, I observed that Martin smiled whenever he described an attempt by anyone in his life to take more from him than he thought the person deserved. I recalled that he'd smiled when counting up Lila's fur coats and when describing his daughters' many demands; also, when he talked about the extravagant cost of Lila's therapist, who, as Martin saw it, had in the end condemned him. He would smile when tenants or building workers sought an extra edge. In each of these cases, he saw someone as out to profit at his expense. Although in nearly every instance Martin had contrived to not yield more than he had wanted to, he smiled just as broadly when, in his opinion, he has been taken by someone as when he hadn't.

In fact, I came to see, that Martin smiled even more broadly when the other person had come out ahead of him. Gradually, I came to notice that he smiled *at no other time*. I began to feel that if I could understand that rare, enigmatic smile of his, I would understand Martin a lot better than I as yet did.

Meanwhile, I resolved not to say anything to Martin that might imply a value judgment about his behavior with people. I would instead simply study his ways of thinking and acting.

But I faltered in this resolve, and a lot sooner than I expected. Martin had just told me the story of a tenant in one of his buildings, a girl from South Dakota studying at the Art Students League and working at night. She apparently knew nothing about rent ceilings, and Martin managed to extract an extra fifty dollars a month from her. If the girl had discovered her rights, she could have recovered a thousand dollars in back rent from Martin and probably additional money in penalties. But Martin felt confident that she wasn't the type to investigate such things and that he wouldn't be found out.

I had mused that if Martin had belonged to any fraternity, its motto should have been caveat emptor. But people like him would, of course, shun anything smacking of the fraternal.

My slip after he had recounted his triumph over that girl began with asking him how old she was.

"Twenty-three," he'd replied.

I commented, "That's exactly Joan's age, isn't it, your older daughter?"

He answered that it was, but with no idea what I was driving at.

I recognized at once that my comment had been a rebuke, and that as his therapist it wasn't my role to chastise him. But I had, apparently, done so obliquely enough for him not to notice.

In the next session, I realized that any such analogy aimed at eliciting sympathy from Martin was pointless anyway. He would have dealt with his own daughter similarly and, in fact, he did. When Joan took a new apartment, he advised her to tell her landlord that she would have the apartment painted at her own expense in exchange for a cut in her first month's rent. With seeming largesse, Martin offered to have his painters do the job for her. She thanked him effusively. "My daughters always kiss me when I spend money on them."

But then, Martin confided in me, he had instructed his crew to apply only one coat of paint instead of two, a savings for him of about two hundred dollars. He told me that though some people could tell, Joan was too young to know the difference.

It was easy to see why Martin's wife had pared their discussions down to practicalities, and why his daughters talked to him mainly about money. Martin offered them nothing except money—no emotion, no sense of joy in being with loved ones, no yearning, no thanks. By withholding affection and interest in everything they did, Martin had reduced them to the role of dependents who spent his money—and who, as a result, were an utter disappointment to him. And whenever he handed over his money to them, it was with a cynical comment.

He never tired of talking about what he considered his family's over-spending, even when the spending was on him. "My wife bought me a pink shirt for my birthday. It's very expensive, and it was with *my* money. It's very fragile. I don't feel right wearing it."

"Why not?" I asked.

"What, to work! And get it dirty? Or should I wear it when I go out with another woman?" He smiled, not at the illogicality, I thought, but at the unfairness of his wife's spending his money on something that he couldn't use.

Hearing him talk about his family, I was reminded of the way boy-hood friends of mine used to describe their cars as "gas guzzlers."

I asked him to tell me about the few women he had gone out with since his separation six years previously. He said that he had met them all through work.

"And you're not seeing any of them now?" I asked.

He shook his head no, and then, right on cue, he listed their faults.

"Grace, she was my secretary before this one. She was just too fat." He made a sour face.

The other two, Mary and Catherine, had been tenants in his buildings. "Mary? She's too old. She's my age."

"And Catherine?"

"She smokes. I hate a woman who smokes."

He winced as he mentioned these women, as if they had put their flaws into his life in an attempt to dupe him.

The story was essentially the same with each of these women and the outcome was identical. Martin had caused each of them to believe that they were unsatisfactory and that he was giving them much more than they were entitled to. Before long, Martin had reduced them all, inevitably, to scream-ing, to cursing at him, to telling him that they despised him, to swearing that they never wanted to see him again.

In the next session I asked him, "What kind of woman do you want?"

"Someone who's attractive and who leaves me alone."

"Leaves you alone?"

"Yes, someone who doesn't need to spend a fortune, and who doesn't constantly ask me for money."

"What I'm curious about, Martin, is why you suddenly want to go back with your wife. Do you love her all of a sudden?"

I could hardly picture him saying yes, even if he did, but he gave even less than I'd expected. He just sat petulantly, not saying anything, so that I wasn't even sure he had heard my question.

The most he could offer was the vague phrase, "It would be a lot better for us to live together."

"Better!" I pressed him. "Martin, why would it be better for *you?*"

He emitted a flurry of answers about pensions, financial benefits, and tax categories.

"I see," I said. "You're saying that there's nothing personal in your wanting her back. You don't especially want to see her or to be with her."

"I wouldn't go that far," he said, waving his hand vaguely.

At best, it was a weak assertion of feeling. But even that much was so uncharacteristic of Martin, he was so opposed to confessing personal desire, that I thought about it later. I wondered, could it be that his wife's wanting a legal divorce had really shocked Martin emotionally by its finality? Could it be that he really did harbor some special devotion for her, even love?

During that first month with Martin, despite my efforts to accept him as he was, he depressed me repeatedly. More than once I caught myself defending the whole human race against his onslaughts, and I realized that I was angry at him for always attributing the worst to people. I thought of him as an oppressor wherever he could be.

But one day all that seemed to change. As a result of a story he told me, I came to see Martin more as a pathetic figure than as a successful manipulator, as someone who saw himself as a victim even when he was totally the perpetrator.

In that session Martin told me with sanctimonious indignation that his tenant the art student had discovered her legitimate rent ceiling and was taking him to court. The girl's boyfriend, a young law student, had done the unimaginable—he had gone to the housing commission and had found out that she was paying too much. Together they had started proceedings against Martin, who would have to make amends, and then some.

"What right did that guy have to interfere?" Martin asked me rhetorically. He shut his eyes and closed his lips tight, like a child hoping that the bad breakfast cereal would go away. When it didn't, Martin said, "It was none of his business."

"I guess this is a classic example of man's inhumanity to man. Huh, Martin?"

Had I blurted out yet another critical comment? Martin really seemed to invite them. I realized that I couldn't go on making wise-guy comments and I told myself to stop.

But, amazingly, Martin agreed wholeheartedly that the girl in checking out her rights had been terribly unfair to him. It was then that I realized what a sorry picture he had of the world. How could he possibly have imagined that this young woman in protecting herself was trying to injure him? And was he so remote from people who cared about others that he hadn't anticipated a well-intended friend helping her out?

It was then that I realized fully that Martin was anything but a potent machine to exploit others. He seemed almost blind to what the rest of the human race wanted or would do. For that reason, he never really got away with anything, apart from making money. And, furthermore, he managed to see himself as the one downtrodden even though he had forced the other person to take defensive measures. I could imagine, only too easily, that Lila, too, had been protecting herself when she had asked him to get out of her life.

Poor Martin did indeed live in an abyss. True, it was one of his own making, but even that cramped, unfurnished apartment of his, compared with those of his tenants, symbolized and was a symptom of the small, unfurnished character of his life. Though his complaints were scattered and never apt, the truth was that Martin's life was bereft of pleasure and of even the barest human companionship.

This realization erased all my anger toward him. I began to see him as a drowning man trying to pull others down with him. When a moment later he turned on me with blame—"How is all this talk about my tenants helping? When exactly do you plan to talk to Lila? What's the point of these questions?"—I felt less hurt than I had when he'd said similar things previously, implying that I was irrelevant and wasting his time.

With this new perspective, Martin lost this power to jar me, and my ease in his presence made possible a host of new insights.

The first of these discoveries, which came at once, was that over time Martin had been systematically making me feel that I was failing him.

With other patients I had often had fleeting feelings that I should be doing more for them or that I should be approaching them differently. I have often wished that I hadn't said something, or that I had, or that I could help someone faster. But with Martin the feeling went much deeper than that. I had begun to feel that I could do nothing right for him, that perhaps I had some psychic aversion to him that was making me totally incompetent.

However, the story of the art student had illustrated that Martin would see himself as the victim, no matter what the reality was. That I should feel like a miscreant had been inevitable—it followed from who he was and how he treated people.

I was then able to realize that I couldn't possibly have helped Martin as yet. He had withheld the information and emotional access that I would need. In fact, instead of committing himself to the therapy, he had devoted his time and efforts to showing me how *I* was coming up short.

I had been receiving what therapists call "an induced feeling," one imparted by a patient and caught like a contagion by the therapist, often without ever being identified.

From there, of course, I saw that I wasn't the only one in Martin's life who had caught the virus of feeling like a failure. Inducing that sense in people was Martin's stock-in-trade. His every relationship—with his wife and with the women he had dated after his separation, even with his children—bore that same stamp. In each of those relationships the other person had come to feel like a woeful disappointment.

I could easily picture how the process worked. Martin, by constant criticism and scowling, by refusing to be pleased with anything, would cause people to doubt themselves, to wonder what was wrong with them. Then, doubting their own worth, they would go on to hate themselves in the relationship, and finally to hate Martin, who seemed always mockingly present as they failed. This hatred of Martin was the visible part of the sequence that had begun by their doubting their own worth and then hating themselves in the relationship.

I took pains to remind myself, "If you feel that you're disappointing

Martin, taking his time and money but doing nothing for him, that is exactly what he makes *everyone* feel. It is the poison he injects in everyone."

I was tempted to inoculate myself against Martin's brutality by focusing on the humorous aspect of his behavior. With his constant complaints and his terse answers he was reminiscent of Molière's miser, who was "so cheap that he wouldn't even give you good morning."

But, I realized, I couldn't afford to inoculate myself. I was not merely another player in Martin's life. I was the person to whom he had come for help, and, painful as it was to deal with him, it would be grossly unfair of me to immunize myself by simply dismissing him as a caricature of a miser.

As a therapist I had to experience the immediate impact that Martin had on me, no matter how unpleasant it was. How Martin made me feel would give me my best leads into how he made other people feel, and into how he was forfeiting everything that he wanted, including Lila.

Generally, the therapist who hides utterly from the sting of induced feelings is denying himself his best firsthand evidence of what the patient is like in the outside world. Now that I had come to see Martin as a very needy person, and with my new understanding of his propensity to make people feel like failures, I felt that I had my balance back.

I had regained the narrow road between feeling too little and too much. To absorb too much would mean suffering a fate akin to that of the renown entomologist, Karl von Frisch, who won a Nobel Prize for his work with honeybees. Over the years von Frisch was bitten so many times that his physicians informed him that his very next bee bite might prove fatal. In the end, he had to let his assistants handle the live bees, restricting his own bee contact to doing postmortems.

Meanwhile, to broaden my understanding of Martin, I kept prodding him to talk about his early life. Before that, the few times I had inquired about those early years, Martin had looked at me, annoyed. "What has that got to do with anything?" he said. But one day, after he complained that his daughter Joan didn't want to see him on her birthday, I was able to learn more.

I'd asked Martin if he had celebrated his own birthdays growing up. He responded with a smile, "No. Never."

"Why not?"

Martin had already told me that his parents were dead, and that his mother had died a long time ago, but only in this session, our seventh, did he tell me that she'd died when he was only ten.

"So what kind of birthday was there?" he asked me, rhetorically. He turned up his palms in a gesture, which I often saw in my own family and which strikes me as a characteristically Jewish way of signaling—empty. Nothing.

"You mean no one celebrated your birthday after that," I said.

He frowned as if I should know better.

"Where was your father?" I asked.

"He was always working. In a restaurant. Twelve hours a day. Six days."

"You were close to him?"

"He hardly ever talked. He mostly slept."

"You mean after your mother died."

"After! Before," Martin said.

He had mentioned having two sisters, but only once, and not by name. Now I asked him, "And your sisters?"

"Gone," he said. "Never there. They were out with bums. They had their own lives. They went away weekends with different men. They could be gone for a week at a time. They had jobs, but I think they thought some man with a big car was going to make them rich."

When their mother died Martin's sister Dorothy was nineteen, and Arlene, whom he called "the fancy one," was twenty-three. With their mother gone they almost never came home, and soon afterward both married.

"Dorothy, she married a hoodlum—a runaround. They lived high for a few years, but he dumped her. I understand her third husband is dumping her now. She has a little money, though. Arlene is working as a secretary again. She hates men."

"Then they didn't take much care of you after your mother died?" I asked.

He smiled broadly, as if I must have descended from another planet and was totally disoriented. "I just about never saw them. Only their clothes—closets full of dresses and shoes. Pretty good for a secretary and someone who worked in a shipping department."

"Boy, that must have been a hard life for you," I said, impressed by the terrible isolation of it.

He just looked at me, as if I would never understand.

"So how did you survive?" I asked.

"Survive?" He didn't grasp my question.

"I mean what did you do all day while you were growing up? You went to school, I guess. Did you have friends?"

He couldn't think of anyone at first. But then he recalled a boy, Arthur, who, like Martin, was acutely nearsighted. Neither could see a ball well enough to play any sport, and they were both utterly excluded by the kids on the block.

I was surprised by Martin's tone as he elaborated a little. "Arthur Rosenthal was a very nice kid. I'd like to know what became of him.

"Arthur and I used to go for long walks across the Brooklyn Bridge. Sometimes we went on it during a rainstorm, and it would shake. I really wonder what happened to him."

But before I could follow up that comment, I realized how much it had surprised me—he had apparently been expressing a nostalgic, a truly romantic longing to see Arthur again. He seemed to have a genuine liking for this boy, unpolluted by his usual cynicism.

I held myself back from asking Martin if he had actually liked Arthur, so wary had I become of his instant reflex to say derogatory things. I wanted to let him live a little longer in the world of liking someone.

Then, to my further surprise, Martin repeated, "He was a very nice kid."

"So what do you mean, you wonder what happened to him?" I asked.

"Well, he was a smart kid," Martin said. "Very smart. He wanted to be a chemist or something. The last I saw him he was thirteen and he was just starting Science High. The family moved away."

"Did you stay in touch?" I asked.

"No. That was it."

I let the subject evaporate, but I felt afterward that Arthur—or rather, that Martin's feeling for Arthur—was a blazon of something that might have been, and perhaps might be: a capacity for pure, unalloyed caring for another human being.

Of course, I planned to ask Martin how his mother had died, both to learn about Martin and to experience him as that ten-year-old boy who was so suddenly bereft. But it seemed inappropriate just then to introduce what might well prove to be the most highly charged subject of his life. There had been a completeness to the session as it was. He had spoken about his early life, and lovingly at that. In discussing his friend Arthur, Martin had put aside his truculence and skepticism. He had talked about someone he had liked, unreservedly, for the first time.

The next time Martin came in he was limping. He told me he had bruised a toe badly when one of his painters accidentally knocked over a table near him. Martin spent half the session haranguing the painter and grimacing over the physical pain, the medical bill, and the fact that, according to his doctor, he would have the limp for a good three months. "I look like an old man," Martin said to me.

Making matters worse, he reported, he'd bumped into Mary on the street, one of the women he'd dated shortly after his separation. Martin said she looked "beautiful, really beautiful." Mary had been strolling up Broadway arm in arm with another man, and Martin hated himself for hobbling along, though he had explained to her that it was only a temporary injury.

When I asked him if he would like to date Mary again, he answered, "I wouldn't mind," which for him was tantamount to someone else's saying, "I love you, and if you won't see me, I'll commit painful suicide."

After some more direct questioning by me, Martin said that Mary was actually a very attractive woman, and that he was becoming sorry that he had broken up with her. There was real wistfulness in his tone.

"But you told me that she was too old and that all she liked to do was to go to expensive plays all the time," I reminded him.

Martin looked at me blankly. Obviously, he couldn't reconcile the two opinions of her, and he didn't try.

On a whim, I chose that moment to ask him what his wife was like when he'd first met her.

He answered at once. "Lila was a pretty girl. She really knew how to dress."

I recalled Martin's constant complaints that his wife spent too much money on clothes. As when he'd talked about Mary, I had trouble reconciling his two descriptions. He certainly had a way of downgrading people viciously, of acting utterly disappointed with them, and then suddenly dredging up fond memories of them when it was too late.

I wondered, did he truly want either Mary or Lila back?

But soon my question was answered. My next sequence of interactions with Martin brought about a startling new insight. I discovered that Martin could romanticize *only people of the past*. He could love no one he knew now, no man or woman in his present life. Only after a person was gone, irretrievably, or seemingly so, did Martin become able to care for that person. And then he seemed to care passionately.

It took the playing out of my own relationship with Martin for me to discover this—an experience that amounted to a miniversion of what had occurred in his life with others.

It was February and near the end of our second month. Martin, who had never missed a session, and had never even been late, called the night before his scheduled hour and canceled.

"I have a closing to go to. I can't make it."

I was with another patient and couldn't talk, but I realized that Martin must have known well in advance when the meeting was to be and, moreover, that he'd had plenty of say over when it was to be scheduled.

That weekend I wondered whether Martin was intending to come back at all.

When he was ten minutes late for our next session I called his office. A secretary told me flatly that he was "at a meeting" and took my name.

After twenty minutes he finally came in, but sat sullenly. He offered no explanation for his lateness and, in fact, didn't speak at all.

When I asked him what he was thinking, he replied evasively, "I have a lot on my mind."

What was it?

"It's not important. I have a few vacancies I didn't expect and a couple of renovations."

"Martin," I said, "Something's going on, isn't it?"

He looked at me quizzically.

He rebuffed my efforts to get him to talk, and said finally, "Look, Doctor, this is pointless. You're not helping me. It's not your fault."

"But Martin—" I started to say.

"I've been coming here for two months, like we agreed. And I just don't see any point to it."

I started to say something else, but then Martin smiled—that rare, enigmatic smile. And at that moment, I could virtually read his mind. With my every subsequent word, I would be fulfilling his dire prophecy that I was soliciting him and was only out for his money. That smile seemed to say that I was offering him false hope, that I was an imposter, and that . . .

Well, when I considered it, what hope had I actually offered Martin? I could make the case ad nauseam that he had never given me a chance, that he had never really told me what he was feeling or volunteered his thoughts. But suppose his problem was such that it precluded his offering me more than he actually did. No, I refused to believe that. There *was* choice. Martin was exercising his will in not telling me more about what he felt.

Then, unexpectedly, he produced a blank check and asked, "How much do I owe you?"

I told him, and he made out the check. Before I knew it, I had walked him to the door, and he was gone.

He had succeeded in demoralizing me. The ten minutes of time that he had paid for, which remained on the clock, only accented my feeling that I had taken his money and rendered him nothing in return. I had entered the lists of those whom Martin had met in good faith and who had robbed him. Now he could flash that ironic smile as he told people of my incompetence, or even my ill will. Martin could impress listeners somewhere with the contrast between how much he had trusted me and how poorly I had done.

Then, as I reflected on his departure, rather ruefully, I pictured him telling his story to whoever would listen, perhaps to those in the smoke-filled back room who played gin rummy with him, if he returned there. He would have an exact tally of how much he had paid for his therapy, how much money he had been cheated out of.

Well, I thought, at least he'll have that story to enjoy. And in my mind's eye, I saw him recounting it over and over, always with that smile. Then suddenly it came to me what that smile meant—it was a signal that Martin flashed in triumph. And the triumph was that someone had yet again disappointed him. I realized now that Martin *wanted* to be disappointed! The feeling of failure that he induced in others he caused intentionally.

Only then, after I myself had entered the ranks of his imagined abusers, did I realize how enormously wrong I had been in thinking that Martin was getting nothing back for his money. True, he didn't get back what the rest of us might expect or want, but he got what he wanted.

Now that he was gone, I saw him in a starkly new way. I saw for the first time that Martin was, indeed, buying something for his money. He wanted that sense of disappointment, and he was ready to pay for it. His money was spent to purchase the proof that people—mostly women, but, as in my case, men, too—were *disappointments*. Martin enjoyed demonstrating to himself that people are takers, that they are all malignant spirits. Had he been able to save up for a whole year to buy a single item, it could have been only one thing—heartless injury, meted out by a person he had trusted and financed.

No wonder he needed so much money, I thought; he needed to continue proving this thesis.

With this understanding of Martin's behavior, I felt that I knew him better. But another question arose. What could his motivation be? Just why was it so important for Martin to refute human decency, to disqualify us all as criminals, as a race unworthy of him?

I could conclude only that he was engaged in a massive retribution against us. But for what? What could *we,* would-be friends, or lovers, of Martin's, possibly have done that required him to discredit us on such a scale?

Well, I would never know, I decided. I realized that my lingering sense of failure was exactly what Martin had intended to impart, but that was no consolation. His need to make me feel like a failure was a symptom of his fundamental problem, and I had done nothing to help him with that problem. I could talk about induced feelings to myself all day, but the fact was that I had failed.

For a month after he left, I wasn't aware of thinking about Martin very often. But he must have somehow remained in my preconscious mind, the way souls of the dead are said to hover near earth until their ultimate release. Then his influence seemed to dissipate, and he was truly gone.

I was so sure that I would never hear from Martin again that when he called about ten weeks later I actually didn't recognize his voice at first.

"Hello. How are you?" he said. "It's been a long time. How have you been?"

As surprised as I was to hear from him, I was even more surprised at what for Martin was such a largess of interest.

After a few words more were exchanged, he said, "I'd like to come in and see you." We made an appointment.

When he came in a few days later, I had the sense that in those ten short weeks he had aged. His face looked even more pinched, though he had gotten a suntan somewhere. The thin strand of hair that he had combed over his bald spot was as untrained as all those people in his life who refused to do his bidding.

"I thought I wouldn't mind our talking some more," he began. Then he mentioned an apartment in one of his buildings that would be perfect if I had a son or daughter who needed one.

I declined his offer.

"Fine," he said. "It's just that I was thinking about you."

"Really. What were you thinking?" I asked.

"It's not really important."

He said that the week before he had gone out to dinner with Lila and "put my cards on the table." He had asked her to take him back, but she had remained adamant about not wanting him. She was only concerned about nailing down the divorce. She had quoted her therapist again, which had produced an argument.

"Believe me, Doctor," Martin said to me. "That woman sounds like an idiot next to you."

"But Martin, you gave me to believe that I was completely wasting your time," I said.

"No, not exactly," he interrupted me. "I thought it over. I decided that you weren't bad."

"You decided!" I echoed him.

Then I thought but didn't say, "Just the way you reconsidered Lila after she was gone. And Mary, when you met her in the street. Just the way your old friend Arthur seems terrific thirty years later."

What I did say was, "And suppose I still can't give you what you want."

"No, I'm sure you can. I told you, you're certainly smarter than that woman Lila talks to. Maybe you can figure out what she's telling Lila against me."

Again Martin sounded pathetic. And he certainly didn't look like the domineering patriarch that his tenants must have considered him. Before me sat a small, stooped, insignificant-looking man, with arms far too frail for his body, as if he had never lifted anything. His shoulders were hunched, and as he stared through almost blind eyes at me to discern any sign of sympathy he might elicit, I felt truly sorry for him. If a person's life was utterly botched, as Martin's was, there was certainly no sense blaming him for doing the botching. Ahead lay only the penalty—for Martin it loomed as confinement to a life unrelieved by human caring, unless he could change enormously.

Again I heard Martin say, "You're certainly smarter," if anything, more pleadingly than before, and I wondered, how had I, one of his castoffs, come back into his esteem.

It was then that I realized the startling fact that Martin could romanticize only people of the past. Such a recovery as mine in Martin's eyes was the *rule* in his life, rather than the exception. When he was finished with people and they were gone, that was when Martin thought most of them and when, as much as he could, he truly romanticized them.

The propensity to do this is an incredible mechanism, not uncommon in the human psyche. But in Martin it was so remarkably pronounced as to be the very essence of his nature. What Martin wanted with Lila and Mary was the *past* person back, not the one he had come to know. In his mind, his present wife—Lila-of-now—was demanding and hysterical. But Lila-of-the-past, she was another person; she and only she was the one Martin wanted.

It was the same paradox with Mary, only to a lesser extent. Martin liked the Mary whom he once knew; he imagined that he had just met *that woman* on the street, and he wanted her. But the Mary who might actually come back to him, in person, or in the form of some other woman who might want him, a present-day Mary? No, Martin would find such a person too old and riddled with faults and not even give her a chance. The only way to qualify with Martin was to be irretrievably gone. Gone, like his friend Arthur, who seemed like such a "nice kid" from a distance, and "gone," as I had been, for ten weeks.

I had a renewed status with him, but only because I had been out of the picture. Martin had made no real comparison between Lila's therapist and me; he'd said nothing suggesting that he'd reviewed our sessions and decided that I was really more insightful than he'd thought. My rise in his esteem had owed wholly to my scarcity value, which, by definition, couldn't possibly last once I started with him again.

That unconscious mechanism of chewing up the present and yearning for the past was so strong, so intrinsic to Martin's nature, I realized, that I myself would surely fall prey to it again. As long as I hadn't yet committed myself to taking him back, my status was still at its zenith. For that reason, though I knew that I was going to, I hesitated before telling him so. Capriciously, an utterance of the ancient Roman gladiators stole into my mind: "We who are about to die salute you."

Then, perhaps because my own mind had reverted to antiquity (in the vein of a tendency of Martin's), I thought about those ancient Greek myths in which the gods devise exquisite and perpetual tortures for mortals. I wondered, could Zeus himself have devised a worse one than to dull a man to all pleasure in people set before him, while tormenting him with images of opportunities missed in people who once wanted him but were now gone forever? To be able to love what we *can* possess—is not that virtually the aim of life, the definition of mental health?

Martin repeated, "Look, all I'm asking you to do is to figure out what Lila wants to hear."

I told him that we'd been through all that before and that I wouldn't help him manipulate another person. I said that his only hope with Lila was to improve the relationship by improving himself.

"Improving myself? Does that mean doing what Lila's lady therapist says I should do?"

"No, it means trying to understand yourself and what's going wrong with Lila. And maybe with other women in your life as well."

Then when I seemed not to be bending, Martin suddenly switched and said, "All right, all right. So what if I come in and try to do it your way?"

I knew that he was paying lip service to me, but I also thought that at some level he probably did yearn for something real, and that this was the most he could say.

I decided to put it to the test.

"Martin," I said. "Let's see how it goes. You'll come in here twice a week again. But we have to work differently."

He asked me what I meant.

"I'm going to give you some assignments," I told him, "and you'll have to do them as well as you can. If you won't do them, we're wasting our time."

"And if I do them," Martin said, "then we go back to our deal?"

I looked at him quizzically, and he explained. "If you think I'm changing, then you talk to Lila. Okay?" he pressed.

It was the most leverage I thought I could get, and so I agreed.

Then Martin asked me what my assignments would be like, and I told him.

"For one thing, I'll ask you to talk about particular topics—your past, your relationships with women. If you refuse, we haven't got a chance, and you'll have much less chance with Lila. We've got to understand precisely how you deal with women—and why. The why is important so that you can get a grip on what you're doing and change. Otherwise, no woman will want you."

"All right, fine," Martin said. "We'll do it your way."

I could only hope that before my status with Martin waned I could make a real connection with him and free him from his torture.

Of course, my conception of Martin as a man accursed, though it dramatized him to me, was not the whole story. Like all who appear that way, Martin was, without knowing it, renewing his own "Greek torture" by an unconscious, repeated pattern. He was not merely the mortal condemned, but the god who condemned him.

That weekend a curious conception of Martin came to my mind: that his crime was *condemning himself by condemning all others*. As before when I had worked with him, I wondered what in his early life had driven him to adopt such a mode. Perhaps I too had profited by our time apart—the key questions about the thrust of Martin's life seemed to me clearer than ever.

What force in Martin's early years had led him to see people as so disappointing, and if they weren't already, then *to make them* into disappointing figures? What kind of perverse wish in the young Martin could possibly have motivated him to discount all humankind, to downgrade people as if they were imposters—and, inevitably, to turn them against him?

I determined to find out whatever I could about Martin's early life, even though he obviously didn't want to talk about it. Almost surely, Martin had begun downgrading people during his early childhood, about which I still knew very little. My first assignment for Martin would be for him to talk a lot more about that period, especially about his mother's death—he could hardly stay detached about that.

I decided to give him this assignment the very next time I saw him, while my status with him was exalted, before he tore the "new me" down in his mind, as he surely would. Now, while I still had the dual standing of present and past figure, I had my best leverage with him.

When I next saw him, Martin came in furious at one of his superintendents, a spy whom Martin paid extra to report to him when apartments emptied out or when a tenant tried to turn an apartment over to a friend. Martin told me that he had to stay vigilant so that people wouldn't beat him out of his increases. But he'd discovered that this superintendent had failed him. The superintendent had let a young man sneak in when the boy's elderly aunt had died, and now it would be hard to evict the boy. Martin felt cheated out of his rightful choice of a successor and out of money. To Martin it felt like rape, or worse, because the youth gave boisterous parties with women, drinking, and sex—it felt like repeated rape.

Martin seemed unstoppable on the subject until I barreled in with my own agenda for the session.

"Martin, your assignment today is to answer my questions."

"Okay."

I knew that I would be asking him some hard ones, and I had decided that it would be easier for him if I just asked them rather than couch them in euphemisms.

"How did your mother die?"

"She was killed in an accident."

"An accident! What kind of accident?" I asked him.

"An auto accident," he said listlessly.

"Really! When you were ten?"

"That's right. A hit-and-run driver. They never caught him."

"Did she die right away?" I asked him.

"No. For a while she was in a coma, in the hospital."

"How awful!"

He nodded. "At least she was in her new navy dress with the floral design. She got to wear it once, that one time," he said.

"Did you see her before she died?" I asked him.

"Yes. I went in with my father. She died at five-fifteen in the afternoon."

"Did she ever regain consciousness?" I asked him.

"She didn't open her eyes, but I thought she smiled at me when I went in with my father. They sent us outside her room. Then the doctor came out and told us. They couldn't do anything. I guess they tried."

He seemed to be reviewing the experience, and I asked him what else he remembered.

"I guess I cried a lot. I was a kid. I ran in there and threw my arms around her, and I wouldn't let go of her. I remember that—like yesterday. My father didn't know what to do. Not that he ever really did know much about what to do. So they pulled me away from her, and that was that."

"And your sisters, where were they?" I asked him.

"Dorothy was out with some guy—a bookie, I think. She was gone for the weekend, to Atlantic City. It was a Friday night. Dorothy and my mother had just had one of their big arguments, and my mother was all upset. That's why she stepped in front of the car. She didn't see it. Arlene was off somewhere, too. She and Dorothy came back the next day. They were all there at the funeral."

"Where did it happen, Martin?"

He reeled off the bare facts, almost as in a telegram.

"About two blocks from our house, on lower Broadway. She was crossing a big intersection. We were living in a project, paying sixty-five a month, just north of Chinatown. My mother had just come out of the A and P, with a lot of groceries. She was supposed to go to the movies with some friends of hers that night. That's why she was wearing her good dress. I was home."

"I can't think of anything more terrible," I said.

Martin just shuffled in the high-backed armchair that he always chose to sit in.

He had still showed little emotion. Although his story screamed its horror, Martin had evidently so embalmed the details in his memory that the words seemed bloodless coming from him.

He said that after his mother died, his sisters had tried to console him.

"They stayed home a little more for a while. They would switch weeks taking care of me. You know—one week Arlene, the next week Dorothy. They acted like they wanted to talk to me a lot. I guess they thought that kind of thing would make me feel better. My aunt, Lily, came over a lot too; she was nice.

"To this day I'd like to get my hands on that driver, but no one really saw him. A checker in the A and P thought it was a black car with Jersey license plates."

Then Martin asked me, "Hey, do you want to make a million dollars right away? You've got it if you can find the driver, the guy, or it could have been a woman, for all I know. But it won't be easy. It was thirty-eight years ago."

The ironic tone of his delivery didn't fool me. I had no doubt that Martin meant the offer and would have made good on it. I had the sense that he'd brooded about it over decades and had made the offer before.

In the next session, when I interrogated Martin further, he supplied a few more details. Martin said that his father had worked around-the-clock as a waiter in a delicatessen nearby. He'd always been a quiet man, but after Martin's mother died, he withdrew entirely. Martin remembered his father coming home only to sleep until it was time to work again. As Martin put it, "My father had nothing left to say."

From what I could gather, Martin's sisters had remained attentive to him for only a few months and then shuffled off again into the world. "They didn't miss more than a few beats," Martin said, smiling sourly. "They wanted their good time."

While going to high school Martin worked as a delivery boy. Afterward he had registered in college "because my mother would have wanted me to." But he never actually went—he was working too hard.

At eighteen he got a job in a pawnshop and started to make good money. Then came the real estate boom in New York City, and he invested with a friend. They soon split up, and Martin established his own office with only a secretary.

Lila had loved him because he seemed so timid, and he was in his late twenties when he accepted her suggestion that they marry. Their daughters were born soon afterward. There was still no male in Martin's life, except for his father, who cut a sorry figure in every respect. Nor had things ever improved for the man: He had developed severe kidney trouble, and after a slow but steady decline, he died when Martin was thirty. "I want to tell you," Martin said to me. "Lila was very good to my father when he was sick, always calling him and going over there."

Then, for no evident reason, Martin abruptly drew the curtain on our conversation.

"So where is all this getting us? What has this got to do with anything?" he said, disgusted.

"I'm trying to understand you," I said.

It was only the third session of our new regimen, but once again I could hear the clock ticking.

I had planned next to look into his attitudes toward the women in his adult life, and I introduced that topic with a question: "So, would you say that Lila was definitely the person closest to you in recent years?"

"No. Mary was very decent, too." Martin was not in an agreeing vein.

"I see," I said. "But you never really gave either of them much of a chance, did you Martin? That's what really interests me—why you cut everybody out so completely."

"Look, Lila had eighteen years to have her chance," Martin said.

I knew that Martin really believed this, even though he might have abused Lila every day during that whole span of time.

It might have been annoyance at Martin surfacing again, or the old feeling of hopelessness, or the sense that I was under time pressure with him—or some combination of these—that next motivated me. But in any event, I suddenly felt that my only hope was to get tough with Martin, to level with him about how he treated people. He acted so oblivious that anything less than firing at him with an elephant gun was sure to fail, and so I had nothing to lose. I would confront him head-on, and let the chips fall where they may.

It was almost as if Martin had at the same time elected to sidetrack me utterly from any further perusal of him, because he asked kvetchingly, "Look, do you still think that I can get Lila back?"

"You mean Lila, the way she *used* to be?" I countered.

"What do you mean?" he asked me.

"The Lila you once loved," I said. "The Lila you married and wanted. The Lila you thought you would always love. Or do you mean the Lila who spends all your money?"

"I don't know what you're saying," he protested.

"Come on, Martin," I pressed. "You know that if Lila said, 'Martin, I love you. Come home,' before long you would criticize the hell out of her, you would kick her brains out—"

"I would not."

"Maybe not the first day, Martin. But certainly the first month."

"I never touched her. I never would."

"No. Not physically, Martin," I said. "But you would certainly end up telling her that she's not your type. She loved you, but you broke her spirit. And you'd break it again."

"Why do you say that?"

"Because that's your style, Martin, if you want to know."

He leaned forward, and I had the sense that he was actually interested in what I had to say, more than he had ever been. Doubtless, his motive to learn what he could was to retrieve Lila, but at least I had his attention.

As a way of keeping that attention, I decided to speak slowly and to remain cryptic. I had noticed that when Martin had been easily able to grasp what I was saying, he had been quicker to dismiss me.

"Martin," I went on. "You want me to bring the old Lila back across the time warp. You don't want the Lila that you know now. You don't want anyone who's in your life *now*."

"What do you mean?" he asked.

"Martin," I continued, deliberately shifting over to another plane so that he would have to listen. "There's a play called *Liliom*. They based the musical *Carousel* on it—"

"So what!"

He was angry, but at least he was engaged with me.

"In this play," I went on, "Liliom is a dumb laborer. He's in charge of a carousel. He treats everybody like garbage, his wife, his kids—he couldn't be worse. Then he gets killed, and in heaven he suddenly cries for the family he has lost. He begs to go back. He says he'll be different. But when he's allowed to come back from the dead and to see them, he's not there twenty minutes before he's treating them like garbage again. They're not the nostalgic past anymore, they're back in the here and now, and so all their value is gone. His own family can't wait for him to disappear, once and for all. They just can't take the abuse."

"I'm not like that guy, if that's what you're saying," he interrupted me.

"I'm not so sure. Your mother—"

"Don't bring my mother into this." He was shouting. "I'll tell you something, Doctor. You can believe this or not, I don't care. I don't give a damn what you believe. But you know when I started making money, real money, I had only one wish. I wished that my mother was alive so that I could have given it to her."

"I realize that, Martin," I said. "I certainly do believe you. But after your mother was long gone, Lila was there, right in front of you. You could have been better to her . . . a lot better."

I deliberately didn't explain anymore to him.

At the end of the session, when Martin said, "Thank you," I wasn't clear whether he had said it sneeringly or not.

He had shown almost no feeling apart from that annoyance when I had mentioned his mother. But it seemed pretty obvious what he must have felt as a child. Back then he had ample reason for his cynicism—for his disbelief in the durability of human goodness. The world had done him a rotten turn. Beyond loving him, his mother was the one person who sympathized with him or even paid attention to him.

In the next session Martin told me of her many visits to eye doctors and optometrists with him. She would assure him that his acute nearsightedness was no real liability, that the children who laughed at him for holding the page so close were envious of his brilliance. "And besides," she'd all but promised, "they say that as people get older, these things clear up."

Her death must have meant that even the firmest promises may lapse, and that the sturdiest and best of us are as frail as the human eye; one should count on nothing. And so Martin became a money-making machine.

At least such an explanation seemed inviting as the answer to why Martin disdained intimacy and disparaged those who sought it with him— in short, why he was so crusty and sour.

But my learning these facts about Martin's childhood was a far cry from getting him to convey what he himself really felt about anything—as a child or even now. It was as if fear, pleasure, love, anger all lay entombed in his silence—and converted into monolithic disappointment, which he would soon again train on me. He rebuffed alike my efforts to commiserate with him over his lonely childhood and my sympathy with him now.

One afternoon Martin came in, looking dapper in a pin-striped blue suit, and told me that he was taking Lila out to dinner at a rooftop restaurant overlooking the city. He was planning to entreat her to accept him back and, for no reason that I could fathom, he imagined there was a good chance that she would. When I asked him what he planned to say to her, he just shrugged.

I was careful not to blemish his optimism by any further comment, but I was hardly surprised when he came in the next time, saying that she had turned him down flat. She'd insisted on the divorce, saying that she had consented to see him only because her lawyer, "another goddamn woman," had said it would save them both a fortune if they could agree to terms before the lawyers met.

Martin looked bedraggled that session and like a man just going through the motions. It was as if coming to see me was an afterthought—and pointless. When he mentioned Lila's leaving, he shook his head sadly, though once he smiled faintly at the folly of her choice. Then he called her "stupid," as if in leaving him she were a child riding her bike into traffic. When he explained that she was getting older and less attractive, and would never find a husband, I resisted my impulse to ask Martin why he still wanted her. But by then I already knew the answer: that Martin didn't really want her. Her desirability to him resided in her being a reminiscence of the old Lila, a remnant of the woman he could never have again. For that reason alone, if he could have enticed her into returning, he would beat her senseless for not being the romanticized Lila of the past, but just a human being, like himself.

I had once again come to feel that my trajectory with Martin was set. We'd had a brief upward interlude since his return, during which I think he genuinely esteemed me. Within a short time we had reached our maximum point, and now, as on the parabolic arc of an object fired into the sky, we were commencing our rapid and only too predictable descent. I badly needed something to divert our course.

I decided to try out a method I had recently devised. It had to do with habitual behavior, and I had used it before to help people break particular habits—both physical, like smoking or drinking too much, and undesirable personality habits, like being continuously critical or repeating oneself to the point of driving others away.

I'd noticed that during the earliest weeks, when a person resists an unwanted habit, two things happen. First, the impulse to indulge the habit wells up, becoming hard to resist. Nearly all of us recognize this as our experience and that of our friends. The urge for the drink or cigarette becomes desperate. Or the person feels that if he doesn't make his usual critical statements, he is going to burst. At these times, people are prone to rationalize, telling themselves nearly anything that will allow them to go back: "I can't correct my office staff if I don't criticize them." "The statistics against smoking probably aren't accurate."

But, secondly, in these moments a whole different set of thoughts, often "crazy" and seemingly unrelated to the habit, assails the person. For instance, one woman, when she stopped smoking, felt inexplicably ugly and awkward. Another woman, who withheld all criticisms of others, felt sure that people were starting to think she was stupid. And a man who held back from repeating himself, even when he wanted to, suddenly felt like a little boy no one would take seriously.

The patients who reported these momentary impressions considered them ridiculous and wanted to dismiss them. But after a while I had begun to see that these "crazy" thoughts bore highly significant meanings.

Instead of having patients dismiss these thoughts, I urged them to record them carefully. I was becoming sure that such thoughts or, more usually, wisps of ideas, were far from unrelated to the people who had them. In fact, these impressions seemed to encapsulate the very reasons why the people had started these habits in the first place.

After only brief discussion it came out that the woman who felt unattractive when she first stopped smoking had started the habit as a teenager. She had taken up smoking in order to look sophisticated and because she thought it made her look graceful, like a 1940s movie star.

And the woman who felt stupid when not criticizing others was also experiencing her earliest reason for the habit. In the strict household where she'd grown up, those with status constantly told others what they were doing wrong and what they should do; insight was defined as being able to correct others.

The man who repeated himself had older brothers who really didn't listen to him, and it took repetition for him to get any of his ideas across. He'd apparently continued the practice on into adulthood, and was now using it with people who heard him clearly the first time.

In each case these "crazy" thoughts provided remarkable glimpses into the person's early life.

I had gone on to make still other discoveries of what had motivated people to begin habits by studying the flash impressions they had when first breaking the habit.

I came to see that the significance of these illusions far exceeded their relevance to the habit in question. Often, getting a patient to stop some behavior and study these thoughts was my *only* way of learning truths about their childhoods. These thoughts gave me precious insight into how my patients became who they were—and into what they wanted even now. They were photo images of the person's life long ago. With such knowledge the patients could attain their goals or feel free to replace them.

Because these thoughts accompany deep pangs of hunger for the habit, I call them "hunger illusions."

But in Martin's case, which behavior should I isolate?

I was confronting a pattern of demoralized and demoralizing behavior. With my goal of helping Martin appreciate people in his present life and enjoy them, instead of despising them and turning them into failures, I decided to take the clearest strain in that pattern: his practice of bad-mouthing people. If he stopped that behavior and I could examine his thoughts while he hungered for it, we might learn a great deal.

I decided to ask Martin to stop disparaging the people in his life. I would ask him to refrain, consciously and deliberately, from saying a single bad word about Lila or anyone he dealt with.

I wondered, what would Martin feel if instead of continually verbalizing "You're not it" in his diverse ways, he forced himself to say nothing negative? Or going further, as I thought about it, suppose that he forced himself to tell such people—his wife, his daughters, even me—what he *liked* about us. Exactly what would he experience?

If bad-mouthing people was compulsive for him—and I felt sure that it was—then what would he experience when he stopped? In Freud's language, if he was "repeating rather than remembering," what would he remember?

When I first considered asking Martin to do this, I felt an immediate misgiving. Historically, we in the role of therapist avoid suggesting life decisions for patients for a number of reasons. The therapist's aim is to instill independence—not dependence. Besides, patients have the moral right, and obligation, to run their own lives. But here I was not asking him to make a long-term commitment of any kind. I was merely asking him to act differently for a while, in order to surface whatever truths were being buried, and reburied, by his compulsive contempt.

For an afternoon, as I thought about these ethical considerations, I imagined that they were the reason for my hesitance about approaching Martin with my request. I grappled with my misgivings, telling myself that I wasn't really suggesting a life strategy to him, but merely asking him to try something unusual so that we could uncover important data. I was asking him to change only so that we could determine why he behaved as he did and where the pattern came from.

I even told myself that after a few weeks or perhaps a month, Martin could, if he wished, go back to disparaging people. He could compensate for his month of "good behavior" by becoming twice as nasty as he had been. I wasn't out to control his life, but was doing no more than a physician does who requests a patient not eat or drink before a sonagram or some other diagnostic procedure. This argument convinced me.

But with the removal of my ethical scruples, I was surprised that I still felt wary, almost afraid to challenge Martin this way. I hesitated to divest him so completely of his cynicism, I think, because I sensed that Martin *needed* to put people down, and that if he stopped abruptly, he would feel incredibly vulnerable. Picturing him without his armor of sneering and cynicism, I actually felt sorry for him.

If I was right in my concern, Martin would relive something akin to the naked terror of his childhood, the unhappiness that must have motivated him to renounce humankind in the first place. But, I then realized, it was this very expectation, that Martin's withdrawal would produce a replica of his early life experience, which made it mandatory for me to go ahead. I decided that I would.

However, our next session didn't seem the time. As soon as he came in Martin told me that his younger daughter, Anne, had let slip that Lila was involved with another man. Anne had begged her father not to say anything, and he'd agreed not to. Anne had told her father that the man's name was James, that he managed a supermarket, and that the relationship had gone on for over a year.

"How old is he?" Martin had asked.

"Older than you, Dad. He's a quiet guy. Mom says he's in love with her."

"She probably met him in the supermarket," Martin observed to me ironically. "Lila's really a genius. Maybe he makes thirty thousand a year. I'm not surprised."

"Not surprised!" I exclaimed.

"Well, I always knew she had poor judgment."

"Do you feel betrayed?" I asked him.

He didn't respond.

It was one more in the skein of disappointments that he perceived as his fate.

Martin hadn't actually thanked Anne for the information or said that he wanted to know more, but after dinner he had given her a few hundred dollars. They thus struck an unspoken deal that he would pay her for information in the future.

I couldn't tell whether his daughter had initially "slipped" to defy her mother or simply because she knew it would bring a reward. But whatever his daughter's motive, Martin's deal with her was like many he'd made with his superintendents who exchanged information for cash. Anne had, in effect, told him that a new tenant had moved in.

Although he went through the session without divulging a single feeling about his wife's actions, he was unquestionably in pain.

But in the very next session I was able to wedge an opening and put my plan to study the hunger illusion into practice.

Martin, as usual, was disgruntled about everyone he mentioned—a superintendent was lazy, his secretary was too slow-witted to tell him things, and his tenants were "compulsive." When I asked him to explain that last comment, he said he had plenty of drunks in his building and "compulsive smokers." "If there's anything I hate," he said, "it's people who are compulsive."

I asked him why on earth he would care.

"Because they're going to burn down one of my buildings some day, I'm sure of it." Then he said drily, "They're goddamn compulsive about everything, except paying their rent on time."

Then I saw a way of setting the stage to give him my ultimate assignment.

"Martin," I said. "You're a compulsive yourself. You compulsively say bad things about everybody."

He looked at me, puzzled.

"Well, am I wrong?" I asked. "All I ever hear you do is to attack people and act disappointed. You've put down how many people so far, and you've only been here"—I looked at the clock conspicuously—"for twenty minutes."

"So what!" he retorted at once. "People get what they deserve."

I had committed myself to my collision course with him, and I rushed ahead.

"Deserve! Your whole way of describing the world is a crime. Never an encouraging word—that's your motto."

"That's not true," he protested. "I want Lila back."

"No one would guess that, Martin," I said. "All you can say about her is that she's expensive and that she's stupid."

"So what's the point?" he growled.

"The point? No one could possibly want you the way you are—that's the point. You could spend five million dollars on a woman, and she'd still be sick at heart. She'd either run away or stay and feel like a prostitute. You make people feel so unwanted that—"

"That's a lot of shit."

"You can say what you want. But that attitude won't get Lila back. And it's not going to get you any joy in life. Unless you change, you're a hopeless case. With all your money, you'll just go on with no friends. And if you ever want somebody like Lila to be close to you, they'll run the other way."

I felt as if I had ambushed him, but I truly could see no other way.

Just then, he surprised me by asking, "So what are you saying I should do if I want all this joy?"

He had put a sarcastic spin on the question, but I decided to ignore his tone and take him at face value.

"We've got to find out why you're so negative," I said.

"You're the doctor," he said. "You tell me. My eyesight isn't that good."

"Well, I've got a way to improve it," I said.

He smirked, as if I'd lost my mind.

"Martin," I said. "Remember your promise to do some assignments for me. Well, now I have the most important one of all. It may sound offbeat to you. But I'm pretty sure that when you do it, we'll get some very important understanding."

Then I told him. "I want you to spend six weeks not saying anything bad about anyone. I'll be asking you what comes to your mind—even your smallest thoughts and feelings—when you do this. I want you to tell me what they are. If you do this, we can learn a tremendous amount about what's really going on inside of—"

"But that would be false," he interrupted. "Anyway, what you call negative is just telling the truth. Are you asking me to lie?"

"It may feel that way to you, Martin, but I don't see it that way. And I'm certainly not asking you to do it forever."

Martin began to pout—that childish look again, of shutting his mouth against the medicine. But I had to insist if I were to give him what I considered his best chance to help himself.

And I added that I also wanted Martin to force himself to say something good about Lila every day—and about at least one other person.

"But why?" Martin asked. "How will that help?"

"It's like asking you to jump off the roof, isn't it?"

"No, because I won't do it if I don't want to."

"I know, Martin. You have options, but so do I. I told you when you came back that if you refused to do my assignments, we'd be wasting our time. If you won't try this, I feel I have to stop working with you. Our work would be pointless. It wouldn't be fair to you."

Later, I realized that Martin must have been surprised at my willingness to stop taking his money, which doubtless clashed with his assumption that the whole world was strictly mercenary. He may even have felt baffled by the implication that I might really want to help him.

Martin was all the while fingering the knot of his blue tie, which was under his navy cashmere pullover. As at the start of every session, he had folded his jacket neatly and draped it over a chair. Now in agitation he yanked the tie out and it dangled in front of the sweater. A Freudian might have said that Martin was symbolically exposing himself, which was precisely what I was asking him to do.

A long pause followed, during which I sensed that Martin was contemplating whether he would be better off without me and my assignment.

I was the one who broke the silence by resuming my case. "Look, Martin," I said. "If someone offered you ten thousand dollars not to say anything negative for a month, would you do it?"

He didn't reply, but I thought I saw him resisting a faint smile, as if he'd anticipated where I was headed.

"Well, this is a lot more important to your life than ten thousand," I said.

"Okay, I see that you think this is important," he said, hunching his shoulders and putting his palms up in front of his face, as if to stop the battering. "But why?"

"I want to see what happens to you when you fake trying to be another kind of person."

Again he asked, "Why?" but I didn't halt my presentation.

"No bad words about anyone," I said. "I want you to say something good about Lila—even about me—every day. You won't die, Martin, I promise you. And I want you to keep careful track of your impressions, of anything that feels different."

"I don't see—"

"We've already said you don't have to do it. There's no law that you have to come here."

"And suppose I slip?"

So he was actually considering doing what I asked. I rejoiced as I told him, "Martin, I expect you to slip. It's okay, as long as you try."

"And I should report to you, is that it?" he asked condescendingly.

"You've got it."

He stopped once more, and then said, "As I recall, the deal was that I would do your assignments and try things your way. And after enough of that, you'd call Lila. So if I do all this for a month and a half, then will you call her?"

Once again, a bargain. I should have realized that Martin would never do something for nothing, even to save his own life. Like any canny negotiator, he had drawn me out first to learn my terms, and now he was spelling out his.

The six-week interval I had chosen was arbitrary, but Martin clearly intended to hold me to the letter of it. Now I hoped it was enough.

I hesitated, first out of uncertainty and then on purpose. To start with, I was momentarily unsure, because I didn't regard it as my province to solicit an outsider and bring her into the case. But even after it occurred to me that Martin could be the one to call Lila and could do so with no problem, I still delayed in answering him. This time I was using a salient pause, the way Martin himself might, to underscore that we were about to strike a carefully considered deal—one that we were both honor-bound to keep.

"Okay, Martin, after six weeks if you call Lila and ask her to come in, and if she's willing to, you bet I'll talk to her. And I'll even say that you're trying like hell to change."

"It's a deal," he said.

This time, speaking Martin's language, I put forth my hand instinctively, and he grasped it.

"Trust me, Martin," I said. "You're battling a compulsion, one that's ruining you. We may learn a lot this way. I know it won't be easy, but it's only for a month or so. Let's start right now."

Martin agreed.

During the remaining half hour Martin spoke slowly; sometimes he faltered. I could see that he was on guard against nasty remarks, but they darted everywhere below the surface of what he allowed himself to say.

For instance, when he commented that Lila and he weren't "seeing eye-to-eye these days," I could tell that he was holding back some fierce comment he wanted to make about her.

And I could tell that Martin wanted to bad-mouth the tenants in one of his troublesome buildings. The comment he actually permitted himself was surely lame alongside the one he wanted to make: "I'm concerned about my building on twelfth street. We have a lot of poor people and they don't all have steady jobs."

Since he was already feeling some deprivation, I took my first chance to ask him what reactions he had. "How do you feel right now?" I asked him.

"Okay."

"Martin, just now while you were talking, did any strange thoughts pop into your head?"

"No."

"Is there any feeling you had, even for a moment, that seems strange or unusual? Anything come to your mind?"

"No, nothing." He looked at me askance as if he wondered why he had to abide by the rules of a game that was so foreign and pointless.

"Martin," I said before he left, "I really mean it about our deal. I want you to keep up this regimen of not bad-mouthing people. And please don't forget, if you have any strange thoughts or feelings about anyone, or about anything that seems suddenly missing in your life or wrong, I want you to write them down—this is very important—and tell them to me."

He nodded, indicating that he would.

I wasn't sure what was going through his mind. If he expected me to predict what he would experience in the upcoming weeks, I couldn't, because I didn't know myself.

In his absence I realized that Martin had no idea how hard it would be for him to keep his part of the deal. People seldom realize how dependent they are upon their habitual behavior—how jarring it is to stop nearly any pattern that they've relied on. Martin had no real commitment to therapy anyway, and I half expected him to come in and say that the whole thing was preposterous.

I was pleasantly surprised when the next time I saw him he said he had kept up his half of the deal. He'd done what I'd asked. But, he assured me, he'd had no unusual thoughts or feelings.

A few times during that session he lapsed into disparaging people, but I stopped him. He winced but did his best to comply.

Then, perhaps unconsciously, Martin found a way to bend the rules. Though he didn't characterize anyone as wrong or ugly or abusive, he told one story after another in which a bad opinion of the person was the only conclusion that one could draw.

He had started to say that Lila had "no conception of money," when seeing the look in my eyes he curtailed himself.

"All right," he said, "I won't say what she is, but she had a guy do her kitchen for four thousand dollars and I could have had someone do it for half."

I didn't react.

Perfecting his device almost at once, he began leading me to derogatory conclusions the way a prosecutor leads a jury, presenting damning evidence and leaving the rest to his audience.

He said, "I'm upset because I found out that one of my painters—this guy Morris—has been making private deals with tenants to do their work during hours that I'm paying him for."

"What kind of work?" I asked him.

"Painting. Bookshelves. Bureaus. The tenants' own property. He's a real . . . uh . . . well, you tell me."

I commiserated with him. "It's painful to be cheated, isn't it?"

"So what about the guy, what do you think of him?"

"The same as you do, Martin, I have to admit."

Although he had stopped belittling people in so many words, Martin was still doing so by implication. Never is the flexibility of the human mind more on display than when it wants to indulge a forbidden desire. At such times even the brightest and most honest people may become prone to fooling themselves. Martin, who was in other ways extraordinarily rigid, had shown that flexibility, that curious combination of resourcefulness and self-deception so often employed by people to get around their own promises. When I realized that he was defeating my aim while technically abiding by the rules, I decided to tighten the screws the next time.

As soon as I saw him I began pushing the second part of the assignment, which was for him to say positive things about people. But when I asked him what he liked about Lila, he would say only that, "She was a very good mother raising the kids."

"Was?" I asked. "What about Lila now? Let's talk present tense," I said.

"Okay," he said grudgingly. "She *is* a good mother."

I told him I was sure there was more to her than that or he wouldn't want to live with her for the rest of his life. But he offered nothing more.

In response to my further inquiries, he mustered precious little favorable about his secretary and his daughters, and what he did say seemed to make him very uncomfortable. Again Martin assured me that he'd had no special flashes of thought or feeling, no unusual reactions at any time.

I was pleased that Martin was sticking with the experiment so far, but I realized that it still made no sense to him, and I worried that he might stop complying at any moment.

In the following week, the third of our experiment, Martin bore almost no resemblance to the man I had known. Without access to the identity of the cynical victim with everything to say, he now appeared confused, self-conscious, and out of whack. He fidgeted a great deal, and a curious sterility of subject matter set in. A few times he forgot what he had started to say, as if wires inside of him were short-circuiting. There were hints of annoyance. "I'm a man of my word," he said, "but this isn't easy, because whether you like it or not, people are really pretty . . ."

Again he must have seen a look in my eyes, because he stopped himself abruptly. Later in the session, he sniped at me again, saying that I was ruining his style.

"So what is it that you feel I'm ruining?" I asked him.

He wouldn't answer.

We were both acutely mindful of how long Martin had been subjecting himself to the rigors of my assignment. I started to commend him on how hard he'd been trying, but he looked at me blankly, as if I were kidding.

In our second session that week I had an impression of Martin as having regressed to some kind of childhood state without knowing it. It was a vague notion and made little sense to me at the time, my only identifiable evidence for it being the quirky outfit he wore that day.

It was a hot and dazzlingly bright day in June. Martin, who had always worn a conservative jacket and tie, came in wearing blue Bermuda shorts and a yellow T-shirt, but with them he was wearing black business shoes and high navy socks that reached his gnarled knees. He waddled slightly. He looked like a camper who had downed a serum that suddenly added forty years to his appearance. He explained that he had just walked across Central Park.

Not wanting to make him self-conscious about his outfit, I didn't mention the way he was dressed; it represented such a radical switch that I suspected it resulted from some inner change that would show itself in other ways. However, during that session I began seeing him as a little boy playing the lifetime part of cynical veteran.

Still Martin didn't let on that he'd had any unusual thoughts or feelings if in fact he had, but there were other visible changes. With the pressure on him mounting, Martin was becoming surly toward me, a reaction not unusual for people giving up long-standing ways of acting. He made a number of snippy comments and was evidently furious at me. He told me that he was sick of saying good things about people who didn't deserve them and that he hadn't come to me to learn the social graces.

I told him that it wasn't my purpose to teach them to him. I resisted adding my own snide comment that it wouldn't do him any harm to learn them anyhow.

Later he said, "Doctor, you've got a ridiculous picture of people."

When I asked him in what way, he just smiled.

Then he told me, "I'm starting to forget things. I mean things I never forgot in my life. I missed a meeting. I lost some tax papers. Yesterday I lost my keys. I don't know what the hell's happening to me. This is a fucking stupid idea, if you ask me.

"And the worst thing is, I can't sleep," he said ruefully. "I woke up two or three times last night in a sweat. I haven't gotten a good night's sleep the whole damn week."

I asked him if he was having nightmares, and he thought a minute, and then said no.

I wasn't sure whether to believe him or not, but one thing was sure. By then I felt real admiration for Martin; he had unusual tenacity. It seemed out of Martin's world to resume his old behavior deliberately without telling me, as some people might. He was keeping his promise steadfastly, and at great cost. I felt sure that he was at the brink of a crisis, and whatever else about him I disliked, I truly admired him for the courage to go to that brink.

In that session I saw Martin without his glasses for the first time. The heat seemed to be making him unusually uncomfortable, and he removed his glasses and wiped them with his handkerchief. I couldn't tell if it was his acute nearsightedness or his newly induced confusion, but as I watched him wipe his glasses while trying to keep me in view, I suddenly thought of a baseball catcher who, having shed his mask, was peering into a brilliant sky for a white baseball lost in the sun. I recalled Martin's telling me how ostracized he'd been for being a nonathlete. Well, my system was apparently divesting him of the alternative he had adopted, perhaps back then, and once again he seemed a little boy lost.

It occurred to me as Martin left my office that in his quirky camper-businessman's outfit he must have elicited many a comment on the sarcastic streets of Manhattan.

The fourth week was almost more than Martin could take. He came in at his wit's end. "I never should have agreed to this," he said. "I don't see doing this anymore. I wake up six times a night, Doctor. I've gotten emotional."

He told me that he'd woken up repeatedly the previous night during a thunderstorm. "I felt like kicking something, I was so upset. I never felt like that before. What was it, the rain? I never minded the rain before. What's happening to me here?"

"Six weeks is too long," he said almost pleadingly. "I proved I can do it. All right? I'm telling you I just can't sleep anymore."

I sympathized with his upset. Then I asked him to be more specific. Had he suffered any nightmares?

"No, not that I can remember," he said.

I asked him if he could be more specific about his daytime experiences. Had there been any unusual thoughts or feelings that he could remember—possibly even farfetched moments of thought about what might be going wrong.

Again he said there hadn't been.

I had no doubt that the strange upset, the new emotionality he was reporting, that feeling of sudden vulnerability was a direct consequence of giving up his long-standing defense of bad-mouthing the world and keeping everyone at bay. It was as if everyone mattered more than they had in a long time. People—or at least something—was penetrating his shell. And though he still couldn't pinpoint anything in particular, aside from the stormy night, I was hopeful that he would.

After Martin had gone that day, I realized how much I really wanted to compliment him for honoring an agreement whose consequences had beset him like a fever. But I couldn't. I pictured him smiling cynically if I had, as if I were attempting to manipulate him. Martin had a way of mocking warmth toward him—of making a kind remark seem counterfeit, like a cheap con. I realized that in refraining from complimenting him I was obeying an order that Martin himself had subtly given me.

In examining my own experience, I could infer the impact that this particular trait of Martin's must have had on others who had known him longer. It was another way he downgraded people and implied that their sincerity was unconvincing. His smirking disbelief in anything positive must have stopped others from offering him spontaneous kind words—or even from offering him any warmth or appreciativeness they might feel. By this habit of his, Martin had certainly made a jagged bed for himself to lie in. Even if he were to change his own ways at once, he would still have to face the inhibitions that he had created in other people, inhibitions that might be slow to disappear.

Understanding this, I resolved not to succumb to his indoctrination. I would compliment him on his fortitude the next time I saw him, no matter what his response.

He certainly deserved a compliment. The more I thought about it, the more I marveled at this incredible commitment to a form of withdrawal by a man who had no real interest in therapy—or in improving himself, for that matter. At first I thought he saw this loyalty to his therapy as simply "the cost of doing business" because he wanted Lila so badly. But then I began to see that it was something else entirely. Once Martin had committed himself to his deal with me, and extended his hand on it, it had become a promise to himself, a matter of personal honor.

Martin wasn't so much the sort who kept promises to others as he was the kind of person who fiercely kept promises to himself. Once he told himself that he would do a thing, he *did* it, no matter what the cost. He was one of those—and they exist in every generation, as if spontaneously created—who would virtually die to keep any resolution he made to himself, and this was one.

It struck me that this fortitude, his utter commitment to a promise to himself, was in itself a piece of data that I had gotten for his efforts and mine.

He came in the next time in business attire and with a black briefcase full of papers; it was as if he were shuttling between the zany and the conservative.

"Doctor," he said. "I've been obsessed. Is that the word you use?"

Then he told me about the black cat that had somehow strayed onto the baseball field. Martin had been watching the game on TV, preparatory to going to sleep. He said with great feeling, "The poor cat seemed terrified. It ran everywhere. They couldn't catch it. Then Tony La Russa, the manager, picked it up and handed it to someone.

"I thought I'd forget it. I couldn't sleep for a while thinking about that cat, worrying. But then I said, 'This is crazy,' and I fell asleep.

"I didn't think about it the next day, not once. That was about two weeks ago. Then I thought about it a few times and I said, 'Aw, the cat's all right. It was okay.' But I couldn't be sure.

"And then I started to picture it running desperately—as if I could see its eyes. Running desperately everywhere, and all the people were laughing."

By the time he reached that point, Martin had a hunted look in his own eyes, a startlement that I had never seen there before. "Doctor, this isn't good," he said. "I don't think about that cat just five times a day. I mean fifty times a day—*all the time*. I've got a closing to go to this evening. We worked like hell to get the papers ready. My secretary's picking me up right on the corner. I know I'll be thinking about that cat every five minutes. Every five minutes? No, no every two minutes. I think I'm going crazy."

I assured him that he wasn't. But after a few moments it occurred to me that his obsession had to be related to my assignment—a part of him was breaking down fast. I was struck by the irony that Martin, who had always been so afraid of being robbed of his money, was now being subjected to an even greater theft. This theft of mine was not of his money but of his aggressive shield, of the hardened outer layer that had become part of his organism, and which defended him against—against what? Here I paused. Against intimacy and the very perception of decency and warmth in others, I thought. Apparently, at least some genuine caring on Martin's own part had begun to penetrate, though I had no idea what these images of the cat could mean.

My further questioning yielded nothing. Martin would have liked me to turn off the spigot of his obsession, but I couldn't. And though his long-distance caring for that anonymous cat was hell to him and profitless thus far, it had humanized him a little. I wondered what was coming next.

When he pointed a finger and warned me, "I have only two more weeks of this," I told him I realized that.

Then suddenly, without any deliberation, I heard myself ask him, "Martin, can you come in three times a week for those two?"

He instantly said, "Okay," and I was not surprised. Apparently, some preconscious recognition of a new camaraderie between us had just descended upon us both, and had given me the latitude and the incentive to ask him.

Minutes later, when I had the thought that he'd complied simply so that I would have no recriminations afterward, I decided that now I was the one being unduly cynical. I felt absolutely sure that Martin had softened toward me, as I had toward him. Maybe he actually liked something about himself as the pained but sentient being who cared so much for a strange cat. Or possibly, through his own experience, he understood that I might care about him, apart from his being a paying customer, a "tenant" in my office. The reciprocal nature of Martin's roles in the two relationships—the one who cared and the one being cared for—was, however, as yet utterly nebulous and undefined to me. I was unable even to see these reciprocal equations until they became unmistakable soon afterward.

The July Fourth weekend was blisteringly hot, and the streets of Manhattan were thinly peopled. On Monday evening, after some light rain, there came a great thunderstorm, the kind that could uproot trees and swell rivers, but which hardly affected the city, except to cool it down and improve the water supply. I paid little attention to it. But it touched off the profoundest revelation of Martin's adult life.

The following day Martin appeared to be in shock. He told me he'd slept only an hour the night before. Then he brushed back his hair nervously and announced, "I had a terrible dream last night—unbelievably bad."

When I asked him what it was, he mimicked me—" 'Tell me about the dream, Martin.' I knew you'd want to know."

"I can't sleep anymore," he said. "I had the dream during the storm, and I woke up terrified. I tried for hours to get back to sleep, but I couldn't. The dream was terrible—just terrible."

I waited. I could see that he intended to tell me the whole dream—or at least as much as he could remember.

He began. "I was looking for my dog, Jill. I haven't thought about Jill in years. She was lost. A woman said, 'Oh, Jill was in my house, but she's not there now.' I realized that I was responsible for that dog.

"I was downstairs and I told a man. He said, 'Don't bother. Leave her out on the street. That dog is too old and scraggly. She's lame. She's no use. That dog is mean. She went that way.'

"But I wanted her. I ran down the stairs and around the bend, but I didn't see her. I started knocking on doors. And I was inside, asking people about her when I heard the storm outside. And I started to get desperate and I opened a screen door and went into the yard.

"Then I saw her. I knew it was Jill right away by her black velvet ears. I could recognize her timid movements.

"And a woman picked her up, and I was going crazy, and the rain was just starting, and the thunder. Then Jill snarled. She never used to snarl like that. And I saw she was old and wrinkled and frizzy and lame. And then the woman got afraid and put her down and Jill ran away."

By then Martin was brushing his wisps of hair back hard and repeatedly, presumably the way he had in his childhood when his hair was a tumbled mop.

"I followed her down the street, but I knew I couldn't catch up with her. And I tried to call her name—'Jill, Jill.' But no sound came out of my mouth, and she was running away."

As Martin said this, the pale surface of his face seemed to be fragmenting. He could pretend as much as he wanted that he felt nothing, but I knew he was near tears. This was one time that I didn't have to ask him how he was feeling.

"But then she stopped running. And she called my name, Martin, Martin, *my name,* in a high-pitched voice. She was scared that she'd be all alone.

"There were people there, and I said to them, 'Did you hear her? She spoke, in a person's voice.' And they did. They were astonished. They said they did.

"Then Jill stretched her legs out and began moving her head gently from side to side, the way she used to when she wanted food at the table."

Now Martin was sobbing convulsively, and he made no effort to stem the tears or wipe his face, anymore than a baby would who didn't know or care. He continued sobbing for a while and when he stopped I asked him if there was more, and he said yes, but he needed time to resume.

Then he said, "And I went over to her. She started to crawl to me on her belly the way she used to. I saw she had a bad leg and she was old, but I picked her up. I told her 'You're mine. Don't worry, Jill. I know you're not mean. I will never part with you again. I will care for you forever.'"

He looked at me through tears as he assured me, "And I will. If I only could."

Then, trying to rally his composure by mustering a more or less objective statement, Martin said, "I woke up thinking the storm caused the dream." He observed that the pelting rain and the thunder he heard in the dream must have been the rain and thunder outside.

Again I waited. The first comments people make about their dreams after recounting them are often as revelatory as the initial thoughts they have upon waking up. The events and characters in any dream, together with their linkages, have particular meanings to the dreamer that no one else can fully guess. These subterranean passages are potentially best understood by the dreamer himself, who has built them, and the dreamer is best able to furnish needed links when others say the least.

And so I waited awhile after Martin stopped talking, and then said what I hoped would be least intrusive. "Is that as much of the dream as you can remember, Martin?"

"Uh, there was one other thing."

"What was that?"

"Out in the street, I was chasing the dog, there were a lot of signs that said, ALTERNATE PARKING."

The parking signs didn't mean anything to him, and he couldn't think of anything else, and moments later he asked me, "Do you really think there's anything in dreams? You know my grandfather was a farmer in Vladivostok, and he used to tell people what their dreams meant. He was uneducated." Martin smiled.

I didn't smile along with him. I could feel us hurtling away from the planet on which this intricate and highly charged adventure took place.

"Any other thoughts about the dream?" I asked him.

He shook his head no.

I would have to be more specific. "And the dog, what does she make you think of?" I asked him next.

"My dog. Jill was my dog; we were very close. I hadn't thought about her in years. She loved me all right. She slept in bed with me, a little black-and-white mutt, mostly a fox terrier and spitz. She was mine. I found her in the street. My sisters didn't let her eat at the table, so I would take food back to my room. She depended on me. I guess I love animals, huh? I'm worried about them all over the place these days."

"Your dog had a limp?" I asked.

"No, not at all."

"Was she mean?"

"No." He seemed surprised—and defensive. "Definitely not! She was scared, that was all."

I waited.

"She would lick my face," he said. "She was afraid of everybody but me and my mother. She was never nasty, never. She never bit anybody."

Something prompted me to echo, "Never bit anybody," and Martin snatched a tissue and stopped tears from emerging.

After that, he didn't speak, but it was obvious that a video of thoughts and ruminations was running fast forward through his mind. He brushed his hair back needlessly. Once again I imagined that I saw before me the contracted and quivering face of a child—of the little boy with the mop of tousled hair who had owned Jill and had been owned in turn by that beloved dog.

Then he told me how he had found Jill. He'd seen her as a stray puppy in a neighborhood alley. They took to each other at once.

He said, "She would run around so much when she saw me that my sisters said she was crazy. I was always caring for her. One day she was gone. My mother had lent her to the neighbor's kids for the day, but she was very unhappy, and she ran away and came back. About six blocks, to our building, up three flights of stairs, and right to our apartment door. Not bad, eh?"

"Not bad," I agreed.

"We kept her after that," Martin said.

"You saw her when she was old, like in the dream?"

"Yes, I took her with me when I left home. I was seventeen, she was thirteen. But she didn't look anything like that," he hastened to defend her.

I asked him about other events in the dream—the characters: the first woman, the man who told Martin not to bother about the dog, and the woman who picked Jill up and then was afraid of her. But they brought nothing to Martin's mind. Then I asked him about the buildings, the storm, the streets, even the screen door. But they conjured up nothing either.

Suddenly, he became very embarrassed about having showed so much feeling, and I told him I was proud of him for such depth of caring, no matter that it was in a dream. Disowning my comment, he countered that she was a wonderful dog.

Talking about the dream led Martin to remember some more about his childhood, and I went off in that potentially useful direction with him. He remembered the dog's being with him and his mother for long stretches when his father and sisters were away. He had especially cherished the dog right after his mother died.

I learned some more facts, but as he presented them, I was struck by how much less feeling he endowed his actual memories with than the dream. If anything, I realized, he had fled into talking about his life to escape the deeper reality of the dream. It was as if the emotions of his real life could not pass into his consciousness but had emerged in the dream.

Toward the end of the session, I realized that I still had absolutely no idea what the dream meant, and I wasn't sure that I ever would. However, of one thing there could be no doubt. The dream itself, and all of Martin's newly erupted emotionality attendant upon it, had come as a result of his carrying out my assignment. His abstaining from acts of cynicism had caused some important truth, still masked, to erupt in that dream. I knew we would be coming back to that dream. But for the moment I let it rest.

Hours after Martin had gone I remained struck by how much emotion he had felt in my presence. He had been so drenched with sadness and sympathy that it was hard to remember how stinting he was with people.

It was another sweltering night. The moon was big with a reddish glow, and the tide of life seemed full. It crossed my mind that Martin had been under the sway of that moon, but he was no lunatic. With his snarling contempt for everyone, Martin had perhaps been denying what he wanted most—intimacy with Lila or someone like her, perhaps with his children, or with at least one or two friends, like his boyhood friend, Arthur.

If so, his very occupation contributed to his torture. In his buildings on every floor lovers were finding eternity in one another's bodies and voices and smiles. Martin could not help but know this, and the more conscious of it he became, the worse his privation would be, the more he would suffer unless he allowed himself to join in.

I pictured him alone in that dingy apartment of his, biding his time until sleep gave him parity with those who declared their loves and their needs, and who took at least some of what was there.

In having his tragedy burst into consciousness, he had suffered the full brunt of it, unprepared. In that dream he was telling me all about it, but so far I had no idea what he was telling me. Both he and I were like people hearing the music of a forgotten song and were as yet unable to recollect the words.

Thinking about Martin's dog, I imagined that, like his boyhood friend, Arthur, she had remained pristine in Martin's love because she had not been around long enough for Martin to see her as violating him. Jill and Arthur had vanished from Martin's life before they could diminish in his esteem, as Lila and Mary and others had—before Martin could perceive them differently. His mother, too, had vanished early. Whatever else Martin had felt about her from day to day, he had loved her unfailingly since her death. But she wasn't even in the dream, so far as I could tell.

That seemed odd to me. I think because Jill was so clearly in his childhood, and because the whole dream was so emotional, I had a sense that logically his mother should be there. The only other time Martin had ever shown any real emotion was when he'd spoken about his mother.

I reviewed the dream characters in my mind, looking for her. Was she the woman who picked up the angry dog and then put her down in a hurry? That didn't jell. Nor did the other characters seem right: the woman who'd said that Jill had been in her house; the man who had told Martin to forget the dog; or the group who'd heard Jill speak. In none of those characters could I find Martin's mother, or Martin himself, for that matter.

Then I found them both at once. It all became obvious so quickly that I was startled. His mother was Martin himself looking for that lost, lame, snarling dog. In the dream she had not been dead at all, but alive, lovingly alive—she was the one hearing the storm, opening that screen door, and running through the streets, desperately searching for her son.

"I saw that the dog had a bad leg," Martin had said. "She was wrinkled and old. But I recognized her at once. I told her, 'You're mine, Jill. I know you're not mean. I will care for you from now on?" And Martin's sadness, his gush of sorrow—his mother was sorry that she had abandoned him. She had finally come back. Martin's whole life had been a bad dream, as he wandered the streets alone, unable to come inside out of the storm. Finally the long trek was over, for her and for him, and he had to cry.

Realizing this, I recalled Martin saying defensively, "No, she's not mean—not Jill." He was telling his own story. What else could it be? No wonder Martin had been obsessed by that cat a week earlier, as it scooted desperately to the right and left in front of millions, looking for its home; it had been as helpless as Martin himself, ready to settle for just a place to hide. He had been able to worry about that cat and to weep for the dog as he had never been able to weep for himself.

The dog's limp affirmed it. Martin had complained to me twenty times that his limp had made him feel old. After that, I had not a moment's doubt that Martin himself was the snarling, lonely creature whom the world misunderstood. Without his lifetime camouflage of cynicism, his truth had emerged in this sense of himself, first as the cat in the stadium, and now more specifically as the dog whom someone had finally brought home. In the dream that "understanding someone" was Martin himself: He had promised never to leave that dog—never until he died.

I felt quite sad myself as I thought about all this. Martin had negated the very possibility of a warm emotional life since being young. Then all of a sudden he had permitted himself the experience he had always yearned for—but only in a dream and with his and his mother's roles reversed.

If only Martin could feel in waking life, even in moments, the tenderness of that dream. I needed him to see himself as forlorn, abandoned, yearning for a home and all the while appearing mean and scraggly. The courage on his part to accept this image of himself could transfigure him. With that, he could pursue what he really wanted but had made impossible to attain. The dream had transfigured him, but fleetingly and in such a disguise that he could easily negate it. I thought about the statue in Shakespeare's *The Winter's Tale,* the perfect likeness of Hermione descending from the pedestal after decades and becoming real. I wanted no less for Martin.

But now I was the one doing the dreaming. I realized with a thud that Martin had contracted to only about ten more days of effort—of therapy altogether. After that, if Lila turned him down—and I was almost sure she would—he would revert to his harsh identity and very likely never again be touched as he had been. If only I could remove some color from that dream and instill it into his waking life, he might become a different man.

By then I felt sure that I understood Martin's meanness, his disbelief in human goodness, and his cynicism. He had been saying since he was ten, "World, I *hate* you for what you did to my mother." He had been hissing this message at whoever drew close, and he would punish anyone who did not back off.

An hour before he was due, I felt hurried. I knew that I had to keep

Martin a prisoner in the painful underworld of his dream, whether he liked it or not. Once he quit therapy, I could hardly call him up and plead with him to discuss it. Any minute away from the dream and its associations was to be a minute lost—that was how I felt.

On the other hand, I dared not move too fast. For a therapist to simply announce an interpretation is worse than useless. If the interpretation is true, then the patient is inhibited from the more authentic experience of reaching it on his own; and, of course, if it's false, then he is sent off in a wrong direction. The ideal approach would be for me to question Martin rather than direct him. That way he would make the best use of whatever emerged.

When the bell rang I reminded myself of the adage, "Make haste slowly."

Martin arrived, again in a business suit, this time looking quite assembled. It was as if he'd strained to put himself together mentally and in appearance since I'd seen him last.

After he draped his jacket over a chair in his usual ritual, he commented, "It's nice and cool in here," and then asked me what kind of air conditioner I had. I told him, and there followed some chitchat about how people were suffering as a result of the greenhouse effect.

To my surprise, he said it was a good thing.

When I asked him why, he explained that it would save him a fortune in heating bills over the year.

"Are you really that indifferent to whether other people suffer?" I asked him.

He nodded that he was.

When I introduced the dream again, he protested. "Why are we making such a fuss about that dream? This is silly."

I chose not to explain. "Look, Martin," I insisted. "You'll be leaving soon if you want to, and we may never see each other again. But while you're here, I want you to stay with this."

"If you say so, Doctor," he replied with mock docility. He sat sprawling in an unusually relaxed posture.

It occurred to me that telling me the dream and weeping over it had been a catharsis for him, and he no longer felt tense. But then I realized, that wasn't Martin. Far more likely, he was trying to tell me by his behavior and appearance that I hadn't fazed him, like a fighter who smiles after taking a solid shot to the head.

As I had before, I asked him if the characters in the dream reminded him of anything, or anyone real.

"Yeah, alternate parking reminds me of my sisters alternating weeks with me. That's where I learned the word 'alternate,' " he said, as if nothing could possibly be more irrelevant.

"In the dream, how did Jill get lost?" I asked him.

He smiled as if to say that the question was stupid. But I then insisted that he make up an answer, *any* answer, as if he were writing a story or a movie.

"Okay," he said. "I guess no one was interested, so she got out the door."

I waited for him to go on.

"No one gave a damn," he said.

"But in the dream you did, Martin."

"I know, but I couldn't do anything."

"But then you found her," I said.

"That was great," he said sarcastically.

"How did you know the dog wasn't really mean?" I asked him. I was content to elicit grudging cooperation, even nasty cooperation. I had to be—he was growling like that dog.

When again he didn't answer, I told him that I was touched by how important that dog was to him. Then, still hoping that Martin would offer more, I explained to him that in a dream, a dog could represent an actual person. Even an object could be a person—anything could be.

"I'm sure your uncle in Vladivostok knew that," I said. Then I asked him, "Who do you think that lost dog could have been?"

"I don't know," he said. "Do you?"

"And how on earth did you know it wasn't mean? Maybe it was."

Again he didn't reply, and I accused him of not cooperating and refusing to play the game.

"Okay," he said. "She growled a lot and showed her teeth, but it didn't fool me."

"But the lady who picked Jill up and dropped her in a terror . . ." I started to say.

"That was a *mistake,*" Martin corrected me. "The woman made a big mistake. Jill wouldn't have bit her . . . Look, Doctor, this is ridiculous. How do I know? It was a dream."

"I realize that," I said, "but you're helping me a great deal by saying all this. Please keep going. Tell me whatever comes to your mind, that's all I can ask, and all you can do. I really appreciate it." I could hear myself virtually begging him to keep talking, and I sensed my own panic that if he stopped trying to form mental connections right now we were lost.

"How did I know?" he said, repeating my words. "Scared can look mean in a dog. It didn't trust anybody else."

"Why not?" I asked.

"Why not? The dog wanted me, all right! No one else would do. Only me."

"You mean all those other people were substitutes?

"Jill didn't want them," he said. "They were shit. But it was a dream."

By then I couldn't imagine that Martin failed to see that in talking about Jill he was talking about himself. He spoke even more fluidly, more soulfully as that dog than he'd ever spoken for himself. But, apparently, he didn't know.

I had a rogue image of seeing a Hollywood shooting script with the bold letters "POV, dog" (point of view, dog) on it as Martin went on. From the vantage point of that tiny dog, I could see those adults hulking into the sky. They were threatening to pick him up, much as Martin's father and sisters must have surrounded him when he was a little boy. All the dog could do was to snarl and keep them at bay, but the dog was scared.

About then came a specter of recognition that I had been wrong about something—the phrase "dead wrong" wounded my mind. Though I as yet had no idea what I'd been wrong about, I began to feel that I'd been painfully out of joint with some premise of mine.

Setting aside that concern for a moment, I went back to Martin's dream.

"I guess the storm made it worse for the dog being out there," I said.

"I guess so," Martin replied flatly.

"But you sure were in a hurry. You ran frantically everywhere to find that dog," I observed.

"Yeah, I was," he said.

"You really felt close to that dog, didn't you?"

"I like dogs."

"Did you ever get another one?" I asked, and then was sorry that I had involuntarily steered him away from the dream.

However, I was caught short by the force of his reply: "No, never. I'd never have another dog. No, I never would."

Such finality certainly suggested that there was more to be looked at here, and I invited myself forward.

"That's interesting," I said. "Even though you love dogs that much—"

That seemed almost more than he could bear. "If you're telling me to get a dog, the answer is *no,*" he shouted. "Jill was my dog and that's it."

"Okay." I backed off. "About that dog in the dream, she limped, right?"

"Yeah. Maybe an accident or something, I don't know."

"Do you know anyone who you think is old and scraggly and lame?" I asked him.

He looked confused.

"Well, do you know anyone who people might *think of* as old and scraggly and lame?" I asked him next.

"You mean *me?*" he asked incredulously.

"Yes, you. You must have told me twenty times how old and bedraggled that limp made you feel."

He nodded.

"And everyone thinks you're nasty, and you do snarl," I reminded him.

"So we could be the same character, you think."

"Well, you sure do act mean, Martin," I said. "You act so nasty. What's that song? You're 'meaner than a junkyard dog.'"

"So I'm the dog?" he said, as if absorbing the idea, but still not showing any feeling. It was as if only the words had gotten through.

"That's what I was thinking, Martin. You're the dog, keeping everyone back. Let's face it, you're acting like an old, scraggly, bad-footed dog. Everyone thinks you're mean. And you *are* mean, Martin. You're cheap and you're selfish. But if you could come inside, Martin, if you could only come inside. That storm is fierce out there."

"Okay."

Then suddenly his imperturbability was gone, and Martin looked as stricken as he had after telling me the dream, though this time he was holding on manfully.

I waited, and then said, "Martin, I understand. You don't have to talk right now. I promise you that if you let me I'm going to help you come inside. You don't have to keep running. I'm going to show you how to come inside."

This time he wasn't crying, but he squinted and wiped his glasses, and I could tell that he was feeling what Wordsworth described as "thoughts that lie too deep for tears."

I went very slowly. We had to live through this together, with Martin as the dog, out in the storm, and me—at that moment, who was I? I likened myself to his deceased mother, returned and rushing feverishly through the streets, looking for her lost urchin son, and promising to bring him home. Realizing this, I was surprised at my own words, at my maternal role. But I knew that I had his attention, and even a glimmer of his faith—and nothing else mattered, though, of course, I realized, I was hardly the mother he wanted.

And then as Martin sat there, fusing himself and that dog in his thoughts, or so I imagined, another answer came to me. I recognized where I had been wrong, the premise of mine that was off course.

I had imagined that Martin had been snarling at people to punish the world for taking his mother from him. But now I realized that the reason for his nastiness was even simpler—or at any rate, more primitive. Martin wasn't merely getting even with people for what "they" had done to his mother. He had been rejecting people fiercely, one by one, because they were *not* his mother.

The real threat to the dog was that people would *console* that dog—console Martin—that he would accept a sorry substitute and betray his mother, and if he did, then . . . then he would never see her again. She would never come back.

So Martin had become and remained the snarling guardian of her place. Not his sisters with their alternate parking, who tried to console him, not Lila, nor anyone since, would cajole him, would hoist him aloft and bring him home. He was preserving his mother's place. He was guarding the faith. He was magically keeping her alive.

"Martin," I said. "You don't have to growl anymore. You're not fooling anyone."

"What do you mean?" he asked.

"Martin," I said. "What happened was terrible. But your mother's not coming back. Never, Martin, great as she was. There's no sense pushing everyone else away to keep her place open."

"I know that," he said.

And then he let himself cry.

We finished the session with little more said.

In that emotional session Martin had momentarily accepted that he was still cynical and savage to people in accordance with a childhood impulse to reserve his mother's place for her. But my interpretation, very lightly made, offered little more than a line of sight between Martin's behavior now and the wish he'd had in childhood. For all the emotional impact of that session, I could hardly expect Martin to make use of that momentary understanding or even to remember it.

For that I still needed him to see the past up close so that he could understand more deeply why he negated people—and the sheer pointlessness of doing so.

In our next session I went back to that era of Martin's life in which his mother had died. He first remembered a curious form of upset occurring right after her death. When his report card came, no one had looked at it or signed it.

"In the beginning, I was glad," he said. "It didn't matter that I got a couple of 'unsatisfactorys'—that's what they used to call it. But then I got really miserable. No one was going to look at my report card at all. Never. They should have done that. I needed a signature."

"They certainly should have," I said.

"Yeah. I finally got one of my sisters to sign it."

He could vividly remember both sisters devoting time to him, asking him about his clothing.

"And how did you treat them?" I asked.

"Lousy. They were insincere. I always knew a phony. Even my dog knew a phony—fast."

Both sisters, but especially Arlene, would put out a cheek for him to kiss, and he would refuse. He mostly stayed in his room alone when either one was there cooking for their father. Once he consented to go out to dinner with Arlene and her boyfriend. "The guy tried to talk to me. He asked if I liked baseball. He offered to take me to a game, but I said no."

Martin would stay in his room listening to the radio a lot, thinking about his mother, and hating his sisters for how they had treated her and him.

"Did you sometimes wish she'd come back?" I asked him.

"Of course not. I knew dead was dead."

"I know," I said. "But you were only ten—a child can't help imagining, can't help wishing."

"Maybe I did."

"Everyone else was like counterfeit money," I said, unconsciously choosing from the vernacular I thought he would best understand.

"That's right."

"And they still are—in your book. Even me, Martin."

"Maybe," he agreed grudgingly, but I think he still took some pleasure in indicting me.

"You decided never to give anyone a chance," I said.

He didn't respond.

That session initiated our final week, and Martin talked a lot about Lila and his chances with her. What he said implied that in his heart he knew they weren't good. I reaffirmed my promise to talk to Lila if she was willing and to listen painstakingly to whatever he suggested as a way of approaching her. I told him, as I had often, that he'd put in heroic weeks of self-discipline, and "I know it isn't easy," I said.

I was surprised to hear him say, "It's not so bad."

When Martin was gone I imagined him using that exact phrase with the adults who sought to solace him, to tell him they knew how upset he must be, after his mother had died.

In thinking about him shortly before he arrived the next time, I realized that though his sisters had had their own courses of life to follow, they hadn't been in reality nearly as heartless toward him as Martin had led me to believe. They had, after all, rearranged their lives in an effort to comfort him, though not permanently, of course. I wondered if any fathers or sisters could truly have broken through Martin's willful isolation enough to reclaim him.

And, obviously, his sisters were stricken too, which Martin himself never mentioned or even considered. Imperfect as they were, they had fallen victim to Martin's bitterness. After his loss he had refused to let them comfort him or to mother him in any respect—"doggedly" refused. I didn't blame him, but I could certainly sympathize with their suffering first a mother's death and then the utter failure of being unable to take up any of the slack with their kid brother. Martin had been no joy, sulking and always retreating when they made their best efforts.

I realized that Martin might do well to reconsider his sisters someday. Beyond the benefit of having sisters once again if, indeed, he had been too harsh in his judgment of them, it would be part of his own cure to relent—to forgive and find forgiveness in the world. But now was certainly not the time for me to present this. Martin had no sympathy for his sisters at all. Well ahead of forgiving his sisters even a little would be the recognition that those in his present life merited far more humanity than he gave them.

It was the session before our last, and obviously we couldn't do much more in the time left to us. It would be enough if Martin could see what he was doing—turning people into disappointments in order to exit them from his life—and that his secret ritual of rejecting all "substitutes" for his mother was pointless. It would take a lot longer for him to see that he could still come in out of the storm—that by trusting he could find trust; by loving, find love. However, perhaps by using whatever sway I had with him, I could get him to consider—

The doorbell rang.

He came in briskly, and I could see that he had something on his mind. When he sat down he asked me if I was a man of my word. I told him that I definitely was, and I asked him if he had doubted it.

"Good," he said. "Because Lila agreed she would talk to you."

I repeated that I would, and he immediately exchanged his inquisitorial tone for one verging on the pathetic. "I don't think I have much of a shot," he said.

Then he told me that he'd called her and invited her to spend two weeks with him in Europe, but she'd turned him down and laughed at him. He said, "Every year Lila wanted to go, but I was busy, and she would act hurt and cry. Now I want to go with her, and she says no. Can you understand women?"

Had he truly believed that she might join him, despite all he knew that had transpired! But then Martin was a believer in the past over the present.

"Well, whatever Lila says or does, we'll see," I said. "You may be right, but I certainly won't break my promise."

"What are you going to tell her?"

"Should I say that you love her very much and that you'll continue to work on yourself?"

"You think that would help?"

"It can't hurt. I don't know if it will help. Conceivably. Is it true?"

"I do love her."

At that moment my phone rang, and my answering machine cut it off quickly. "Maybe that's Lila," he said, and then smiled as if to camouflage his fantastic yearning with humor.

"Does she even know my name?" I asked him.

"I think I told her your name," he said. "Maybe not."

"That's it? Don't you have any more ideas about what else I might say to her?" I asked.

"Tell her that she's making a mistake with that guy, the supermarket manager."

"Martin, I can't talk about someone I never met. Isn't there anything more I can say about you?"

"Yeah, that I love her and I'll do what she wants."

I told him that I seriously wondered if Lila would believe that.

"You're right," he said. "Okay, what would you say?"

"I'd say that you discovered during your work with me that you snarl and that you're nasty and cynical. If it were up to me I would tell her that you never gave anyone a chance. No one can remain loving and kind, or even decent, in your book. Certainly not a woman—it isn't just her. But I would tell her that you found some things out and you're going to change—"

"Won't that turn her against me?"

"Why? She knows how tough you can be. Everybody knows. But I'll tell her that you're really not mean underneath, that you're scared, like Jill. Maybe I'll tell her that you *are* Jill, maybe I'll tell her the dream—"

"No, don't," he protested.

"Okay, I won't But why not?"

"I don't know how she'd take it."

"How would anyone take it—the way you loved that dog?"

I could see that he suddenly felt sad, and he wasn't desperately trying to hide it.

"Okay," I said. "Martin, if you don't want me to, I won't tell her the dream. I have a better idea—I'll tell her how tough it was on you when your mother died, how's that? I'll tell her how you kept everybody away from you, even people who wanted to love you, even people who did love you. I'll tell her that up until now you couldn't trust anybody, you were afraid of love. But now you can really love Lila. And every time you snarl, you'll think, 'I'm scaring people away but I really want them.' "

"By the way," he said. "I'm sorry I yelled at you the other day when you told me to get another dog."

"That's okay."

"It's sensitive with me, because my daughters always wanted a dog and I didn't want one. That was a big argument. I guess that's why I jumped at you."

I wished that I could return to talking more directly about Martin himself. I suspected that soon even the hope of Lila would be gone. But as yet, his hoping for Lila provided an incentive for Martin to think about himself in a way he ordinarily would not. However, when he dropped the subject of Lila, he then seemed bent on talking about his dog, the real Jill, whom he loved so profoundly. He told me that when she became old he had brought her to his office with him; he had felt good when she was there.

Aside from her affectionate nature, I realized, Jill was the only figure who had been a part of his early household before his mother's death and who had remained. As he told me about the dog's death at a very advanced age, it struck me that he had imbued that dog with more than a little of his mother's fervent affection for him.

"People told me to get another dog right away," he said, "but I wouldn't."

The same theme! It was as if Jill had been so linked to his mother that he had to keep her place open too, in order to keep his mother magically alive.

I told him that I could understand why he had refused to get another dog.

"Why?" he asked, as if I were disparaging him.

"You couldn't replace Jill," I said. "Never."

"That's right. I thought it wouldn't be fair to Jill. I couldn't look at another dog, even though I like dogs. A tenant of mine on Riverside Drive has a dog that looks just like Jill. It upsets me since the dream."

"That's why you're such a killer to people, Martin," I said.

"Why?"

"You won't take anyone but the original—your mother. And Jill, who was a part of her. You want your mother, you want Jill. And you got into a frame of mind of thinking that way all the time. You want Mary back as she was before you ditched her. And you want Lila the way she was twenty-five years ago. And if you can't have that, you curse whoever comes along."

"I know what you're saying."

"I'm saying that it's time to grow up. You're smart, but you cheat people. And nobody's coming to find you out there. Nobody cares. No, that's not true—I do. And some other people would. Possibly even Lila, but definitely your daughters."

"Why do you think my daughters do?"

"Well, you are their only father."

He looked at me, as if trying to pretend that I was having some kind of seizure and that my words bore no relation to his reality. And, indeed, for a moment I did feel like one of those soapbox orators in Hyde Park, in London, with a crowd gathered around on a Sunday watching him for their mirth while he attempted to rally them, pleading with them to act in a way that he considered to be in their best interests. However, even as I had this picture of myself, and of Martin as a detached multitude, I knew that he was really hearing me, I hoped with the force of a multitude.

"Listen, Martin," I concluded, "if you don't change, you'll stay all alone—on Sundays, holidays, every day with no friends, no love. You'll be that dog in the dream. Not the real Jill; she had you. You have nobody. But if you come in—"

"All right. I get the point. I think you're right. What next?"

"I'll talk to Lila, and I promise you I'll try hard. But you're the one that has to turn your own life around. You're the only one who can do it."

I knew that I'd said all I could, and more.

During the last session before my showdown with Lila, Martin and I were slightly less at cross purposes.

I asked him if he was eager to return to his cynical, greedy, bad-mouthing self as soon as the hour was up.

When he didn't reply, I told him, "You really worked like hell to do what I asked you. You gave me a terrific six weeks. But it's over. We learned a lot and now—"

"What do you want me to do? You're the doctor?"

"Me!" I said with some surprise in my voice. "I'd love to see you keep going in your new direction—to save yourself, to make real friends, maybe to fall in love—"

"Then you don't think it looks that good with Lila, do you?"

I realized that I had implied this, and not wholly by accident. Not wanting to mislead Martin, I told him simply that I didn't know for sure, but that we'd find out soon enough.

Then perhaps for the last time I tried to convey to Martin the alternatives that lay open to him, the life that cynicism was sure to go on producing, and the more personal and rewarding life that he could still have. I wished that I had the power of the Dickens's ghost who conjured up the outcomes for Scrooge, but I didn't, and I wasn't sure how convincing I actually was.

He said that Lila would call me the following week, and that after I'd seen her, he would be in touch to find out what had happened.

At the door he cautioned me, "Do your best," as if I might easily neglect him. He had forsworn cynicism for a time, but he still harbored disbelief in the genuineness of other people.

I half expected him to promise me a bonus if I did well. I remembered that million-dollar offer he had made for the name of the hit-and-run driver.

I assured him, "If there's any chance, I'll certainly ask her to reconsider."

But then I told him that if Lila had really made up her mind, nothing I said could make any real difference.

He nodded. He knew that but didn't want to know it.

Lila did call a few days later, and after eliminating times when we were unavailable, we agreed on an evening hour. She sounded rather impersonal, somewhere between linear and cold.

The bell rang at the moment that we'd agreed on, and I was surprised to see a couple at the door. The woman was fiftyish, slender, and attractive, and she seemed full of color; she wore a brown raw-silk jacket over a yellow silk blouse and a sleek black skirt. A long scarf with a brilliant floral pattern, knotted elegantly around her neck, picked up the gold of her reddish hair and the flashing green of her large crystal earrings.

I was so stunned at the contrast between her and the colorless Martin, especially in view of his nebulous description of her, that for a moment I took no notice of the man she was with.

The woman stepped forward and introduced herself as Lila, and a smile came and was gone.

I invited them in.

Lila entered and beckoned the man to follow. He was very Irish looking, with a handsome, mobile face, slightly overweight, his hands dangling limply at his sides.

She introduced him as James and we shook hands.

"Is it all right if James comes in with me?" she asked as I headed toward my office. "James and I have no secrets from each other."

I acquiesced.

Obviously, James wasn't just moral support. Lila was putting the matter of her reconciling with Martin beyond any doubt, showing me in advance that there wasn't even an ember of hope for him, that if I had any notion of arguing his case, it would be so much breath into the wind.

Inside my office Lila sat on my couch and James sat deferentially in a chair off to the side.

Lila began, "James has never met Martin. And he doesn't want to either. James is a widower. He has two wonderful children. He's a very hardworking man, and he has been very good to me. James is capable of real love, and I guess very few men are."

It was a well-rehearsed preemptive strike—and effective. While she shot out these compliments of James, he listened without expression.

I sympathized with Lila. Where was I when her husband was crushing her? And though I believed that Martin could repair himself, why should she stake her life on that meager prospect? And if her heart was already elsewhere. . . .

I had an impulse to abbreviate the session and get out of there. If it were my own case I would never have pleaded it against such opposition. Who can oppose love—even professed love? But I couldn't quit there and then. I owed Martin a try, an effort, if not comparable to the one he had made, then at least my own best effort.

However, I could hardly talk about Martin and Lila as a couple with his replacement in the room.

I looked over at James, the silent partner, and he suddenly appeared a lot bulkier than he had. The picture flashed through my mind of him putting a store thief in a headlock, and the stolen steaks tumbling out all over the floor.

"James," I asked him, "would it be all right with you if Lila and I spoke alone for a while?"

He looked over at her.

"Maybe you could wait outside?" she said.

He left. He seemed totally overcome by her intellectuality and her verbosity, and if she said that he was a good man, then he would be one.

I escorted him to the waiting room. There I pointed to a few magazines, but I pictured him just sitting quietly, not wanting to be presumptuous. He was quite a contrast to Martin.

When I returned to my office Lila was sitting with her legs crossed and leaning on her elbow. This posture and her intense countenance were as if to say that I was a teenager who had brought her home after a date and definitely wasn't going to get anywhere.

And things went from bad to worse when I brought up Martin. I began by telling Lila that, in my opinion, Martin had really tried hard to change, that he had put in an unbelievable effort "and it's because he wants a chance with you."

"That's good," she said. "Then maybe he'll be good for someone else." She paused for a moment and added, "Think badly of me if you want. I have absolutely no sympathy with him."

If there was ever a closing remark, that was it.

Still, in deference to Martin I felt obliged to see the session through. I asked her, would she consider going with him to talk to a marriage counselor before giving up the relationship forever?

"Of course not. I tried to get Martin to see my therapist a hundred times, years ago, while there was still hope. I begged him, but he didn't even hear me."

"You're sure you don't love him?"

"Of course. I don't."

"How can you be so sure?" I asked.

She made a wry face, which I took to be disgust at the idea and mockery of me for asking the question. It seemed fatuous to me, too. I felt like a robot carrying out Martin's wishes.

In case the matter was still in doubt, she crossed her legs the other way and added, "Martin blamed me for everything bad that ever happened to him in his life. I'm really not interested in any way. I worked very hard in art school, and I have my own life and my own friends. I'm a very serious painter."

I dared not let on that I'd had no idea.

"Have we covered everything?" she asked.

"Well, you did come here, I thought that maybe—"

"I'm here solely because my children never had a father, and they deserve the one thing he can give them, which is some of his money. I want a decent settlement for them for my having put in twenty-five years with that inconsiderate animal.

"Let me be honest with you," she went on. "I'll listen to whatever I have to listen to, to accomplish what I want."

"I understand."

I thought I really did, but she snapped, "No, you don't. You can't. Do you want to know the worst part?"

"What's that?"

"My daughter Anne is just like him. All she thinks of is money and deals, and coming out ahead of people, and I blame Martin for that more than for anything."

"I'm sorry," I said to Lila, noncommittally. However, I didn't disbelieve her.

"Anne doesn't want me to marry James because there's no financial future in it, even though James would really be good to me and to her, too. So the least Martin can do is supply enough money so that his daughters won't have to be embarrassed about themselves. I want them to find a little more happiness than I found, and Martin is going to help them if I have anything to say about it. Have we covered everything?"

"I guess we have," I admitted.

"Doctor, I didn't mean to give you a hard time, I really didn't. You have a hard enough time with him, I'm sure," she said as we both stood up.

"Well, you certainly were clear," I said.

She smiled. "By the way," she said. "I don't know if Martin told you. I have ten paintings in a show all this week and next. I'd love you to come and see them. They're at the Chase Gallery. Four of them are already sold. There will be a lot of nice people there; you might really enjoy meeting some of them."

She was obviously trying to soften the impression that she had made. I had no doubt that Martin was her worst subject.

"Really. That's exciting," I said.

"Yes, it is. Thank you."

I told her I appreciated the invitation. Of course, it would have been traitorous to Martin to go. Nor did I confess to Lila that Martin had never even mentioned her ambition or her career.

As soon as he heard the click of my office door opening, James sprang to his feet attentively.

At the door, Lila thanked me, and he said good-bye courteously. She said that they were returning to the gallery for some kind of celebration.

After she'd gone I permitted myself to feel the shock of her visit. She was staggeringly different from anything that Martin had led me to expect. She was much more attractive and honest and well grounded than he had any idea of. It was as if his camera lens was simply not up to the task of seeing her.

Of course, the meeting had been a debacle. Momentarily, I wondered if I could have approached her otherwise, but I couldn't think of anything else I might have said. Clarence Darrow could hardly have done more if he were simply dropped overboard in mid ocean, and that was how it felt. The marriage didn't need a doctor, it needed a coroner.

I wondered how Lila would fare with her loyal James, and what he was really like. I had seen only a mask of compliance.

Then I remembered the obvious, that Martin's relationship with Lila was to continue, and that some mutation of it would always go on because of their children. I hoped that he could redeem them and learn to deal with Lila more effectively.

My train of associations halted at the thought that I would have to give him the verdict.

I called Martin right afterward and we set up an eight o'clock time to meet a few days later. He didn't ask how it had gone, and I didn't volunteer any information.

On the day of our appointment I had been downtown, and I took a cab back through a downpour and sudden afternoon darkness. As the cab went past Roosevelt Hospital, I thought, as I often do, of people who would never get a second chance, and I wondered if Martin would give himself one. When once or twice our cab skidded slightly I asked the driver to please slow down, but he spoke little English and either didn't hear me or acted as if he didn't. I wondered if I would have any more success communicating with Martin.

Inside my office he began with a single word: "So?"

"It didn't go well, Martin. I tried, but it seems that Lila really wants to end it."

"Did she say why?"

"The same stuff you've heard. You didn't take much interest in her life. You supported her financially, but she wants a lot more."

"Well, I'll give her more. Couldn't you tell her that I'll do absolutely anything she wants?"

"I told her that you've been working very hard to change, and that you would do almost anything if you could have one more chance with her."

"And she didn't care?"

"She's very angry, you know that. And you also know that there's another guy in the picture. That always makes it tough."

"Okay, then that's it. If that's her choice, then so be it. So there's no deal. It's not the first closing in my life that fell through at the last minute."

I knew there was lot more pain than his intonation or words suggested. But I could also sense that something was different about Martin. He cared a flicker less than he had, I could tell by his tone. Perhaps he had allowed himself to anticipate what seemed painfully evident, that Lila would never be back. And perhaps along with that discovery, he had come one degree in the direction of realizing that it was just as well, that his life was ahead of him and not over and done.

"So it looks hopeless, huh?" he said, nodding his head slowly as if assimilating the fact even further.

"Not for you, Martin," I countered. "Certainly not for you."

When he asked me what I meant, I started to explain to him that he still had in front of him the possibility of life and love, of friendship, of nearly anything he could want. But I knew as I spoke that I must have sounded like the vain multitude who had sought to console him after his mother's death, and something told me to stop abruptly.

"Maybe," he said sadly, "and maybe not."

"Martin," I said sternly, "you can certainly go back to living in the past again, if you want to. You can tell everyone, 'You're not it, I want Lila.' Or, 'You're not it, I want my mother.' Or you can give yourself—"

Once again I stopped myself abruptly, deciding that preachments wouldn't help. I had conveyed all I could. The rest was up to him, that was all there was to it.

Then to my surprise he asked me, "How did you know that dog was me?"

"Martin," I replied. "The cat was you also, by the way."

He looked at me confused.

"The cat who didn't know which way to go in the stadium. It was a real cat, I know. I hope it's safe, too—"

"That's funny. I hadn't thought about that cat."

"No, not since the dog. But the cat was also you, all alone out there, homeless, desperate. I'll bet it tried to claw whoever picked it up."

"I wouldn't be surprised," he agreed.

"I hope it's okay," I said. "I mean the real cat."

He nodded.

"And I hope that you're okay, that you save yourself, that you get what you want."

"And how am I going to do that? Go on in therapy with you?"

I had to meet that caustic innuendo head-on, by interpreting it. "I guess you think I'm hustling business, that I want your money, and that I don't give a damn what happens to you. This is my way of getting rich, sitting with guys like you and robbing them, conning them."

"I didn't say that."

"Well, I'll tell you one thing. I'm sorry about Lila, but it looks as if she's your past. There's only one way that you can ever feel that anyone is ever coming for you, that people really want you—take it or leave it."

"What's that?"

"You've got to go looking for them, the way you went looking for that dog in the dream. Really put yourself out. Love first, worry later."

He sat nodding his head sullenly. I couldn't tell whether he truly believed me or was thinking, "What a load of hard-sell crap this guy is trying to foist on me!" Maybe he couldn't distinguish either.

It was possibly our last round, and I decided to throw every punch I could, so I said to him, "Look, Martin, put it this way: If your mother was looking down from heaven, or if she could have anticipated what would happen to you after her death, she would not have wanted this. That's for sure."

"What do you mean?" he asked aggressively.

"For you to turn into a snarling, distrustful, lonely, miserable character, without anything except money. She would have wanted—"

"I understand. You don't have to give me a lecture."

"Martin," I said. "You've heard the phrase 'abject poverty'?"

"I think so."

"Well, you're an example of *abject wealth*. You have money, but you're lost, and the question is, Do you want to come home? Do you want to learn how to make a home for yourself?

"I'll tell you what, Martin, if you believe in what we've done, and you want to go on working with me, you can call me. Don't decide anything on the spot."

He said that was fair. We shook hands, and he left. I had no idea whether he would call, though I certainly hoped he would.

To my delight, he called the next day, and we agreed that after our vacations in August, we would resume work on a twice-a-week basis for as long as it took. We set a time for the first session of our new enterprise.

I knew during that hiatus that Martin would under no condition change his mind about working with me, so steadfast was he to anything he promised that he would do. Indeed, Martin's power of resolution, honed by loyalty to his mother in those early years, had worked greatly to our advantage already. It had given him fortitude to combat his own worst tendencies during those fateful six weeks that he first abstained from cynicism.

I worked with Martin for four years after that. Especially in our first year, when his divorce from Lila went through, Martin was dismal so often that I wondered if he really wanted to climb back into the human race at all. On the surface Martin surrendered Lila stoically. But her going out of his life reactivated his contempt for everyone and later brought back the wistful reverence for the past that was so important for us to analyze. During that year Martin let practically no suggestion of mine pass without referring to himself as "too old" to do whatever it was. I often had to remind him that resorting to that argument was simply another way of preserving his mother's place.

I did my best to sustain a dual emphasis in our sessions—dredging up his early life to keep his motivations vivid, while also pointing out that he didn't have to go on making his present life a sorry replica of his childhood.

In a dramatic session Martin recalled that after his mother died, he had "stopped believing in life." He said that for years after she died "whenever I had a good time, I would think of her." Martin's mother had left some fruit in a bowl for him the morning before she died, and he had actually kept it for years in a wooden box that somehow got lost when the family moved.

One of my major aims was to help Martin broaden his life and start relationships, but he opposed me at every turn. Whenever I said anything that smacked of "you can do it," Martin would become downcast and tell me that I had no idea how bad things really were.

By our second year Martin became able to truly understand that he was at heart less crusty than lonely, but that recognition made little difference in his behavior. He remained reluctant to allow himself any real happiness in a relationship, as if still believing that this would be the ultimate betrayal of all he stood for.

He often rebuffed me bluntly when I was optimistic. Though I felt stung, I took solace in his ongoing willingness to come to my office dutifully and on time and to make up any hour that he'd had to cancel for business reasons. I realized that I was the only living being with whom he had ever talked about himself. Although by general standards I still knew relatively little about Martin, from his point of view he was unclasping the book of his secret soul for the first time.

Our third year began with Martin still very often curt and sullen and with almost no ongoing life between sessions. I persuaded him to keep trying with his daughters, saying that, "Even though they aren't friendly right now, they may be glad you care enough to try." Martin could understand that easily, very likely because as a young adult he must have felt the same way. By his efforts his relationships with both of his daughters improved, and I could see how pleased he was. After that he heeded my words more, but he still resisted acknowledging that he trusted me or respected my opinion.

During that third year, at my continued urging, Martin began talking to more people. He forced himself to go to a few social gatherings; however, he never made overtures to start relationships, and when people expressed interest in him he seemed unaware of what they wanted. More than once he reported to me a remark made to him by someone that seemed to be an invitation to start a friendship. However, Martin remained deaf to all such implications.

Sadly, I realized that even if Martin conceived of a friendship or a love affair, it would have to come about by the other person's virtually using duress to get through. He was still utterly grudging about admitting people into his life. I realized that I would have to prod him even harder if this were ever to change.

An incident pointed this up. A woman had relocated to one of his buildings from Chicago, and Martin described her as attractive and showed evident interest in her. Days later, she shyly complimented him and virtually invited him to call her if he wanted to. Doubtless because the invitation had registered and flustered him, Martin had been worse than indifferent toward the woman. He had pretended that he was too busy to see her and had made a vulgar comment about her availability. Not surprisingly, she immediately withdrew, and soon afterward Martin saw her coming and going with a steady boyfriend.

I decided not to let the incident pass.

When he admitted that he might have liked spending time with her, I confronted him with what he had done.

"If your aim was to make her feel rotten, you certainly did a good job," I told him. At first, he simply tried to refute me, and then he said he didn't care. However, I reminded Martin that he'd just said he did care. I insisted that it was one thing to hurt someone if he really wanted to, but to punish a woman he was attracted to simply because she wasn't his mother didn't seem fair.

Before he could manufacture things wrong with the woman, I told him that he was deliberately cold toward everyone, including me, that he welcomed no one. He seemed taken aback by my accusation that he would crush anyone who wanted to be his friend; I was sure that he heard me better than when I had been as blunt on previous occasions.

I had let out all stops, and for weeks I kept assailing Martin's bleak outlook by pointing out his own selfishness—and his inertness. He was getting only what he deserved. In this effort to dramatize how he had closed down his life, I noted to him that he was so reluctant to extend himself that the only women he'd ever gone out with were those with whom he'd been thrown together and who had then pursued him.

That fact was undeniable. After Lila, who had proposed to him, he'd been involved with only three women: Grace, Mary, and Catherine, all of whom he had seen every day in the course of his work. By implication, he would never have another relationship unless a new woman whom he saw every day chose to pursue him. I pointed out that this was yet another instance of keeping his mother's place sacrosanct. He obviously felt that he would be betraying her the least if he made none of the advances.

And I stayed tough with Martin, often returning to his passivity. Once I even likened him to a rattlesnake, that relied for his occasional dinners utterly on the creatures who chanced to run over it. Tears came to Martin's eyes at the implication that his victims fared no better than creatures eaten alive.

Finally, as we entered our fourth year, I began to see a real effect. Martin stopped insinuating that I was against him, and at times he even granted that I had made a good point or had said something interesting. Ordinarily, a patient's relationship with a therapist is a model for other relationships. But Martin's case was exceptional. The problem remained that Martin could still accept more from me when I wasn't warm than when I was, and yet warmth from people was exactly what he needed.

I pointed out to Martin how self-defeating this was. I told him that if he went on distrusting those who came toward him, and eliminating them for their very warmth, then quite obviously he could expect no more from life than the solitariness that he already knew. By then he could see the dilemma, and also the plain truth that by how he conducted himself, he was going to resolve it one way or the other inevitably.

It might have been coincidence, or the result of our work together, priming him, but a few months later he met another woman who he said he liked a lot. She was an accountant about his age, whom he had met at a neighborhood diner where some local real estate people convened for afternoon coffee.

When Martin admitted a feeling verging on infatuation for this woman, I asked him how, if he were to be at his worst, he would insult her and drive her away. I often ask such questions of patients as a form of "self-unfulfilling prophecy," on the grounds that clear recognition of our harmful impulses is the best defense we have against succumbing to them.

I was surprised when Martin volunteered that he realized that he'd offended her already.

He quickly added, "I know I did it, okay? I can see what I'm doing."

He said that the woman, whose name was Margie, wanted to rent out her summer house in nearby Connecticut, but she didn't know how much it was worth. She'd asked Martin if he could help her assess it. Naturally, he would have to ride up there with her to see the house. In fact, he'd almost suggested that, but before the words came out, he'd said something else—a cold rebuff.

"You really ought to pay an agent for that kind of thing," he'd told her, as if implying that Margie had wanted only to get something for nothing from him.

She had thanked him politely, and that was that.

Martin was irked with himself and nearly hadn't told me the story. He worried that his mode of parrying people who came toward him was so ingrained that he could never change it. I tried to explain that he was for the first time seeing himself at his worst and that this was a necessary stage, but he appeared inconsolable.

However, a few days later he mended the relationship with Margie and helped her rent her house. He began dating her and meeting her friends. I noticed almost from the start that Martin expended a special effort that seemed to spring from the feeling that this would be his last chance. Not that he became a sensitive wooer; his lifetime of guardedness had left him without the awareness and the habits that many men acquire. But Margie seemed a forgiving person, whose own first marriage to an alcoholic had disposed her to appreciate sober, plodding, responsible Martin.

Usually when I pointed out to Martin things he did that reduced intimacy or pushed Margie away, he was grateful. But at times he became suddenly crestfallen or flared up in anger. One day he raged at me, "You can't teach an old dog new tricks," and I reminded him of that revelatory dream of four years earlier, which was still inspirational.

"You *are* an old dog. And you *can* teach *yourself* new tricks," I shouted back.

With unaccustomed geniality, Martin extended his hand to me at the end of that session, as he had long ago when we'd agreed on our deal. I took it firmly. We both seemed to be saying, "We've come a distance, and we're going to stick it out."

Shortly afterward, Martin went on a binge of spending money in ways he never had before. He took a bigger apartment and decorated it, with the help of Margie and of his daughters, who both liked her. That spring he went with Margie to Europe, staying a week in Salzburg, the city that her parents had fled shortly before the Second World War. When he returned, he told me that he and Margie were talking about living together.

The following week, in May, almost four years after we'd begun the final round, Martin said that he wanted to stop therapy. As I often do with patients, I wished that I could have gone further on his pilgrimage with him, and I felt sure that I had more to offer. But I could also sense that Martin had deliberated on this decision, and I certainly didn't want to imply that he would collapse without me.

I had in the beginning wondered if Margie was really special in his life or if she were in some respects "accidental," the first woman whom he could appreciate with his changed emotional perspective. But time had shown Martin that he was truly happy with her, and I rejoiced.

A few weeks later we said good-bye. I had to chalk up any misgivings I still had about his leaving to my own perfectionism, a trait I had wanted Martin to recover from in his own life. He would take his chances like the rest of us.

I saw Martin only once after that, when I met him by accident in Central Park. We were both walking dogs. Martin was with a few people, and taking my cue from him I did not stop to chat. Whether he stayed with Margie or not, I don't know. In fact, almost on a par with asking him how that relationship fared, if I had been back in my privileged position of asking him anything, it would have been whether that snappy little fox terrier with the black, pointed ears was his.

A few psychoanalysts with whom I discussed this case have, not surprisingly, called it Oedipal. In the respect that Martin was a male who longed for his mother and seemed disinclined to let go, it was surely, in their lingo, a classic instance of a "mother fixation." But as for the analytic premise that Martin must have unconsciously wanted to sleep with his mother and kill his father, and that his mother's death prevented him from resolving this, who can say? Such conjectures are nearly always read into these cases and not evoked from the patient in so many words. Apart from their speculative nature, it seems to me, such interpretations suffer from being reductionist and far too limiting.

Martin was, rather, a victim of his own demand for perfection, for the revival of a life that in retrospect seemed ideal, and which in his case ended in a minute. Unlike Martin, most of us suffer slow attrition of our childhood dream. We have years to exchange our hopes of idyllic life for the new and less pleasant discovery of life as it is. But as surely, though with better alternatives, we, all of us, dreamed of perfection once. The sense of ourselves as abandoned here on earth, the idea that the fundamental promise of life—or at least the one we imagined as tots—has been savagely broken, this universal appears to me to be far bigger than the Oedipal idea.

It seems to me that what really matters is how we handle this existential disappointment. Do we disdain the leftovers of our dream, namely our life on earth? Or do we decide that, in spite of all, it is still magical good fortune to be alive? That was Martin's essential choice, and it is ours, too.

···5···

The Hidden Messages

*W*e next need to look at the anatomy of compulsions—at the structure of a compulsion, at what drives it and how a compulsion operates in the personality. With proper understanding we may also see how to break a compulsion.

To analyze a compulsion we need to investigate the simple "habit"— the building block, the stuff of which every compulsion is made. A compulsion, as I said earlier, is a habit—and more. It is a habit whose special function is to rebury some horrifying idea; that is, to keep the idea from becoming conscious. The compulsive activity accomplishes this by offering a symbolic solution to the problem; it numbs the unconscious dread in its underworld and keeps it there.

For instance, Jonathan's running out of the dormitory room and "proving his masculinity" in the gym allowed him to remain unconscious of his homosexual urges and of their attendant terror.

A compulsive habit differs from an ordinary habit in that it is driven by just such a powerful unconscious dread. Such a dread does not go away easily. This may be verified by anyone who tries to banish a compulsion. Refraining from an ordinary habit will do away with the impulse for the habitual activity after a time. After an initial increase in desire to do the thing, which is inevitable when attempting to break a habit, if one has the fortitude to go on resisting the impulse it will appear less frequently and be weaker. Further resistance will do away with the urge entirely, and eventually it will feel utterly natural to live without the habit.

Compulsions, on the other hand, may not be defeated by so simple a strategy. Even if one manages to refrain from a compulsive activity for a long period of time, the urge for the activity, though weakened, will not die. After months or years the compulsive urge may recur in full force—and often quite unexpectedly. A person must do more than refrain from a compulsive activity in order to break its hold. So long as the unconscious conflict and the underlying dread remain, the source has not been uprooted.

With an ordinary habit, the monster to be defeated is the impulse for a particular behavior, nothing more. Resisting the impulse defeats the monster after a time. But with a compulsion the monster has a much more tenacious and manifold grip and merely resisting the one activity is not enough to break it.

When I treat a patient who is fighting an urge for some unwanted activity, neither of us are likely to know at the start whether the activity is a habit or a compulsion. The practical test is whether persistent refraining annihilates the urge. If it does, then a simple habit has been broken and the problem is solved. If it fails, and the person can't escape so simply, we know that this patient is up against a compulsion. He or she still has some critical unconscious conflict and a dread that must be attacked by further measures.

Often in this context I am reminded of one of the ordeals of Odysseus, as told by the ancients and set down by Homer. Odysseus had to steer his ship past the Sirens, sea creatures whose voices were so melodious that no one could hear them without drawing too close and being swallowed up by the ocean.

Odysseus, having been forewarned of the danger, ordered his sailors to bind him to the mast and then to plug their own ears with wax. Odysseus alone was to hear the Sirens' song. Anticipating that, wooed by the Sirens' song, he would order his mariners to row closer, he warned them to disregard his entreaties and to keep a steady course.

Upon hearing the melodious music, he frantically signaled to his men to approach it, but they kept rowing as they had been bidden. Not until the ship had passed well out of range of the Sirens did the mariners release Odysseus and allow him to resume command.

The analogy to inner drive—with its hypnotic, melodious, and often self-destructive lure—masked by illusion, is unmistakable. We who wish to break any inveterate behavior pattern—habit or compulsion—can know in advance that as the urge rises, its "song" will sound sweeter than ever, and yet we must keep rowing.

If we are breaking a habit we will find ourselves safely out of earshot of the Sirens' song. If, on the other hand, our activity was compulsive, though the song becomes discontinuous and weaker after a while, merely disregarding it for no matter how long will not end it. We will need to take other measures.

Virtually any habitual activity can become compulsive. A person has been doing something for years—reading, playing billiards, smoking, or exercising—on a daily basis; then suddenly a deep, seemingly unsolvable problem sets in, and the person begins employing the activity as a distraction and escape. Before long they are doing it compulsively, and the threat of not doing it for a few days or even a few hours becomes very upsetting.

We might say that while the activity was still a habit, the urge for it was "local"—that is, a sheer product of prior repetition. But once the activity has been borrowed and used to distract oneself from some deep concern—as many people use physical exercise to suppress and "solve" a desperate fear of getting older—it becomes a full-fledged compulsion.

The science-fiction writer Ray Bradbury presents a beautiful example of a compulsion that sprang from very reasonable origins, In his short story "The Fruit at the Bottom of the Bowl" the protagonist, William Acton, commits a murder, and has twelve hours alone in a room with the corpse to remove his fingerprints from whatever he might have touched.

Acton begins his cleaning in quite logical places, but despite his urgent desire to hurry away from the murder scene and never return, he becomes obsessed with the need to be sure he has left no trace anywhere. Hours pass as he wipes more and more items on the chance that he might have touched them. At the end of twelve hours Acton has polished the whole house to a brilliance and the police find him in the attic wiping music boxes and stowed away cases of cutlery.

Bradbury concludes his story: "On the way out of the house, Acton polished the doorknob with his handkerchief and slammed it in triumph!"

Acton's dread of being caught took on a life of its own. Or was his motive unconscious guilt and the desire to be caught? That is left to us to surmise. In any event, Acton's compulsive need so took over his life that reality was consigned to a very backstage role in his thinking. And this is often what happens when compulsions become severe.

Now let's pause to examine some basic truths about ordinary habits.

We get a tremendous head start toward understanding compulsions if we examine the properties of habits in general. Indeed, such knowledge is indispensable, because every compulsion is also a habit—a lethal form of habit.

Of even an ordinary habit we might say that repeating the activity "beats a path" in the mind. Not literally, of course, but this is how it feels. Doing a thing over and over justifies it, makes it feel right to the person, and necessary. We believe most in what we are least conscious of doing, and habitual activities become completely unconscious after a while.

Of course, not all habits begin in childhood, though many of our old reliable modes of acting did have their earliest traces back then. However, every habit began with a problem that demanded conscious attention. The person thought about some challenge, took outcomes into consideration, and after trial and error found a solution. The original challenge might have been to talk or to tie a shoelace or to get attention. Whatever the puzzle was, the child or adult solved it by some consciously chosen activity.

The early solution was crude. The chosen activity was burdened by waste motion and inefficiency. There were lapses of performance, and the person still had to do plenty of thinking each time the challenge arose.

Then, with repetition, the person, still needing plenty of thought to do the thing, began smoothing it out, paring off waste motions and excesses. It was as if the mind had solved the problem of what to do, had closed the book on that question, and was now working on the problem of how to do the thing smoothly. After many more repetitions the action came to look suavely efficient.

In trimming the activity by repetition, the learner of the habit was making it seem almost instinctive, like the natural thing to do. Eventually the habit, which evolved out of much conscious thought and effort, resembled an instinctive piece of behavior. Lower animals run or fly or protect their young, or make provisions for young that they will never see, with that same suave efficiency, without ever having done the thing or seen another creature do it. But it takes tremendous practice for a human being to make behavior efficient, immediate, and automatic—to learn a habit.

Think, as a metaphor, of a primitive society faced with the challenge of crossing a fast-flowing river. Some genius among them conceives of an idea, and soon the members have built a crude bridge to arch the water. Its construction took considerable time and thought and the bridge itself is unwieldy, but it works. Replicas are made for other rivers; perhaps some collapse, and subtleties are added along the way. Soon the need for a bridge is not even reviewed, the issue is how to build an efficient one and fast. Eventually, construction is completed quickly; the bridge does the job with suave efficiency.

Products that do the job well survive; those that do not are discarded.

Habits, too, undergo a survival-of-the-fittest challenge. Those that seem to serve the child well are kept and not even reconsidered. He or she speaks fluently, ties shoelaces while thinking about other things, and has automatic devices such as raising a voice or making a gesture to get another person's attention. Activities that don't seem to serve are discarded and never become habitual.

The home environment, how the parents and others treat the child, is critical, because the child solves problems based on observations of the parents. If yelling is necessary in the home or the child will not be acknowledged, the child may become a shouter. If deference and quiet speech are the way to beat out one's siblings, then the child may solve the problem of getting accepted by those tactics. If topping people by clever insults wins approbation, then the child becomes a smart aleck and may feel helpless without a barb.

Good habits or bad ones may be discovered in the home according to what challenges arise and what works. And those behaviors, whatever they are, become habitual as a rule.

An exciting aspect of habits has to do with the *decline of consciousness*. There is undeniable benefit in not having to reconsider the circumstances that led to the adoption of a habit back in the past. Without this decline in consciousness of the activity and of its rationale, there would be scarcely any value in having formed a habit in the first place.

As William James taught us, a person incapable of forming habits would be at an utter loss. Unable to act without deliberation, such a person would lack the time and energy in a day to carry out more than a handful of behaviors as complicated as tying a shoelace.

Exactly what does it mean to say that the person is no longer conscious of doing the thing or of why the habit was originally adopted? Does it mean that nothing is left of that original thinking and feeling and that now the activity is truly mechanical?

In the latter half of the nineteenth century, when habits were first written about extensively, this is precisely what was believed. Students of habits assumed that once a habit is formed, it makes no difference why it was begun or what the child wanted or feared during the learning stage. From the fact that repetition of the habitual behavior annihilates all consciousness of doing the thing, it was assumed that the history of the habit, the features that led to its acquisition, had also disappeared.

These early students of habits believed that once a habit is acquired it doesn't matter anymore what the child thought when he or she first adopted the behavior.

For example, three girls in different families learn to be extraordinarily polite and never interrupt another person. All three were taught the habit of attentiveness. The first girl was given to believe that she wasn't too bright and that if she spoke people would see how stupid she was. The second was simply slapped for talking back, without any explanation. The third was revered by her immigrant parents, but she observed that they were very hurt when she contradicted anything they said.

These three women, who acquired the same habit independently, all became unduly polite as adults. As grown women they appeared quite similar: They would listen politely when spoken to and never contradict the other person. None of them gave any thought to why they did this.

Are these three women, then, truly the same in their habitual politeness? Now that they "behave" automatically, has each of them truly discarded the highly individual history present when they adopted the habit, leaving them with only the habitual behavior itself?

This was the conclusion drawn by the early writers on habits, including William James. When these writers exhorted people to form good habits, they insisted that it didn't matter why people acted properly.

These early psychologists assumed that once a person was no longer conscious of why he was doing a thing, or even that he was doing it, all memory of and associations with the past were wiped out. No one imagined that a person engaging in a habitual behavior could have been carrying pain or a sense of inadequacy or any self-image problems that had begun in the past. The idea that people might have been visualizing their childhoods unconsciously, that traces of their childhoods might still be present in the psyche, though unseen, simply hadn't occurred to the early thinkers.

During the nineteenth century and early in this one, writers on habits didn't even consider that what ceased to be conscious might exist and be unconscious—namely, a sense of why the person was doing the thing.

Did each of the three women still harbor childhood memories, distinct in each case, urging their particular brand of "politeness"? Does it make any sense to say that these present acts have childhood motives?

No one considered the question before Freud's emphasis on the unconscious, and James in his private notes called Freud "a regular *halluciné.*"[1] Still, by the middle of this century, the descendants of the early habit theorists could not escape Freud's influence. They felt forced to rebut explicitly the idea that present acts could have past motives.

---

[1] Ralph Burton Perry, *The Thought and Character of William James* (New York: George Braziller, 1954).

No, wrote psychologist Gordon Allport, the motives and memories associated with the original learning of a habit are gone like breath into the wind. Once a habit is learned it runs on its own. The habit assumes what Allport called "functional autonomy." Allport argued that the "go" of a habit is totally in the present and does not derive from the past.

However, it turns out that much of the early motivation for a habitual activity does remain. In fact, a little picture—what amounts to virtually a cameo image of why the person began the activity long ago—has become unconscious but remains associated with the habitual behavior.

Apply this to the three women with the habit of listening politely. They were, as adults, doing the same thing, but for very different reasons, and they still harbored very different memories that gave meaning to what they did.

The quiet habit of deferring to speakers, which looked the same, was in reality totally different for all three. These women were not acting mechanically but with profound emotional content—a content that was different for each and that radically differentiated the lives of the three.

In these instances and, remarkable as it seems, always, there is more to a habit than meets the eye.

No habit—and certainly no compulsion—ever becomes a truly mechanical act. The circumstances of its learning—how the child perceived himself and others and why the child chose the activity—remain associated with even the simplest habit. The only change that occurs over time is that this picture becomes unconscious. I have seen the proof of this with hundreds if not thousands of habits.

The ideal way to surface these long lost pictures is to refrain from the habit, as Martin did, and to study closely every thought that comes to mind in connection with the urge to resume the behavior.

Immediately upon refraining from any habit, the impulse for it intensifies. The person feels what I call increased hunger for the habitual activity. And along with this spurt of hunger *come long lost memories of a time when the habit was learned.* These memories emerge into plain view and can be seen with the clarity of a photograph, if only one knows what to look for.

When a person first stops a habit, along with the bursts of impulse to resume it there invariably come to mind reasons why he feels he ought to resume it, to indulge the urge once more. The person imagines that it would be wrong, immoral, or even dangerous *not* to do the thing—and unquestionably right to do it.

The person himself may imagine that he is simply inventing reasons on the spot to justify going back to the bad habit. However, these reasons are deeply rooted in the person's history. If rather than simply dismissing them as lame pretexts to resume the habit, we *study them* closely, we may be amply rewarded.

I call these thoughts, which flood the mind during the withdrawal period, *hunger illusions*. They are prompted by hunger for the habit and come to mind predictably in conjunction with that hunger.

These thoughts seemingly invented on the spot are actually part of the habit. They are barely disguised memories of why the person adopted the habit in the first place.

Hunger illusions reveal a mode of thinking that has always been there but has been unconscious.

Now let's look at the three women who learned the habit of polite listening and never interrupting a speaker. The first woman had acquired the habit at age six, when she had gotten *the idea that she was stupid*. Seeing her family smile condescendingly at her remarks and show obvious contempt for her, she had stopped voicing her ideas altogether. All three, let us say, are patients of mine, which gives me the latitude to question them.

"Come on," I encourage the first woman, "People break in all the time at these office meetings. You have ideas of your own. Speak up."

As soon as the woman states an opinion, however, or even contemplates doing so, she feels that her ideas are stupid. She imagines that several people in the room are laughing at her or holding her in contempt. Were I to busy myself trying to override this perception, I would fail to recognize it as a *memory* of exactly how she was treated—the very memory that motivates her now to be so quiet and "well-behaved."

The second woman, who became an overpolite listener after being slapped for volunteering her ideas as a girl, physically cringes in front of me when I exhort her to confront her boss. She draws back from me and covers her face with her hands. However, she resolves to confront him the next day and tell him what is on her mind.

She does this, and when I next see her she reports how she felt while speaking up. "I know it's silly," she admits, "but I had the sudden picture of his going berserk and smashing me in the face."

"Is he really that kind of man?" I ask her.

"Not really. He doesn't seem to be . . . But maybe he is," she says slowly.

Again a memory—this time *the memory of being physically abused*—has surfaced disguised as a present fear. What seems like a bizarre explanation for sticking with a time-honored habit is really the vignette that has, over two decades, remained attached to this woman's habit of perennial deference.

For the third woman, whose immigrant parents worshiped her but felt incapable of raising a child in the new country, the memory was different yet again. This woman had throughout her childhood *recognized her parents as fragile* and easily wounded. Hers was a loving family, but she was always afraid of hurting them. The woman's early life had been given over to taking pains so that they would not worry about her.

This woman certainly doesn't think about her parents when she's at work dealing with high-level executives. But her nonassertive style still holds her back. As her therapist, I exhort her to speak out to a rather stiff vice president, a woman who runs the show too much and has not nearly our woman's talent.

"What good are your insights if you don't volunteer them?" I ask. "That deference of yours is only leading to frustration and it's costing you prestige and money in the long run."

"I know you're right," she replies reluctantly. But then, right in my office, as she starts rehearsing her new habit-breaking performance mentally, a look of pain comes over her. "I don't really want to *hurt* the woman," she says. "I'm afraid I'll crush her."

Each of these people has given us in disguised form a memory—their memory of their childhood reason for adopting the activity, which they have sustained over the years. Each has reported a personal illusion that is part and parcel of the habitual activity and that has been its unconscious motivation all along.

Though the reason for an inveterate habit recedes from consciousness, *it has always been there*—as if waiting to surface when the habit is interfered with.

These women don't interpret explicitly for us: "I dare not speak up because my parents slapped me," or, "because my parents thought I was stupid," or, "because my parents were too insecure not to feel crushed when I disagreed with them."

However, those motivating memories are there nonetheless.

Stopping any habit is a kind of trauma. Just as blood rushes to a wound, heightened awareness rushes to the mind the moment a habit is resisted. The person who is trying to break a habit has a special chance to see why he has been engaging in the habit all along, and even why he began the habitual behavior in the first place.

The thoughts that accompany the hunger illusion are commonly dismissed as sheer rationalizations—as nothing more than lies that the person tells himself. But they are "lies" with deep personal meaning and a long history.

And often these hunger illusions are clearly not rationalizations. A person merely rationalizing could produce far better justifications for the behavior than those that come to mind. Take the woman who was slapped as a child, and who as an adult could recognize a fear of being struck by people when she first began to express opinions. Even as she imagined that the person might hit her, even as she saw herself cringing, she simultaneously recognized that this wasn't going to happen. She realized that her boss was not the sort to strike anyone and certainly wasn't about to slap her for merely disagreeing with his opinion. She was in the position of knowing that her fear was unwarranted and yet being unable to avert that fear.

Another example of such a seemingly free-floating thought occurs in a story often told by members of Alcoholics Anonymous. A man who had been dry for three weeks said sincerely to a roomful of people, "I'm really worried that if I don't sit down and drink with my family and friends during Christmas, they'll think that I'm a snob and that I hate them."

Everyone in the room laughed out loud at that one. "But it's only July," someone reminded him.

Obviously, if the man were merely inventing an excuse to justify his drinking, he could have done a lot better than that. But the thought came from the very center of his being. He uttered it with genuine conviction, even though a moment later he knew as well as anyone that it was utterly illogical. Just as with the woman who feared being slapped, the hunger illusion described a past scenario that the person was not consciously remembering.

The man had begun drinking in his teens to get close to people and to prove that he was not a snob. He had been the only one in his crowd to go to college, and he had taken plenty of kidding about it. Over the years, his drinking had retained much of its original purpose for him: It was an unconscious device for him to draw closer and prove that he was "one of the guys," even though he was a top executive who lived at a level quite above that of his friends.

As in these cases, time and again the ideas that come to people's minds when they break habits make no sense even as excuses. They are anachronistic reasons for the activity, reasons that the person had had in the past when he or she had begun the behavior.

But whether they seem to make sense or not, these past images often emerge so vividly into the mind of the person breaking a habit that they temporarily obscure judgment. We must learn to recognize them as what they are: pure visions of why the habit was inaugurated and what it means.

I have spent twenty years studying the illusions that come to people when they first break habits. Often the dramatic glimpses that they allow into the person's past have stunned my patients and me. The person has not remembered ever feeling a certain way, seeing himself or his parents or others in a particular light. Then the hunger illusions bring the feeling back.

A woman reported that when she stopped smoking, she at first felt immature and less capable than the others at a staff meeting. She was in actuality far more capable and was their superior, and she knew this consciously, so the illusion at first made no sense to her. It was an anachronism, as all these illusions are—a flash of memory into why as an adolescent she had begun smoking, namely, to look mature to older girls.

This woman had totally forgotten the days in her teens when she had tried to copy Ingrid Bergman in *Casablanca* and had posed with a cigarette in front of the older girls in the sorority, trying to look elegant and sophisticated. Her study of the hunger illusion brought those memories back: the feeling of awkwardness and not knowing what to do with her hands; the teenage sense of immaturity; and the worry that she would not be cosmopolitan enough for her newfound friends.

Hunger illusions, which can give us magical glimpses of a person's childhood and what current behavior meant in the past, have not been examined previously for several reasons.

First, many people think, understandably, "Why take the time to study the nonsense or the empty excuses that people make up to justify resuming a bad habit?"

Secondly, and even more pertinent, is that these illusions are considered *dangerous*—in a sense, like enemy propaganda. Is not the whole idea to rebut as fallacious any argument in favor of the habit?

And so when someone, the alcoholic or gambler or smoker or habitually interruptive talker, starts pleading why the habit may not be so bad, even well-meaning listeners tend to shut the person up. Members of self-help organizations are often almost reflexively ready to discourage any argument for the undesirable behavior. It is felt that to make the activity look appealing, or even not so bad, might threaten the "sobriety" of at least some in the audience.

With the popular view that studying a person's arguments to resume a bad habit is useless, and that even listening to them might be dangerous, it is not surprising that hunger illusions have not received attention.

Every habit, no matter how automatic it seems, contains *as part of it,* the vignette that was present while it was being learned. And because the habit contains that vignette, breaking the habit *will weaken the particular imagery connected with it.*

It is because habits contain memories and secret motives that breaking habits severs connections with the past. Breaking habits (or compulsions) weakens the grip of the past.

Let's go back to see what this must mean for some of the people mentioned.

Think about the woman who muzzled herself for years, imagining that she was stupid and that other people would ridicule her. Her unconscious memory of being considered stupid was part of the habit. Maintaining the habit was keeping alive that unconscious appraisal of herself. By suppressing her own opinions in company she was renewing her perception of herself as stupid.

Breaking the habit would eradicate that source of the woman's low estimation of her own intelligence. This is why speaking up would raise her self-esteem.

Analogously, for the second woman there were associations to being smacked. Muzzling her thoughts was keeping alive that unconscious memory and the woman's apprehensiveness. Speaking her mind would cut off that old source of fear.

In the case of the third woman, what might seem like the identical habit of not speaking out was associated with an excessive concern that she would hurt people badly. Her exaggerated idea of the fragility of others and her assumption of responsibility to protect people at any cost was built into the woman's habit. Breaking that one habit, therefore, would release her somewhat from this picture of other people as so needy.

In each case, breaking the habit would cut off the supply of particular ideas associated with the habit—ideas that were, strictly speaking, part of the habit.

We have all noticed how after changing certain habits, we start to see ourselves differently and feel almost magically transformed. This is because habits are repositories of ideas. They carry ideas along with them. Our every habit continually supplies certain impressions to the brain—impressions about ourselves and about how other people perceive us and what they will do.

Take the case of children who because their parents are abrupt with them begin to talk very fast. Their sense in the home is: "I have limited time to get this said, so I'd better hurry." As adults, many of these people still talk much too fast. When they first slow down, breaking their habit of speedy chatter, their illusion is that they sound pompous and that no one will give them the time they need to finish a thought.

The very habit of talking too fast has kept this impression alive and so, after they break the habit and master the technique of speaking slower, they come to feel more confident of themselves and better assured that their listeners will give them the time and attention they need and deserve.

Though most impressions we have are sustained by many habits, not just by one, every single habit contributes to our outlook. It is as if every habit spills its particular colors into the pictures of ourselves and others that we hold.

Remarkably, people are constantly reproducing aspects of themselves—virtues, vices, fears, ways of perceiving others and themselves—by multitudinous, ongoing habits.

Over the complex network of highways called habits a person constantly transports replenishments to the citadel of the mind. Habits are both expressions of the person's intricate picture of life and the source of that picture's continuance.

The human outlook, including unconscious perceptions and behaviors not reconsidered for decades, is completely alive and we renew it unknowingly. In essence, the psyche, our outlook—our picture of ourselves and others—has not congealed and never does.

It is interesting to note that people who break habitual patterns sometimes have highly revelatory dreams. This is most likely to occur when a person stops a compulsion or an addiction, where the satisfaction being denied pleads most for continuance. But I have come to see that, especially with nonintrospective people such as Martin who don't put emotions into words even in their own minds, dreams often tell the most articulate story.

In Martin's case, his unconscious dread of being alone, with no one to care for him, found expression in an eloquent dream. He had been trying to cope with that dread by symbolically keeping his mother's place open for her, which he did by snarling at all possible replacements. When he stopped his habitual disparagements, the whole worst-case scenario surged into his consciousness, not as free associations in waking life, but in a nightmare.

The hidden scenarios that come to a habit breaker in dreams are not always so disguised.

Some years ago a man came to see me whose boss insisted that he either go into therapy or leave his job. I could see at once that the man was a poor listener who snapped to defend himself against even the slightest implication of criticism. He obviously couldn't bear being caught in error and almost instinctively fought anyone who implied he'd done anything wrong.

The man couldn't remember his childhood at all, but there had to be a reason why he would wriggle out of every criticism as if the critic were demanding his life. At my request, he forced himself to remain silent when people criticized him or made suggestions.

Soon after that, in my office, as he tried to get through an hour without rebutting me, I asked him what thoughts were coming to his mind.

"None," he shot back instantly.

But later that week he had a vivid dream of being in a room clinging to a teddy bear while his parents and sisters took turns mimicking his grip on the bear and laughing at him.

In describing the dream to me, he recalled having actually been mimicked by his schoolteacher father, while his mother had just smiled and said nothing. He then recalled that his father had often mimicked him and his siblings. The father had once stated openly that the best way to correct a fault was to see it committed by another person. Of course, my patient had felt preposterous on those occasions and had reasoned that if his own family held him in such contempt he was totally unacceptable to the world.

Defending himself in adulthood was truly a compulsion; he was symbolically averting the dire consequence of being caught in error. He was trying to keep suppressed his unconscious dread of being mimicked and laughed at, of forfeiting the love and protection of everyone significant to him. This man's unconscious association of being ostracized for an error had dogged him for decades.

After seeing this, he became able to admit his mistakes instead of arguing his way out of them. Following other changes, he saw that in real life mistakes are not fatal.

I sometimes think of breaking even a single habit as akin to toppling over one vehicle that carries supplies to the mind. Of course, this could be good or bad. If a habit is beneficial, it carries with it desirable associations, and breaking it would be a loss. For example, the habit of honesty is likely to transport optimism, and the recognition that at least some other people are also honest, and the notion that honesty ought to be rewarded. In such a case, the true corruption of spirit would be allowing that behavior to lapse.

The miracle is that even with ordinary habits there is an "acting rather than remembering" that goes on constantly. What differentiates a compulsion from a simple habit is, for one thing, the dread that compulsions spring from and, secondly, that the compulsive activity is a symbolic solution to a problem rather than a real one.

Ordinary habits cope with life, for better or for worse. Ideally, only a small fraction of a person's habits are designed to cope with unconscious fears. Compulsions, on the other hand, are purely symbolic solutions, which is why they so often appear deranged and pointless. Virtually by definition, compulsions are unsuccessful activities.

When we look at compulsions, benefiting from what we now know about habits generally, we can see why a person with a compulsion should try to stop the compulsive behavior entirely. Because unconscious dread is always a motive for a compulsive activity, the activity itself not only conceals the dread, but renews it; compulsions are reinfecting agents.

They also renew the sufferer's sense of helplessness. The choice of dealing with a problem symbolically rather than actually is an admission of being overwhelmed by the reality. It is an admission to the self. Every compulsive activity spills the message of personal incompetence into the brain of the compulsive person—and it does this over and over again.

Still worse, behind many compulsions is the blind terror that the child experienced and the adult would not. To the child, any act that might incur humiliation or loss of a loved parent feels like psychic suicide. Think about the boy ridiculed for mistakes by his father while his mother indifferently stood by. Because he was utterly dependent upon his parents for love, friendship, guidance—for everything—he could not endure losing them as allies. To him there seemed no alternative to defensiveness, no options; throughout his childhood his refusal to admit mistakes was a pertinacious, desperate act, a seeming necessity.

Over the years that early prospect of total loss if he were caught in an error remained a feature of his defensiveness. When as an adult he compulsively fended off criticisms, even well-intended opinions, it was still *with the desperation of the little boy* who stood to lose everything if proved in the wrong.

Nearly all compulsions preserve the childhood nightmares that initially gave rise to the compulsive behavior. The person's very engaging in them prevents him from appreciating that times have changed and that the age of utter helplessness and dearth of resources has passed.

As another example, Jonathan's very compulsion to conceal from himself what he construed as homosexual feelings reinfected him with "homosexual panic." By compulsively fleeing from any recognition of those urges, Jonathan continued to load homosexuality with the horror that most young boys feel when first facing the fact that they might be gay.

Likewise, Martin's compulsively denying all other human beings access to him—his withholding, crustiness, disparagement of others—kept him feeling as desperately in need of his mother as he had felt on the day that she died. Back then he had understandably imagined that he would never find love, commitment, affection, loyalty in another soul. He had indeed faced a future that seemed joyless and bleak, as he fought to keep his mother's place open in the event that she might return to him.

But in reality only Martin's immediate future had to be so barren. His real prospects improved steadily. Well before he became an adult other people might have been there for him if he had allowed them in. What prevented him from seeing this was no longer the reality but his own compulsive behavior, which renewed the bleakest perceptions of childhood.

Compulsions nearly always do this—restore the worst expectations of childhood and prevent the sufferer from making an accurate appraisal of his life. This is the main reason why people with compulsions typically feel far more precarious and without resources than they are.

Regarding any compulsive activity, we might ask, *Why this particular activity?*—drinking or belittling people or nonstop talking or compulsive secrecy or running out of rooms.

Since each life is different in its details, the possibilities of actions that may become compulsive is never ending. But always the choice of compulsion has to do with the perceived "success" of the activity somewhere along the line.

Deidre, an attractive girl who was neglected at home and made to feel stupid, discovered that acting sexy brought instant attention. As an adult, even in sedate company Deidre now uses flirtatious innuendoes and sexual appeal compulsively to compensate for what she considers her below-average intellect.

Anne, also neglected as a child, was rewarded for charity and sensibility. Anne now compulsively props people up in conversation, praising others too much and overlooking people's selfishness and coarseness toward her. Anne is *compulsively forgiving*—that is, she is afraid to be anything else. People consider Anne kind, but her generosity brings her no pleasure.

Both women act compulsively. Both are motivated by an unconscious dread of being cast off in contempt. Deidre cannot truly enjoy her sexuality and Anne cannot enjoy her kindness because both are acts of fear.

These two women employed their compulsive patterns to dull pain in childhood, to eke out whatever limited status they had in the home. That the two women are today acting compulsively might go unnoticed if we think of compulsions only as single, aberrant activities and not as whole styles of meeting the world. But, as I illustrated especially in Martin's case, compulsions may be networks of behavior, and may indeed sometimes masquerade as a whole personality.

As with the two compulsive people whose stories I've told at length, Deidre's and Anne's compulsions were handy; as girls the two were virtually invited to act as they had. The modes of behavior that became compulsive were chosen to solve gnawing problems—ones that seemed unsolvable in any better ways.

I could hardly have overlooked the importance of availability in my work with addicts. For many addicts the combination of despair and a readily available drug drew the person in and made him or her compulsive. Hard drugs were almost irresistible for kids who could not conceive of ever feeling good about themselves by taking another route, such as slogging through school or finding a career.

At least some of these kids who resorted to drugs were unconsciously hoping to be stopped. But no one was there to show them a better way.

Even the most idiosyncratic compulsions were adopted because at one time they appeared to work. Now of course the same behavior only pushes the problem out of consciousness and aggravates it, but the instant relief afforded by the behavior keeps it going.

Many compulsions are adopted originally by imitation. The child acquires them after seeing a parent act in some way—for instance, bragging, or never admitting a mistake, or shunning intimacy or drinking or pursuing money as if it were life itself. Being rewarded in the home for doing what Daddy did might be the launching pad for acting in ways that become compulsive. Certain compulsions are a social heritage—as, for example, the compulsive shunning of minority groups or unfavored people. What drives the behavior is a dread of being ostracized, and perhaps hated by all who matter, as would have occurred in the person's childhood.

In other cases, the motive is dread of resembling a parent who was held in contempt by others or by the child himself. For instance, a boy becomes compulsively meticulous because his father was irresponsible and incompetent and was jettisoned from the family.

And even if the parent provided neither example nor counterexample, the important thing is that the activity now compulsive once solved a riddle and was nurtured and stressed on that account.

Once a pattern is acquired, the person resorts to it almost instinctively to solve new problems as they arise. A teenager might have begun drinking because he was far behind in school and felt stupid. Years later, he drinks because a woman rejects him. Some day, if he is still alive, he may drink in order to forget his wasted life. New problems, same solution.

Compulsions may be regarded as generalized though faulty problem-solving techniques.

Reinforcing certain adult compulsions are social invitations to behave in particular ways. Commercials that encourage drinking rather than think-ing, and those that invite millions to seek fun and solace at the racetrack or gambling casino, induce at least some fraction of viewers to indulge com-pulsively.

This is apart from the issue of blame. Only a tiny minority of watchers become compulsive. However, the better we understand how compulsions develop, the more able we are to enjoy existence in its diversity without being ourselves swallowed up in some solitary, repetitive endeavor at the expense of the rest of life.

This understanding of how a compulsive activity gets chosen can help a person diagnose his own compulsions. In a later chapter I will discuss the exact procedure for removing a compulsion, either alone or in therapy or with the aid of a self-help group. One thing is sure: The optimum first step is to try to stop the compulsive behavior. Doing this is ideal both to lay bare the compulsive dread and to help recognize its inappropriateness.

Of course, the dread does not dissipate instantly, nor does the sense of helplessness that the person must confront. More needs to be done, and as those in self-help groups who cope with compulsions know full well, those early days of withdrawal are full of pain and illusions.

Once the dread is identified, the next step must be to remove its underpinnings systematically, to alter the whole life-style which has been continually bringing the person's past into the present.

Consider a compulsive gambler, a man whose dishonesty, whose disdain of people who work hard for regular but not spectacular pay, and whose braggadocio reinfect him with misery. His compulsive gambling is a desperate attempt to compensate for a life that seems wasted and hopeless and for mental faculties that he secretly feels are not nearly up to par.

For this man the gambling is a last-minute rescue effort, an attempt to justify a misspent life. This motivation may be unconscious, obscured from his consciousness by the gambling itself, which floods the day with its details. Stopping for even a short time forces the man to see these details, and the next step must be for him to change, one by one, those and other behaviors that have been sustaining the illusion and the sense of fraud.

No matter what the compulsion, the ideal blueprint for change is, in short, to stop the behavior, face the underlying dread and sense of inadequacy that motivates it, and, finally, to identify, one by one, the lesser behaviors that support this dread and to discontinue them.

In theory a person can do this alone, though it is much easier to describe the process than to carry it out. A friend or a therapist, or especially a self-help group, can assist greatly by offering warmth and encouragement during the dark and lonely period of withdrawal.

Always the Sirens must be faced, but rather than pretend that they have no song to sing or no lure, the ideal method of stopping their voices forever is to listen to their song closely, to write down the words if necessary. For in those lyrics are the story of the habit, of what drives it, and even why it was acquired long ago. And such knowledge, especially in the case of a compulsion, is invaluable in seeing what a person must do next.

The durability of outlook, including the unconscious fears of the compulsive person, are thus subject to reinterpretation. We can accept the notion that much is unconscious and the metaphor of a layered psyche, not just in the compulsive, but in all of us. However, nothing has congealed, and what the person does in daily life matters a great deal.

The person with a compulsion is regenerating his whole psychic structure, unconscious fears included. In fact, all of us—not just sufferers from acute compulsions—are creating ourselves in our own image, day after day, year after year. As every personality does, the compulsive's owes to the momentum of his own behavior.

With this in mind, our next century of psychology can progress further, past Freud's discoveries. I think that we will see the psyche more as organic, as constantly evolving, than as congealed. However, our very approaches and ways of thinking, some commonplace today, Freud introduced and made second nature.

Freud's phrase "repeat rather than remember" turns out to have far greater sweep than even he imagined. He taught us that everything a person says and does is meaningful and a potential source of vital information—even the rantings of a drunk or the babblings of a psychotic person. In studying what seem like the obviously made-up excuses and incoherent logic of people breaking habits, we are acting in accordance with this dictum of Freud's.

Though such study leads us toward conclusions beyond Freud's, he would have approved of our method of investigation. And perhaps in the end we might have convinced him of the continuing plasticity of the psyche, even in the case of the compulsive person who feels hopeless and incapable of change.

While reading the next case, which I will present in some detail, think about the person's behavior as not merely symptomatic. The woman, Marianne, after being violated sexually when quite young, changed her whole mode of reacting. Her dread of such an event recurring was both conscious and unconscious. She certainly remembered the event—it remained terrifyingly vivid to her. But it also became an unconscious motive for a whole pattern of compulsive behaviors that she maintained, refined, and added to.

As a result, Marianne's unconscious dread of a traumatic event recurring became sustained by the very activities that she first adopted to protect herself.

But this is always what gives traumatic events their lasting force. It is not simply that they are shattering to the spirit, which they are. The adoption of a network of behaviors to avoid any repetition at all costs becomes paradoxically the greatest cost to the victim.

If after being betrayed we never trust people again, then by our very guardedness—by our evasiveness, withdrawal, secrecy, or whatever it is that we do routinely to avoid subsequent betrayal—we unwittingly renew our worst fears of being betrayed. Not until we venture forth and trust people again will we stop sending to our own mind the repeated message that all people will betray us.

This is analogous to what almost all country folk know about horseback riding. If after suffering a bad fall, a person shuns horses, the fear of horses will increase and remain. As psychologists, we now know the reason—namely, that every avoidance aggravates the terror and sustains it. The person's choices, understandable as they are, become the agents of renewal. By each avoidance the person is whispering to himself, "Look out, or the exact same thing will surely happen again."

Concerning victims of sexual molestation, the identical principle holds. The horror of the event is of course significant in itself. But the victim's natural adoption of a wide range of activities, whose single aim is to avert repetition, becomes the supreme hazard, because such activities keep the unconscious memory alive; they reinfect the person with unconscious dread of the same thing happening again. They thus limit the palate of a life.

This explains principally why it is so important for rape victims to talk about their experience to a compassionate listener as soon after it has occurred as possible. Not only will this reduce self-hate. The victim who can find solace in others, and by mourning keep the event at a conscious level, where healing can occur, is the least liable to withdraw and to suffer over the years.

Just as much of Martin's whole life-style, and not merely a single activity, was compulsive, so in this next case a network of behaviors were driven by unconscious dread. Marianne, like Martin, was phobic about giving herself the kind of life she most wanted. For years she had compulsively kept a safe distance from reminders of a trauma. Her relinquishing some of that distance was a feat of courage, one that put her back in possession of the truths that she needed for a much better life to come.

···6···

The Cover-up

Isabel: With an outstretch'd throat I'll tell the world aloud

What man thou art.

Angelo: Who will believe thee, Isabel?

My unsoil'd name. . . . Will so your accusation overweigh.

That you shall stifle in your own report.

—*Measure For Measure*
Shakespeare

The earliest cover-up, and also the first rationalization by humankind, may have been contained in the act of burying the dead. I would imagine that primitive people couldn't stand the sight or smell of someone recently deceased, and they especially didn't like the dead person looking at them. Moreover, they didn't like the thoughts that a corpse must have invited— thoughts about their own end, I imagine. So they decided that it must be good for the dead to be shoved into a hole and covered over with earth.

Having adopted this practice, it took only millennia for people to make an institution of a "proper burial." By the time of the Trojan War, when the Trojans begged Achilles to release the body of the slain Hector and stop dragging it around the walls of Troy, the Trojans did so because they believed that without a proper burial, their Hector would never rest in peace.

When the ancient world was at its height, it was also expected that people speak well of the dead. The ancient Romans needed only to whisper two words to remind their citizens of this rule. *"De mortuis"* ("of the dead"), they would say, which everyone knew stood for the proverb, "Of the dead speak nothing unless it be good." Thus to the practice of covering up corpses with dirt "for their own sake" was added the custom of covering up their reputations. And for the most part we still regard it as befitting our humanity to do both of these things.

Doubtless, there is genuine fellow feeling in those customs today; after all, to die is to leave behind a defenseless body and reputation, both of which need protection. And, of course, there is also the matter of sanitation. However, our ancestors were very likely, I think, motivated originally more by concern for their own ease—and by the attendant desire to be sure that the deceased would not return to haunt them—than they were by concern for the person who had died. Theirs was a cover-up in the most literal sense.

The forces of light and dark—vectors of human history—were played out at a very particular funeral on a day in 1975.

It was actually a very bright day. No leaden clouds clogged the sky, to befit the sad occasion. The sun glazed the roofs of the dark vehicles that wended their way slowly through the streets toward the cemetery. The route took the cortege through a bombed-out slum, and toward the end of the journey the only signs of habitation were some stores selling funeral bouquets and various oddments.

At the cemetery the seven black autos went through an iron Tudor gate and along a dirt road. They stopped a discreet distance from the grave and the people got out and walked slowly, in little groups, to the grave site. The undertaker was already at the head of the grave, and the minister was the first to reach him, with the crowd gathering behind him.

Most of the mourners were already assembled when a yellow cab drew closer than the other vehicles, and a tall, slender woman with a very erect carriage hurried to join them. In her long black coat she could have passed as a mourner, but she was definitely not one. A black felt hat was pulled over her face, low enough to give her an aura of mystery, but not so low as to conceal her cerulean blue eyes.

She was there in time to see the six pallbearers, three on either side, carry the coffin from the hearse to the grave site. The men placed it on a mesh of heavy canvas strips over a metal framework that outlined the top of the grave. The opening in the earth was thoughtfully covered over with a patch of artificial grass. When the minister began to address the group, the grave diggers, in overalls, in the background, put out their cigarettes and stood at attention.

The minister spoke from notes obviously supplied by those who had known the deceased. He described Mr. Mack as a loving man, one who had devoted himself to his profession and to the betterment of others. Then he read some scriptural verses familiar to most: "I am the resurrection and the light. He who believeth in me shall not perish." He lamented the tragic death at seventy-four of this "child of God."

Well, what else could he do but lament? thought the tall woman in the black coat who had arrived separately in a yellow cab, which had pulled up some distance away and was waiting there.

She watched, her eyes narrowing with many emotions as, one by one, speakers came forward to say how much they had loved and appreciated the deceased. A woman with gold-rimmed glasses talked about the dead man's dedication. She said that Mr. Mack had called to see how her mother was faring during her final illness, and on more than one occasion he had delivered medicines himself. Next, a man with a basset-hound face extolled Mr. Mack with great solemnity.

The tall, dancerlike visitor who had come by cab recognized the deceased man's brother. He was the only one she knew, though he had shaved off his beard and it had been many years.

She glanced over at the coffin and wondered if she would recognize the druggist who rested inside that box. Mr. Mack had had a huge torso and giant hands. How could she be sure that he was really in there? Then, as she had ten thousand times before, she experienced him grabbing her long, loose hair, fondling her breasts, and pressing himself against her as she stood helplessly, not able even to scream. She had been eleven then.

Another speaker was on stage—the minister again: "Let us pray. Let us give thanks for the life of . . ."

The woman had been young then, delicate, impressionable, her body hovering on the cusp between childhood and adolescence—she was just as Julia, her daughter, would be very soon. She could now appreciate how fragile she had been then—only through photographs and by looking at Julia. He had been drinking, the monster had been drinking; she had become able to interpret that only years later from the memory of the smell of his breath and the corded red veins in his forehead she had seen as he held her in his grasp. He had asked her to sniff something, which, as she had deflected her face from it, had made her cheeks tingle. He had moved his body up over her, and she was helpless, absolutely helpless, in trying to push him away. He had tried to rape her. It was then that her blouse had ripped—

Everybody at the funeral was praying now. "Let us give thanks for the life of . . ." the minister was repeating, "as we commit his body to earth." He said something further about the sad, unfortunate loss of "this fine man."

When she had realized that her blouse was being ripped, she had managed to lurch forward by a stroke of good luck, knocking over a column of medicines that had seemed to her then as tall as a building. "What the hell!" he had exclaimed in injury, as they went hurtling to the floor. A table, too, was overturned, and she had screamed and scrambled to her feet and escaped. Fortunately, the pharmacy door had not been locked. She had wondered years afterward if she had raked his face with her short nails, and hoped she had.

She was dimly aware of the Lord's Prayer being run through, and listened carefully to the benediction as if it were a final confirmation that he was gone. Around her, people were red-eyed and weeping. "So you're really not out there anymore. You're really not," she said to herself with militant simplicity.

"The Lord give you peace," said the minister to the assemblage. The funeral director touched a lever with his foot, and as the rough-wood box containing the coffin slowly descended a symbolic distance of a yard or so, she muttered to herself, "May you go all the way to Hell."

Some of the people threw flowers onto the wooden box, and then the little assemblage dispersed, and people, mostly in twos, made their way to the vehicles that had brought them there.

On her way back toward the cab, the woman had the impulse to ask the grave diggers to open the box so that she could make sure he was dead. Or maybe she could kill him again, kill him not just for that afternoon, but for those years of distraught silence that had weighed her down.

"Sorry about that, lady," the cab driver said, making his best surmise from the evidence. How could he conceivably know that she was not under the common blanket of sorrow that day?

Actually, her performance that day was the result of two powerful forces. One was her own impulse to go to the funeral and denounce him once and for all, as if by that open declaration she could terminate her own suffering. The second force was her husband's profound entreaty that she not do anything radical or outspoken, that she stay home altogether.

Going to the funeral but saying nothing had emerged as a compromise between her and her husband after a battle between them that had lasted well into the night.

My involvement in the case began with a call from the tall woman's husband three days after she went to the funeral.

"I'm Dr. Alan Zeiss, a psychiatrist and psychoanalyst," he began. After portraying himself as a practitioner and teacher at a leading orthodox Freudian academy, he said that he was calling for his wife, who had agreed to see me. Then he told me about her attendance at that funeral and said, "She went there deliberately to upset me. I'm afraid that she does a lot of things for that reason."

He went on to describe her as "extremely argumentative. She has a lot of unresolved rage, and these days she's expressing it all over the place."

I immediately wondered why Dr. Zeiss hadn't referred his wife to an analyst from his own highly orthodox Freudian institute. It is common practice for psychoanalysts of that school, most of whom who are men, to send their wives to fellow practitioners from their own close-knit academy. Actually, I had always considered this practice to be ingrown and unwise. At worst, it seemed to me a way of making sure that an ally of theirs would handle the case—it was a symbolic method of keeping their wives at home under psychological "lock and key." But even at best, keeping the person so close deprives the patient of a point of view sharply different from their own.

I inwardly applauded Dr. Zeiss's entrusting his wife to me as an authentic act of letting go. He must have known full well, since he chose me, that I was not a Freudian. Indeed, I was very far from his camp, in that I interact with my patients more than the Freudians do, and see people as freer and as more responsible for their own actions.

Moments later, however, I began to suspect that he had another reason for choosing someone outside his realm.

He said, "Above everything else, it is important to me that I can depend on your confidentiality. My wife and I must both feel free to tell you everything, with the absolute knowledge that you will tell no one else."

I promised him that he could count on that.

He went on. "I should tell you—my wife certainly will—that she was once my patient. It is imperative that this remain secret. Of course, Marianne will be telling you about us, herself, but this fact must remain strictly confidential."

"Everything she tells me will be, if we work together."

"There is no 'if,' " he said. "She has promised to call. That is not my concern. Frankly, what I'm worried about is my professional status if this thing gets talked about."

So this was to be no routine therapy as far as Dr. Zeiss himself was concerned. I was to be made privy to information about Dr. Zeiss or his wife, which if it became the property of his immediate "countrymen," could cause him acute embarrassment. Indeed, I was already privy to it. He had obviously chosen me because he considered me far removed from the theater of his operations. He added that he had decided on me after reading an article of mine and determining that I was quite sensible.

It was obvious why Dr. Zeiss was so concerned. He had violated the strictest Freudian taboo, and would lose all standing at his institute if he was found out. Freudian analysts have dubbed such relationships, of analyst with patient, "incestuous." By their most orthodox standards, sleeping with a patient, even years after the treatment is over, or marrying a former patient, is an abuse almost tantamount to sleeping with a patient during treatment.

Most other therapists would certainly agree that sleeping with a patient during treatment is akin to statutory rape. In the therapist's office the patient suspends disbelief and distrust and, in reliving his or her early life, becomes utterly vulnerable. The therapist who approaches a patient sexually is exploiting this trust and doing violence to the patient. But as for a posttherapeutic relationship, not all therapists are so stern as Freudians are. We consider every case to be different, though even in a relationship begun years after therapy is over, there may still be exploitation. Ideally, sex with patients—past, present, or future—is to be avoided.

Dr. Zeiss spoke quickly to extenuate his behavior, striving to make clear that it was as aboveboard as any such act could be. "Marianne was my patient for only five months and, of course, I did not touch her during the treatment. When I realized that I was falling in love with her, we quickly terminated, and I married her a few months later."

"I see."

"However, we have not been exactly happy. Not even from the beginning. She has deep depressions, and then acts out impulsively. I must admit that I underestimated the depth of her impulse disorder when we married. Of course, I recognized that she needed further treatment, but I guess I didn't think it through. Nor did I discuss our relationship with anyone from the institute.

"But her continuing problems have caused us both great turmoil," he went on. "I still believe that if she can cope with certain of her childhood fantasies, she can become a very healthy person. Is there anything in particular that you would like to ask me now?"

"Thank you. No. I'm sure that she'll tell me whatever it is that I need to know, if and when she calls."

"She will call," he said, this time with some irritation. "By the way, she has the illusion that she was badly molested as a child. By the man whose funeral she insisted on going to—"

"You're saying that it didn't really happen?"

"I think it's an illusion. Marianne has quite a vivid imagination, as you will see. Such illusions are, of course, common among young girls, as you certainly know. The poor man died last week. She brings her imagined past with this man wherever she goes. She insisted on going to his funeral to denounce him, to make a big speech that he was 'scum,' or something like that—in front of his own children and friends. That's typical Marianne—always doing things regardless of their consequences."

"Did she?"

"No. She finally consented not to. We agreed that she would go, since it meant so much to her, but that she would not make a spectacle of herself. She would simply go and witness the proceedings."

I declined yet another offer by him of diagnostic information about his wife. I had a sense that it wasn't easy for him to turn off that spigot. In fact, I was becoming annoyed with myself for having engaged him on the phone for as long as I had, and especially for having encouraged him by asking questions.

Again he beseeched me not to tell anyone that his wife had ever been his patient, and I assured him that I would protect his secret. I underscored this assurance by telling him that I realized that such information, if made public, could be ruinous to him.

Despite an occasional moment of condescension and annoyance toward me, I realized that he was relying on me heavily. I recognized, too, that he had chosen me more out of necessity—because I was remote from his world—than because I was high on his list of experts. The orthodox Freudians have often regarded the rest of us as "in the provinces"—to use a term that Freud applied to Carl Jung when the latter defected. From their point of view, we who question any of their tenets are not doing the quintessential work. And yet, Dr. Zeiss had to rely on me for that very reason—namely, that I was "in the provinces." Such a compromise would be enough to account for at least some of his irritation toward me.

Although Dr. Zeiss had insisted that his wife would call, it is never a sure thing that one person heralded by another will follow through. And after that conversation, obeying some habitual law of economy, I gave not a single thought to Marianne until I actually did hear from her.

She introduced herself on the phone, and we set up an appointment.

She was a willowy, tall, and ethereally pale woman in her mid thirties. In spite of her shoulder-length, honey-colored hair, she looked a bit boyish.

She wore a long, loose, crimson silk shirt, obviously expensive, black leggings, and black lizard flats—an elegant punk look. She wore oversize sunglasses.

Almost at once there was a strained silence.

"What brings you here?" I asked her.

"Besides my husband, you mean?"

"Yes," I said.

"Well, I really don't know what else to do. I'm confused. I've been doing crazy things. I'm not even sure I should be married. My life is a mess, and so is my daughter's, and that's my fault. I've done it to her. I thought I was helping her, but I've made a mess of her, and I can't live with that."

She told me that her daughter, Julia, had just turned eleven. "I thought when I married Alan that Julia's life would straighten out, that she'd just go to school, have friends, and be happy, that I could give her some quiet, comfortable years."

"And it's not like that?"

"Definitely not. It was a dream, I guess. I don't care what happens to me. But I don't want anything to go wrong with Julia."

Then she removed her sunglasses briefly to daub her lower eyelid with a tissue. From the redness of her eyes, I surmised that she'd been crying before she'd arrived.

"We'll try to figure it all out," I said, as reassuringly as I could. "Let's start with you, though I would like to hear all about Julia. You say you're doing crazy things. Like what, for example?"

She shot back a volley of them. "Okay. For example, marrying Jeff, my first husband. And maybe marrying Alan. For another thing, I've been saying things lately that I can't believe I said, and I scared the hell out of some street person who tried to wipe my windshield."

I chose what seemed to me the simplest item on the list, and asked her to tell me some of those unbelievable things she was saying.

"Well, for example, I told those analysts that I was sick of pushing Madame Smyslov's wheelchair."

"She's in a wheelchair?"

"No. And she's not a 'Madame' either. I call her that. But only in private to Alan, until I made that remark in front of all the analysts."

"She's Alexander Smyslov's wife?" I asked. I knew him to be the renowned psychoanalyst of the old school who headed the institute and chaired the meetings.

"Yes. When she talks, everybody listens," Marianne said sarcastically. "We're supposed to worship him, and Madame too—Sonya. It was the other night, they were back at our house, about six of them. Alan asked me to drive her to the Metropolitan Museum of Art and back, and said that I'd learn a lot. I said that—in front of all of them, out of the blue—'I'm sick of pushing Madame Smyslov's wheelchair.'

"They were all so shocked, I thought they were going to pass out on the spot. It was in our apartment. They didn't say a word, but it was obvious what they were thinking. A few minutes later they all left. I know they think I'm losing my mind."

She seemed close to tears. "It just came out," she said.

In the silence that followed, I got a sense that she didn't want to talk about that incident anymore right then.

"And the street person?" I asked. "What was that about?"

"Oh him! We were in the car with Alan. I was driving—Alan's eyes aren't so good, and when Julia's with us I do the driving. We were stuck at a light, and I see this man, this *derelict,* going up to people's cars and wiping off their windshields, whether they wanted him to or not, and demanding money. He went up to two cars in front of us. One woman actually opened the window and gave him a quarter.

"I said, I must have shouted, 'Don't come near my car. Get your fucking hands off my car.' But he didn't even act like he heard me, or cared.

"Alan said something like, 'But, dear,'—he always says that. Anyhow, I got so furious that when the guy got directly in front of our car I switched the gear into neutral and stepped on the gas. The engine made this terrible whir. Then he jumped back, as if he heard his death in that sound. And I really could have killed him. The guy ran away, and then I switched back the gear, and took off when the light changed.

"I was furious for an hour. Julia thought the whole thing was funny. I think it scared the hell out of Alan, but I really didn't care. Who the hell is that guy to touch my car when I tell him not to!"

"It doesn't sound as if you regret it. So what bothers you about it?"

"How furious I was. And Alan says that stuff like that isn't good for Julia. He's probably right. She's got her own problems. I hate how murderous I can get. I feel just *compelled* to do these things. Do you think I'm going crazy?"

"So what scares you is how fast you go into these states of rage, is that it?"

"That's it exactly. I think things are under control one minute. And the next minute—wham! I've done something berserk."

"I see. You mean, it's like being in a car that's stationary. Then a minute later it's going sixty, and you don't know how it got up to that speed?"

"That's right. And it's happening a lot more lately. I can't even tell you about everything I do right now. But Alan's right, when I'm with Julia it can't be good for her."

"Let me see then," I said, and then asked her, "By the way, what should I call you, Mrs. Zeiss, or Marianne, or what?"

"Oh, Marianne, please. I hate when people call me Mrs. Zeiss."

It was a stronger answer than I had expected, and the flash of intensity in her tone was a small-scale instance of that sudden passion she had been talking about.

"All right, Marianne, let me say this. One thing is certain. You're not just going from zero to sixty with nothing in between. Something is working you up to that speed. I'm certain that there's a lot going on in between the calm and the storm, and we've got to understand what it is. We've got to understand you—"

She looked at me curiously.

I tried to clarify. "There's a lot happening that you have feelings about, and you may not be aware of those feelings. If you're bursting out like this, then one thing is sure: You're feeling squeezed—"

"Squeezed! Am I! I don't know whether to stay with Alan, for one thing. We're not really that happy together. For a year I tried real hard, but I do these sudden crazy things. More than I did."

"Tell me a little about you and him."

"He said he told you how we met."

"What he told me makes no difference. I'm interested only in what you tell me. I won't be talking to him about you again. So this is strictly confidential."

"All right, so you know the major thing about us. He was my doctor. I'd been going to him a little under a year. I was having affairs with several men at the time and working in an ad agency. I do layout and design. Actually, I'm pretty good at it. That may sound surprising, but I am. I've always had an excellent color sense.

"I was having too many affairs. I never stayed out all night, though. I was always home for Julia. We had a housekeeper, and I never missed a day at work. But my life was a mess.

"So, anyhow, one day I was very upset, and he asked me would I give up all those men for someone who really loved me. And I said I would, and he said he loved me and wanted to marry me."

"Were you surprised?"

"Yeah, I was. Of course. I was honored. I couldn't believe it. I couldn't understand why he wanted me. I said I wanted to think about it. Then the next time I saw him, I said yes."

"Did you love him?"

"I don't know. I don't really think so. But I thought he was the kindest man I ever knew. I'm not the sort to live alone all my life, and those other men weren't asking me. At least not the ones I wanted to. And I felt sure it would be good for Julia. At least I thought so at the time."

"And now?"

"Now I'm not so sure."

"What's wrong with Julia?"

"She's doing things. I'd rather not discuss it. So Julia and I moved in with Alan, and I think she thought he was neat. He would tell her a lot of stories. But now she's not so sure either, anymore. It's gotten tough. She knows I'm unhappy. She sees."

"You say you didn't see why Alan wanted you. Have you figured that one out since?"

"I've asked him that question. All he says is, 'I love you. You're pretty and you have a wonderful mind,' but I don't buy that. It doesn't sound right."

She didn't elaborate, and a little later I asked her, "Do you enjoy sex with him?"

"My God, I didn't think I'd be talking about all this so fast!"

"Don't answer me if you don't want to."

"You won't be talking to Alan, will you—about any of this?"

"Absolutely not," I said, my tone verging on that of one who has been insulted. "This is absolutely confidential."

"I almost believe you."

"That's up to you. I hope you can believe me—"

"At first, sex with him was a lot of fun. Not the best, but the idea that he was my analyst, it was kind of dramatic—like we were doing something wrong whenever he touched me. Nobody could know. We only had intercourse a few times before getting married."

Suddenly her expression dropped, and she was silent.

I asked her what she was thinking.

She looked almost like one startled out of a reverie. "Oh, I was remembering a phone call to an ex . . . an ex-lover. Daryl. When I told him that I couldn't see him any more. That I was getting married. . . . Naturally, I didn't tell him how I knew Alan, or for how long. 'Oh, God,' he said. "I'm sure he's a wonderful lover, because you are, I'll . . . I'll . . . always miss the taste of your clitoris, and your fantastic orgasms, especially that one on my living room floor.' All right, so you know." She raised her voice, and I had the impression that she was almost—angry.

I asked her, "What do you mean—'So I know?' Know what?"

Now she seemed puzzled.

"I think about Daryl a lot. He's a good guy, even though maybe he won't amount to anything."

A loaded silence followed.

Then she said, "Alan doesn't believe in oral sex. He's of the school that it's a perversion. He thinks it will keep me immature. We always do the same thing, and we never talk during. . . . So I guess I'm pretty impulsive to have said all this the first time I ever saw you, huh?"

"I certainly didn't draw that conclusion. It's important that you tell me everything."

"Everything!"

"Well, whatever you can. Whatever you can allow yourself to tell me."

"I hoped I'd enjoy sex with Alan more as time went by."

"But you're not?"

"Not yet." She shook her head as if she might be sorry that she had revealed so much, so soon.

"So," she summed up. "I don't know which way to turn or what's wrong with me. But I've got to stop acting so crazy. Can you help me?"

"Do you feel okay having talked to me about all this?"

"All this!" she said, with a smile that seemed close to a sneer.

I didn't call the smile to her attention, much less ask her what it meant. It seemed clear that she had to go at her own speed.

"Do you think you can help me?" she repeated.

"You mean help you not feel so crazy or act so impulsive?"

She nodded. "And help me be a better mother."

"If you can understand yourself better, what you really feel in situations, you won't feel so out of control."

"Okay," she said listlessly, and I realized that she felt I was right.

"What's the most impulsive thing that you fear you're on the brink of doing these days?" I asked her.

She sat for a moment, thinking—and I had the impression that she was reviewing many possibilities.

Finally she said, "I'm afraid that if I get this job I'm going for, I'll find myself having picked up Julia and my worldly goods and stormed out of there."

"You mean leave Alan?"

"Yeah, that's what I mean. I've often thought that if I had a good job I might have left already."

"You've been looking for jobs?"

"I blew about four interviews lately. By saying stupid things. That's another example of my impulsiveness. But maybe it was for the best."

Our time was coming to a close, and I asked her if she wanted to come in regularly, a few times a week, or if she wanted to think about it.

"I guess I should say, 'think about it.' "

"You should? Why?"

"Because I'm always so impulsive."

"Okay," I said. "Call me when you feel like it. And, of course, even if you do come in, you can stop at any time. This isn't a locked-in commitment."

"Okay, let's quit the kidding," she said. "I trust you. You make a lot of sense, and I don't make any sense lately. So I might as well trust you. Alan says I'm supposed to go into therapy three times a week, so let's set up a schedule."

"Twice a week will be fine," I said at once. "You'll be doing plenty of thinking about yourself in between anyhow, and if an emergency comes up, you can always call."

"Okay, that would be better." She smiled broadly.

We found two hours, Monday and Fridays in the morning. I wished her a good weekend, and she was gone.

The instant she left, I realized that I had set the pace at two sessions a week instead of three, not because I knew for a fact that two was the ideal number, but rather because I wanted to exempt us from Alan's overshadowing directive. His signature in her life was all too pervasive.

I had the sense that her enthusiastic agreement with me might have been for the same reason. Perhaps even that small differentiation from Alan was meaningful to her. It said that she and I together could do what had to be done, and that ultimately she, on her own, would do what she had to do for herself.

Actually, all I knew for sure thus far was that if Marianne blew up as often as she reported, she must have been catering to Alan—and, doubtless, to others—far too much between outbursts. I certainly didn't know why or how. But at least my immediate course was set—to learn about her life and to help her surface whatever was going on in her private experience between those outbursts.

When she came to my mind the next day, I remembered her sitting and thinking right after I'd asked her what impulses she was afraid she might succumb to. After a full thirty seconds, she had offered to me her fear of leaving Alan precipitously. But that long delay before she spoke, when I thought about it, implied that there was a lot else, very likely concerns more urgent to her.

Then I remembered that she hadn't even mentioned going to that funeral, or being sexually molested as a child, and I knew that I would have to bring those topics up before too long. It might well upset her if she got the idea that I was holding information about her in reserve—and especially such loaded information.

Apparently, when Marianne went home after that first session, Alan had asked her if I seemed competent. She had answered sourly, "Probably not, but why should I go to a competent person? I'm not that competent, myself."

When she reported this the next time I saw her, and I commented that she had really let him have it, Marianne justified her response at once. "Well, I'm sick of his messing into my affairs. I know he really meant me to tell him everything that went on."

She spoke briefly about the collapse of her sexual life. "I really don't like his touching me, except at certain times it's okay."

"Can you say why?"

"Well, he's always studying me. 'Did you have an orgasm?' 'Was it good?' 'Was it better than last time?' "

Then somehow she got to talking about Julia's father, Jeff. "He was good to look at. He had a wonderful face. I think he really loved me, too. But he was a flake."

"In what way?"

"Well, for example, when I met Jeff, he had a huge apartment and no furniture in it. We lived there for a year. Neither of us even bothered getting any chairs or anything. But we had a lot of fun. It was a camp. Then I got pregnant with Julia and we got married.

"But he kept losing his jobs. Meanwhile, I had a career going. Jeff went out to California to look for work—as a scriptwriter. He ended up working in Beverly Hills as a restaurant manager. I couldn't leave my job. Julia and I wouldn't have been able to eat on just his salary. I was at J. Walter Thompson's—making good money. So we got divorced. He still talks to Julia a lot on the phone, and she goes out there sometimes."

Then Marianne surprised me by concluding, "Jeff's the only kind of man who would have someone as unstable as me."

Already, in one and a half sessions, I had gotten the sense that Marianne considered herself damaged goods. I wondered if the molestation was a factor. Had it really occurred? So far, I had no reason to consider that it hadn't. Though Marianne was mercurial, I hadn't seen a single sign that she suffered delusions or that her imagination played such tricks on her.

I was deliberating about how to bring it up, and approached it by asking generally about her childhood. She told me that she was an only child, and that she had grown up in Summit, New Jersey.

"My father is a lawyer—a real wimp. But he would do anything for me. Well, he would do anything for *anybody,* I think. We were comfortable financially—better than most, I imagine. I went to Summit High School. I had friends. Not a lot, but some. I was a good artist even then, and I majored in art at Montclair College. My father wanted me to be a good citizen—just like him and Mom."

"What did that mean?"

"Go to church. No disruptions. No fights in public. No trouble. Dress down. Don't give them anything to hold against you. So that was the way I lived." She said this last with resignation and, I thought, a good deal of sadness.

"Your parents are still alive?"

"Yes. All Julia's grandparents are. Both sets. And they're all good to her. My father's retired. My mother managed a dress shop in Summit, and now she's part owner of one in Miami."

"You could talk to them easily?" I asked. I was edging closer to the "incident," still hoping that she would bring it up herself.

"Yeah, I could. Whatever it was, they would always tell me not to worry. Like I didn't do so great in school. I'm really not very bright. They always told me not to let it get me down."

"And if you were really in trouble, or something terrible happened—"

"They were there, smoothing it out."

"Can you think of an example?"

She gasped audibly, and for an instant I thought I saw a countenance as morose as those that Michelangelo had painted in his depiction of the damned. But then she composed her face so quickly that I wasn't sure whether I had imagined that expression or really seen it.

She answered my question calmly, almost lackadaisically. "Well, I failed algebra, and when I came home with my report card, I thought it was the end of the world.

"My father was home already, and I showed it to him. He was always calmer than my mother. And he said, 'Don't worry. It just means that you haven't done enough work.' He told me not to even mention it, and they'd get me a tutor. Which they did."

I felt sure that I had been fobbed off by that example, which, though it was doubtless the statement of a truth, was a tame replacement for whatever else it was that had flashed into her mind and fazed her utterly. The horrendous sexual abuse, I imagined. I felt almost certain of it.

"Were there any other examples?" I asked her.

"There were, I'm sure, but I just can't think of them. My parents were very good to me. They still are. They're sort of patiently on my side. Always offering me money. They've put away money for Julia's college."

"That's nice for her," I remarked, realizing that Marianne wasn't going to tell me just then what had so disconcerted her. If I were right, and the molestation memory had haunted her before she reburied it, I would do well to go far in the direction of not being an assailant myself. "Who goes softly goes far," runs the old Italian proverb, which I resolved would have to govern my curiosity.

After she left I wondered if, having heard what I had from her husband, I had only imagined that expression of acute dismay, if I had only read it into her face, when I had asked her for an instance of how her parents were there for her when she was in trouble. How could I be sure either way, when those oversize sunglasses so masked her real expression? I had been tempted several times to ask her to remove those glasses, as I had done with others in my office. I've never had a problem with such a request. But that Italian proverb—not knowing Italian, I could recall only the rhyming words, *piano* and *lontano,* ("softly" and "a long distance")—and I realized that the most I could do in Marianne's case was to comment upon the difficulty of talking to her through those sunglasses. She would remove them when she was ready.

At that point I also made a note to myself that the bigger an event actually was for Marianne, the more languid her tone seemed to be when she recounted it. I cautioned myself not to underestimate the importance of any comments that Marianne made about herself in that lackadaisical tone. If anything, when she said something very blankly, I should give it an extra moment; her very flatness might itself be a cue that it mattered a great deal. But as to why she had adopted such a mechanism, as yet I had no idea.

Two weeks passed, during which I desisted from steering Marianne toward any subject matter. She dictated all priorities and trusted me where she chose to. I didn't relish the role of possessing facts about her that she had never presented to me in a session. It seemed unfair for me to have them, and if her husband ever mentioned to her that he had told me about the molestation and her going to the funeral, she might consider me devious for not having brought those events up with her directly. It was a calculated risk for me to remain silent, but still I felt that it would be the best thing for Marianne in the long run if she could divulge things to me at her own pace and use me as she chose. Anyway, I consoled myself, no matter what Marianne elected to tell me, I was learning about her.

It crossed my mind that in assuming such a passive role, I was conforming with the practice of those in her husband's and Dr. Smyslov's retinue at the institute. Orthodox Freudians have been known to say almost nothing for months or years so as not to inhibit the patient's free association process. I was hardly more active during those weeks than they would have been, though I imagine I felt more restless in my chair than analysts truly inured to the method must feel. I was using such noncommittal silence only in hopes of evoking better communication between Marianne and me.

Meanwhile, those sunglasses stayed on. Even on one especially dark, dreary day, with poor visibility in the streets, she wore them. On that particular day, Marianne seemed a bit ungainly, as if she had just grown up, and I felt a touching, elfin quality in her.

Marianne had been telling me about her childhood, and I was getting the impression that both her parents were formal, capable people who related to her with their heads instead of their hearts. They stressed good manners and nonassertiveness above virtually everything else.

Marianne had kept her room clean; she had said thank you to nearly everyone for nearly everything; she would call to offer condolences and a helping hand whenever a relative got sick. Her decorum was exemplary at school. Her parents had indoctrinated her so deftly that she could not remember even once having been corrected for misbehavior. When she remarked, "I was trained never to hurt another person's feelings," I thought to myself: "The basic formula for getting sexually molested and not wanting to make a fuss."

I heard some irony in Marianne's portrayal of her mother—her garish engagement ring, her out-of-date bouffant hairdo—heavily sprayed—her harsh voice when she wanted something. Marianne said, "And my father always went in circles to do right by her."

"How?" I asked.

"Oh, I don't know. She would tell him anything, and he'd do it. Rush out for ice cream in the middle of the night. Pick up the pieces of a glass she broke. It was ridiculous."

"Did your mother expect the same from you?"

"I didn't actually have that much to do with her. My father was home with me a lot more than she was. He was really the one I talked to, I guess. We were both out to please her."

On that dreary day I mentioned, Marianne began by telling me that she'd been quarreling badly with Alan "for a week or so." She hadn't mentioned any arguing the last time I had seen her in the same week, but something told me not to ask her why she hadn't brought it up.

After recognizing this constraint, I became more aware than ever that Marianne was sending me a signal not to remark on anything before she did—*"never to molest her,"* I thought—and I mused about how the word "molest" has lost its general meaning in recent years, having become overidentified with specific, sexual molestation.

I came to see that Marianne felt molested by Alan in a variety of ways; for instance, by comments of his that she would usually let pass. He had often said derisive things about her first husband, Jeff, which had stung her, but she had never spoken out. Alan had called Jeff "immature" and "unstable." But on the Monday night before our session she had exploded at just such remarks.

The fight had begun when Alan characterized Marianne's marriage to himself as her "first adult relationship."

"He said it was a real test to see if I could stick with something real," she said. She had become furious and had lambasted Alan for putting Jeff down. She had retorted, "Jeff is a wonderful man—and very kind. Who the hell are you to call him—to call him anything? He's Julia's father."

Eventually, Alan's pleas of "Darling, you misunderstood me," had quenched her fury. Or else her fury had spent itself. They had sex and went to sleep. The next morning was pleasant, and it seemed to her that she had forgiven him.

But then, hours later, after another job rejection, she had come home extremely touchy. They'd had a dinner guest, "a starchy old analyst who flirts with me. I hate the fact that Alan doesn't even notice that the guy is interested in me. Alan thinks the creep is a genius just because he talks slow and has some kind of theory. I'd like to fuck him just so I could tell Alan about it, just so he'd notice something."

I merely listened.

"But, of course, I wouldn't. Anyhow, as soon as the guy, Jack Nandor, that's his name, left I asked Alan, 'Why do we have to keep it so secret that I was your patient?' 'Darling,' he said, 'let's not go through all that again. You know how important it is to me.'

"So I said to Alan, 'I don't get it. You're always talking about going right to the truth. But we're constantly telling a lie, aren't we? It really bothers me that I can never tell the truth.' Then Alan told me that his friends all like me, which I don't believe, that things are going fine, and that I shouldn't shake anything up.

"But I did shake things up—at least between the two of us. I don't know what happened. I think we both had a drink or two. We got into a huge fight after that. We were both crying."

"Did Julia get into it?"

"No. No. She was sleeping over at a friend's house. But Alan and I are fighting a lot more than we ever did—and worse. The one good thing about Alan is, he agrees we should never fight in front of Julia. And we don't."

I wondered whether Marianne's seeing me, and finding if not support, then at least not condemnation, was fueling these recent outbursts. No, I corrected myself—at most, her seeing me was simply freeing her to indulge in them.

It began to seem obvious to me that certain feelings of Marianne's, which had amplified inside of her by being unexpressed, were finding an outlet. However, I was just as sure that they were not being surfaced in their real form, but had undergone transitions before finding the light of day.

I pondered the various accusations that Marianne had already made— against Alan and his friends and against her parents. They seemed to have certain strong strains in common. Sifting through those anecdotes, I asked myself, "What was their general theme?" As if Marianne had heard my question echoing in the room, she said, "I hate cover-ups!"

Then, near tears of rage, she added, "I don't want Julia to be like me—unhappy."

But when I asked her in what ways Julia seemed unhappy, she said only, "It's my fault. I know it is."

We got no further that session. But the theme of "cover-up" had been imprinted in my mind, along with that of "molestation," and I felt certain that they had both long been incised in hers.

Marianne's marriage to Alan became more fitful during the next month. Their arguments were long and loud. The tenor was the same—she did the shouting, and he did the assuaging, by telling her that she was overreacting. His very calming her—"Darling, don't lose your temper, be reasonable"—fanned the flames every time. Marianne would repeat, apropos of the merest criticism of her—and there were many—"You're so fucking perfect. I'll never be what you want. Maybe I'm not what anybody wants."

It humiliated her that he granted his friends and their wives the right to ask her questions that were supervisory in essence: "Did you have your résumés reprinted on better paper, as I suggested?" "Don't you think that you should change to another cleaning woman, since you can't get this one to come on a regular schedule?"

Marianne found such condescension almost unbearable at times. Still, she obeyed what she knew to be a desperate wish of Alan's: She never told his friends off.

The nearest she came was at a dinner party one night while the group was chatting about a colleague who was just getting on his feet again after his second heart attack. At the table, a few of the senior analysts interrogated the man's wife about her behavior over the years, and one of them virtually told her that if she had treated her husband better, he would not have had either of his heart attacks.

Marianne, who surely identified with the downtrodden woman, was hard put to keep her mouth shut. She perhaps managed it only because she heard one of the analysts, who had previously been silent, take the woman aside and warmly tell her that she should not blame herself and that she had been a wonderful wife.

That night, when they got home, Marianne berated the accusers to Alan, but he defended them as "only trying to be helpful." They had another heated argument.

Still, when I thought about Marianne and Alan's marriage, it seemed more cold than hot, despite their quarrels. The image came to me of those fights as the breaking up of ice on a river, which froze again each time, but sooner or later it would not refreeze, and the river would become a torrent.

Of all the indignities that Marianne suffered at the hands of Alan's friends, those that cut deepest were slurs on how she was raising Julia. One came from no less a personage than Madame Smyslov herself, who was—as Marianne put it, "graciously"—still talking to Marianne after her wheel-chair comment.

During what had begun as an innocent chat at an institute luncheon, Mrs. Smyslov remarked that Marianne wasn't nearly involved enough with Julia's daily life. Madame Smyslov boasted that when her daughter was Julia's age, the girl had taken private lessons in piano, tennis, swimming, and ice-skating—in just about everything—and that Mrs Smyslov had kept a close watch over her progress at each. Mrs. Smyslov said that she had monitored her daughter's practice hours and had spoken regularly to her instructors. Mrs. Smyslov concluded chirpily, "It's not good to raise your daughter too loosely."

It was obvious why such a lecture had been so hurtful to Marianne. She was already agonizing over what she saw as Julia's growing unhappiness, and she already blamed herself. Marianne felt her daughter's pain far more keenly than she did her own, and it was much worse for her to think that she was failing Julia than that she was botching her own life.

"That really was a low blow," I said, almost before I realized that I had said anything. Then I hurriedly explained, "It should be obvious to anyone how important your daughter is to you."

"That's true," she said slowly, and I thought with a note of appreciation. "And Julia is so unhappy."

Though she had said this before, she seemed to be rediscovering it as she thought about her daughter.

And I found myself repeating a question, with a freshness that I truly felt once again, "But what makes you feel that Julia *is* so unhappy?"

This time she said, rather mysteriously, "We have the same sickness. I know we have."

I urged her more than I had about anything else before. "I wish I knew what you meant about Julia. Or at least that you could tell me a little more."

She didn't reply. Then, to my surprise, she took off her sunglasses. It was the only time she ever had, except to wipe her eyes. But it wasn't because she suddenly trusted me, or liked me any better.

On the contrary, it was to get a better look at my eyes, so as to gauge my reactions. But that look of hers gave me the impression that I was a being whom she had never seen and didn't like. For a full ten seconds she surveyed me this way without speaking. Obviously she had something on her mind that she was very deliberately concealing from me.

At that moment I felt more shut out of her thoughts than I ever had before—I likened myself to the derelict who had been about to put his hands on her car when she had gunned the motor.

★ ★ ★

During the next session she abandoned her sunglasses entirely. They gave way to the occasional use of ordinary steel-rimmed glasses. Her blue eyes were quite beautiful, their color accented by triangular Indian turquoise earrings, which she wore for the first time. During that session I may have only imagined a look of humorous restraint, as if she thought of herself as taking a chance.

She talked more about why she'd married Alan, and when she mentioned that "Julia needed a father," I thought of the question, "Julia did or you thought that you yourself did?" But I didn't ask it.

When I finally inquired about her women friends, she mentioned having cut them all out except for one or two, whom she saw on special occasions. She blamed this on Alan's view of the others as bad influences. Her closest friend, Sarah, a successful investment banker, he had condemned as incapable of forming a lasting relationship with a man; and another friend, Susan, he had stigmatized because she drank too much.

But Marianne recalled hilarity when with these women, and feeling free in their company. So saying, she resolved to see them more often—it would have to be alone, she added. She glanced over at my eyes, I thought, to see if I considered it okay. But I am sure she found no sign either way.

I felt that I had a much better chance of getting to know Marianne, now that I could see her eyes. But when I asked myself why, I decided that it had nothing to do with my improved ability to read her. It was because of a real change in her attitude, which was only signaled by the removal of those glasses. She had trusted me by that act of self-exposure and, whereas distrust breeds continued suspicion, even such a small act of trust might open the portals for her to place more confidence in me.

A week or so later, she again discussed Julia, but without mentioning any serious problem. Though I realized that Marianne felt put upon in the marriage and downgraded by Alan, I could see that he, too, must have felt real injury. He was trying hard to create a setting for Julia, arranging outings on Sundays that the three of them could enjoy. They went to zoos and museums and movies.

But to say that Marianne and her daughter were strongly bonded and that they ostracized Alan would be putting it mildly. They often ate dinner without him when he was due home from work shortly. They shared a trust, a very language of understanding together, and even when he was with them, they often excluded Alan by references that they didn't bother to explain to him.

I had at first thought that cutting him out might be Marianne's reprisal for Alan's condescension toward her when they were with his colleagues and friends. But then I came to recognize it as something deeper, as a byproduct of how she regarded him and men in general—namely, as creatures who should never be allowed too close. Marianne and her daughter were like a sealed-beam unit that was part of a working engine. They had joined the household as one and would, if the marriage failed, leave it as one—that was only natural. But the extent to which their containment excluded Alan had evolved out of Marianne's character and, so long as that exclusion persisted, it would stunt any hope for a true family of the three of them.

Marianne's tacit exclusion of Alan was manifest in many small, as well as big, ways. One day she disparaged Alan for the way he dressed, saying that his clothes were "boring beyond belief."

"He thinks that the only place for color is a necktie. Like those congressmen on those TV hearings. They all dress dull, and then their personality splashes out in a red tie; it's like their mistresses, and their outfits are their wives."

I asked her how Alan had reacted when she had offered her suggestions, assuming that the real problem was his indifference to her. But she surprised me by saying, "I never told him. He wouldn't listen to me, anyhow."

I told her the obvious, that she wasn't giving him a fair chance, and when she debated this, I added that she wasn't giving me much of a chance either. "There's a lot you're deliberately not telling me."

"You're pressing me," she said.

"Not at all. I'm simply commenting on your choice."

When she questioned me as to how I could believe anything she said anyway, and added that she might be making it all up, I told her that this was a given in psychotherapy. "We therapists can only go on what the person tells us. That's obvious." I added that the only way she could ever come to trust me was by confiding in me.

After she had left, it occurred to me that Marianne's doubt of her listener—her distrust of me or Alan or of anyone—was inseparable from a profound self-doubt. For some great reason in her history, she doubted her own credibility—her ability to report events and to be believed.

A few weeks later we met outside my office quite by accident.

My apartment building, on Central Park West, had been selected for a one-minute scene by the location crew of a Hollywood film. By nine o'clock on the appointed Friday morning, equipment trucks lined the side street, and when I got to my lobby door a few minutes before our scheduled session, the shooting was in progress inside. A smart-looking woman in her early twenties with a walkie-talkie asked me politely to wait with the crowd, and I saw Marianne also waiting, looking dramatic in a black cape.

However, after seeing me, she appeared very uncomfortable, as if, I thought, she had imagined that I existed only inside my office, at most the incarnation of an understanding voice, but a being without physical presence. Many patients feel this way about their therapists, and they certainly have the right to construe us as they wish. I felt a bit uneasy myself at the idea that I was troubling her. But, of course, I could hardly resolve myself into a dew while I waited for the next break in the shooting.

Then I realized that Marianne, having married my predecessor, Dr. Alan Zeiss, would, quite understandably, want to sustain a very sharp demarcation between herself and me. Our meeting outside the lobby was considerably stickier than if we had met in passing on the street, where she could simply nod and keep on walking.

That decision of Alan's to exploit the impression he had made on her as her therapist as a head start to romance had left many aftereffects, none of them good. He had, in the language of his institute, "exploited the transference"—he had confused her unconscious and made my task harder.

I was wondering whether I should start the session by bringing up our meeting outside and asking her what feelings she had about it. This is often an ideal thing to do after chance encounters with patients if one suspects strong reactions, or even weak reactions, that might fester if unmentioned.

Just then, the seemingly very capable young woman in the crew, after hearing something over her walkie-talkie, said to us, "All right, you can go in now. Sorry for the delay."

About four of us went in, past the spotlights and huge reflectors set up in the lobby. The throng of film aficionados, eager for a glimpse of the shoot or of one of the stars, surged closer as we left the space.

A minute later, almost by the way Marianne sallied into my office and sat down, I realized that she had an agenda of her own—and something very definite to say.

Her first utterance confirmed this. "I want to talk to you about Julia."

"Sure. Go ahead."

"She's the only thing I've done that's really important to me. Whatever I've done wrong in my own life, I can live with that." She hesitated.

"I know how important she is to you," I said.

"Julia's very unhappy," she said flatly.

"Something has just come up, it sounds like," I said.

"Eleven-year-old girls don't often give each other Tourneau watches, do they?" she asked.

"It's conceivable," I said. "But no, I guess they don't."

"A three-hundred-dollar gift! Come on! Julia is stealing things from stores. She has been for some time—soap, a blouse, a scarf, a bracelet. Then this. In the last few months it's gotten worse."

"You've asked her about those items, I assume?" I inquired.

"Always: 'One of my friends gave it to me.' I didn't want to really press her. Who? Stacey? Where would she get a Chanel scarf with a Saks Fifth Avenue label on it? Maybe I wanted to believe Julia, but I know. I've known for six months.

"She's really smart. But she slipped up. I brought her downtown with me to pick up my watch after a repair. A Tourneau watch. And the next thing you know, like the next day, I see her with one of her own. How the hell did she do it? I could never have done that. What causes a child to steal? It's *pain*. Only an unhappy child would steal, I know that. A very unhappy child."

"Yes, if it's true, I agree that it does suggest unhappiness. But it's something that can be dealt with," I said. "She's asking for something—"

"You see. You understand!" She sounded exuberant at the idea that I did.

Then she said, "Will you treat her? Look, I think she should come in and see you, instead of me—"

"Wait, wait. That's not a good idea for a lot of reasons."

"Why not?"

"I'm not quitting on you, and you can't quit on her, and I'm sure you don't want to, anyhow. If she does need therapy someday, that's off in the future. You have to deal with her," I said.

"I can't. It's impossible for me to—"

"Why not?"

"George, that's the curse. *I've been stealing all my life.* Ever since I was a child. That's what I haven't told you. I thought I'd never tell anyone. Even if I got caught, I'd face it alone. I know how horrible and lonely it is to feel an absolute compulsion to grab something in front of you, to snatch it—a scarf, a ring, a handkerchief . . . a . . . a little box of tissues if it's loose on the counter, or an eye pencil or a comb. And to feel, every time afterward, such despair, such *misery*—like you're not part of the human race. To hate yourself.

"My God, I didn't want Julia to hate herself. I thought maybe even if my life was a mess—and it has always been—I'd make her life right and orderly. She's a bright child, George, very bright. She has a hundred and thirty IQ. Alan says that's almost a genius. It's like a curse on me that she steals. That's the only reason I'm telling you about myself—not for me. We've got to help Julia."

"Does Alan know about this?"

"About Julia?"

I nodded.

"No. He doesn't. I thought of telling him, but she would feel so terrible."

"Does he know about you?"

"Are you crazy? That would be his proof that I'm crazy. He thinks so, anyhow."

"When you were his patient . . ." I started to ask, but she broke in.

"I was thinking of telling him when he was my therapist. We talked about crime once in a while. Maybe I would have told him sooner or later. Maybe not. But then he proposed, and I accepted."

Then, as if telling me about Julia and herself was like removing the sliding panel from a whole crate of fears, Marianne asked me questions in such a flurry that I was hard put to remember them. "What is she stealing for—love, even though I always tell her I love her? Did she inherit this from me? Why do you think she does it? How can I deal with her when I do the same thing myself?"

I asked Marianne if she was positive that her daughter had increased her stealing in recent months.

"I think so. I can't be sure. My God, if she ever found out that I steal."

"You're sure she doesn't know?" I asked her.

"I don't see how she could. I'd rather go to jail than see her end up like me. I've already decided that if she gets caught and I can, I'm going to take the blame."

"Slow down," I said, rather crisply. "There's a lot we don't know yet. She certainly knows that you and Alan aren't getting along. Her world is shaky—that may be aggravating the problem. But stealing is not inherited through the chromosomes. You didn't bequeath to your daughter a gene that says, 'Steal!' You say you've stolen all your life. But millions of children steal at one time or another—maybe most do at some time in their lives— and the great majority stop."

"What can we do?"

"The important thing is that you told me this about her—and about yourself. And the other important thing for the future is that you not panic. You and Julia are *not* the same person. It isn't even sure that you're stealing for the same reason."

"I realize that. Can you help her?" It was as if Marianne had switched the entire beam of possibility from herself to her daughter, and Julia was the only one who counted. But both mother and daughter would suffer in consequence of such self-abnegation on Marianne's part.

I came in hard. "Think of it this way, Marianne. I'm going to try to help you, and you're going to help Julia. You're the only one who can. And you will."

"One thing I should tell you. I've always had a great fascination with crime—and with criminals. I mean murderers. Serial killers. Could that be important?"

"Did you ever know any?"

"No," she smiled. "I mean, reading about them, in the news and in books. Real ones, though."

I told her that I couldn't integrate that fact as yet, but I was glad that she'd told me, I wanted her to tell me everything.

I had taken pains all along not to say anything that might make me seem too intensely reactive to what she told me. Several times she scrutinized my face, almost certainly to determine if I had been shocked. She had a habit of trying to gauge reactions to her, like a cat putting weight down gingerly on planks of wood to see if they were secure.

Then, abruptly, she dropped the subject of her stealing, and of her daughter's. In conformity with giving her all the leeway she asked for, I inquired no more about what she had told me.

I had been expecting one kind of revelation and had received quite another. Instead of answers, I was being confronted with more questions. That weekend I did plenty of thinking about what Marianne had told me. I believed her implicitly that Julia hadn't seen her steal or seen items of Marianne's that she knew to be stolen. Nor, I was certain, had Marianne ever given Julia the license to steal, in words or by implication.

But I had many times seen the transmission of ideas and of actual behavior from one person to another without those ideas or behavior being performed or even mentioned. Indeed, instances of such transmission come as close to illustrating extrasensory perception as any I have ever seen.

Examples came to me readily. For instance, it is not unusual for a woman therapist very early in pregnancy to have patients dream that she is pregnant. In cases I had seen, the therapist had indicated nothing that she could think of, and yet—What had her patients recognized? How had they known, without even knowing that they knew? Conceivably, the woman had become somewhat more maternal toward these patients. Or had hinted unconsciously that she might be taking a forced break in the therapy, perhaps by pulling back to reduce the intimacy. The sensitive patient had seen the data and deciphered it in the dream, retaining the conclusion without realizing what it was based upon. But this is conjecture.

In any event, transmission is far more subtle than the identification of the means of transmission. We feel truths and, here, Marianne's stealing might have been one.

But not necessarily, I then thought. It might be that only the *ingredients* of the kleptomaniac were transmitted, the conditions. Marianne's attempts at submission to people failed because of a very poor ability to tolerate frustration—a catering but essentially choleric makeup—followed by the eruption of the attitude, "I want something now." Though Julia never actually saw her mother steal, she saw her mother blow up repeatedly, act on the premise, "Let the world go hang."

At such moments, she could have inferred her mother's pessimism, her mother's essential disbelief that honest effort over time was right and would win out. Very possibly, Julia surmised her mother's disbelief in herself, in her own credibility, in her own future, and Julia stole—stole, because, why not?

There might even have been some inherited biochemistry contributing to both Marianne's and Julia's inability to wait. However, no one can know that for sure in any single case, and of course even most children with poor tolerance for frustration do not steal.

On the other hand, it struck me that many children who have stolen when very young have been caught and punished—or at least redirected. And on that score Marianne had already defaulted. She had not been as stern as most mothers would be, perhaps because she saw herself as a thief and did not want to be hypocritical. If so, a cost of Marianne's own poor self-appraisal, combined with her conscious detestation of being fraudulent, was the inability to pounce on her daughter for stealing.

In that respect, it seemed to me, she might well be "transmitting" the problem. Even if Julia had been no more prone to stealing than any other boy or girl, but had merely toyed with the act, she was deprived of a mother who would set her straight.

I recalled a favorite concept of the great anthropologist Ruth Benedict that any individual can choose as actions "only a small segment of the great arc of human possibility." Culture, one's own society, which stimulates and encourages certain acts and trounces us for other acts, plays a critical role. Benedict was fond of calling human nature "plastic" and describing culture as doing the early selecting of what we start out doing.

Benedict's theory fit here. In many cases, stealing has been one of those behaviors tried in childhood. If your mother was Ma Barker, who taught her sons to pull holdups, you grew up in one kind of society. Most of us started our lives in quite another way. But, I could now see, if your mother was Marianne, incapable of condemning theft, you were somewhere in between. If this were so, then even without unconscious imitation on Julia's part, her own stealing did derive, though indirectly, from her mother's stealing.

I realized that, even though direct imitation was unlikely, Marianne was, paradoxically, doing havoc to her child by a kind of "fair play" that was anything but fair.

I was, of course, eager to convey this idea to her and to have her consider it.

April was in its promissory glory; the morning was resplendent. Marianne arrived early, looking very attractive in a black linen suit with white piping along the collar and around the cuffs. Her large silver necklace hung in several layers. I thought of her as a bit off chic, in the direction of artistic.

"No more cameras?" she asked, smiling.

"I see you're dressed for them," I said.

She explained that she had just come from a job interview at a breakfast. The group had found her credentials to be adequate.

"Their art director is leaving, and they want two people to fill his spot. I would be one, and I would also deal with some clients. It's a small firm, but they have some good accounts."

She said that the two partners both liked her. "John, he's about forty-four and very attractive. He's divorced. He has a daughter in ———"
She mentioned a very fancy private school.

I sensed relief and an ease in her style, but didn't know what to attribute it to. Possibly, her telling me about her daughter's stealing, or about her own, had helped her. I hadn't offered her any insights, but at least I knew and nothing was different.

She readily went back to these subjects, saying that she could hardly absorb the "incredible horror" of Julia's "doing what I did."

I agreed that, obviously, stealing wasn't what anyone wanted for Julia. But Marianne's phrase "incredible horror" implied nightmarish associations, and I asked her why she had used the term.

"Because if Julia feels anything like the way I do, it's incredible horror. That's why. Because I didn't even really *want* the things I took, and I suffered so much for them."

"Yes, you said you always suffered after taking something—"

"No matter how cheap the thing was. But I felt worse when it was expensive. I felt like I wanted to kill myself. I once took something, I forget what, and I had it under my coat, and I stood in the subway, watching trains and imagining myself jumping in front of each one. It's amazing that I didn't."

"What's your earliest memory of stealing something?"

"Oh, maybe I stole crayons in school, like most kids. But I didn't steal seriously until I was eleven or twelve."

"What kinds of things did you take?"

She rattled off a breathtaking history of thefts—of items always stolen one at a time. The list included scarves and skirts and blouses and fountain pens. The exception to the one-at-a-time rule was a fine pair of shoes that didn't fit.

"Did you try to take your own size?" I asked her.

"I don't remember. I was still growing, I think."

She said that in college she had stolen textbooks, whether she needed them or not. "My one rule was, I always stole from stores, never from a person. And I don't think I ever stole anything without feeling terribly sad, I mean miserable, for a few hours or a whole day.

"I once wore a whole outfit to a party where everything was stolen, and the boys said I looked great. The girls did too."

"What would you tell yourself, or think, about why you did it?"

"I'd say, 'Why should this store have the dress? Why not me? I want it. They're rich.' One day, I put everything I had taken into an old tattered suitcase. There was so much stuff I could hardly jam it all in, and I drove across the George Washington Bridge with it. I was going to drop it overboard into the Hudson. But there was too much traffic. So I left it on a street corner, somewhere in Harlem. I guess some poor person found it, maybe. I swore I'd never steal again."

"How long did that last?"

"No time at all. You guessed it. I was back grabbing things. Don't you think Julia must feel awful?"

"Possibly. I'm not sure."

"I used to say to myself, 'They won't notice, and they don't care, anyhow.' I used to have dreams that I got arrested, that I was in court and the judge would point to me and ask me, 'Is everything you're wearing here today really stolen? Is that what you're telling the court?' And in the dream, I would laugh and giggle, and the judge would laugh, too. It was a riot, but I'd wake up depressed. Can you make any sense out of that? Sometimes everyone in the court would be laughing. It was a comedy, the human comedy."

But then her face froze, and she said. "There was always this terrible pain. I don't want Julia to feel that pain."

"In other words," I said, "you stole, and right afterward you felt terrible—sometimes almost like jumping in front of a train."

"But I'm not clear. Did you feel guilty or were you afraid of getting caught?" I asked her.

"Guilty!" She enunciated the word sharply. "I never felt guilty. Never. Not for one second. That's your word, George. I'm surprised at you for that. You're being very moralistic. Criminals don't feel guilty or spend their lives worrying about getting caught. You don't understand the criminal mind. I do." She sounded almost proud of that understanding. "I never felt guilty—I mean, I never felt guilty until now, with my daughter."

"Then the great sadness," I protested, "that 'suicidal' feeling you described. How would you explain that?"

"I can't. I never could. I guess I just felt that I had a curse. Or there is a curse in the world somewhere. I was sad about that. Do you hate me? No, I guess you're not allowed to hate your patients."

I bypassed that last observation and honestly responded to what I perceived to be her real question. "Hate you? Not at all. I'm only sorry you've been so alone. In such pain for all those years. Even if it wasn't guilt, or worry about getting caught, it certainly was pain."

"That's very nice of you to say." She said this so dryly, I wasn't sure whether it was sarcastic or not. But then I saw that she really meant it. She sat there impassively, absolutely still, and tears rolled down her cheeks.

I asked her what she was thinking.

"I don't want Julia to be so alone, and she doesn't have to be. She has me. I can understand."

"I know you can," I told her. "Do you think she'd feel better if she knew you knew?"

Marianne breathed audibly but didn't answer.

After a while, still looking at the wall, she said, "Maybe."

Although she intoned this single word without emotion, or perhaps because she did, I felt sure she'd given the question a lot of thought even before I asked it.

Later, as she handed me a check for the month, signed by Alan, she said, "I'd really like to be paying you myself. That would make the most sense. And I will be soon. Very soon."

I took that to mean that she felt sure she'd be working soon and that she was coming to regard her therapy as worthwhile enough for her to pay for it. But the comment also had overtones of threat to the marriage. I wondered if she meant that she would soon be living alone again with her daughter, and paying for everything.

We were entering our fifth month, and though Marianne had trusted me with much, she still hadn't told me about the sexual abuse she had suffered. But I sensed that we were heading toward it. It crossed my mind that her husband's belittling the event, holding its very existence up to question, must have jarred her repeatedly. She must have wondered, suppose she trusted me with the story and I, too, disbelieved her.

I conjectured that Marianne thought it would be taking a great risk to tell me about it. But on the other side, now that she felt closer to me, her daily decisions not to entrust the story to me could be demoralizing her. She was prolonging the horror of the event by continually deeming it unspeakable and, at the same time, she was reconvincing herself that I would perhaps be unsympathetic—or would disbelieve her entirely, as her husband apparently did.

That I knew something about her, which, theoretically, I shouldn't have known, remained troublesome to me and complicated the issue. As it was, I worried that when Marianne finally told me and I mentioned Alan's allusion to it, she might feel betrayed that I hadn't brought it up myself. But however much I wanted her to tell me about the incident, I realized that it was still best to wait until she got to it.

She continued arguing with Alan, especially because she was now often refusing to go places with him. Alan had always expected her to join him at psychoanalytic lectures and at social gatherings with his colleagues. In the past Marianne had usually given in, even breaking dates with her friends to go with him. But now, since she had admitted to herself how uncomfortable those evenings were, she was turning down more of them. Alan's mode of pressuring her was to call her "immature." He was disposed to see all humankind as on a developmental ladder of mental health on which, presumably, the topmost rung represented full maturity.

However, Marianne had, herself, recently discovered a trump card that she was playing regularly. She needed only to imply that she might let slip that she had been Alan's patient, and he would instantly drop his argument and go along with whatever she wanted. Although Alan was by nature quite demanding, I had to admit to myself that in a way Marianne was blackmailing him, and quite successfully, in those arguments, though she was claiming only what she was entitled to.

In the next few sessions Marianne recalled other occasions when she had stolen. Rarely was her stealing premeditated; usually she took things on impulse. She said that she had sometimes felt a sense of urgency while stealing, though at times she felt nothing at all. But always there was that deep and inexplicable sorrow afterward.

No, that sad feeling was not guilt, she would insist.

Then what was it? I thought that a comment she made once might provide a clue. She had described her sorrow as an ache not just for herself but for the world, because there was something grievously wrong with it. But I could only wonder what she thought was so wrong and how her stealing seemed to address whatever it was.

Then, a few weeks after her original disclosure, Marianne told me that she had been caught once: "It was embarrassing."

She smiled. "I took a porcelain doll from a store. I thought it was just a toy, but it was actually a collector's item—worth a few thousand dollars. An old woman in a shawl, with her hands folded. I got as far as the door."

"The police came?" I asked her.

"Yes, and they called my mother. I guess I was about fourteen. We found some social worker, and he went with us to talk to the judge. Not in a courtroom, but in the judge's chambers. They all said that there was no way I was trying to steal anything, that I had just forgotten to put the piece down before leaving the store. They persuaded the judge, and he let me go."

Marianne looked absolutely grief-stricken. When I observed this and asked why, she replied only that yes, the whole thing was very upsetting.

"What in particular about it?" I asked.

"My parents never even asked me if I really stole or not. Or if I had ever stolen anything before. I said to myself, 'Even if they saw you taking something right in front of them, they still wouldn't believe it.' They didn't really *want to know*. The world doesn't want to know. That's sad, isn't it?"

I agreed that it was.

Instantly, I thought about that dream of Marianne's in which the judge knew that she was a thief, and everyone involved, including Marianne herself, giggled with joy. But though I would have bet that it was related to all this, at that exact moment I could not see how.

Marianne remembered that, after that incident in which she was caught but exonerated, she had stolen much more often. I asked her if the experience of being declared not guilty had actually spurred her on.

"Of course," she said at once.

"Why?"

"Because it meant that nobody gave a damn. Why shouldn't I steal? They didn't want to see it anyhow. And by the way, George, I never got caught again."

The picture of Marianne in the judge's chambers stayed with me. And of Marianne afterward—a little girl, confused and hopeless, running about in a world in which no one sees anything—in which no one cares. She might have been crying out to be seen and punished, but instead she kept discovering and rediscovering with every successful theft that there was no justice on earth.

Marianne had obviously left the stage of innocence too soon—and entered a world of cynicism where she still dwelt. But what had hurled her into that lonely world at so young an age? And how could I help her? Certainly not by proving that all criminals are apprehended. Marianne herself was living testimony to the contrary.

In order to help her I would have to understand the key events that had driven her to her particular view and that had inured her to so unhappy a life at so young an age.

Then it dawned on me that Marianne was subjecting her daughter to the identical experience that she herself had had. By disregarding Julia's stealing, she was plunging her daughter into the same kind of indifferent world that she had grown up in. I hoped that even before I understood what was going on with Marianne, this insight would give me leverage to help her give Julia a better chance.

In the next few sessions we talked extensively about why Marianne became so furious with Alan these days. Their fights were becoming more embittered. True, Alan was presumptuous and unduly fearful in telling Marianne how to behave in front of his friends, who were all colleagues as well. But Alan had always been that way. He would plead with her not to counter when his colleagues gave her meddlesome advice and not to sit in company resting her face on her hands and covering much of it while they spoke: "You look so depressed that way, dear, and you're not."

"But I am, when they come over."

"Not really."

"Don't tell me, 'Not really,' " she would say. "How the hell do you know?"

"Well, you don't have to announce to everyone, 'You're boring me to death.' "

"Well, they certainly aren't interested in my opinions on anything. In my *lay* opinions."

Irksome as Alan's expectations were, as boring as those "professional evenings" were, Marianne and I came to see, they cut especially deep because her parents' expectations of her during her childhood had been much the same as Alan's were now. Their premium was almost entirely on looking good.

Marianne was realizing increasingly how fearfully conformist her parents had always been. Their bugaboo, "the neighbors," held them in awe, and their cardinal rule was never to discredit themselves.

From their point of view, their home was a showcase, and any visitor could inform against them if he or she saw something amiss. They would start when even a delivery boy rang the bell, and would dicker for a while over who should admit him to their spotless kitchen. The one who took on the assignment was the one who felt readiest to face the outside world. "It was like one of those war movies," Marianne once said, "where someone has to volunteer for a dangerous mission and might never come back."

The more Marianne raked through her early life, the more she came to loathe the relentless good manners and suppression of self that had governed it. Of course, now it was too late for her to tell her parents what she really thought of their performance or to defy them. But she could defy Alan. She was finding it increasingly hard to comply with his requirements and those of his circle.

One night during an institute soiree, Marianne had almost burst trying to show respect. About a dozen highly respected analysts and a sprinkling of the most promising trainees had been invited with their mates to Madame Smyslov's impeccable Park Avenue apartment. The occasion was an American visit by a psychoanalyst from Berlin, Dr. Wierstrasse, an old friend of Dr. Smyslov and, according to Marianne, a man who seemed even more doddering than his eighty-two years would imply.

The group could not have revered him more. Wierstrasse had personally met Freud, and he was so frail that the company were sure they would never see him alive again. Both his frailty and his fame commanded docility from everyone there.

Toward the end of the evening, while munching her supermarket coffee cake, Marianne had found herself very interested in the topic that Weirstrasse was discussing with the masters of the institute. It was crime. The analysts were giving their psychoanalytic profile of the as yet unapprehended perpetrator of a string of major robberies that had been dominating the media. They hesitated before no inference, no matter how groundless, drawing conclusions from scraps of evidence that they had read in the paper. From the words of a note the criminal had left they inferred an Oedipal conflict. From the style of the handwriting, reproduced in the newspaper, especially its forward slant, Wierstrasse concluded that his Oedipal conflict was still unresolved.

They all asked Dr. Wierstrasse to go into more depth about the robber's childhood, and with the help of Dr. Smyslov, he did. The two traded insights into noted criminals of the past to document their insights. Wierstrasse felt sure that this particular criminal would be caught because of a trait that psychoanalysts call "undoing," a mechanism first identified by Anna Freud, Sigmund's daughter and a psychoanalyst herself.

Marianne and the lesser figures listened politely. The fledgling analysts, the wives of the old guard, and the few businessman husbands of the women analysts who composed the audience were not expected to have ideas worth presenting.

Marianne found the evening especially difficult. She had a great many thoughts about what was being said. She had long been fascinated by criminality, after all, and had read a great deal about criminals and their motives and careers. Only with great fortitude did she restrain herself.

In my office I think Marianne half expected me to have as little interest in her "untutored" opinions as the others had shown the night before.

After telling me about the conversation, she commented, "I think I really have some insight into how criminals think." She stopped herself abruptly.

"Really!" I said, and told her that sounded interesting.

She needed no more invitation than this. "Yes," she said. "Actually, I understand them a lot better than those analysts do. Maybe better than almost anybody.

"This bank robber. Oh, he wants the money, all right. I'm sure. But he loves reading about himself, too. That's why he writes those notes to the police and calls them. You know, Dillinger did that. He put in calls to Melvin Purvis, who was assigned to his case—he called him from all over the country. And Leopold and Loeb, after killing that boy, they sent notes to the police and even went to his funeral. I understand that."

"You do?"

"Yes. You see, the key thing about a lot of these criminals," she said, "is that they're making an announcement."

"An announcement?" I echoed her. "What are they announcing?"

I hoped that she was going to tell me something vital about herself, perhaps even give me the key to her stealing that I had been looking for.

But again she exclaimed only the fact: "Believe me, I understand this a lot better than those analysts do."

I did believe her. She had never before said anything so emphatically. In that moment, I had not a scintilla of doubt that she knew something that neither I nor the rest of our profession knew. I imagined her sensing it, knowing it by proxy, whatever it was, the way a mariner who has almost drowned can forever interpret and understand the blind ocean and what wreckage means better than the rest of us can.

"Those criminals are announcing that *there's no one out there,*" she explained.

"What do you mean?"

She looked at me intently. "They know this 'crime does not pay' stuff, it's a joke."

"Why a joke?"

"A joke because most criminals don't get caught. There's no one to catch them. There's nobody out there," she repeated.

"Look, George," she said, "when I was a little girl, I used to believe that God or society or someone would punish the wicked, and that they'd lose everything and have a rotten life. But I found out better. Half the time, the worse somebody is, the better the life they end up having. I'm telling you there's nobody out there to punish evil."

"What about the police?" I asked innocently. "Or the FBI?"

She laughed sardonically. "Maybe one out of ten crimes is solved, do you realize that? The police can't do everything. People don't give a damn unless they're the victims themselves. Your average person could see his neighbor getting robbed, and he wouldn't even turn around. Criminals know that. This is the real truth. They're the only ones telling the truth, really."

"The truth!" I was startled.

"Yes. They're announcing it all the time—that evil triumphs. And that nobody really cares enough to stop it."

"You mean that the world is chaos," I said.

"Exactly. Chaos." Again that decisive tone.

"And that's why you steal—to announce that?" I asked.

"I think so. At least it's a factor."

"And Julia, too. You're saying that she knows that."

"Maybe." She seemed taken aback, and she dropped her impersonal tone. "But Julia's life doesn't have to be chaos. She has me. That's why her stealing is so different . . . so . . . tragic."

"It's tragic because you love her, and you *are* there. No. I take that back," I said. "Not really there."

"What do you mean by that?"

"Well, you know she steals, but you pretend that it's not happening."

"I don't pretend anything."

"Marianne," I insisted. "You say you hate cover-ups. But you're engaged in a massive cover-up yourself. If Julia is really stealing, she *is* in a chaos, because you insist on pretending—"

"What do you want me to do? I can't be a hypocrite. How can I punish her for doing what I've done all my life?"

"I didn't tell you to do anything. I merely said that so long as you're silent, you're telling Julia that no one cares. She's in a world with no one out there—just the way you were, growing up."

"Well, right now, she's away for two weeks with her father, in California. There's nothing I can say to her, anyhow."

"Marianne, you're her mother. It's up to you. You asked me how you might be passing 'the stealing gene' along. I'm just pointing out a way that you might be. Maybe if you weren't stealing, yourself, you would have jumped in before this."

Marianne's comment about theft being an announcement that "there's nobody out there" stayed with me, of course. She had not spoken in the personal terms that patients most often use, "I was lonely, I had no one." Rather, she had expounded in universal terms, framing her conclusion not simply about herself, but about criminals in general. It occurred to me that if her thinking were taken one step further and applied to everyone, and not simply to criminals, it might pass as the premise of existentialism—or, more precisely, as the philosophy of the French existentialists.

But though Jean-Paul Sartre had made precisely the same assumption, that evil may well go unpunished, that, in effect, "there's no one out there"—no higher punitive power to enforce justice—he proceeded quite differently from that first premise. To the existentialists the inherent chaos we encounter does not warrant pessimism. It merely implies that it is up to us, as individuals, to create order out of the chaos we find.

As individuals, Sartre and those of his school have stated, we have the power to create ideal values by what we *do,* and thereby to make our lives meaningful. By striving for courage, we make courage important; by adhering to truth, we affirm the value of truth. And as for love: "There is no such thing as love but acts of loving," wrote Sartre. But acts of love *are* possible, and therefore all is saved. This was the step on which Marianne faltered.

The next day, to myself, I compared Marianne's view with that of the existentialists. Same premise, opposite conclusion. How had she miscarried? Without too much difficulty, I could infer the answer. I could see how Marianne had fallen short of seeing that values, even the world's worth, are created by each individual. For one thing, a great leap of faith is needed to take this next step. For another, a certain amount of security is needed. One needs love, and plenty of it—as a child or an adult—to face up to the fact that "there is no such thing as love but acts of loving." Such a concept comes precariously close to the simple notion that there is no such thing as love at all. As a child, Marianne was simply not equipped with either the logic or the love to make order out of chaos.

Of course, I had realized all along that Marianne's conclusion was too cosmic for a little girl to have reached it by pure thought. She had obviously reached such a vast and lonely conclusion through some hard experience, drawing the generality from a particular in her own life.

This time, as I wondered about her childhood, a different kind of question became silhouetted in my thoughts: What had convinced Marianne back then of the chaos itself, that all was permitted? What had taught her this terrible—but potentially wonderful—truth too early, before she could make the most of it?

Being sexually abused could do it, I had no doubt of that, if it were so. She would have to tell me more, I decided—and soon, or I could not possibly go further with her.

My final thought about Marianne that day was of a supreme irony in her makeup. It was that Marianne, who stole repeatedly, had perhaps a more profound sense of justice, and of disappointment at injustice, than virtually anyone I knew.

Marianne and Alan rented a house in Martha's Vineyard, where they were to spend the rest of August with Julia. I next saw her the following week, a few hours before she was to pick her daughter up at the airport. She told me that she was going to confront Julia on her stealing as soon as the right moment presented itself.

I was leaving New York City myself in a few days, and our next scheduled session wasn't for a full three weeks. That resumption week in September is always chock full of surprises for therapists. She looked wonderfully rested, and her face and arms and hands were a dark tan. I was struck, as I had been when I first saw her, by how straight her posture was, the bearing of a dancer or a young cadet. She did, in fact, look boyish. She said she'd spent a lot of time swimming and playing tennis, and she warmly inquired if I'd had a good vacation.

Then she said that Julia had admitted stealing.

"She had on a lapis necklace, which she said she'd bought in L.A. I asked her how much it cost. She didn't know. Then she changed her story, saying that her father had bought it for her. I told her good, we should get the receipt from him in case it gets lost. We're insured for theft. She turned white. Then I told her, 'Look, if you stole it, even if you stole that Tourneau watch and other things, I won't punish you, but please just tell me. I don't want you to have secrets from me. You never have to lie to me.'

"When she told me about her stealing, I felt terrible anxiety. It was like I was living my own life all over again. All I asked her was why she stole. She obviously didn't want to answer. She just said she didn't know, and I let it go. But she promised me she'd stop.

"Then we hugged each other, and she begged me not to tell Alan or Jeff. I said, 'This is just between us, but I'm going to tell my doctor,' and she said okay. I made her promise me again that she'd stop."

While she spoke, a flurry of thoughts had come and gone too fast for me to be sure what they were. Yet I felt a swell of excitement and knew that at least some of them were important, and I struggled to name them to myself.

I could sense in the unaccustomed softness of her tone and the fact that she allowed her eyes to rest on my face that she trusted me as she never had before. It was as if I had ranged the underbrush and recovered her long lost daughter before she froze to death, and now that Julia was in her mother's arms by the warm hearth, I was welcome too.

I was happy for both of them. Yet at that moment I also worried that Marianne might do what so many parents have done in resignation over their own perceived failures—make a child their exclusive project, their measure of success, while discounting their own lives. I certainly did not want the spotlight to continue on Julia alone while Marianne contented herself in the darkness.

I was delighted when in that same session Marianne went on to revel in her new, honest relationship with Julia. Talking on about it gave us both a chance to assimilate her accomplishment. Only later in that session did I look for ways to return the focus to Marianne.

She was still savoring what they had done. "Julia's very glad she told me, and so am I. We've been much closer," she said.

"She's not alone any more," I said, I thought innocently.

"She was never alone," Marianne retorted. "She only thought she was."

"Well, that's the same thing, isn't it?" I said.

"She has *me,*" Marianne said, disregarding my comment. "Julia is not alone, the way I was."

"Well, you're not alone now either," I said, "even if you were—"

Suddenly, her tone changed. "Not alone! Who have I got? You?" She asked this bitingly.

"No," I said. "You have Julia. Even though she doesn't know about your secret life, you know it. Maybe you owe her a real effort to figure out what's going on."

She smiled. "That's a cheap trick, George," she said.

I didn't know what she meant, and I said so.

"Using my daughter to get to me. It's important that I don't steal for my own sake, isn't that what you mean?"

"You mean, throw away all your stolen booty?" I asked her.

"You'd like that, wouldn't you?" she said.

"In a way," I admitted. "But that's not really what I had in mind. Think how much it meant to Julia to trust someone. Maybe you'll find someone you can trust—"

"You mean *you?*" she said sharply.

"Me or some other great doctor," I said, trying to lighten things up. She didn't reply, but she smiled again.

At the door she said thanks, and I knew she meant it.

When I'd commented that Marianne was no longer alone because of Julia, I'd meant that she could rely on her daughter for inspiration and for comfort. I had seen many a woman whose life had been diffuse and directionless saved by a child—by having someone she loved and was responsible for. But Julia had done something beyond that for Marianne. She had bravely confided in her mother and discovered that any fear she'd had of confessing was unwarranted. Perhaps it was this that gave Marianne the encouragement she needed, because the next time she saw me she finally divulged her dread secret.

"By the way, there is something I should tell you," she said, very blandly, halfway into the session. "I was molested, as a child. Sexually assaulted. It might be important. I thought I should tell you." She paused.

I waited, not wanting to press her on any subject, but especially not on this one.

She continued. "For a time, it tormented me. Then sometimes I wasn't even sure it had really happened. But I'm sure it did." She smiled faintly, but her subject matter certainly didn't warrant a smile on my part.

She stopped again, and I asked her to tell me anything more about the incident that she wanted to.

"Well, we lived in Summit, as I told you," she began. "We were about five minutes from this drugstore." She cleared her throat. "It happened in the neighborhood drugstore. I was about eleven. I shouldn't say that—I was just eleven. It was in March 1948. March eighteenth. The day after St. Patrick's Day.

"My father used to send me down to this drugstore, to Mr. Mack. He was a big, red-faced Irishman. They liked him. They thought he was a nice guy. My mother had bronchitis for months, and he would always recommend things. You know, a certain cough formula, or he would look at your bruise. I guess he was a good druggist—everyone used to say he was better than a doctor. I used to go there a lot when my mother was sick, and he'd always be sympathetic."

Marianne was still talking slowly, lackadaisically. She had a bleak, almost vacant look. But the urgency of what she was coming to was easily inferable from her next comment. "George, please don't interrupt me until I finish."

I promised her I wouldn't.

"Because I'm about to tell you about my first sex experience."

She said this quietly, but with a very deliberate irony, which I have never forgotten.

"Everybody worshiped Mr. Mack," she went on. "We thought he

knew everything. But I was never quite comfortable around him, even before that, even though he gave us candy. He used to comment to the girls about how they were growing up, and it made me nervous. And he was always asking me about my mother and telling me to take off my coat and talk to him awhile. He had this Norman Rockwell print behind the marble counter—of a doctor examining a child.

"Anyhow, my mother was sick. She was coughing like mad, and they sent me down there to get something. It must have been cough medicine, I don't remember what it was, but I came back without it." Marianne smiled insipidly again.

I knew where she was headed, and I girded myself to not twitch or say anything.

"There was a heavy rain, one of those downpours. But it had just stopped, and the air was very clear, like pure oxygen, and the streets were shiny. As I said, the guy always made me nervous, and I hoped some other people would be in the store. I didn't want him to ask me to stay and tell him about my mother or school. Or to ask me to take my coat off.

"I remember looking inside the shutters, and I could see only Mr. Mack in that short, white jacket of his. There was no one else there. He was doing some work with that old mortar and pestle they used to use—I don't know if they still use it. When I went in, he said he was closing up for the night, he was just waiting for me. Someone from home had called up ahead.

"I tried to stay away from him, but he started talking to me. When I backed away, he said I was impolite, and I explained that I was in a hurry. I don't know what happened, but he got mad and came toward me. He said, 'You need affection,' and he grabbed me. I tried to push him away, but he threw me down and he grabbed my breast and tried to put his finger in my crotch. He kept calling me impolite, and for a second I blacked out. I let him. Then he took some kind of chemical, now I imagine it must have been amyl nitrate—you know, what they call 'poppers'—and he sniffed it, and tried to shove it into my face.

"I don't know where I got the strength from, but I kicked him and I scratched him and I pushed him away, and a huge wall of medicines came crashing down, and he was astonished.

"I somehow managed to run past him and to the door. I prayed it was open, and it was, and I ran. But I fell down in a puddle. I looked back, and he wasn't actually chasing me. There was a big field I had to cross, there's a project built there now, but I went the other way because there were people in the street.

"A couple of people saw me, adults on the street, and a man got off a bike and came over to me and asked me if I was all right. I told him I was."

Marianne was by then telling the story at high speed and with great animation. But abruptly she stopped and asked me an amazing question: "Do you believe me?"

I must have looked as astonished as I felt, because she clarified: "I mean, do you believe that this really happened?"

"Of course I do," I told her, still incredulous. "Every bit. I mean, maybe there's some little fact you can't remember but I certainly believe—"

"I remember every detail perfectly. I thought about it a million times," she shouted. "And the details didn't change. The details *never* change. I didn't just imagine it. I didn't."

"Of course not."

She was crying so softly I hadn't noticed at first. The tears melted her mascara, and the hollows under her eyes became black. She swallowed hard.

"Of course, I remember it," she said. "For years it was the first thing I thought about waking up in the morning. Or in the middle of the night. I couldn't look men in the face after that, even boys who were my friends, I was so ashamed. For a while, I worried that I was pregnant, and I said if I was, I was going to kill myself.

"I would go and sit under a big oak tree right near us, and I would wish he was dead. I hoped that maybe I could forget. And then I'd remember that white tile floor and those big old four-blade fans coming down from the ceiling. I used to dream about spiders, and once there was a big pharmacy sign right in the web, and I knew it was him.

"Once I sat under that oak tree during a violent storm, and my girlfriends thought I was crazy, that I'd get struck by lightning. But I loved the storm—I still love storms—it was the only thing that understood me, the only thing I could talk to, the only thing violent enough. I used to sit there as a little child wishing I had brothers or sisters. But now when I went there I wished only one thing. I wished he would die. And then we moved and came to New York City."

"How old were you then, when the family came here?"

"About fifteen. But I still have some girlfriends from there. My friend Susan is from Summit; we were friends when we were in elementary school."

"You told your parents—"

"No, I didn't. My mother was sick, and my father said, 'Don't disturb her.' "

"You're saying that you didn't tell your father either?"

"No way. He was a friend of Mr. Mack. He thought Mr. Mack was a god, because Mr. Mack was so reliable and saved him all that money. He and my uncle used to play cards with Mr. Mack once a week."

"So you never told him?"

"No. I saw my blouse was ripped to shreds, so I hurried into the other room to change, and I used some of my mother's makeup to cover my cheeks because I'd been crying so much."

"But your father knew you didn't come back with the medicine. What did he say?"

"Nothing. Maybe he thought the drugstore was closed. He was tinkering with something at his workbench. I just went inside. I guess I hoped it was a bad dream. But I realized the next day that it wasn't. After that, as I said, it was the first thing I would think about when I woke up in the morning. And I would think about it a lot."

Our session was coming to an end, and I felt that, despite those natural frames that therapy necessarily takes place in, it was a very unfortunate moment for us to stop. It felt as if I were abandoning her. Obviously, I could not salve the hurt, but I felt the impulse to remain available.

That was, of course, impossible, but I told her to please feel free to call me later that day if she wanted to. Then I gave her a number where I was to be that evening and told her that I'd very much appreciate hearing from her if she had the slightest urge to call.

"Don't worry about it," she shot back, quite curtly. "I've lived with this all my life, and I can get through another day with it. Or a year. Or forever."

I didn't respond. Then she said, "I'm sorry. I didn't mean to be tough. I guess I'm a little crazy on this subject. But the important thing is that you do believe me. You don't think I made the whole thing up, do you?"

"Absolutely not," I said.

"Or that I encouraged him in any way?"

"Hey, if it was Julia, what would you say? she made it up, or she encouraged Mr. Mack?"

She looked at me agape, as if I'd just hit her with a right cross to the jaw.

"Well, you *were* Julia once. And there's still a lot of Julia in you. That's what makes you such a loyal mother. Call me if you want to," I said, disregarding her peppery rejection of my offer the first time.

She didn't call, and I hadn't expected her to. I realized that the mere fact of my being a man must have made it hard for Marianne to reveal need to me. At least, thus far in our relationship, in her eyes I still had some inevitable commonalities with Mr. Mack, as did any man who put himself forward sympathetically.

In the next session she said that she had told only two people about the attack over her whole lifetime. One was a man she had met at a sales meeting in Chicago, a married man whom she had spent the night with. "He didn't get too involved, and I knew he wouldn't."

The other was Alan, who had become so coldly clinical that she stopped abruptly. He told her about Freud's "seduction theory," that young girls are strongly prone to fantasies about being sexually intimate with their fathers, and sometimes other adult men who remind them of their fathers. Alan explained, quite accurately, that at first Freud had believed that these things had actually happened, but that later he had revised his view and decided that they had occurred only in the girl's teeming mind.

Alan had given her this protracted explanation on a night when they were in a hotel room in Washington, D.C. That night Marianne had conceived a hatred for him that she had vowed would be timeless—much like her hatred for Mr. Mack, I thought.

"I refused to have sex with him when he approached me a half hour later, and he was astonished. I guess he thought he won me over with that explanation. He got all upset. I went into the bathroom. He thought I was putting in my diaphragm, but I was masturbating, and I went right to sleep. I don't hate him, though. He's a decent guy. He really loves me, I think. He's just a wimp."

She told me the whole story of the attempted rape again the next week, and then the week after that. She wanted so much to talk about it that I could hardly believe her secretiveness over the years. But that very suppression of the event must surely have added to its eruptive force as she went over it with me.

I had no doubt that the whole episode was a primary cause of her distrust of genuine affection from a man, which she took to be possibly counterfeit or dangerous. As part of its fallout effect she had never let herself get romantically involved with any man who was intense and who was truly in love with her, though there had been a few. For husbands, she had chosen Jeff, who seemed always in transit and uncommitted and who had warned her that he didn't want to settle down; and then Alan, decent but detached—a man she was hardly acquainted with and one who certainly did not know her as a flesh and blood woman, so riveted was he to his theories.

After that, no matter what her topic—Julia, Alan, her ongoing attempts to land a job, even her relationships with women friends—I kept looking for other ways that the event had possibly affected her. What I could see was a pervasive secretiveness and a readiness to withdraw from all but Julia when things didn't go smoothly.

Besides putting her in shock, I had no doubt that the molestation had made her prone to withdrawal and to distrust people. Trauma experts who talk about the need for rape victims to begin therapy as soon as possible after the event might have been talking about Marianne. If only some loving adult had pressed her to talk about what had happened, she might not have surrendered so much hope.

As it was, thanks to Mr. Mack, she had turned from a joyous child into a bland one, taking less part in school activities and becoming quiet with her friends.

I could see in Marianne still subtler vestiges of the incident, excesses in her style that I would not have understood at all if I had not known about the assault on her and its horror. In my own mind I called it a rape, even though there was no actual penetration. The impact was certainly the same. In fact, at the time, Marianne herself, stunned and baffled, worried greatly that she might be pregnant. She even told me, "After that, I wouldn't go to a doctor for years. I thought he might know and ask me about it."

Within a month of the session in which she told me about the event, an incident occurred in Marianne's life that might have seemed meaningless, or at least inexplicable, were the episode not in the forefront of Marianne's consciousness—and mine.

Marianne and her friend Sarah were at an Italian restaurant from which Marianne had called Julia on a pay phone. She had been talking only briefly when a man "practically shoved his way into me because he wanted me to hurry. I shouted at him that I'd wrap the phone around his neck if he didn't step back and give me room. Everybody laughed, and the guy shuffled off.

"Sarah said that I'd make a good executive, that I didn't accept sexism. But then she said the guy wasn't all that obnoxious. He must have thought I was crazy. I think talking about Mr. Mack got me thinking again, maybe extra sensitive. Could that be?"

The question evoked in me a host of associations to that rape, and suddenly her whole "Don't crowd me" style made more sense than it ever had.

"Wait a minute," I said. "Don't you remember that guy in the street trying to wipe off your windshield, when you stepped on the gas? That was no joke."

"You know, I actually thought of him as like a rapist. These guys . . . You mean I'm oversensitive about people getting too close to me?" she asked.

"I could understand it if you were," I said.

Marianne had been well aware that her reactions to me were sometimes excessive. True, those various men who crowded her were vulgar and unfeeling. But the images that came to her mind, of murder and butchery, were reactions in part to unconscious memories, and neither Marianne nor I had any doubt that they included memories of Mr. Mack.

Apparently, Marianne felt suddenly concerned about her tendency to recoil when men came toward her emotionally, because she asked me, "Do I act that way with you?"

"What way, Marianne?"

"Treat you like Mr. Mack?"

I certainly didn't want to foster a cover-up, but I was reluctant to indict her.

I hedged. "Well, you sometimes can be a little snappy. Maybe if I say something warm sometimes, you push me away."

"I realize I do," she said, and we let it go at that.

Little by little, Marianne filled out the picture of how her early life had been marked and marred by the incident. She said that she used to be religious and say her prayers, but that she had stopped after the rape. "All I could think of was hoping he would die, and it was wrong to use prayers for that."

Another time, she asked me, "Does this sound crazy? I was afraid that everyone would find out."

"Not crazy at all," I assured her. "The terrible thing is that you actually treated the experience as if you had done something wrong."

When she said, "You really understand, I can't believe it," I observed to myself that it was the first time that she hadn't rebuffed my sympathy, and I was glad. Marianne was starting to look at the unfairness of her plight, not just as the victim, but from the vantage point of an adult looking at a poor girl who had suffered acutely.

One day she came in with a memory that she felt sure was relevant. "In my teens I would keep my coat on in people's houses. I was famous for it. My friends kidded me for not wanting to take my coat off—or at least some kind of jacket or sweater. I had this girlfriend, Vivian. Her parents were rich, and they had this basement setup where the kids could go to play.

"We spent a lot of time over there. There was a movie projector, and they had easels for the kids to paint on. The room was blue with recessed lights. It was fabulous, and her parents were terrific. I think they ran a mail order business out of the house, and they were very wealthy. Vivian and her sister were nice. But they would all kid me about not taking my coat off even when it was hot indoors.

"One day they were really kidding me, and Mr. Andrews—that was her father—told them to shut up. He said I could dress the way I wanted, and they shouldn't mention it again, ever. He said they were . . . they . . ."

She was crying, so suddenly and so profusely that she had not even thought of trying to control the tears. I had no idea what they meant, but just handed her a tissue.

"He said it was no way to treat a guest. He was furious. Oh, my God, I don't know what's gotten into me." She said this last at very high speed, staccato, in obvious haste to get the words out and not break down in the middle.

"Do you want to tell me what's so upsetting?" I asked her, as she wiped her eyes.

"I don't know," she said. "He was a very kind man."

"And keeping your coat on," I asked her. "What did that mean?"

"The significance is that it was after Mr. Mack, and he was always asking me to take my coat off so he could look at me. So I guess it affected me longer than I thought," she said, forcing a smile.

"But I take my coat off now, everywhere."

I asked her, "What about those sunglasses that you have on so much?"

"My God, do you think that could be the same thing?"

Of course I didn't know for sure, but I wondered aloud whether those sunglasses could stem from that same impulse to cover up.

She nodded. "I'll bet they do," she said. "Should I stop wearing them? Oh, I know you don't give advice. All right, people always complain about them, though you didn't. Did they bother you?"

"Well," I said, "I imagine that they must give a lot of people the idea that you don't want them to get too close."

"Did you feel that way?" She seemed genuinely concerned.

"A little," I admitted. "I can live with it, but it can't be good for you to do anything that renews your own sense of danger."

The session ended without my learning anything more about those tears that streamed down her cheeks when she thought about Mr. Andrews, who had so staunchly defended her right to keep her coat on.

When at last Marianne told me about going to Mr. Mack's funeral, it was almost anticlimactic.

I let her know that Alan had mentioned it on the phone, but I added that I wasn't interested in what other people said about my patients.

Then I held my breath, anticipating that she might consider one or both of us to have betrayed her. However, she seemed indifferent to what Alan had told me.

She explained, "I decided to go to that funeral after a discussion with Alan. Susan had told me that Mr. Mack was at St. Elizabeth's Hospital and that he was near the end. I actually toyed with the idea of going to see him in the hospital and telling him off. But I figured I had waited this long and a month or two more couldn't hurt.

"I decided that I would go to his funeral and denounce him to his own family. I would tell his two daughters what a filthy lowlife he was. You know, one of his own daughters didn't even go. She must know. Maybe he tried to fuck her, too.

"Alan begged me not to go. He kept saying, 'Let it rest.' That's his philosophy of life. We had several big arguments. He started them. He'd ask me if I was going, and when I would say, 'Definitely,' he would ask me why I had to go. 'Because people like you don't really believe it happened,' I would tell him. Then he would say again, 'Let it rest.' "

They had finally struck a deal.

"I would go, but not say anything. I would just enjoy it. I would just watch and listen and *enjoy* it. Alan couldn't understand that. Can you?"

"Very easily," I said. "It's the next best thing to killing him yourself—"

"You get it. But I had to wait too long."

"Did you enjoy the experience?"

"Not really. I guess I just don't like anyone's funeral if I don't like his. But it was something I had thought about so much."

★ ★ ★

That weekend—we were well into our second year—I kept picturing Marianne as a teenager, sitting alone under that oak tree thinking about Mr. Mack and consoled only by the vindictive beating of the rain. By then we had gone over the episode innumerable times, but it was almost as if the more I learned, the more I sensed the absence of a very important piece of the puzzle. Indeed, that piece was so thoroughly missing, with all its traces, that I couldn't identify precisely what I was searching for, not even well enough to formulate a useful or valid question about it.

I was in a Broadway theater, stirred by a revival of the Eugene O'Neill play *Emperor Jones*. The first act ends with Jones, the self-styled emperor of a little island, running for his life from the natives. Jones can hear the steady beat of the drums of his pursuers off in the distance. The director of that production kept those drums going throughout the intermission; it was quite effective, with the result that the audience, too, felt pursued.

Most left their seats, and I found myself alone, responding to those tom-toms and thinking about Jones—and also about Marianne, interchangeably. Was not she, too, royalty, as all children are at the start, but driven forever from grace? Again that missing piece mocked me by its absence. I tried to call my wandering thoughts together, but I might as well have attempted to summon back the audience departing through the many exits.

It seemed only moments later when the bell rang and the crowd returned. Then, just as the theater went dark, a whole new perception of Marianne's childhood came to me.

Perhaps because Emperor Jones was an utter stranger among natives on an island, an old question about Marianne became prominent: Why hadn't she *ever* gone to her parents and ended her terrible isolation? She had actually taken great pains to slip out of her torn blouse and to hide signs of injury by applying makeup, so that her father would never find out what had happened.

Previously, I had glossed over this question as if I knew the answer. Many girls, and adult women, too, feel too ashamed to talk about a forced sexual experience. They imagine that silence will help them get over it faster. I had unthinkingly construed Marianne's secrecy as a natural, though especially sad, part of the tragedy.

But that night in the theater I felt sure there was more to Marianne's secrecy than that. The trauma of the rape alone would not have separated a girl so completely from her parents if she had always felt truly close to them. Even those little girls who felt responsible and sinful, if the relationship at home was good, would almost surely, over a period of months or years, break down and talk about their pain. In this respect, a child's response to a rape, as to any other tragedy, mirrors what that child's life is already like, at least to some degree.

What struck me now was the enormity of the fact that Marianne had made a life's work of guarding her secret and of bearing it all alone. Moreover, the aura of distrust about her seemed enveloping, so much so that I doubted that it could spring from one event, no matter how awful.

As I thought about it, I could only conclude that at the time of the molestation Marianne had had a lot less faith in her parents than she had let on. She had often said that she wasn't close to her mother. But her father— now I realized that something must have been very wrong in that relationship, too. Undoubtedly, even before the rape, she must have despaired of reaching him—of his hearing her out and believing what she said. Otherwise, Marianne at age eleven would undoubtedly have rushed to him and told him when tragedy struck, instead of feeling forced to live alone with her experience over all those years.

I then saw the rape not simply as causing Marianne's distrust of all men, but as accenting a distrust that was already there. Marianne had felt terribly misunderstood and uncared for *well before the rape*—I felt certain of it. She had felt ignored and unworthy. She had felt unloved even by her father.

No wonder she didn't expect people to believe her now—and was so astonished when they did. She had been reared by parents like Alan, who discounted what she said. She was far more used to people like Alan than to those who accepted her, as I did.

Of course Mr. Mack's violation of her was every bit as horrible as I had thought. But its *lasting* power, its impact of isolating her utterly, even into adulthood, derived from Marianne's own vulnerability at the time it happened. Mr. Mack had delivered his blow to *an already wounded person*. Marianne, feeling unable to confide in her parents, lacked the resources that at least some other girls in her position could muster.

And if she had told her father, outright and at once, how would he have reacted? The answer to that question would succinctly summarize Marianne's entire home experience.

I was stunned by the force of my conviction that all this was so, and I wondered where my discovery had come from. Marianne's parents' stress on propriety, her own secretiveness, and the fact that she had opted not to tell them about so dire an event—these were all evidence. Still, I felt sure, I must have observed something else in my recent sessions with Marianne that had brought the whole picture into focus. I strained to identify what it was, but I could not pin it down.

The play was again on stage. I'd already missed a few lines, and I thought no more about Marianne at the time. But it is always disquieting to know something and not know how we know it. And not until two weeks more had gone by did I identify that elusive piece of data that had told me what I now knew.

I had remained hesitant to ply Marianne with questions about the Mr. Mack episode and her long silence after it, still hoping to learn what I could more gradually as facts emerged.

We were talking about some friends of hers in Summit, and when she mentioned Vivian's father, I brought up that incident when he defended her right to keep her coat on. This time she was barely able to restrain her tears.

I asked her why she felt so moved by his taking her part.

"Because he liked me and he understood me. So did Vivian's mother."

"In some ways, I guess, they were every bit as understanding as your own parents, weren't they?" I said.

"More. I could say anything to them." She stopped, and I could see that she was uncomfortable. However, rather than attribute that feeling to anything we were saying, she ascribed it to the atmosphere in the room.

"It's hot in here, isn't it?" She looked over at the radiator, and I got up to make sure it was off. It was.

"I have the idea there was a lot you couldn't say, even to your father," I suggested.

She nodded. "That's right. There was a lot I couldn't say. They were both so uptight and scared." Then she looked startled. "How do you know?"

"Well, you never told him about Mr. Mack, and you're always so surprised when I completely believe what you say, when I listen—"

"What has Mr. Andrews got to do with it?" she asked.

"You were so moved by him," I said. "I got the sense that his reaction to you was unusual. I mean, that you weren't used to someone so involved with you, to someone defending your rights so staunchly—"

"You're pretty smart, aren't you?" she said saucily, but with good spirit.

"Well, I didn't really figure it out," I confessed. "It sort of came to me gradually."

Then I explained to her that almost every child has had the experience of seeing startling novelty in a friend's home, of seeing life as the child had never seen it, never even imagined it, before. "It usually comes as a shock," I said. "For one child, it's the shock of seeing a friend's parents kiss, if the child's own parents never did in public or if they silently detested each other. For another child, the shock might come after seeing a grownup admit a mistake to a child. Or it could be seeing another kid's parents look up a word in a dictionary."

I told her that I remembered my own astonishment when I first heard classical music filling up an apartment, since there was never any played in my home.

Then I explained that if we look back at our surprise, even years later, it can tell us a lot about our own household. While growing up we think that what happens in our home is the only way, that it's universal. "And if you were so stunned at Mr. Andrews, I realized a few minutes ago, then you didn't really expect any adult to fight for your rights."

"No, I didn't."

"Which might be a reason why you never told them—"

She fidgeted in her chair, and I stopped abruptly. I had the impression that I'd said more than enough for one day.

By then Marianne was seldom invoking her lackadaisical tone with me. But in its absence, I realized what it meant. It was a shield against the experience of reporting something of great import and having the other person disbelieve it or treat it indifferently. Marianne would affect blandness specifically when conveying a loaded truth; then, if the other person disregarded her, it wouldn't be nearly as painful.

I didn't mention that mannerism of flatness or my discovery about it to Marianne. But I took it as a signal of her new trust in me that she had dropped it and that she now spoke to me with steady animation. She had always been an inwardly copious person, full of emotions, associations, and ideas, and I felt sure that her newfound freedom of expression would extend itself to at least some other people before long.

A few days later, Marianne reported that she'd caught Julia stealing again. This time it was a music cassette that Marianne knew Julia was planning to buy with her next allowance. Seeing the cassette on Julia's desk two days before her allowance was due, Marianne had exploded and Julia had confessed to stealing it. Marianne then scolded her daughter with a ferocity that startled both of them.

"What's so bad about taking a five-dollar cassette?" Julia had pleaded with mock innocence.

"Bad! It's bad to be a thief. In this world, you're either a thief or you're not. And if you're a thief, you're a *freak*," Marianne had expostulated. "It's wrong. When you walk into a store, I don't want you walking in like a freak. Why couldn't you wait three days and you would have had the cassette legitimately!"

In my office, Marianne repeated to me what she had said so often before: "I won't have Julia being the way I was. She told me yesterday that a couple of her friends steal, and I told her that I don't give a damn about what any other kid does. I told her that the next time I catch her, it will be a lot worse for her. She swore to me again that she'll stop."

A month or so later, Marianne told me, "I've got some very interesting information for you."

She said that she and her friend Susan had been talking about dishonesty in children. Susan's eight-year-old son had been lying to her regularly, and Susan had asked Marianne what she would do if her child did something like that.

In the past Marianne would have been at a loss. But having loosened a bit toward people, and perhaps because she now saw a young girl's dishonesty more as a sign of distress than as a heinous crime, she sought to allay Susan's chagrin by telling her that many kids experiment with dishonesty.

Marianne went on to say that she felt convinced that a child needs firm boundaries. She encouraged Susan to put a high premium on honesty and to insist on it. Then Susan mentioned that her husband felt the same way, and she seemed reassured.

"But *then*," Marianne said, "Susan reminded me that apropos of what she called a dishonest stage in kids, *I* used to *steal* as a little girl. Of course, she had no idea that I'd kept going as an adult—she only mentioned it to show that kids go through stages and come out of them. I asked Susan what she remembered, and she said that I always used to take things from the neighborhood drugstore. I would even take things for her, like lipsticks that she wasn't supposed to have, and cigarettes for some of the other girls. I didn't remember that. But when Susan said it, it came back to me.

"So *that's* what I wanted to tell you. I *did* go back into Mr. Mack's store. I went back a few days later, and he wasn't there, and I grabbed something. I didn't remember any of that until Susan reminded me.

"I still forget a lot of the details, but I remember Mr. Mack's big, pale face, and the swing of that huge body. He would come over to me and say, 'What have you got there?' And I would say, 'Nothing.' But he knew. It could be a perfume or a lipstick I already had—often things I didn't even want. I always waited until other people were in the store. Once I took a vial of something, I didn't even know what it was, and he came toward me and said it was for somebody, to put it back, he didn't have anymore. And I said to him, 'Grab me. Just grab me again, why don't you? Why don't you call the police, I'd like to talk to them.' He didn't say a word. He just walked away."

"So that was your revenge," I said.

"I guess so." She smiled broadly.

I said, "It wasn't really much revenge for what he did to you," and she agreed.

"No, and he was certainly lucky that my parents were such uptight people and that I never let them know."

I thought again of her sneaking into the bathroom that night and applying her mother's makeup to cover her bruises, and of her stashing away that torn blouse, and of her thinking up a quick excuse for returning without her mother's medicine. Her parents, in blindly worshiping "respectable" people like Mr. Mack, were almost Marianne's enemies in such a situation—or at least, she thought so, or she would have turned to them for solace and perhaps even real revenge.

Marianne said that she felt sure she'd never stolen from stores before Mr. Mack. "It just wasn't the way I was brought up."

But she had promptly made up for lost time, visiting his store every few days and leaving with something.

"Mr. Mack got to know why I was there, but he couldn't say a damn thing," she told me.

Sometimes she had watched him afterward, from across the street, as he went to the shelves where she had stood, and scoured them to see what she might have taken.

"Did it help?" I asked her.

"Possibly. A little. But it was never enough. I think I told you I always felt terrible ten minutes later."

"Even after taking things from Mr. Mack?" I asked her, a bit surprised.

"Yes. Even with him."

I asked her to describe that experience again.

"It didn't matter what I stole. Once the rush was over, it was always the same. I don't remember when I started going to other stores, but it was the same everywhere. I'd sometimes go in not intending to take anything, but then I would, and before I knew it, I was gone with it. I was good at stealing. But after it was over, I always felt unbelievably miserable."

Recalling Marianne's blasting me for suggesting that the feeling might have been guilt, this time I simply asked her if she had any idea why she had felt that way.

"None. But you can't believe how bad I did feel. By the way, a few weeks ago, I felt like taking something from a store, but I didn't, and I got over it fast. I forgot to tell you that. I'm sure I'm never going to steal anything again."

I asked her why she was so sure, and she said she didn't know.

Then a curious question came to me, which at the time seemed more capricious than apropos of anything Marianne had been talking about. But I asked it anyhow: "Marianne, have you ever felt like stealing anything from me—from my office or maybe from my waiting room?"

She responded in that familiar, bland way that I hadn't heard in months. "Well, actually, yes. When I first came here, it was in my mind, even though, of course, you would definitely have known it was me."

"What went through your mind?"

"Well, I like those old-fashioned ceramic elephants you have in the waiting room. They look like a mother and daughter. Anyhow, the little one with the missing tusk being protected by the big one. I used to think about grabbing the little one."

"What stopped you?"

"I don't know. And please don't analyze why I would take the little one and not the big one. Because it was lighter, that's all. I don't know what stopped me, but I never have the urge anymore."

"Have you any idea why not?" I asked her.

"No, I really don't. Oh, I know you don't accept that answer. All right, you're always telling me to say whatever comes to my mind, and I'll tell you the first thing . . ."

I waited.

Then she said, "Because you wouldn't be surprised. You *listen* to me."

"You don't want to steal from me because I listen to you?"

"No, it's not that either, really. It's just that I wouldn't be proving anything. . . . Come on, I don't know where this is all going. I don't even like the subject of my stealing from you. Let's change the subject."

We did. Marianne was about to return for a third interview at an ad agency that she was talking to about a job, and she felt confident that she would finally be back at work soon. She wanted to talk about the interview, which was coming up the next day.

After the session, I felt great elation at having linked her stealing to Mr.

Mack's abuse of her. She, too, seemed more confident—even optimistic. But, as I thought more about it, I realized that I still didn't understand how the rape was connected with her continued stealing, though I suspected that it was. If Marianne had come to hate men after her experience with Mr. Mack, that certainly would have been understandable. Even so, simple revenge against one man, or even *all* men, was insufficient explanation of a lifelong pattern that extended to people, men and women alike, far removed from Mr. Mack.

We were headed toward some bigger discovery, but it was hard to tell how near or far away it still was.

Marianne got the job; she would start right away doing the layout for a series of perfume ads and attending meetings with the client. Alan wasn't overjoyed—it meant that Marianne would do some traveling, and with her new financial independence she would be less reliant on him than since the day they had gotten married.

She still accompanied Alan to a fair share of gatherings with his psychoanalyst friends, where she still sat obediently, regardless of how she felt about what they were saying. Few in attendance knew her as an individual, or wanted to; that she had gone back to work drew interested questions from only one or two.

But, in their defense, Marianne, being so reluctant to talk about herself, was an unwitting accomplice to being overlooked—to being regarded as the wife of a rising participant in the institute rather than as an individual very worth knowing.

Marianne soon impressed people on the job with her creativity and she fit in well. Almost from the start she was given more responsibility.

And she began to see me more as an ally—to trust me more.

I assumed that this owed partly to the good discussions we'd had about Mr. Mack and about Marianne's stealing. In telling me about her stealing, it was as if Marianne were finding a kind of redemption, like a repentant sinner. In a sense, she could relive those lonely, "nefarious" acts of hers with me at her side—entering stores, seizing objects with me along with her, leaving with them, and then sharing her sadness, oceanic and still inexplicable.

Although I obviously hadn't intended my improved relationship with Marianne to diminish Alan's status with her, I was afraid that this was precisely what was happening.

One night, after a quiet period, Marianne was more brutal toward Alan than she had ever been; it was as if she'd saved up all her venom for months.

They had just spent time with his fellow professionals, and as always, Marianne had squelched her opinions all evening. But on this night, as soon as they had closed the door of their apartment, she had gone on a tear, telling him how much she detested his friends and why. Nothing Alan had said could slow her down.

I could sympathize with Marianne's frustration. But her rage toward Alan that night reached a level certainly not warranted by anything they had said or done. It was as if she were drawing her intensity from the past—from that inveterate hatred of Mr. Mack and possibly others—and directing it all against Alan.

I didn't make that interpretation outright, but when she quoted Alan as having said that she didn't really give his friends a chance, I didn't oppose him.

"What kind of chance?" she asked me.

"You'd have to express your real opinions and see how they reacted."

She glowered at me.

Then I did interpret. "Maybe you had good reason not to confide in your father. Though maybe even *he* would have backed you up more than you realized. We'll never know. But as for these people, we don't know how they would actually respond to the real you—"

"So you *agree* with Alan," she said, murderously.

"Not always, of course. But this time, maybe he's right, that you're not giving them a chance—"

"You son of a bitch," she said, and then caught herself and laughed, as if taken aback by her own ferocity toward me.

In commenting upon Marianne's silence with a collection of "fathers," I felt that I was virtually talking about that long, bitter silence she had maintained in her own home.

It seemed almost coincidental when, a week later, Marianne broke her silence about the past and talked about Mr. Mack to her old friend Sarah. But I was sure that it wasn't coincidence. Our work together had invited her to speak out, and Sarah, being a very old friend and a woman at that, was the natural choice.

Marianne had often discussed office politics with Sarah, who was a highly paid executive and knew the ins and outs. She had welcomed Sarah's insights and encouragement.

On this particular night, after a few drinks, the two of them had begun talking about how different the world was from the one they had looked ahead to as children. Sarah, who was from Chicago, was once again recalling how her own childhood had changed when her father, a successful businessman, had run off with a young secretary and left the family with very little money to get by.

She had said, "My sisters and I grew up in a hurry."

It was a perfect lead, and this time Marianne told Sarah about Mr. Mack and what he had done to her. Seeing Sarah quite moved, Marianne strained her memory for details, not just of that fateful evening, but of her reactions later. Sarah could hardly believe that Marianne had told no one at the time and only a few people over her whole life. She applauded Marianne's going to the funeral and said that she wished she could have gone with her.

"I told her about my robbing Mr. Mack, and she strongly approved. But I didn't want to tell her that I'd stolen from other places after that."

"Why not?"

"I didn't think she'd understand. I don't fully understand myself."

I let that subject go. I could see that Marianne felt greatly cheered by having allowed a good friend into her secret world, and I was glad to see her bask in that feeling.

She said, "I know it sounds crazy, but the whole incident actually feels more real to me now. As if I'm surer that it happened. Oh, I always knew it did, but it seems more flesh and blood now. I didn't cry at all when I was telling her. Don't you think it was good that I told her?"

I agreed that it was. "There's no reason why you should have to be so silent. You did nothing wrong."

"It seemed different when I was telling Sarah," she said. "Something else came to me that I hadn't remembered before."

"Really! What was that?"

"I think I told you that it was raining that night. It was a silvery rain. It was just stopping when I went home."

"You did."

"There were only a few people on the street. I remembered the face of that man on the bike who asked me if anything was wrong, if I needed any help. I could see his face vividly. He looked so shocked when he saw me."

"Yes, you mentioned him."

"It poured again later that night. A big storm. I remembered when I was telling Sarah that I thought the sun was never going to come out again—like in one of those end-of-the-world movies. And when the sun did come out the next day and there were the usual people on the street, I was really amazed."

"That's very sad," I said, caught up in the vividness of her recall.

"Yes, it was like it shouldn't happen. That people shouldn't just go on—"

"You mean, go on as if nothing very unusual had taken place?"

"That's right. As if the world didn't give a damn."

Talking about the rape to Sarah had been a giant step forward. Not only had doing so buoyed Marianne's spirits, it had actually enabled her to see the past somewhat differently, as talking about long ago events to new people often does. After telling Sarah, Marianne became softer toward herself and more accepting of her own vulnerability.

I recalled a paper written in the 1940s by the interpersonal psychoanalyst Harry Stack Sullivan, in which he talked about repression as a relative phenomenon. According to Sullivan, we don't simply repress memories or not. Rather, we repress partially and selectively. The very shape and detail of a memory is influenced by the person we are talking to.

In thinking about this, it occurred to me that I could learn something more about Marianne by reviewing the way she remembered the incident for Sarah and for me. When telling Sarah, Marianne made even more of that man on the bike than when she had mentioned him to me.

In fact, every single time she had ever talked about that horrible evening, she had mentioned him. I wondered about this man—he was an invariant, no matter which other details went in or out of her account. I think I sensed even then that his existence meant something special to her.

Several weeks later Marianne trusted another audience with her story, an audience that I never would have expected her to confide in.

"I told them all," she announced.

"Who?"

"Smyslov and the institute," she stammered.

"And they didn't believe you?" I was almost afraid to ask the question.

"Maybe a few of them didn't. But the rest *did.*" She piped out that word "did" in a treble.

"A man named Dr. Miller—he's a creep—had just given a speech at the institute on Freud's theory of hysteria. He said that little girls only *imagine* that men—like, for instance, their own fathers—molest them. During the question period, someone in the audience asked Miller if Freud really believed that all stories of childhood molestation were figments of the imagination.

"Miller said that Freud had originally believed his patients when they said they were molested as children, but then he changed his mind and decided that for the most part these things didn't really take place."

Marianne raised her hands in ironic resignation.

"That was it," she said. "That was the end of it. Everybody just let that answer go. I couldn't believe it. They all went on to the next question as if they were totally satisfied.

"Afterward, there was a reception at the home of one of the other big shots, Dr. Nandor, I think I mentioned him."

I nodded that she had.

"He has all these lush armchairs where you sink in and can't get up.

And these black-and-white photos of singers and music people on all the walls, with their autographs and little notes to him. His wife is a singer, retired, but a lot younger than him, and she said, 'Well, there must be some girls who really do get molested? What happens to the ones who do get raped and are telling the truth? What happens to them?'

"Smyslov told her that the unconscious doesn't know reality from fantasy. The woman said, 'I don't understand,' and I saw her husband give her a sharp look, as if to say, shut up, you're not bright enough for this company.

"So I said, 'I was sexually assaulted, and it was real. How many of you in here believe that?'

"For a minute, no one said anything. Then some very old guy, he's really a very dear man, Louis something, said, 'Marianne, if you say so, I do. It must have been terrible. How old were you?'

"I told him eleven, and said it was a druggist right in the neighborhood, that everyone thought was great. They listened to me, but they were twitching in their chairs. Smyslov's wife left the room, and I could see that Alan was desperate for me to shut up, but I decided I'd give them every detail. So I did."

Suddenly, Marianne was fighting tears. She said in astonishment, "They were incredibly sympathetic. They all believed me. And the old man said, 'I'd like to give you a hug. You went through so much.' And I said, 'Louis, please do,' and he hugged me." Here Marianne smiled. "And just then, that was when Madame Smyslov came back into the room. They were all so human, except her, of course, that I couldn't believe it."

"So the world isn't all that bad," I said, not really knowing what to say.

"It's crazy, isn't it?" Marianne agreed. "I can't believe they were so decent. They're not all bad, I guess."

"You gave them the full story, huh?"

"Yeah," Marianne said. "They liked that man on the bike. He was . . . he wa—." Then, as if some phantasm had condensed from nothingness in front of her, Marianne stopped fighting to regain composure, and she gave in to an onslaught of tears.

Whatever it was that halted her narrative, it seemed so vivid and palpable to her that I had the urge to ask her not what she had just thought of, but what she had just *seen*. I waited before saying anything, and then went back and asked her about that unforgettable figure.

"Did you just realize something about that man on the bike, Marianne?"

"I don't know. I told you he was zipping right along on the other side of the street. When he saw me, he rushed off his bike, and he came over to me, and he asked me what had happened. I told him, Nothing, but he said, 'Come on. It isn't nothing, it can't be. How did your clothes get so ripped? And your face is all red. Are you hurt?' And I told him, 'Not really.'

"Then he said, 'I can leave my bike here and walk you home. I have . . .' " Marianne continued to cry. " 'I have two daughters, they're a little older than you. They're away in college, and I know they don't always like to talk. You don't have to talk. But I'll walk with you if you want me to.' "

Marianne sucked in air, as if she needed it for the strength to continue. "But I told the man, no thanks," she said, "and so he left on his bike. But he looked back once to be sure I was okay."

"He sounds like a wonderful person," I said, "that man. But what upset you so much when you were talking about him? Do you remember?"

She just looked at me as though I ought to have figured it out. And maybe I should have.

"Because he cared so much," she said.

That instant I remembered Mr. Andrews and how his staunch defense of Marianne had made her cry. And now she was crying because those analysts had been so unexpectedly warm. And the man on the bike—they were all saying the same thing. There are people who care, even though you don't believe it.

"Marianne, did you actually try to tell your father that night?" Even as I asked the question, I knew the answer was yes. My own conclusion stunned me. And I did not even yet know how I had reached it.

Marianne didn't answer me right away. She ran her fingers through her hair and looked perplexed.

After a while, she said, "I guess I did." She seemed startled. "Isn't that amazing? I didn't remember that until just now."

She paused again, and looked away for a moment as if revisiting the scene. "Now that I'm really thinking about it," she went on, "I can picture my father looking shocked when I walked in that evening. Obviously, he must have seen that something terrible had happened, that my eyes were puffy from crying and my clothes were a mess."

Again she waited, as if more seemed to be returning to her.

I didn't want to press her, and yet I knew that this part of her story had to be told. It was the key to everything that I'd been waiting to discover. And, in a sense, she had been waiting, too.

"Do you remember what your father *did* right then?" I asked her hesitantly.

"He ran over to me, I think. He asked me what was the matter—I guess he thought I fell down or was beaten up by a bully, or something. And now I remember, I told him, 'Mr. Mack tried to rape me.'"

Suddenly I realized what had already suggested this, and had brought the memory back to Marianne at the same time. It was that man on the bike. Obviously, if that man riding along across the street from her could see Marianne's condition in the semidarkness, and it looked serious enough for him to go over to her, then her father must have seen it, too.

"What did your father say?" I asked Marianne.

Now her answers came quickly, as if the first few jolts of remembrance had brought the whole scene back.

"Well, he asked me if I was hurt, and I said, no. It was stupid of me to say that, wasn't it? Now I realize that I should have said, yes. Instead, I tried to tell him how Mr. Mack had tried to feel me up, but my father didn't want to hear it. He pulled back. He asked me if I was sure. I could see that my father was in a panic. He pointed to my clothes and asked me, 'You're saying that Mr. Mack did that?' and I said, 'Yes, he did.'

"Then my father said, 'I need time to think. Get changed and come back in here.' He was trying to fix an old radio. He liked to do that kind of thing, and as I left the room I heard him going back to it. As I told you, it had rained that night, and I could hear a lot of static. I imagined that my father was working on the radio while he figured out what to do about Mr. Mack.

"But when I came back in, all changed, with a new blouse and makeup on, he said, 'There, you look a lot better,' and he didn't say anything more. No," she corrected herself. "Actually, I think he said, 'We can't do anything tonight, and I want to sleep on it.' But, of course, I was sure he was going to do something—"

"And he didn't?"

"No, the next day he didn't mention it. I still figured he was deciding exactly what to do. Gee, I guess I really hadn't remembered the whole thing at all the other times I told you about it, George. I hadn't remembered a thing about those conversations with my father."

"That's okay," I reassured Marianne. "You remember it now. So you and your father discussed it after that, I assume."

"I brought it up. Or, I mean, I tried to."

"When was that?"

"Well, the next day when I saw he still wasn't doing anything. I guess I had some really weird ideas about what he was planning. I was actually afraid he was going to kill Mr. Mack. After that, my father wasn't around for a week or so—"

"Where was he?"

"He just wasn't around the house very much. Maybe he was avoiding me."

"And you didn't tell your mother either?"

"No, my father asked me not to. He said he'd handle it. I did bring it up again later, during breakfast on a Saturday. My father was all dressed up in a tweed suit, the kind he wore when he was going out to some big event, or with a client. My mother was going with him.

"I started to ask him what he was going to do about Mack, but he signaled me to wait until my mother was out of the room. She would always have breakfast with us but get up every few minutes to go put on makeup or do her hair.

"I waited until the next time she left the room, and then I asked him, 'Daddy, what are you going to do about Mr. Mack?' He asked me, 'What do you want me to do?' Of course, I was too young to have any exact concept, but I knew it should be something pretty serious. I told him, 'The worst you can.' Then he said, 'I only want what's best for you. Would you like me to go to the newspapers?' I told him I didn't know. But he answered his own question, and said, no, that he thought that would be a terrible embarrassment for me.

"Then he asked me, 'Do you want me to go to the police and press charges?' and I said, 'Definitely yes.' He said, 'You'd have to testify in court,' and I said, 'Fine, I wouldn't mind.'

He said that I'd need to be examined by a doctor. I think I said okay. But then he looked very concerned, and he said, 'I see you don't have those black-and-blue marks on your neck and your arms anymore.' I didn't know why it mattered, but he explained that without those marks the jury would have nothing to see as evidence. My father said, 'It would be your word against Mr. Mack's.' I remember he said, 'I'm a very good lawyer, but I'm not sure we have a case.'

"Then my mother came back in, and they went out to some kind of community meeting.

"By the way, George, even though my father told me not to say anything in front of my mother, I'm sure she knew the whole story."

"Why do you think so, Marianne?"

"Because he always told her everything. And she never insisted that I go to that drugstore again, even though they both used it."

Marianne paused for a moment. "You know," she said, "I remember something else. Can you believe it, my father went and played cards with Mr. Mack after that, a number of times?"

"So you were completely betrayed," I said, summing up.

"Yes. Now that I think about it, yes I was. I was betrayed! And for years, I really believed that my father only wanted what was best for me."

"It's pretty shocking to realize all this, isn't it?"

"It certainly is. Why do you think I forgot about it like that—such a big thing?"

"Because it was a lot easier to blame the whole thing on Mr. Mack over all those years. You didn't need him. He wasn't your father."

Suddenly she looked furious. "Well, I don't need my father either. I never did," she said. "And now I hate him more than I ever did, and I've always hated both of them," she said.

"Well, now it's obvious why you thought that none of those analysts would believe you," I said.

Marianne didn't seem to hear me. "Maybe I'll never talk to my father again," she said, as if discovering that possibility for the first time. At that moment, I pictured her not at Mr. Mack's funeral, but at her father's.

I realized now that Mr. Mack was not the sole culprit, and perhaps not even the chief one.

Hours later, I felt as if Lee Harvey Oswald's long sought accomplice had come forward and confessed. I was perhaps more stunned by the discovery than Marianne was. In a sense, she had always possessed the memory, although she had long ago lost touch with it consciously. For me, it was a totally new fact, one that went far to explain the real basis of her expectation that no man could be trusted and why she thought there was no justice in the world. Moreover, it was the key to why the rape had taken such a terrible toll on her.

As I had suspected, it was not only Mr. Mack's violation of Marianne that made her cynical and an isolate. It was a combination of that act and the fact that there was very much wrong in her home. However, I had underestimated the enormity of the injustice done to her. It wasn't simply that Marianne had been vulnerable at the time of the rape and unable to speak out about it. The reality was far worse. She *had* endeavored to speak about it and had been turned away.

Before that fateful night, even Marianne had not realized how unloving her parents were. Not until she had gone to them and found them utterly disloyal could she know. How could she possibly come away from that evening untainted by cynicism and despair, or without the sense of herself as damaged goods?

Her reawakening to the truth had come gradually. Her telling that psychoanalyst "family of fathers" had almost surfaced it, and now in my office it had exploded into her consciousness, never to be forgotten again.

More technically, she had broken a pattern of compulsive avoidance of intimacy—a pattern of ritualized avoidance aimed at protecting her in an unloving home. Her secrecy, her distrust, and her stealing were all "compulsive adjustments" to the idea that there was indeed nobody out there who cared or mattered.

As always, the compulsive person's own behavior becomes a continuing cover-up. Marianne was protecting not just herself but the image of her parents who had so betrayed her. Nearly always when a child exempts parents for crimes against him, an aim is for the child to not feel orphaned—to preserve the illusion of having parents there. And in acute cases like this one, the child's aim is virtually to preserve his own sanity.

I felt sure that I had truly grasped the significance of that man on the bike. He had been over those long years a witness to how visible Marianne's physical injuries actually had been and, by implication, how traitorous her parents had been.

If that man had not come forth, Marianne would have been better able to pretend to herself afterward that her parents couldn't have seen anything, that they hadn't known. The truth would have been harder for us to discover. But he *had* come forth. He had survived Marianne's attempts at repression over the ages, remaining a messenger in perpetuity.

I came to see a number of Marianne's traits as fallout more of her experience with her father than with Mr. Mack. Her expectation of being betrayed, especially by a man, and her hatred of cover-ups, for instance, must have evolved, or at least been greatly accented by her father's betrayal of her.

After that session, when Marianne would use her favorite phrase—"there's nobody out there"—we both recognized that in its tragic overtone, it referred to her parents. Regardless of whatever cosmic truth there is in that statement, for Marianne it had this special meaning.

She would often use this phrase, and once after she used it while speculating about what her life would be like if she left Alan, I interpreted it in the terms that had made special sense to her long ago.

"Wait a minute," I said. "The man on the bike was out there."

She knew precisely what I meant. I was accusing her of undue pessimism.

Another time I asked her why she hadn't let that man get off his bike and escort her home. Marianne recalled that her parents had warned her not to trust strange men, never to get into cars with them or to be alone with them.

"But maybe I should trust the next guy on a bike," she said, and we both smiled.

I hoped that by that she meant men in general.

Of course, we continued talking about that betrayal by her parents and what it had meant to Marianne. One day, she said, "I guess I half expected it. That's the way they were all the time. They would smooth over anything not to be embarrassed or to have to take action."

"You saw that even before Mr. Mack?" I asked her.

"I'm sure I did." She recalled that her father would get terribly apologetic when he had to complain about anything outside—about being overcharged at a restaurant or being kept waiting at a doctor's office. And, in fact, on that very night of the molestation, when her father was tinkering with the radio, he had chosen to work on it because he hated to take things back to stores and say they didn't work.

Sadly, Marianne remembered that after her experience with Mr. Mack, her father had pulled away from her. Soon afterward, he had promised to take her ice-skating at a nearby rink, but as the evening came he kept looking out of the window at the weather and finally decided there was too much snow. Marianne said, "The weather really wasn't all that bad."

Her father had consoled her by promising to reschedule their date, but he had never followed through. "I brought it up for several evenings, but I always ended up going with my friends. Then spring came, and the ice was gone, and that was that.

"I guess he was afraid I'd ask him about Mr. Mack," she said.

It crossed my mind that the explanation might be worse, that possibly her father considered Marianne flawed by what had been done to her, or that he himself felt ashamed and humiliated, as many fathers do when their children are sexually abused. It seemed pointless for me to speculate. But whatever he felt, partly because of him and partly because Marianne herself withdrew, even their very limited relationship had dwindled sharply after that day.

★ ★ ★

Later it occurred to me to ask Marianne if her father had known about her stealing, too.

"No, that definitely not," she said at once.

He obviously hadn't wanted to know about that either. On the afternoon that Marianne got caught, the police had called him at his office, and he had gone down to the precinct. That night he had simply asked her, "Are you guilty?"

The instant Marianne had said no, he had said, "That's enough for me." He had turned the case over to another lawyer, a specialist in defending juveniles, and then came the conversation in the judge's chambers. Marianne remembered that the lawyer had begun by saying that she came from a fine family, after which her father had protested her innocence. The whole meeting had lasted only about ten minutes. Marianne had lied to the judge, who had said he believed her implicitly, and that was that.

I asked Marianne what her parents had said to her afterward.

"Nothing. They never mentioned anything about stealing again. It was foolish of me to get so depressed, wasn't it?"

I asked her what she meant.

"To want a fair world. To want justice. It's idealistic," she said, criticizing herself.

"Marianne, we know you're an idealist and a romantic. That's no discovery. You always were. That's why you're not a natural thief," I said.

When she asked me what I meant, I explained that in real life, thieves are seldom romantic. "Maybe Robin Hood was, or François Villon. But they're in years gone by, and we don't really know. But you're not like—"

"What's so different about me?" she asked defiantly, as if I were disqualifying her from a federation she cherished.

I did my best to convey my own idea of how she was different from nearly all people who steal. I told her that with all her stealing, she retained an intense concern for right versus wrong, a firm ethic. I said that she seldom rationalized or did what inveterate thieves nearly always do—affect indifference about other people in order to cloak their actions, and finally become truly indifferent to justice.

"Marianne," I accused her, "you have the most burning sense of justice of anyone I know."

I'd had that conviction about her for a long time, but the idea was new to her, and she seemed taken aback. However, she quickly accepted it.

"Well, I think it bothered me every time I got out of a store with something because it was so unfair," she explained. "It didn't matter what it was—a ring or a scarf or lipstick—I would think it really belonged back in the store. That doesn't make any sense, does it? Do you think maybe I wanted to get caught?"

Suddenly, I recalled that dream of hers in which the judge said that he *knew* that Marianne was a thief, and the whole jury knew. I reminded her of it.

"So what were they all laughing about, and you, too?" I asked her. "You were laughing right along with them, every bit as much. Don't you know why?" I had just realized why myself.

"I think I do," Marianne said. "Because I was glad. I was glad they all knew. Because there was justice in the world. I was relieved. I felt great."

That had been precisely my inference. "You were laughing with pleasure," I said. "The long pretense was over. In your dream world, justice prevailed. That was all you ever truly wanted, *justice,* wasn't it?"

"I know," she said. Then she started to digress. "I once read that people who steal are calling out for something—"

"Well, I don't know about thieves in general," I broke in. "They're all different, I guess. But you certainly were crying out for justice. You were saying, 'Look, nobody sees anything, and I wish they did.' "

"You mean my parents?" Marianne asked.

"Them to start with, certainly. But anybody. Marianne, do you remember when we talked about you possibly stealing something of mine?"

"Vaguely."

"You said you wouldn't steal from me because I *listen* to you. That says something. Maybe you stole from the world because it wouldn't listen. But now it *is* listening. Do you hear me, Marianne, the world is listening—or at least some of us are. If you talk, we'll listen."

"I believe you."

That evening, I thought about that judge who had let her go. He probably had imagined that he was doing her a good turn by believing her. But in actuality he was merely confirming to Marianne that one's deeds in the world leave no traces and therefore mean nothing. The judge had simply taken his place on a long line of those who had participated in the cover-up.

If any adult had taken an interest in Marianne—parent, friend, Girl Scout leader, teacher, storekeeper, or even that judge—it might have made a great difference. Back then, an adult with the integrity and courage to hold Marianne responsible for her stealing and to talk to her might have found it relatively easy to reach her. Any such person would have done her far more good than an army of well-intended adults who merely stepped aside.

And I think that if, while in her teens, Marianne had found such a strong and compassionate adult, Marianne would have readily spoken about Mr. Mack to that person. She had been bursting to talk about him for years—to voice her despair about her parents and about the world in general.

However, no such person had come forward, and Marianne had only reinforced her isolation over the years by her silence—and also in part by her stealing, which was a clarion call that no one heard.

What Marianne and I had uncovered together we would never forget. It would be wonderful to add that our discoveries suddenly liberated her to trust men, to love unreservedly, and to expect loyalty from people until they showed bad faith. But the early hope of psychoanalysis—that the surfacing and reliving of traumatic events would eradicate their stigma—has proved too optimistic. Marianne still had more than her share of distrust, especially of men and of people in authority. She was in large measure a solitary person who disbelieved in the good intentions of others.

The rest would take time, but at least she saw the path ahead and was moving along it. Among the benefits of our work already were that recovering the truth about her early life gave Marianne a sense of fullness. She was softer and more open than she had ever been. Already she was trusting "strangers" with her secrets. And as people genuinely listened to her, she was fast coming to think of herself as worth listening to, as believable. All this was surely related to the fact that she no longer had the slightest impulse to steal. Nor did she ever again. Though problems remained, the whole function of her stealing was gone, and this in itself delighted her.

After several years of our working together, the main immediate question was whether she should stay with Alan. "Perhaps I married him because I wanted to get through to someone who wouldn't believe me," she once volunteered.

I suspected that there was a lot of truth in that.

And another time Marianne said, "I wanted to convince Alan of what had happened to me when I was his patient. Maybe I thought I could do it by marrying him. But now I think I never will."

I didn't respond, having no desire to forecast the future. But Marianne might have been right about that, too.

Basically, very little had changed between Alan and her, and I was not surprised when she reported that Alan was starting to beseech her to change therapists. If he saw the great growth in Marianne's confidence, it did not mean the same thing to him as it did to her or to me.

From Alan's point of view, he had married a woman who depended upon him for stability, a woman essentially timid though given to occasional impulsive acts. He felt that Marianne had needed him to support herself and Julia, whom he genuinely cared for, and though Marianne was never governed emotionally by economic need, it seems likely that Alan thought that he had that grip on her and that he felt bolstered by the idea.

Still, looking at it from Alan's point of view, I could imagine that he now saw himself with a woman who had much more confidence in herself and much less time for him. As a result of doing well at her job, Marianne already had a good income, enough for her to give Julia all she needed. And after her great revelations to the institute analysts about Mr. Mack, she was making some incipient but real friendships with a few of them. She was no longer the old-style wife Alan had counted on, and he must have sensed that she was taking seriously the option of leaving him.

Indeed, Marianne began threatening this during arguments. In the middle of one fight she actually began ransacking her closet and hurling her clothes on the floor, as if preparatory to packing her suitcases and walking out. She and Alan made up that night, but he remained terrified, perhaps sensing that such threats also served as mental rehearsals for leaving.

A few days after that particular argument, Marianne came in saying that she'd had a long discussion with Alan in which he had begged her to see another therapist before making any radical move. She had felt profoundly insulted and had countered that I understood her better than anyone ever had. She had retorted to Alan that she would leave him before leaving me, and in my office she sounded closer to storming out than ever.

"Would that be one of your famous impulsive acts?" I asked her.

"I guess it would," she conceded.

Marianne did care for Alan in a way, and she appreciated his loyalty, as far as it went. She realized that he deserved better than to have her leave in a huff.

I asked her whether she might declare a moratorium on deciding whether to stay or go, and she shot back, "Yes. Sure. For five hours."

"That's just what I'm saying, Marianne. Maybe you ought to be on guard against doing anything right now that you haven't really thought out."

She and Alan had another long conversation and Marianne decided to wait. But she reported that Alan had pleaded that he would never have a fair chance with her if she kept talking to me.

"This time he admitted that he could see wonderful changes in me. He said that everybody could. But he still begged me to stop therapy for a while until I decide about my marriage. I asked him to see you himself, but he wouldn't."

She seemed caught between two giant forces.

"If I leave Alan, he said he would always feel that it had been your influence," she said.

"Would it be?"

"I don't think so." She hesitated. "Well, maybe. But only in the respect that you helped me to see so much about myself. It really has nothing to do with you. And, anyway, your influence is certainly a lot less than his influence was on me when I married him in the first place."

★ ★ ★

Marianne came in late for the following session and looked quite shaken when she sat down.

"I've reached a decision," she said.

I assumed she meant about Alan.

"I know I don't love him, but I think he's right when he says I'm torturing him."

"How, Marianne?"

"By being with him and constantly threatening to leave him. He says he loves me very much and it's more than he can bear. We've been very artificial together—he says he's always afraid of offending me, that I've gotten so oversensitive. We just aren't natural. We've lost whatever we had, and that wasn't much anyhow. So I've made a decision."

"What's that?"

"I'm going to stop therapy, and I'm going to get my own apartment. Julia and I will see Alan a lot, but we're not going to all live together right now. Not until I know what I'm doing."

Marianne was doing her best to look unemotional. She spoke slowly and evenly, as if attempting to prove by her manner that she wasn't just acting on a whim.

I had the impulse to plead with her to reconsider. I wanted to spell out the task that she still had ahead of her, and to warn her to go slow. But I had no right to do any of that. I could see that she was quite nervous and unsure of herself, and I surmised that any strong presentation by me might have tipped the delicate balance of her decision.

I felt as if we were two sparrows who had miraculously survived the first phase of a long flight over a great body of water and had just rested on an island before going on. The remainder of our flight would be easier, but Marianne had elected to stop. Not to stop, I corrected myself—only to choose another direction, one that I could not take with her.

I felt tender toward her, and then I realized that I already missed her. But if I saw her as fragile, that was only because of what I knew about her history. I looked closely at her for one of the last times, and it was obvious that she did not see herself as delicate either. She had just left work, and looked all capability in her cream-colored satin blouse and slim brown skirt.

Her amber necklace and big carnelian earrings were in the primitive style, which was her favorite.

"I guess you and Alan have discussed it," I said.

"Yes. We both felt bad, but we agreed that it would be best. Julia and I are leaving next Friday. We're going to stay with Sarah and her husband until we find a place. Can I come in for an hour now and then, maybe every few months or something like that?"

"Of course."

However, eight months later, when Marianne still hadn't contacted me, I began to doubt that she ever would. My experience is that patients respond very differently to treatment after it is over. Some bore everybody by talking about their therapy nonstop, the way zealots do about their religious conversions. They stay in touch with the therapist, and they become walking ads for that person and for the process.

Others resent their former reliance on a professional whom they had to pay. They do everything possible not to be reminded of that interlude of dependency; this includes never talking about their treatment and avoiding all contact with their therapist. Interestingly, it seems that the degree to which therapy has actually helped the person does not put him or her into either camp more than the other, and of course most people fall in between these two extremes.

I was starting to conclude that Marianne might be in the category of those who are glad for the benefits, but want to sever from the experience. Perhaps her very reason was the desire to forget a time when she was quite different—unformed compared with the person she became.

When I finally did hear from Marianne, I was surprised and delighted. She looked cheerful and said she was very busy. She and Julia were living in their own apartment, and she had a housekeeper five days a week. She said that she wanted to discuss some touchy office politics, which we did for most of the hour. When I asked her about Alan, she was brief and evasive, saying only that the relationship was "the same."

During the session I sensed that she was keeping me at a distance, training the discussion on office strategy and not voicing much feeling about anyone. I had the impression that it was important to her to be sure that I was still there, but she was also resisting anything that might look like reliance on me emotionally.

Another year went by before I saw Marianne again. She was warmer this time, talking about Julia and her job. She said, almost reportorially, that a divorce from Alan was "in the works."

I asked her how she felt about it, and she said that he was a "decent guy," but that it was definitely the right thing to do. "I never really loved him," she said, "and it really wasn't fair." She said that she often missed me and our work together, and I told her that I felt much the same way about her.

Not until five more years went by did I hear from her again, and for the last time—a brief note saying that she had liked an article of mine, which she had read in a popular magazine. She had come across it by accident while she was waiting her turn in a beauty salon. She commented only that things were going well, and that Julia had been accepted at Amherst and would be starting in the fall.

After that, Marianne assumed a quiet repose in my memory. I remember thinking of her once when a feminist friend of mine observed that women in one's past may disappear if they assume their husband's names after marriage, and that doing so is like volunteering for oblivion. As I thought back about women whom I had known personally and as patients, among those who came to mind was Marianne. I felt absolutely certain that whether she married again or not, she would keep her name very much alive. That seemed almost to go with her nature.

Then, in 1984, the much publicized Masson controversy broke out. Not only was it on the tongues of my fellow professionals, but the *New York Times* gave it enormous play.

Jeffrey Masson, a brilliant young scholar, was privy to seldom seen documents of Freud and his contemporaries. Masson charged that archivists had systematically covered up important psychoanalytic papers, some revealing abysmal failures of cases that had been celebrated as successes and, in particular, papers dealing with Freud's so-called "seduction theory."

It was well known that Freud had originally posited that neurosis derived from children's real sexual experiences with adults. Nor did this idea originate with Freud. Masson cited an early-eighteenth-century psychiatrist, Ambroise Tardieu, as having written that "somehow these children kept their knowledge of the horrible crimes that had been committed on their bodies sealed off from the world."

However, as the psychoanalysts in Marianne's circle had mentioned, after a time Freud had retracted his original seduction theory, substituting for it a new thesis—namely, that his patients had only *imagined* their early sexual assaults and were lying to him, consciously or unconsciously. In fact, this new formulation became the very basis of Freud's Oedipus theory, which stated that all children fantasize sexual acts with the parent of the opposite sex, and that their psychic future is determined by how they resolve those fantasies.

Masson, alluding to this second theory of Freud's, in effect accused Freud and his followers of a wholesale cover-up of real abuse of children by adults. This was, of course, a serious charge. As if being molested in childhood were not horrible enough, Freud's theory encouraged adults, including analysts themselves, to dismiss people's accusations as if they were only statements of what the child had imagined.

It seems unconscionable that when such a child finally goes to a psychoanalyst, either early in life or later, and reports having been seduced, the analyst construes it as nothing more than a fantasy, and a commonplace, predictable one at that.

Were children only imaging their abuses, or had the deeply revered Freud made an error that was very costly to all who had truly suffered? Masson's book, *The Assault on Truth: Freud's Suppression of the Seduction Theory,* became a great topic of conversation, not just in the field but among thousands of literate people. Psychoanalysis quickly ousted Masson from his niche in its hierarchy, but the controversy continues to rage.

Among those who feel strongly about the issue are feminists, who have long argued that sexual violations of women are much more prevalent than people admit. Feminists have had their troubles with Freud, who was distinctly patriarchal, and Masson gave them plenty of tinder to set new fires in the Freudian dominion.

Naturally, I could hardly think about the Masson controversy without remembering Marianne, who had, indeed, kept the knowledge of a horrible crime committed against her body sealed off from the world.

To me it seemed obvious that even if seductions are on occasion only imagined, the abuse of children by strangers or by adults in their own home is often very real. Anyone who makes such a charge deserves to be heard. Indeed, few among my own colleagues, even among staunch Freudians, automatically attributed their patients' accounts of having been molested to mere fantasy.

Marianne's case also reminded me of how dangerous it is to attribute positions to people without asking them. Marianne herself did that in assuming that the psychoanalysts she knew would disbelieve her, in a homogeneous mass, if she told them what had been done to her. In reality, they did not, but responded to her individually, as human beings moved or not moved by her account.

Nor was it Alan's psychoanalytic persuasion that kept him aloof and deaf to her tragedy. Rather, it was Alan's own character, his nature, which spoke as her adversary.

I wondered whether Marianne had been following the controversy in the *New York Times,* where it had received steady comment for months. Perhaps she had even read the book.

One evening during this period, my recollection of Marianne became so vivid that I could almost see her sitting next to me in an automobile. I was driving some psychologist friends back from Nyack on a Sunday evening. When they began to talk about Jeffrey Masson and Freud's seduction theory, the discussion became heated. Several of them seemed unswervingly Freudian, bent on believing whatever he had said.

One of those Freudians maintained, "Freud's discovery that children develop their character structure largely out of their fantasies was a great contribution."

"But how can you tell fantasy from reality?" someone asked him challengingly.

"You can't tell," said the Freudian. "That was what Freud pointed out in his letter to Wilhelm Fliess, and I think—"

"Well, I think Freud's seduction theory, which puts it all in the mind, was his greatest act of violence against women—"

"Now you're overstating what he said."

I vaguely sensed someone turning toward me and asking, "Isn't that right, George?" But I merely recorded the words without construing their sense until later.

In the darkness, we were approaching the George Washington Bridge, and its great arches loomed against the meaningless sky. Almost hypnotized by its filigree of cables and the cityscape ahead, I thought of Marianne driving over it on such a night, twenty years previously, with a suitcase full of stolen items in the back of her car and the plan to jettison them and start a new life.

As we went on to the center span under the necklace of lights, I had the fantasy of stopping and hurling that suitcase over the railing, and I fervently hoped, as Marianne must have, that there would be time to stop, and a place. But the traffic kept surging ahead, like time itself, and there was none.

"George, you've been so quiet. What do you think of Masson?" the person asked, more insistently this time.

"Sometimes things really happen," I said.

...7...

Breaking Compulsions

*I*n this chapter I want to set down a series of steps for combating compulsions; their rationale derives from what has already been said. The whole procedure may be carried out alone or in therapy or with a self-help group.

Any such outline, like a map for an explorer, is admittedly easier to set down than to follow. Yet millions of people have overcome compulsions. The journey must be somewhat different for every individual. Each person needs to face his own set of enticements and to overcome them. These enticements draw their shape and sustenance from the person's own highly individual history.

The secret is always to analyze them and lay bare the real fear, after which you can break the compulsion, as you would a habit, by refusing to give in to it. Indeed, the essence of the method is that you are turning the compulsion into a habit by depriving it of its special functions, after which you can break the hold of the activity.

Before elaborating, the steps are briefly:

1. Identify the compulsive activity or pattern that you want to stop.
2. Stop it if only briefly in order to decipher it. Ask yourself what you truly dread and are evading symbolically by the compulsive activity.
3. Ask yourself, Under what basic misconception have you been living? Try to answer this question in as much detail as possible.
4. Answer the question, How has the compulsive activity masked your dread or appeared to solve some problem?
5. Stop the compulsive activity once and for all. This will be feasible, though it was not previously. Now you can do this in weeks or months by determined effort.

Granted, after you have broken the compulsion, you may find yourself facing some discontent with your life. You may dread looking at this underlying problem, but it was always there; only your awareness of it is new. There would be considerable benefit to you in going on to root it out, because this problem has been limiting your life for years.

Finally, you are in a real position to do something constructive on that front. After stopping the activity you are like someone who has just removed a blindfold. However, what you choose to do once you have liberated yourself from the compulsion is beyond the scope of this book, and is of course your own private matter.

Now let's look at the five steps more closely.

1. Identify the compulsive behavior. This is, of course, quite easily done if you have been agonizing over the compulsive activity, as many people do for years.

Harder to identify are those pervasive compulsive patterns that may be almost coextensive with the personality. It might take years for a man to appreciate that talking much too much and too fast and exaggerating make up a compulsive pattern. Or for a woman to appreciate that her fiery disagreements with men she is attracted to are compulsive.

Only when the sufferer tries to stop the activity and sees how hard it is, may he or she realize that it is a compulsion rather than a bad habit. Besides the terrible feeling of urgency there is unanticipated anxiety, a feeling of loss, that is quite marked. These are signs that the pattern has been compulsive.

2. Next, stop the compulsive activity if you can, if only for a while, as an aid to identifying its function.

When you do this your urge for it will immediately become much more intense.

As the urge mounts, ask:

What would it give me to resume?

What seems suddenly missing in my life without the activity?

Answers may come to you that sound outlandish:

"If only I could check the gas jets once more, I would be certain that I wasn't going to die or kill someone."

"Without betting on any baseball game today I feel that my life is empty. I feel stupid and without a purpose."

"Tonight, as I resisted my compulsive impulse to brag and exaggerate and talk about myself, I felt invisible. It was as if no one cared about me, as if I had no business being in the room with those people. I felt unnoticed."

Listen to these reactions. They offer glimpses into yourself that are of inestimable value. You are experiencing "hunger illusions," which contain vital truths about the compulsion, about what it means and why it started.

Studying these reactions will teach you what is really driving you to the compulsion. In order to decipher the deeper meaning of these flashes of thought you will need to ask yourself certain questions—and to ask them insistently, perhaps over and over again.

When you pose these questions to yourself, if no answer comes to you at once, push yourself to make up answers. The first thought that comes to your mind under this instruction to fictionalize may itself hold the secret of the compulsion.

Good follow-up questions to ask yourself are:

In exactly what way do I feel frightened?

Exactly what terrible thing do I think will happen to me now that I won't engage in the behavior?

Why will it happen?

What do I feel other people are thinking about me?

In connection with each of these questions, ask yourself what comes to mind about your childhood. Did anyone treat you as you now expect to be treated? Did you have the picture of yourself that you now have? Why? Who was that person? In what circumstance did the thing occur?

Don't dismiss whatever comes to mind.

Probe deeper into your glimpses. Ask yourself, Why does this seem so? Press for as much detail as possible. You will flesh out the picture if you do.

For instance:

"I feel that if I don't make sure that the gas jets are off, I will die."

"Why?"

"Because I'm careless. I don't deserve to live."

"Why not?"

"Because I'm not a decent person. I know this sounds ridiculous. I don't even know why I'm saying this—"

"No matter. Just keep voicing the first thought that comes to your mind, no matter how bizarre or irrational it sounds."

"All right. I deserve to die because I'm not a kind person."

"In what way not kind?"

"I don't know."

"Make up an answer."

"My mother always told me I wasn't kind."

"When?"

"When she said she had headaches and I was playing too loudly with my friends, or just singing to myself. She would look desolate. She would tell me that I was young and I had my whole life ahead of me and that she was getting older. She said she couldn't take all this racket.

"Now I remember. That was why I rarely invited friends over, and I never announced it when I had a good time. I played everything down. I expected to be punished—well, I guess actually I thought that I was killing her.

"You mean I check the gas jets to be sure that I'm not killing my mother? Actually, I am enjoying a good relationship with a lover, and I guess I feel in jeopardy, that all this happiness can be taken away from me at any minute. My compulsion has been at its worst recently."

Persistently asking why you have your particular reaction when you stop the compulsive activity even for a time will often reveal its meaning. Other good follow-up questions are:

Why do I feel in jeopardy at this particular moment?

What does this feeling of danger that I have remind me of, especially in my childhood?

At what other times do I feel this way?

After abstaining from the compulsion for a time, the impulse for the activity will predictably become almost unbearable and the sense of privation will be enormous. It is then that many hidden and unexpected thoughts will come to mind. But they are not dross. They are a treasure.

A woman I mentioned earlier, Deidre, who flirted with men compulsively, forced herself to stop for a time. When she did so a flood of self-denigrating thoughts came to her mind. She felt dismayed by the idea that she had nothing to offer in the way of ideas, that she was so dull that she had to either flirt with men or die alone.

Deidre recalled compliments from her parents for being pretty, but they had no interest in what she had to say. She could recall once yearning for them to ask her opinion about a camp counselor whom she knew better than her brothers did. But they asked her brothers and never turned to her for her opinion. And she did not volunteer it.

Deidre discovered that her compulsive flirting was based on the expectation that all people would feel about her the way her parents did: that she was dull and that her real worth to people now was no different from what it had been to her parents. She had begun flirting early in her teens: she was pretty and it got attention; the boys wanted her; and the girls admired her.

By stopping herself from flirting she had forced fragments of its rationale, a glimpse of her early childhood, into her consciousness, and for the first time she got insight into what she was doing and why. The discovery made her furious, and she never forgot it.

In another case a man of thirty, who told tall tales and bragged about his exploits compulsively, at first felt "nonexistent" when he stopped doing these things. When he asked himself what the experience reminded him of, he at once remembered himself as a little boy. His father had died when he was three and his mother had encouraged him to make big promises and "be a man" long before he was able to. He apparently had developed bluster before acquiring much else in his personality.

And consider this contrasting case, also illuminated by stopping the behavior and studying oneself without it. A young internist, esteemed by fellow professionals, was compulsively reticent and often did not inspire from patients the confidence that his skills truly merited.

This internist came to see that he compulsively avoided owning up to his own attainments or excellence. In fact, he was so timid that he virtually concealed from acquaintances that he was an internist with superb credentials.

Breaking this pattern meant pushing himself to speak confidently, to profess being good at things when he really was. One night at a dinner party he was giving, he mentioned that he had built some bookshelves that his guests were admiring. He then forced himself to add that he was a good carpenter. His guests were duly impressed, but he instantly went into a near panic.

After interrogating himself silently, two questions yielded answers that surprised him. When he asked himself what he imagined his guests really thought, he "saw" them laughing at him and considering him a fool—a "jester" was the word he used. This surprised him, because he recognized that they would never actually think this, they were not cruel or mocking people.

He could also honestly say that when he heard another person speak of him as capable, he felt no such derisive contempt.

Then why this idea that they considered him a jester? he asked himself. While still in the throes of discomfort about what seemed to him like an embarrassing fit of braggadocio, the internist asked himself what the whole experience reminded him of.

The answer came barreling into his mind. He remembered his father at his worst.

An event of one particular evening when he was about eight flashed into his mind. The young internist recalled his vagabond father, a man who talked big and delivered nothing, boasting about a fortune he expected to make with a new store he had not yet even bought and couldn't afford. A little family group was sitting on the porch and his father was called inside to the phone. When his father was out of earshot, the boy's mother and the rest of the group, including two of her sisters, proceeded to mock his father and call him a loser.

Apparently the father had frequently predicted great business successes for himself that had never come to pass, and everyone was disgusted with him.

The internist would never have recalled any of this had he not forced himself to resist his own compulsive reticence by speaking well of his own performance. His biggest fear was of being considered an imposter, as his father had been, of being mocked and talked about derisively behind his back. It was the dread of this that had over the years kept him compulsively low-key and had cheated him out of the assertiveness, self-respect, and respect from others that he truly deserved.

Only when he broke the pattern did the fear and the vignette contained in the compulsion come crashing into his consciousness. And once the internist appreciated that he had this motive he took pains never to lose sight of it.

Resisting the compulsive behavior and studying every thought that then comes to mind—ideally, by writing them down or by saying them into a tape recorder—lays bare the true motivations for a compulsion better than any other conceivable method. This method capitalizes on the fact that every compulsion retains its memory and keeps that memory unconscious so long as the concealing compulsive behavior rolls along unmolested.

Deliberate interference with the compulsive activity, coupled with painstaking inquiry and careful recording of what comes to mind, exposes the anatomy of the compulsion and shows its function in the personality. Anachronistic motives and vignettes emerge to be seen when the person stops the behavior.

To answer the question, What is truly dreaded and being evaded by the compulsive activity? is a giant step toward depriving the compulsion of its long-standing value.

Surprisingly often, the "irrational" flashes of fear or expectation that come to mind are glimpses into one's early history, into how one's life seemed when the compulsive activity was begun. And even when they are not, those unexpected thoughts reveal the true motive for the compulsion—that is, what the activity is covering up and appearing to remedy, though of course it never actually is a remedy. I call this mode of studying hunger illusions "the method of magnification," because the method of questioning oneself in this way magnifies the minutest clues so that you can draw inferences from them.

3. Next ask yourself, *Under what false premise have you been living?*

Behind every compulsion is some irrational fear—that is, some misconception about oneself based on childhood—that the person is suppressing. The inquiry already conducted will reveal this fear, which you will now recognize to be a misconception. Let's look at some examples:

The woman who compulsively checked her gas jets realized that her mistaken assumption was: "I do not deserve to be happy, and other people, or Fate, will strike me down if I enjoy my life."

For Deidre:

"I have nothing of interest to say, and the only way a man could ever want me would be if I enticed him with sexual favors, or at least promises."

For Anne, mentioned in a previous chapter:

"Unless I am helpful and prop people up emotionally, they will not tolerate me because I am dull and plain."

For the internist:

"If for even one moment I am not deferential and do not play myself down, people will mock me and hate me as they did my father."

For the gambler:

"To think of myself as an unaccomplished person, instead of a genius with a master plan, would be like death."

Having spelled out for yourself the misconception being hidden by your compulsive behavior, state for yourself its alternative:

"No one will strike me down just because I am happy."

"I need not play my talents down to anyone. Real friends will delight in my pride in what I do well."

As another example, recall the draftsman who discovered his dread that even the slightest artistic license with his drawings might be conspicuous and result in his being put to death. He profited greatly by writing down every day, "In my life now I can break rules and not be sent before a firing squad."

It is helpful if you can see in what way your misconception is an anachronism, as when the woman who stopped smoking recognized, "I am mature even without a cigarette in my hands."

However, expect that for a time what you now know to be false will go on feeling like reality. The illusion holds on for a while even though you know it's an illusion. This is because, for a time after you first curb the compulsive activity, the remaining impulse will go on making its purely emotional case, bringing the memory with it.

During this time your identification of the misconception as such will coexist with your continued belief in it. You will know that you are subject to an illusion, and you will know why, but the illusion will hold on nevertheless. You are in effect suffering from a form of double vision.

For instance, even after Anne could honestly say, "I am worth more to myself and to my friends if I express my real opinions than if I don't," she still had lingering emotional doubts. She understood her misconception intellectually and even recognized where it came from. But still, the instant she disagreed even with her best friend, she experienced a momentary anticipation of being utterly rejected.

If simply glimpsing the truth were enough to change an outlook then the insight alone would be curative.

However, as the poet Edna St. Vincent Millay once put it, "The heart is slow to learn / What the swift mind beholds at every turn."

Recognizing the truth, however, does deprive the compulsive activity of much of its force, but what you know will help you to resist subsequent urges. Now each time you resist the compulsive urge it will bring you closer to feeling and actually experiencing the truth as well as seeing it.

For instance, the truth is that you have the right to people's respect even if you don't flirt with them or prop them up. And how else can the former concentration camp victim teach himself to appreciate that he is no longer in prison than by taking the liberties to which he is entitled?

Knowing the truth will make it much easier to resist your compulsive urges. As you do this, what you only contemplated at first, you will come to feel genuinely. Whatever misconception drove you to the compulsion will loosen its grip. Over the months that follow, the impact of your new knowledge and of resisting the compulsion will combine to break whatever hold it had on you.

4. Answer the question, *How has the compulsive activity masked your dread or appeared to solve some problem?*

This question is usually easy for certain compulsives, such as alcoholics or addicts, to answer. The drink or drug or pill has created an instant sense of euphoria or dullness and has either erased the problem or made it seem unimportant.

In most cases the compulsion has also been serving to distract you from what you are truly afraid of. Engaging in it has kept you busy thinking about other things. Most addicts spend enormous time getting the money for their cherished substance, finding people to sell it to them, checking the prices and quantity of what they buy, and worrying about their future needs.

Similarly, compulsive gamblers, by losing themselves in the details of their gambling, avoid facing the truly important aspects of their lives. Actually, every compulsion provides some form of distraction. Workaholics, compulsive joggers, and "exercise freaks" find in the details of their activities distraction from whatever they are really afraid of. Concern with the gas jets or with lining the furniture up perfectly or with cleanliness similarly distract the person with details of the task.

Ask, *How does the activity seem to solve the problem?*

For instance: What are you really cleaning up when you wash the floors repeatedly? What are you really afraid of when you count your money or set aside time to fill in the *o*'s and *e*'s in your newspaper?

Any answer you can find may help you see through the impulse when it comes again. To know that by making sure the gas is off you can't stop Fate's reprisals for having a good life will help when the urge to check them comes again. To realize that you can't atone for outliving your mate no matter how spotless you make the floors can take some of the impetus out of cleaning the floors.

Exposing your compulsive activity as a false cure will surely heighten your appreciation of its pointlessness and make stopping easier. You can certainly proceed without perfect understanding of the role of the compulsion, and you may have to. But recognizing the symbolic value of your activity will help nullify your motivation for it.

The more you know about your compulsion the better, though whatever you discover, you will still need plenty of willpower to stop the activity. By your work you have at least made stopping feasible. You have deprived the compulsion of its mystery and of some of the secret power that it had over you, and having done this, willpower will be enough.

In some special cases, you now stand aghast at the brink of what you've discovered. You've come upon a reality that seems devastating. You may feel tempted to say, "This is no misconception. My life *is* a hopeless tragedy, it doesn't just seem that way."

For instance: "Now that I'm not compulsively playing bridge all day, I have to face the fact that my husband doesn't love me, that he never loved me. It kills me. But it's reality."

Or, "Why shouldn't I use drugs? What chance for happiness do I have? I'm in a hated minority group and I never had a break."

And recently a woman who would compulsively try to regulate the entire lives of her three adult daughters, with the result that they all withdrew from her, complained to me, "Doctor, you tell me to try seeing them without criticizing anything they do. How can I? Their homes are a mess, they're all destroying their marriages and ruining their children. I have nothing to live for."

People who resist compulsive urges often imagine that they have come face to face with some painful and unmovable reality. However, there is always a better solution than flight and surrender to the compulsion. What seems like a final stage is virtually never one. Anyone who makes the case that facing reality is worse than giving in to a compulsion is rationalizing or suffering from acute demoralization—or both.

There is no psychological condition that is best dealt with by flight and surrender. In fact, flight always makes a person feel less able to cope with a reality. Facing any predicament reduces it somewhat. Once you absorb the full reality, you will see alternatives.

For instance, the woman's avoidance of her problems with her husband by hiding in bridge clubs could hardly have helped the marriage. Maybe things could be made satisfactory. And if indeed the relationship has lost all worth, she need not prolong it. Naturally, all these solutions are easier described than reached, but a lifetime of absorption in a circular and repetitive activity is almost akin to premature death.

Even where a reality is indeed awful there is nearly always a range of ways for coping with it. Conceivably you need help in finding another solution. But of course, people paralyzed, and even those with fatal illnesses—in extremes of all kinds—still vary in what they make of their lives and how much they can enjoy them. An incredible range of possibility and texture, more than any individual can ever live long enough to savor, can easily pass through the needle's eye of whatever mobility remains to us.

If when you stop your compulsive behavior your dilemma seems insuperable, keep looking at it. This promises a much better future than succumbing to another compulsion.

5. Stop the compulsive activity once and for all. Having prepared yourself properly, you can do this now. You know why you engage in the compulsion, what its costs are, and why you want to stop. You can recognize your illusions as such, though they masquerade as reality. In moments it may still seem to you that by not engaging in the compulsive behavior you are risking friendships or your reputation or even your life. Yet you know this is untrue and that you must go on resisting the urge.

Especially at this juncture you need faith that, if you continue holding out against the impulse, the hazards you face, being only imaginary, will vanish.

Dorothy, a woman who had a compulsive need to show herself as generous, determined to combat her newly discovered dread of being considered selfish. Every six months the club to which she belonged asked for volunteers to house visitors from out of town. Dorothy had never failed to raise her hand, and would play hostess to a few people, sometimes quite thanklessly. She realized that the majority of the members, many with more time and wherewithal than she had, had refused to help out even once.

As part of her battle against self-imposed servitude Dorothy resolved to make no such offer the next time. She very much wanted to break her feeling that it was necessary for her to volunteer so much. She considered her resolution utterly reasonable, and a few friends cheered her on. The morning of the meeting one of them even called with some last-minute encouragement.

At the meeting, when volunteers were called for and Dorothy did not raise her hand, she experienced her old terror that people would despise her for being selfish. As she had in recent weeks, Dorothy could once again see her hypochondriacal mother calling her selfish, and then her father coming home and asking her, "Were you a good little girl today?" With great sadness she could hear herself answer, no. She was well aware that her mother had never enjoyed her and had not wanted children in the first place.

However, when not enough members offered themselves, and a second, more urgent, call for volunteers went out, Dorothy managed to resist that one, too.

After six months of holding out, Dorothy was stunned that she could ever have pictured those club members as she had. By then she had abolished her illusion that she had to do everything people asked of her.

Along the way, several club members had actually expressed disappointment in Dorothy for doing less than she used to. Of course she was hurt, especially when she realized that these people said nothing to other members who had never done a tenth as much she had. By always saying yes, Dorothy had actually trained these people to expect her to contribute tirelessly. However, after a while Dorothy had so altered her outlook that even those comments did not make her doubt herself.

Whatever your compulsion, it is a sure thing that you will feel in danger, even wrong-minded, when you first stop the activity. But knowledge is courage. Even as rogue images of danger or wrongdoing on your part come to you, you can see through them. You can recognize those images as merely memories that your mind superimposes on your present life. Knowing this will help you stay on your course.

Though these enticements and these images that come to you are yours alone, millions have taken similar journeys. As predictable as these illusions are now, they will as predictably come less frequently after a while. Then the day will arrive when you can hardly remember them and when your newly opted for behavior feels utterly natural:

"Was there really a time when I thought the whole club would ostracize me for not devoting yet another week of my life to strangers? And did I care? I worried about that even though only a tenth of the members ever played host to out-of-town guests."

"Did I really think I couldn't go to a business meeting without a drink?"

And there's one more psychological truth that I have found helpful to keep in mind early, when personal ghosts assume their most dreadful forms.

To understand it, state what seems like the worst danger you are now facing by *not* engaging in the compulsion.

For instance: "If people don't think I'm generous they will hate me and throw me out."

"If I don't check the gas, I will die, because I don't deserve to be happy."

These statements tell you exactly how you are going to *benefit* if you keep fighting the compulsive urge. You will feel more desirable and less in need of proving yourself by generosity. You will feel more worthy of having a good life and less in danger of being struck down for seeking happiness.

In other words, what you now feel offers a precise prediction of what you stand to gain by breaking the compulsion. These illusions are a reverse measure of what you can expect.

Breaking any compulsion will increase your sense of competency; it will dispose you to feel that you yourself are enough. Whatever the compulsion appeared to offer you you will feel that you already have without needing to resort to the compulsive activity.

What you now know about compulsions—their nature and, in a curious sense, their nurture—you can thus use to break your particular compulsion.

Admittedly, this is never easy. Combating the urge, enduring the anxiety, holding out against the illusions, these you must do alone. But to be less alone, think of the place you are going to, and of the many who have taken similar journeys, who have been equally alone en route, but who have arrived at the promised land. And few proceeded with nearly the insight or knowledge that you can afford yourself.

···8···

The Symptom of Tyranny

So far we have been looking at compulsions from the inside—that is, at the compulsive person as the victim of the experience. However, if we step back a little and look at compulsive people the way their friends or others might, we are struck by another feature of the compulsive: the indifference toward others, and even brutality toward them, that compulsive people often display.

Anyone who has come between a compulsive person and his ritual can attest to their ferocity when thwarted or even questioned. To the compulsive the real stakes in carrying out his ritual may seem so high that nothing must be allowed to stand in the way. With personal security, safety, everything on the line, the compulsive may have no hesitation about shoving others aside or bending them to his own purposes.

As an extreme example, I recall a man, a patient in Hartford Hospital where I worked briefly, who kept compulsively rearranging playing cards on a table. He would put them into different small piles with great speed, shuffling and realigning those piles continually. He did this day after day.

I noticed that on occasion, when a card accidentally fell to the floor, he pounced on it and scooped it up as fast as he could. If the card happened to fall face down, he smoothed it off with his hand and caressed it lovingly; he then put it into a very special pile, doubtless giving it preferential treatment to compensate for what it had suffered.

The others on the ward had learned to keep their distance from him, and the story was that he had driven a fork into one inmate who had come too close and would not retreat.

When this man saw me looking at him, he glowered at me and gestured to me to move back. I duly obeyed. If I hadn't, I think he might very well have assaulted me, perhaps even tried to murder me.

Undoubtedly, if we knew exactly what those cards represented to the man, what they embodied, we would appreciate his proneness to frenzy and his willingness to defend his ritual at nearly any cost. To this man nothing less than his survival or that of the whole human race might have been at stake and justified his desperate defiance of interlopers.

All compulsive people to some degree perceive their ritual as necessary to their happiness or well-being. Let it be challenged and many become surprisingly callous. Their freedom to continue the behavior takes priority over all else. Because of the dread that lurks behind even seemingly insignificant compulsions, the sufferer may become suddenly angry at anyone who gets in the way.

Lovers and friends of compulsive people are often taken aback at their fury. Merely pointing out to a compulsive person that he or she has just checked the gas jets or locked the door or washed his hands, and that it's not necessary to do so again, may be enough to provoke it. The poor compulsive, feeling in inexplicable danger, may whirl on his closest intimate—as if that intimate were a traitor. Minutes later, after he manages to carry out his ritual and feels safe again, he may apologize profusely.

For instance, family members of alcoholics have learned how dangerous it is to tell the person, "You've had enough."

It's just as dangerous to suggest to certain compulsives, "Maybe we can have our friends over without scrubbing the floors."

Or, "Let's go to sleep tonight without both of us checking the faucets a second time to be sure they're off."

As a therapist I have learned to anticipate that when I ask certain patients to try to resist their compulsive urges for a while in order to study them, some will turn on me in fury. Not wanting to admit, "I simply couldn't do what you asked, I was too terrified," the patient sometimes suddenly finds other faults with me.

Just as the compulsive activity is itself symbolic, so are its appurtenances. The cards that the mental patient put into piles were to him more than mere playing cards. I don't know what they signified in his case—people or nations or months of the year or diseases, for example. To one person, a bankbook represents mental capacity; to another, a photo album represents deceased parents and their continued support; to another, cracks in the street represent fatal illnesses like the one that struck down a parent.

To all of us—not just people with compulsions—certain inanimate objects take on human meanings. But to compulsives, because they are motivated by unconscious dread, the urgency of this symbolism reaches its peak.

And it isn't just inanimate objects that take on special meanings: other people do as well. Individuals in the compulsive's life, not just those who make it harder for him to engage in his ritual, but a variety of people, are seen as other than themselves. Not infrequently, they assume dread meanings, with the result that the compulsive may go to great lengths to control another's behavior.

In fact, those who suffer from compulsions, being motivated by acute dread, which they ordinarily do not identify, may become among the most controlling people. Rather than examine their feelings and delve into the nature of their dread, they typically seek to regulate their environment. In the process many become despotic without even thinking about it.

Behind this despotic streak in compulsives is a twofold purpose. The first is the compulsive's desire to clear a path for his repressive activity—that is, to stop others from interfering with his compulsive ritual.

Secondly, and more pernicious, the compulsive's aim is to prevent people from evoking the fear that he has been taking such pains to repress. For what good is the elaborate and painstaking ritual if someone can confront you with your fear? What good is it to pursue money compulsively in place of love if two penniless lovers can delight in their lives? The compulsive workaholic must denounce them as irresponsible and predict misery for them.

This second motive gives rise to the severest tyranny, because the compulsive so driven demands absolute conformity with his values.

Some examples of people who convert their own compulsions into despotism on this account are the following:

A well-to-do man compulsively buys showy items and flaunts them to demonstrate to himself and the world that he has truly arrived, despite the fact that his life is barren of interests and love. When at a party a neighbor innocently wonders why he bought such an expensive car, he conceives a hatred of that neighbor, as if the fellow had called him an abysmal failure at everything that counts. He receives the comment as a deathblow and disparages the neighbor ever afterward.

A woman compulsively readies her apartment for weeks to pass muster with her mother-in-law. When the mother-in-law observes casually that her choice of dark window shades was ill-advised because they keep out too much light, she feels insulted to the quick—as if her mother-in-law had proclaimed her not worthy of her husband. She resolves never to see her mother-in-law again. Though she relents in this, there is constant trouble not just with her mother-in-law, but with virtually everyone. Many people avoid her, and those who put up with her feel highly controlled in what they can and cannot say in her presence.

A man who compulsively works out in gyms to prove his masculinity goes berserk when a gay weight lifter and his lover join the gym one day. It's as if the two homosexual men were informants against the man's method of proving his "masculinity." He immediately complains to the management that homosexuals have no place in any group where he is a member.

In each of these cases an "interloper" unknowingly threatened the success of a compulsive ritual. It wasn't that the intruder made it actually hard for the compulsive person to indulge in the activity, as when a friend beseeches a compulsive person not to do his usual checking up or cleaning. Rather the threat was to the value of the activity. It was as if the intruder had said, "Despite all your pains, your compulsive activity does not prove your thesis. You are engaging in the activity for naught."

The following story—about a compulsive man named Timothy—is to be my last full-length one. I have chosen it to illustrate the narcissism and indifference to others, the dehumanization of people all set in motion once a person becomes compulsive. The activity becomes primary and, especially if the compulsive feels thwarted, performing it becomes all that counts.

As you will see, I myself as Timothy's therapist was hardly a real person to him. Though he spoke to me respectfully, in a curious sense I barely existed. One doesn't to compulsives, quite often, and though the case of Timothy shows these narcissistic features at their zenith, such features are only too often apparent to intimates of compulsives and to those who attempt to help the person.

Indeed, one of the horrors of being compulsive is the isolation chamber that the person creates to live in. It's as if all thought—foretaste, pleasure, and afterthought in life—concerned the compulsive activity. Ideally, the recognition that one is being so swallowed up provides strong incentive for breaking free of a compulsion.

...9...

Tuxedo Junction

*Now she desires no more. So, poor madman, do not follow her and
live in misery. Be firm.*

So wrote the greatest of the Latin
lyric poets, Catullus, whom the an-
cient world admired for his wisdom. However, on that occasion, Catullus
was doubtless saying nothing especially new. The exact same counsel must
surely have been given to the victims of one-sided love affairs since the
beginning of time. Perhaps no advice has ever been both better and more
wasted on the listener.

An exceptional feature of this story is that this particular lover, who
was unloved or at best the recipient of what some psychologists call "inter-
mittent reinforcement," actually came to a therapist for help. He came to
me.

Another was that Timothy O'Donnel, the lover, was himself constantly of two minds, of two recognitions. Even as he doted on his beloved,
rising reflexively to her name as if it were a summons to his young blood,

he could say to me, "She's not even that pretty." And, "I know she doesn't compare with my wife."

However, such was the power of her command that he felt magnetized to her from the beginning.

Timothy was, in reality, an erudite man. He had gone to Princeton, made law review at Columbia, and had for ten years been a senior partner at Jensen, Busby & O'Donnel. History was his hobby. But even if he had never gone to school, he would have understood how Marc Antony forfeited the Roman Empire for Cleopatra better than a college of historians could.

I was struck from the start by how thoroughly alone he was in his monstrous necessity. He knew that he looked ridiculous. He had mortal fears that his carefully-built reputation could come crashing down in a moment if he persisted in his folly, and yet he felt unable to stop.

Timothy O'Donnel's first words after shaking my hand firmly and saying, "Thank you for seeing me," were, "I know that what I'm doing is utterly stupid. I realize that I may be wrecking my life."

I asked him the obvious question: "How?"

"With a woman, not my wife. I'm in love—or, not in love, maybe obsessed is a better word."

"You say, in danger of wrecking your life?"

"Yes. Because it so preoccupies me. I'm insanely jealous, and yet I realize that I can't give her what she wants. What I guess she deserves. I even realize that she's not that nice a person. But I can't stop thinking about her. I got into this thing much deeper than I ever expected to, and now I don't know how to get out."

He was trying to look composed, but he fidgeted a great deal and broke off his own sentences as if better ways of presenting his predicament kept coming to his mind. The result was a disconnected series of false starts, and all I got after five minutes was the fact that he was in jealous pain over a woman.

I tried to get him to be more specific by asking what the woman's name was.

Even at that, he hesitated. But after what seemed like a conscious decision to go forward, because it was the only direction he could go in, he told me, "Karen ———."

Watching him squirm in his chair I had the impression of a big fish twisting on an invisible hook.

After about five whole minutes of this, I told him that I would need a lot more detail, and asked him to go back to the beginning. I had a sense that he felt very relieved at being asked to do this, as if it unburdened him of the need to be selective and stay relevant.

He did retrace his steps, and once he got past a terse preamble, he needed almost no prompting from me to render even the most intimate moments of his clandestine affair.

"Let me begin by saying that I'm a corporation lawyer—actually, a partner in a mid-sized firm. We represent sizable companies—mostly in mergers and acquisitions, or if someone has been wronged.

"I'm a happily married man. Louise and I celebrated our twenty-fifth a year ago, and we have two daughters. One is away at Stanford and our younger just got a scholarship to Juilliard. We all love opera."

"Your wife knows about this other woman?" I asked him.

"God no! She has no idea, though I don't know why she doesn't. After all these years, she just believes me."

A melancholy look came over him. "I think I'm being very disjointed," he said. "I guess that's the way I've been these days. I'd like to go back, if I may, to a very cold, raw night, last March, a little over a year ago.

"I have a close friend, Felix. We both worked for the federal government as assistant U.S. attorneys. It's the ultimate training to be a trial lawyer, but Felix became a judge, and a very fine one. Anyhow, on that night we had both attended a formal dinner at the Bar Association building—you know, across from the Algonquin—for an eminent judge who was retiring. We left there shortly after eleven o'clock, not late. Felix took the first cab because it was going downtown. And there I was, in my evening dress, looking for a cab going uptown. I live at Ninety-fifth and Park.

"I was faintly aware that a woman had appeared nearby. After a few minutes, a cab came, and as it stopped, she ran up to me and asked, 'Which way are you going?' Instinctively, I told her uptown. 'Can you give me a ride?' she asked me. 'There are no cabs.'

"She was looking plaintively at me, and it was pretty damn cold, so I said sure, and she got in. I didn't permit myself to look right at her face, but I could see that she had very narrow hips and a slender neck, and she seemed very supple. I could see her staring at me, and when she asked me what I did, I told her I was a lawyer. She said, 'I guessed it.' She was very intense, almost like a hummingbird, and very childlike, I thought.

"She said that her name was Karen, and I told her my name.

"As we rode uptown, I sensed that I seemed to fascinate her, but then immediately I had the thought that it was silly. But, still, I liked it. She said that I had very sensitive lips. I thought that she was only my older daughter's age, and I just said thanks. Then as we got to about Eighty-fifth Street, she said, 'I've got to get off soon. I'm staying at a friend's house.' I said, 'It was nice meeting you,' and she said, 'Nice, huh?' Before I could say anything, she pressed her lips against mine and kissed me hard.

"I admit that I kissed her a second time voluntarily, and she said, 'You're wonderful.' Then she gave me a card with her name and phone number, and she said, 'Oh, how I want you. I really do,' and we kissed good-bye and she jumped out of the cab.

"No one had ever said that to me before. Going home, I remembered the savor of her hard young body and those words. It was a kind of miracle. I woke up the next day feeling great.

"I tried to forget the whole thing, but she had started some craving in me. When I told Felix about it—he's the only one I ever told about Karen to this day, before you—he said that I was a dreamer, that maybe I got married a little too early, and that I shouldn't take it to heart. Well, he's on his second marriage, and his wife is a big trial lawyer. His divorce was in the papers plenty. He's had his share of excitement. I haven't really had much adventure in my life. It's been very straightforward.

"Anyhow, I didn't call Karen, but I kept thinking about her, more and more—about the way her body moved under that suede jacket and long wool skirt.

"Maybe my imagination played too big a part. She started to seem more appealing—very appealing. I remembered that she had very muscular legs, and I pictured them tapering to slender ankles, and I remembered that kiss. I thought I remembered her tapping on the cold pane of the cab window and saying good-bye when she got out at the light, but later she said that hadn't happened. That's why I say a lot was in my imagination. Doctor, I realize that I'm no longer young."

I figured Timothy to be in his middle fifties. He was slender and wearing a beautifully tailored blue suit, a pearl-gray shirt, and a burgundy tie. He had a pencil-thin mustache, agreeable gray eyes, and a pleasant alertness of expression. His face was deeply lined. I imagined that he could be attractive if one was drawn to this stately type. I wondered, could this Timothy truly have been what that woman was waiting for all her life—an older man of obvious solvency who seemed either too timid or too civilized to look at her face?

"I wanted to kiss her again," he said, "just to see what it was like, really to clear my mind, because the evening lingered.

"After about two weeks I called her, and I started to introduce myself hesitantly. I figured that she forgot me—you know how young people are. But as soon as I began, she said, 'Oh, thank God. I was afraid you'd never call.' I suggested dinner, but she said, 'Just come up here, I'll make you something,' and she gave me her address on Audubon Avenue.

"She was annoyed that I couldn't make it on a Saturday, but we set it for during the week, and I told Louise that I would be with a client.

"I drove up to Washington Heights very early. It was a very rickety neighborhood, poor people, cheap stores, and a lot of street vendors. The buildings were mostly in disrepair, with ornate facades that were crumbling and fire escapes in the front descending almost into the street. I only mention this because I was scared on two counts: scared of seeing her and scared about bringing a good car up there and looking too dapper.

"As I say, I got there ahead of time to see where I could park. She lived in a slightly better place than most, an old white building with a door that was painted over many times but never scraped and an old fanlight window that looked like someone had broken it with a baseball bat.

"I had planned on having a snack before going in, but for security I just parked my car at the hospital parking lot, which was nearby, and then took a cab to her building.

"Fortunately, a street lamp was shining on the door and I could make out her name on the bell. It was printed very small, and when I buzzed, she clicked back so fast that I couldn't shove the door open. I felt like a real idiot. Am I giving you too much detail?"

"Not at all."

"I walked up the three flights. She met me at the door in a crisp cotton dress. I really looked at her. She looked great. Her mouth seemed so luscious. I sat down on an overstuffed wing chair, and we talked trivially for a while, about her artificial fireplace and some inspirational quotes that she had pasted on the walls: 'LOVE CONQUERS ALL.' 'DON'T POSTPONE THINGS UNTIL TOMORROW.' Stuff like that. I complimented her on her spirituality, don't ask me why.

"Suddenly, she said, 'I can't stand all this talk. Come with me,' and she took my hand, and I followed her into her bedroom, primitive—you know, Santa Fe designs, with a carpet that she said was real Navajo Indian. She veered me toward the bed. Seconds later we were kissing, and she was unbuttoning my shirt, and the next instant I was on top of her and she was breathing hard. Her breasts were beautiful, conical, and her nipples stood up, and I kissed them. I never imagined this would matter so much.

"Then my pants were down, and she was on top of me, and I was inside of her with an unbelievable erection, and her hair was bouncing into her cheeks as she went up and down. I never forgot that first time. I could feel the tightening of her pelvic muscles, and I was floating through space, and neither of us could breathe. She came, and when my spasms started into her, she kept saying, 'This is wonderful.'

"And then I held her, not knowing what I had done to my life or was about to do."

"I don't follow you."

"I knew I couldn't just stop, and we did it again that night, and the taste of Karen and the smell of her were in my blood and my nostrils, her taut, sweaty body, and those long muscular legs, and her lips. To me she had become beautiful, I guess because of what she had done for me, and could do. But even though I needed her, I had no place for her. I never thought of leaving my wife.

"Before I left, at about ten thirty—I had to, for obvious reasons—she asked me if I liked her, and I told her that I did more than words could express. She said, 'That's good—you're very good with words,' and we laughed.

"I told her I'd call her soon, and she said, 'You'd better,' and then I put my clothes on and wrested myself away.

"When I reached the street, there was a drug deal in progress, and I was terrified. But the dealer and the buyers separated at the sight of me, as if they didn't know each other and they all just happened to be waiting there. And as I kept going, I realized that my fear was only fear of what I had done.

"Driving home, I remembered the incredible thrill, the whole evening, even the dilapidated front door, and I kept seeing her eyes wide open during sex, as if she was astonished by some miracle, and I remembered her gasping for breath.

"But mostly, I felt like a criminal. I tried to laugh to myself at her coarseness, but I realized that I loved it, and I could see her, over and over again, stepping out of her pants. I kept thinking of myself as having committed a heinous crime. I thought, this wasn't the idea when I married Louise. I had really meant, 'Till death do us part.'

"I vowed that it wouldn't affect my marriage, and the only person I told then or ever, before you, was Felix. We had lunch regularly at the stock exchange, and the next day when I saw him I told him. I think he understood. He never criticized me. I told Felix that even though you're a judge, you're never judgmental, and that I prized him for that.

"Of course, I called Karen right away and sent her flowers, which she said she loved. Let's face it, I was hooked.

"After that, I became desperate to make love to her, even to be in that dingy apartment. I began living not just for those orgasms and to kiss her, but for the whole sordid adventure. I worried about being recognized or that someone might mug me, but the sex made up for all of that, with plenty left over. I talked to Karen on the phone every few days, and I had an extra line installed so that she could call me at my office.

"I would see her once a week, rarely twice, and when I wasn't with her, I would think about her body. When I was with clients, I would think of her shirt open, revealing her nipples, or about her pussy. I would count the days and hours until the next time, when she would say, 'I couldn't wait for you to get here.'

"She would tell me that she masturbated, thinking about me, and once she asked me, 'Do you mind if I play with myself?' and I said it would be okay, and she did, and she wouldn't let me touch her. It was all unbearable, and unforgettable.

"We talked very little about ourselves. She surprised me by saying that she was thirty-eight. She looked a lot younger. She was so waifish. Sometimes I felt sorry for her. She was very exposed to the elements. She said she worked as a secretary and that she was an excellent typist. But she said that she had also been an office manager.

"At that point, she was very kind. She seemed almost able to read my mind, and she massaged me and put a pillow under my head at just the right times. As for cooking, she could hardly put up tea. I would order food to be delivered, and it was the only thing she would let me pay for, except for an occasional gift of perfume.

"The few occasions when we did go out, it was to a gaudy place in the neighborhood for dim sum. She knew I wasn't comfortable there. She liked to trace my lips with her finger, and I loved it, but in the restaurant, it made me nervous. She saw that—as I say, she could read my mind. But she would really have been quite hurt if she knew that secretly I was glad that she lived in a bad neighborhood because I wouldn't be recognized there.

"Sometimes when I got home, I was deeply shaken by the intensity of the sex, and by what I had done. I tried not to think about where it would go, except for the next time. I would immediately start planning when I could see her again and what I would tell my wife. Louise was credulous— or gullible, however you want to look at it. She believed whatever I told her, and that made it worse, in a way. Besides, I knew full well how criminals get careless by repetition. The hundredth time, they feel invulnerable, almost immortal, and I resolved I wouldn't make that mistake.

"It made no difference that Karen wasn't arrestingly beautiful. To me, she was—and, I must admit, she still is. By some feat of resurrection, she had made me reconsider my whole life, think what I might have been and could no longer be.

"Or maybe I could. Can a man live two whole lives? I would ask Felix, and all he would say was, 'Well, you're making a hell of a try.' "

Several times up until then I had tried to break in with a question. If I could learn what Timothy's present problem was, it would help me consider what might be most relevant in what he was telling me now. But each time I sought to ask him something he put up his hands instinctively, as if I were talking during a movie.

I felt the rush of his necessity to recite the details of this affair, like the Ancient Mariner, who needed to tell his story far more than he truly needed any individual to hear it.

Timothy raced on. "We saw each other for a few months, with no problems. Oh, I shouldn't say that. I was always nervous about getting caught. Sometimes the sex was very animal. Karen would rip at my shirt and dig her nails into me when we got going. I'd never had a woman do that. I'd only been to bed with two women before marrying. I had started dating my wife when I was in law school. I loved Karen's savagery, and I joined in, but I didn't want her leaving telltale marks. She would get upset when I asked her not to, and that was a problem.

"And a few other things upset me, too. One was that Karen was very tough on waiters and waitresses. She would get very critical if they forgot a glass of water she had asked for, and that made me uncomfortable. But there was no discussing it with her. So I just accepted her indignation. She would tell stories of people who were rude to her—like a man who got ahead of her on line at the bank. It happens to all of us, but if I didn't act outraged, she would see me as disloyal. I did my best to sympathize.

"On one score she was right, though. She liked to take my hand in the street. That made me nervous, but if I pulled back or demurred in any way, she would get very hurt and angry. She would ask, 'Are you afraid to be seen with me, by some chance?' Of course, I denied it. But I would have preferred to take cabs. However, she liked to walk in the neighborhood. So I went along. I couldn't risk offending her and, besides, what she wanted was small enough and only fair—I realized that.

"And she was also a health nut. She wouldn't eat the skin of a chicken.

She had a sunlamp, and she took every kind of vitamin. That part was certainly okay. But she was vehemently against my cigars. I couldn't smoke one in her presence, and I love my cigar at the end of the day. She said that they were fatal. Maybe she was right. But she also said that she hated the smell, and one night when I got there, she could tell that I'd had a cigar and she wouldn't let me touch her all evening. She established a twenty-four-hour rule. If I smoked within twenty-four hours of seeing her, no sex. She said that she would always be able to tell, and she could. So I obeyed. In fact, once after that when I did smoke, she knew immediately. She accused me, and I had to confess I did.

"None of this really mattered much. I weathered it all. Speaking of weather, I would count the hours, and I would go up there through rain, snow, sleet, fog. I think I would have gone through a tornado. Felix said I was like the postman—you know, who fog and snow can't stop from his appointed rounds. He also said that I must either love her or be crazy, because I would never have gone through a single lunch cigarless for him.

"When she objected that I never saw her on a Saturday, I found one or two, at great cost. Once I sent my wife down to Florida for a weekend, with Mary, our younger daughter, to spend time with my wife's parents. Another time, I actually cut short my vacation with my wife. I didn't want to be away too long—I know that was terrible of me to do. Usually, I just made an excuse and winged it. Making love to Karen was worth it, even though in some ways she was difficult."

Again I sought to break in with a question, but Timothy raised his voice to drown me out. It seemed that to him it was always as if the very next episode in his "love story" were the really critical one, as if what he'd told me were only prelude and the real message was about to come.

I subsided in my chair. I had the sense that Timothy both wanted me there and not there.

He went on, implying by his tone that I should pay special attention to what was to follow.

"One evening, I had really been counting the hours, but when I arrived, she asked me to sit down and discuss a law case with her. She was planning to sue a restaurant for scalding her with hot water and causing her pain and suffering. She kissed me quickly and told me that we had to discuss this, it was on her mind. She felt that the restaurant should pay her at least fifty thousand dollars if she brought the action properly.

"She already had the summons and complaint forms, and she had filled most of them out. She asked me to handle the case. I tried to explain to her that it wasn't the kind of case that our office deals with, and that I really wasn't competent at that sort of thing, that we undertake, almost exclusively, corporate matters. But she got indignant, as if I was copping out, walking out on her.

"I don't know what words I used, but she surprised me by saying, 'Are you calling this a frivolous case, because if you are—' She glowered at me.

"That was, in fact, exactly what I was thinking, though, of course, I didn't say so. What startled me was her use of the word 'frivolous.' I know it's a common word, but it's a special legal description.

"For the next ten minutes she talked straight legalese. She discussed 'gross negligence' and 'punitive rights,' and kept repeating the term 'pain and suffering.' I was astonished. Nothing she said made sense, but it sounded as if it did.

"Then she bragged that she had made money in settlements three different times in her life. She had sued a dentist about a bridge he had put in and had collected twelve thousand dollars for don't ask me what. And there was a whiplash deal in a cab, also settled. I forget the third one.

"Slowly I came to see that she was one of those lifetime litigants that we throw out of our office when they come in on occasion. We're careful never to take a dime from them so they can't sue us. Of course, I was very surprised. But not utterly. I had already seen Karen's self-righteous side, though never like this.

"I did my best to temporize, to give her some advice, and we finally went to bed. She was very passionate. She told me she loved me and thought about me all the time.

"But the whole evening bothered me. As soon as I got to my car, I took a cigar out of the glove compartment. I felt like smoking two at a time."

"What exactly bothered you?" I asked Timothy.

"I wondered if she was using me for my legal knowledge."

"Would that be bad?"

"I guess not. But I didn't like to think of her as one of those people who live mainly to be injured by accident and then collect astronomical amounts.

"Anyhow," he said, and then speeded up as if compensating for our brief digression, "a few days later, I forgot the legal stuff, and all I could think about were those passionate stabs of excitement and her legs intertwined with mine.

"But after that she became increasingly difficult. She would ask me legal questions, and sometimes she would call me up with one. I realized that she had gotten the word 'frivolous' from other lawyers, and maybe even from a few judges. I wondered how many suits she had brought and lost.

"I was still distracted as hell by her. During a meeting while my partners were wrangling over what kind of bonuses we could afford to give the staff, they asked me why I hadn't expressed my opinion. All I could think about was my grinding into her in that Santa Fe bedroom with the artificial fireplace.

"The sex got better, if anything, but she would get angry with me in a moment if I didn't give her the advice she wanted on legal issues. Or if I didn't show enough animosity toward her enemies. She always had a couple of cases going at once.

"Then, one Friday evening, after I had been seeing her for four months, maybe five, she gave me a terrible time. As soon as I got there, she said to me, 'You're married, aren't you? And you lied about your age.' Her face was stern.

"I tried to protest that I hadn't. But she knew. She said, 'You told me that you were fifty-three, but you're fifty-seven. April twelfth, 1933.'

"I wondered how she had found out and could be so sure. She spoke very sharply, 'I don't care how old you are, but I don't like you to lie.' She looked right through me. I felt devastated for a while, but then suddenly I didn't. I actually felt an enormous sense of relief. I told myself, all right, you had your fling and now the relationship is over. Even so, I had gone all the way up there, and I had a terrific desire to make love to her one more time.

While she was bawling me out, I got an erection but, of course, I didn't know what to do with it.

"She sat back, with her legs closed, and smoothed her skirt down over them, and boy, did she berate me. It was a habit I saw plenty after that. She called me a phony, and she said I really should be terribly ashamed of myself. She accused me of misleading her.

"I admitted everything, I had to, and finally I asked her how she knew.

"She got up, went into the bedroom, and returned with a big book. I was stunned. It was *Martindale & Hubbell.*"

"What's that, Timothy?"

"It lists every lawyer in the country. It tells where they're employed, where they went to law school, the year of their first admission to the bar, and a lot of other facts, including their date of birth. It even listed the jobs I'd held and some of the papers I've written.

"I was astonished, and I asked her how she happened to have that book—it's a lawyer's *Who's Who.* She said that a few years earlier she had decided to look for a job as a legal secretary, so she bought it. She said that after our conversation on the phone that week about my office, she got curious to see what they said about me because she loved me. I asked her, 'My age, you mean?' and she said, no, that she didn't even know they had people's ages in there.

"She said that she could hardly believe that I had lied to her, and that when she realized I had, she had cried, not just then but on and off afterward. I felt terrible. Then she said she had reasoned that if I could lie about that, maybe I didn't always tell her the truth.

"Apparently, that brought the sudden insight that I was married. She screamed at me, 'You bastard. No wonder you didn't want marks on your arm and you didn't want to see me on weekends.' She asked me my wife's name, and I told her, but I hated to. I felt as if I were betraying Louise. Then she got ironic. She said now she knew why I was so uncomfortable when she took my hand in the street.

"I couldn't conjure up any defense. All I could think of was the lawyer's trick of asking for a postponement while we gather some important new evidence, and I couldn't really say that. I didn't have anything new to say. I was afraid she would call my wife, and I put my arm around her. I was also horny. I asked her if she wanted to make love, and to my amazement, she nodded yes. It was the most fantastic sex I ever had.

"When it was over, I whispered to her that I was sorry, and I said that I really thought she must have known I was married, but that I hated to talk about it. She swore that she'd had no idea. She said that she never thought that a married man would be in a tuxedo without his wife. I explained to her that it was a party for a judge who was retiring. She asked me, 'And men don't take their wives?' I told her that some did, but a lot didn't, and that mine didn't want to go. She had never met the judge and she had things to do.

"We had sex again, and we were very affectionate. I told Karen that I cared for her a lot. I didn't say so, but I guess I had felt from the beginning that such a time would come, that it was inevitable. I asked her if things could ever be the same between us, and she said she wasn't sure. She said something like, 'You're not what you were.' I told her, I thought light-heartedly, 'Well, I can't always wear a tuxedo.'

"A few minutes later, she asked me, in a really sexy voice, if I would wear my tuxedo again. She said very coarsely, 'I want you to fuck me in your tuxedo.'

"Naturally, I said yes at once. I felt forgiven, and as I kept thinking about it, the idea turned me on more and more.

"She kissed me good-bye very passionately. It was like a conspiracy. On the way home I thought, 'Wow, you really survived a close call,' and I started making up my next week's excuse for Louise.

"When I told Felix about Karen's tantrum, he said, 'She obviously knew that you were married all along. That was just a game.' I differed with him completely on that one, and also with his allegation that Karen had known how old I was from day one. He insisted that he was right and that her sudden discovery of my age was also a game. He argued quite cogently that she must have looked me up in the big book on the night we met. He said women do a lot of data gathering, calling friends and all that kind of thing when they meet a man, and that there was no way on earth she could resist looking me up in a book that was already in her apartment. I called him cynical, and he said maybe, and that was that. But I knew in my heart that he was right.

"My alibi to Louise was another judge retiring, which also explained my tux. I owned two of them—complete outfits, one with stays and the other with buttons. But I decided to go out and buy another shirt.

"On Friday evening Louise and my daughter Mary and one of Mary's friends were sitting down to an early dinner before going out to an eight o'clock movie. They couldn't stop talking about how young and handsome I looked in my tux. That made me feel like an ax murderer, and I guess in a way I was—a murderer in a cummerbund and shiny black shoes.

"Of course, the tux attracted plenty of attention up in Karen's neighborhood. I knew that some people sitting on a stoop were pointing at me, but I told myself they could laugh all they wanted as long as they didn't follow me and hit me over the head. Oh, I should say I made friends with a guy named Willis in the garage. I gave him big tips and he always had my getaway car ready to go. That night he warned me to be especially careful on the side streets, and that put the fear of God in me.

"There were the usual dice games and domino games on little tables, and some quiet drug deals going on. But everyone was aware of me. I was the loudest character there. The good part was that I made it, and when I got upstairs, Karen threw her arms around me and kissed me and thanked me for remembering, and right away I put my hand inside her dress and took liberties that I never did with my wife. The sex was so great that it was as if we were having it for the first time.

"As a rule, we would order in Chinese food, and the deliveries came fast. I was a little paranoid, though there was no need to be. I would give Karen the money and she would pay the boy. But she said that I looked so great in my evening dress that night that she insisted on going out to dinner.

"That was exactly what I didn't want. But I had to. We went a number of blocks to her favorite gaudy little Chinese restaurant, and while she was staring into my eyes and stroking my hand, I saw everyone gawking at me in my tux. I felt like a real freak. Wouldn't anyone?

"I bolted my food down, which isn't like me, but I wanted to get out of there. Karen is a tormentingly slow eater, as if she's evaluating every mouthful for a possible lawsuit. But I couldn't act in a hurry. I knew from experience that if I looked impatient, she would get angry and go slower. Karen has a strong will, and she doesn't really go into motion except in bed, where she's violent. And in the law courts, of course."

Timothy laughed at his own humor and his own plight. He had a boyish open smile. To himself, as well as to me, his whole story was thus far tragicomic.

"After dinner," he went on, "we returned to her place and did it again. This time she pulled me into bed and made me keep my tux on, or as much of it as I could. Not the cummerbund, of course, but she made me stop and put the shoes back on. She got terribly excited, and I think she had many orgasms. Of course, I enjoyed it, even though the outfit got in my way.

"While I lay there afterwards, she kissed me on the eyelids and begged me to wear my tux again next time.

"I couldn't believe it. I protested vigorously. But she said the sex was fantastic and called me a great lover. She insisted, and she got very hurt each time I said no. She accused me of being embarrassed. I finally reluctantly agreed to wear it one more time. But I didn't like it.

"It was a very upsetting walk to the garage, a lot of streetlights were out, and I didn't know which was more dangerous, to walk or to run, so I walked real fast. I was awfully happy to see Willis, who had once told me he was armed, because a lot of garages get held up late at night.

"When I got home, after showering, I threw my tux into a separate bag and got into bed. Louise was really asleep, but she asked me, as she always did, 'Did you have a good time, dear?' which only made me hate myself more. I told her it was fair—I didn't want her to feel that she missed anything." He smiled sheepishly while making this last comment.

"The next day I brought the bag out to the laundry myself. You guessed it. Karen didn't stop. It didn't bother her how miserable I was. She absolutely demanded that I always wear a tuxedo to see her. I tried to beg out. I fought like hell. I asked her if I could at least leave one or two in her apartment, but she refused even that. She said it wasn't sexy or realistic.

"Even when I told her I was terrified, it didn't seem to matter. When

I said it was a big expense of time and money, she asked me sarcastically how much time I spent with my wife and kids and how much money I spent on them. Of course, I didn't want to go into that. She actually said she didn't think she'd enjoy sex the same way if I refused, that she couldn't help it, but that was the way she felt about it.

"I should have broken the whole thing off right there, but I didn't. As Felix put it, she had raised the ante, and I still continued playing.

"By then, I had no idea what to tell my wife. Obviously, I couldn't make the tuxedo excuse every Friday. Felix would kid me. He would ask, 'Another judge retiring? You'll retire the whole bench pretty soon. There won't be anyone left anymore, except policemen and lawyers.' Felix said it was cruelty on her part, that Karen was a cruel person. When I would tell him I didn't think so, he would say, 'You're just not thinking at all.' He said that I ought to protest to Karen, to flatly refuse.

"For a while, I did. I objected every time I saw her, but it was a hopeless cause. She just wouldn't give in. And here's the terrible part. I felt like such a fool that I even began lying to my friend Felix. I told him that we agreed that I would wear the tux only once in a while for variety, and when I was in the mood.

"I tried to make the most of the situation. For one thing, I started renting my tuxes, having them delivered to the office, and I would return them the next day. It was a pain in the neck—I feel better just telling you the story. Thanks for being so sympathetic.

"On the good side, the tux did solve one problem. Any lipstick or perfume that Karen got on my outfit wouldn't be seen at home. I actually suspected her of planting things on it a few times, but I must have been mistaken. At first, I would put the tux on in the office and stop back there at eleven thirty to change back before going home. But I didn't want people to see me, so I began changing in the car going and coming—that also saved a lot of time. As I say, the tuxedos were terrible, but at least they had that one advantage. I guess I tend to see silver linings—my wife says I do.

"But the good side didn't go far. It was a nightmare, let's face it. I knew how ridiculous I looked. And it got to be worse and worse. I began to suspect that people in the neighborhood were expecting me to walk through on Fridays and were laughing at me. Once I tried wearing a long coat over it, but that didn't really conceal it. I felt like a sitting duck—maybe a sitting penguin would be more like it.

"After a month or so, it occurred to me that I wouldn't feel quite so outlandish if I went to better places with Karen, instead of just staying in the neighborhood. I began escorting her to fine northern Italian restaurants—all downtown, none of them near me. Of course, I always kept tabs on where Louise and my daughter were going to be on Friday evenings. But there was still some risk. We know a lot of people. Or, I guess more to the point, a lot of people know us. Once or twice she argued with a waiter, and I was desperately afraid that she might want to bring a lawsuit. That was the last thing I needed.

"One month, I told Karen that I had eye trouble, as an excuse to wear dark glasses, but, naturally, I couldn't always do that. I noticed that Karen was incredibly unsympathetic to what I had reported as very serious. She didn't even ask what was wrong with my eyes. I hadn't really expected her to, but I didn't say anything. And when I took them off, she didn't even comment.

"Going to good places made things easier, in a way. I felt less conspicuous with other people also dressed up—there was even an occasional man also in evening dress. Still, it was pressure, and the instant I got back into her apartment, I would feel suddenly relieved. I could breathe, like a fish returning to water.

"I actually thought I had figured out her motive, and that Karen was really a kind of diabolical genius. I figured that she had insisted that I wear a tux so that I would have to take her out in style. She had anticipated that in my evening dress, I would think big—good restaurants, theater, and what have you.

"Of course I resented it, but I grudgingly admired her for doing it, for keeping me off balance, which I didn't think was that easy. I'm known as a pretty good litigator and a thinker on my feet.

"But, believe it or not, I was wrong even in that. Not long afterwards, she threw me another curve.

"Out of nowhere, she announced, 'I don't really want to go to anymore fancy places. From now on, I'd rather just stroll through the neighborhood and eat at Dim Sum's, or whatever it was called, or on St. Nicholas Avenue.'

"I couldn't believe it. It sounded as if she was saying, 'I'll give up the good restaurants so that you can look ridiculous.' But, of course, there had to be more to it. I realized that I didn't understand her at all.

"I must have looked dumbfounded, because she asked 'Why? Are you ashamed of me? Don't you want to be seen with me?' She reminded me that I hadn't ever wanted to meet any of her friends.

"How could I refuse? Of course, I agreed, though it was the worst of all nightmares. I knew that I would dread every minute that we weren't in her apartment, and I certainly did.

"By then the whole squalid neighborhood was waiting for me to arrive every Friday in my tux. When I would go into that white tenement building in my black evening dress, I had the thought that I had no protective coloring and that I'd be eaten alive. I had the feeling that it was only a matter of time before something really bad was going to happen. Only the sex kept me going.

"Doctor, I was slowly becoming deranged, and I wasn't telling Felix the half of it—the danger, I mean, or how Karen treated me. Also, she was very uneven. Every week I'd go through a war zone and I never knew how she would be when I finally made it—how she would receive me—by being legalistic and calling for a conference, or naked and hot, or like one time, in a fur coat with nothing on under it and desperate for me to play with her vagina. Incidentally, I never had any idea how she got that expensive fur coat—it seemed kind of tacky and loud. But the point is that no two days were the same. It was a lot more adventure than I'd bargained for.

"By the way, about then, Karen got a five-thousand-dollar award from a tailor who she said ruined a dress she was counting on for a job interview that she couldn't go to and that would have changed her life-style. The whole story made no sense to me at all, I couldn't imagine how she got the money, but apparently she did. She showed me her bankbook, where the total had jumped up to twenty-three thousand and something.

"Doctor, I may seem crazy, but the sex and my romantic feelings were greater than ever. I lived for the best of what I could get in an evening, and it seemed worth everything else. In fact, even that was only sporadic. I feel that my life and my sanity are on the edge—and, of course, my reputation. That's why I'm here.

"Timothy," I said. "I don't exactly follow you."

"Believe it or not, I've told you the best of it. The worst is yet to come. I'm afraid that I've gotten insanely jealous, and I'm taking unbelievable risks. If I don't stop, I'll destroy my career and my marriage. I may even get killed.

"The real trouble started about five months ago. I was about to quit, to pull out—literally and figuratively, as Felix put it. I wasn't enjoying my life, except when I was with her. And obviously, I had no future with her. So I went up there on a Friday night with my abdication speech all prepared. I remember feeling like a free man on my way up there.

"When I got to the door, she must have known something was up because I wasn't in my tux. I was dressed appropriately for the neighborhood."

Timothy stopped abruptly and looked at me in bewilderment. "But I guess I really wasn't a free man," he said, "because, obviously, I didn't end it that night.

"Naturally, I wanted to touch her the instant I saw her, but I didn't. I had promised myself that I wouldn't. She looked really great that night, and sexy. I asked her to sit down, and I said that I had something very important to tell her.

"Just then the phone rang, not once but maybe eight times. That was rare. She very seldom got calls. So far as I knew, she had only one friend, Nancy, and she would always answer her calls on the first or second ring and get off in a hurry.

"Karen seemed very jarred by the ringing, but she didn't get up to answer it. Finally, I asked her, 'Aren't you going to get it?' But she just shook her head and told me to go on.

"I was glad she stayed put. I needed her undivided attention and I wanted to get this over with. I started my little speech by telling her that she was a wonderful woman. I said that she was bright and very attractive, but that this relationship just wasn't meant to be. I thought she'd get more upset than she did when she saw where I was heading, but she just listened.

I told her that she deserved a lot more than I could give. I was very emotional when I said that, but she seemed distracted.

"Unfortunately, just then the phone rang again. I asked, 'Who the hell is that?' And she said very flatly, 'I'd better go and get it.'

"She ran into the other room, and right after she said hello, she said, 'I'm sorry. I was out for a minute or two.' Then she said very softly, 'How are you?' Then she lowered her voice and went on chatting, and she giggled a little. I think she said, 'That's wonderful,' but I couldn't be sure. Then I distinctly heard her say, 'I'm sorry, I can't really talk now.' 'Yes.' 'Okay.' 'Me, too.'

"I got very irritated while I was waiting, I didn't know why, except that on the most basic level I don't like to be interrupted. When she came back, I finished my speech. I told her again that I realized that I wasn't really giving her what she wanted. She just listened. She didn't try to refute me in any way, and I found that disturbing.

"She heard me out, and when I was all finished, she remarked very indifferently, 'So I guess it's over.' I didn't know what to say. We were both kind of quiet for a while, and I was really at a loss.

"A little later, she commented, 'I had a feeling that you didn't really want me.' I argued with her that it wasn't that simple, but that got her annoyed. She said, 'Well, it was simple enough for you to come up here every Friday night.' Little did she know. I guess I drew a blank because she said, 'Don't worry. I'm not asking you to leave your wife. I'm not a dependent sort of person.

"I walked over to her to try to kiss her, but she stopped me very sharply. She actually said, 'Please, don't touch me.' She seemed cold and remote, more beautiful than ever.

"I felt near a state of collapse when she got up and went quietly toward the door. There was nothing I could do but walk out, and after I left, she just closed the door and bolted it.

"I was in shock. I knew I had a rival.

"I hadn't expected it to be easy, but, my God, she agreed with me and practically ushered me out.

"It was a bitter cold night, and that braced me up. It also meant that the streets were deserted. When I saw Willis, I figured it was the last time, so I gave him a twenty. He was very appreciative. As I got into my car, I felt that he would miss me more than she would.

"This all happened about five months ago. When I got home, I tried to put it out of my mind. I counted my many blessings. I looked at our big, comfortable apartment on Park Avenue. I love my children—my older daughter was coming home that weekend, and we had a lot of social plans. I tried to tell myself that I had everything, and that going up to that bleak and dangerous neighborhood was pointless. I said to myself, it's worse, it's self-destructive.

" 'Well, Timothy,' I told myself. 'Everyone has some kind of vice, a tragic flaw, and this one was yours. But, thank goodness, you didn't let it defeat you. Just settle down and enjoy your real life. It's Saturday morning. Get some sleep.'

"But I woke up about an hour later. I guess I sprang up because Louise asked me if anything was the matter. I wondered who the guy was, and I told myself, 'Well, if something is starting, it's only fair. You have driven her to it.' I pictured him younger, eligible. I wondered if he was a lawyer. I tried to sleep, but then I wondered if they'd had sex already.

" 'What's the difference?' I told myself. 'If they haven't yet, they will. You don't expect her to become a virgin again, do you?' I remembered her saying, 'Too bad, you're married.' I guess I slept fitfully that night, but it was only the beginning. As I say, I became a near madman."

Just then, Timothy caught sight of the clock behind me, and said, "Oh, my goodness, I've been talking nonstop. Am I running overtime?"

I told him that it was okay, that I had a few extra minutes before I'd have to stop.

"I'm sorry," he said. "But I feel that I've got to confide everything in you."

I said that was exactly what I expected him to do.

"There must be things you want to know," he said, very solicitously.

"There are, but I didn't want to break in on your account," I answered. "The next time you come in, I'll ask you some questions that occurred to me."

"Please do," he said. "It's not likely that I'll forget any of the details by the next time I see you. I just wish I could forget half of it."

A brief, uncomfortable silence followed, during which I reflected that, though he had told me some of his feelings and I could infer others, there was a great deal going on inside of him that I couldn't surmise. I wondered in particular how conscious he was of any anger he felt toward this woman, whose peculiar charm had induced him to walk a tightrope through space for uncertain gain, week after week. I had the impression that at times he was quite angry with her, though he had never said so explicitly.

Our session had, indeed, come to an end, and when I told him so, Timothy said he had no doubt that he wanted to continue seeing me.

"I can't tell you how helpful it is just to talk about this," he said. "Maybe what I told you sounds strange, but it isn't half as bad as the stuff I haven't yet gotten to. You'll hardly believe what I've been doing. I hardly believe it myself."

I didn't look or act surprised. I simply reassured him, "You'll tell me about it next time. Along with a lot else I want to know about your life."

"Of course," he said. "When should we meet?"

We set up a twice-a-week schedule, for lunchtime Tuesdays and Fridays. He warned me that he might have to cancel on occasion. "You know, we lawyers aren't always masters of our time, but I'll be able to give you notice."

I told him that would be fine.

When he was gone, I thought to myself, "You sure aren't master of your time."

The next session, Timothy went right back to his story. He said that after that first rush of jealousy, he had decided to call Karen "just because I didn't want it to end in such ambiguity."

He had asked her if she was willing to see him again.

Timothy said, "She asked me, did I mean just once or more than that. I told her more than that, of course, and we made a date.

"When I went there—in my tux, to please her—I had the feeling that she was at best lukewarm, but I told myself that was only natural. We chatted for a while. I was actually glad when she asked me some technical questions that I could answer."

"You mean legal questions, Timothy?"

"No, actually this time it was about money investments. She wanted to double all the money she had made suing people, and I tried to review for her some different forms of investment—treasury bills, liquid asset funds, you know, that kind of thing."

"You felt closer?"

"In a way. But she seemed very disappointed in the low percentages that money could earn. I explained to her that once you start trying to beat six or seven percent, you really have to start taking risks. But she snapped at me, 'I don't take risks.'

"She seemed surprised when I asked her about that phone call the week before. She said it was Nancy. 'But you usually get off the phone right away with Nancy and say you'll call her back,' I told Karen. She didn't answer.

"When I tried to kiss her, she pulled back and said that, after the way I had threatened her, she didn't feel comfortable with me yet, and I went home without touching her, except for a quick kiss at the door.

"That week I was very upset. I replayed our conversation about the phone call, and the phone call itself, as well as I could in my mind. I felt pretty sure that it wasn't Nancy. And if it wasn't, there had to be a man in her life, exactly as I had suspected. Well, I shouldn't say I was certain, but I strongly suspected it. She simply wouldn't talk to a girlfriend that way, not by lowering her voice or saying those things. Or even if it was Nancy, they had some secret, and there was probably a man in the picture, anyhow.

"For a while, I told myself that if that was the way things were, I could live with it, and I settled down. But then I had the terrible thought that maybe some of those other calls in the past were from the same man. The more I thought about that one, the more it made logical sense. I reasoned, it was too much coincidence that this one time when I was saying good-bye, she was on the phone so long, when all the other times she got right off. If it was a man calling her, then it made sense that she would get him off fast with me there, but with me dropping out of the picture, she would naturally let him talk a little more.

"It was incredibly hurtful to think that there had been another man in her life all the time she was seeing me. It was like we never had anything special. I tried to tell myself that maybe she hadn't been sleeping with him during those weeks when she was sleeping with me. But I realized that Karen was a very sexual woman. I didn't know where to go with that one.

"Pictures started in my mind of this man, whoever he was, making love to Karen in that same bed. Once I woke up with a nightmare of this man on top of her, moving in and out, and she was begging for more. I tried to, but I couldn't see his face.

"I broke down and told Felix my theory, hoping that he would say I was inventing the whole thing, the way he said I invented Karen's greatness. But he just looked at me and said, 'There may be another man. Possibly. There's no way of knowing.' When I brought it up again with him, he would tell me to try not to think about it. I figured, of course, he was right: I would probably never know. But he was wrong about one thing. I couldn't help thinking about it.

"I made an all-out attempt to get back into her good graces. I guess it was my competitive urge, but I felt I had to be her lover again, and knock out whoever my rival was. I would picture another man with his hands on her naked body. I wondered if the guy was my age, but then I figured, probably not as worldly. Then I would imagine that it was some punk kid. It was bad either way, but worse if he was younger—"

"Why was that, Timothy?"

"I don't really know. Maybe because I figured a young kid would take advantage of her.

"Anyway, at that point, I starting sending her flowers again, constantly. For a few weeks in a row, I went up there in my tux and discussed law with her for hours, and money management. I thought she was melting, and finally she did, but it wasn't the same."

"In what way?"

"For one thing, there were no phone calls anymore. Not one. Not even a ring from Nancy. Of course, that made me very suspicious. Why would they stop so abruptly? I figured that she didn't want to take a chance talking to whoever it was, because she knew that I was pretty smart and would figure it out.

"Finally, we did go to bed. She gave herself to me, but she just lay there. It wasn't like before. I went real slow, and then fast, and did everything I could to arouse her, and I think she was pretty moved for a few minutes at one time. But her eyes were closed, and she was still.

"When it was over, I asked her what was the matter, and she said, 'Nothing. It was wonderful.' But I didn't believe her. Her eyes had been closed."

"What was the significance of that?"

"It was different for her. I had the terrible feeling that she was imagining that it was him, the other guy. I pictured him young and handsome and athletic, and I felt old and flabby, and—yes, and near death, unworthy of her. She was just starting out in life, with a lot of sex ahead of her, not with me.

"We kept talking, and I approached her again a little later. We had sex again, but it was the same.

"On my way home, I felt unbelievably bad. I wondered if I had any appeal to her at all, and if I did, what it was. Was I just her advisor and this other guy her real lover?

"I wanted to stop thinking about him, but I couldn't. I could imagine her rushing to the door and kissing him when he got there, and then rushing him into that bedroom. I imagined him rubbing her back and knowing exactly what to do.

"I felt it was imperative to have her back the way she was, that lithe young female who had given me so much excitement, so much to look forward to—and to remember.

"Slowly I realized that my days were still being interrupted, but not by beautiful images—by horrible ones. I was obsessed by terrible jealous thoughts of her with another man. When I would sit in the living room with Louise, trying to read my newspaper, I couldn't help picturing whoever it was up there with Karen, maybe both of them walking around nude and laughing. I could practically hear her saying to the guy, whoever he was, 'This is wonderful,' just the way she said it to me in that cab and fifty other times.

"I would also wonder how she had met the guy, and I would think, it couldn't have been as romantic as the way we met. I know this sounds stupid, but I wanted to be him—"

"Stupid. In what way?"

"Because he might have been some derelict, for all I knew. Why should I want to be him? I did a lot of legal work for her on a case that interested her. It concerned a huge settlement that a woman got in New York City when a piece of stone fell from a cornice and broke her shoulder. Karen had found out that the woman got about six hundred thousand dollars. She said, 'I wish something like that would happen to me.' And I said, 'Doesn't everybody?' and we laughed.

"I told her that I'd look into the details, and I did. The night I analyzed the case with her, we had great sex. She was her old animal self again, really getting into it with me. It was fantastic. I thought she felt that way, too.

"But then, going home, I had the terrible thought that she might have been thinking about that other man all during sex with me, and maybe that was why it was so wonderful for her. I thought, suppose she was imagining him really there with her, while I was going through the motions. It sounds crazy, but the thought stuck in my mind. It just lodged in there. I couldn't get rid of it.

"I told Felix about my jealousy. But I felt too ridiculous to tell him how intense the whole thing had become. As you must have gathered, Felix is pretty worldly, and he tried to talk me out of it. He said, 'Timothy, what's the difference what she's thinking? It was great for you. What more do you want?'

"Then he said the usual thing, you know, that jealousy is only natural, but that I should try to get over it. He was right, of course, but it didn't help at all. I could only conclude that things are a lot easier for him than for me, and I respect him for that. Anyhow, I didn't want to look stupid, so I let it go.

"I was beginning to realize by then that nothing Karen did could satisfy me. When she was unhappy and sex was bad, I was miserable. I would figure that she was in the guy's power, whoever he was. And when the sex was great, I got even crazier. I couldn't get the idea out of my mind that she was thinking about him. I know what you must be thinking— What the hell did I really want? It's a good question. Maybe you can help me figure out the answer. I have no idea, myself.

"Of course, after a month or so of this, I wasn't sleeping enough, and

I looked drawn. And, naturally, Louise could sense that something terrible was going on in my life. She began asking me to talk about it, whatever it was. At first, I would tell her there was nothing, that I was just overworked. But she had seen me overworked before, plenty of times, and she knew there was more to it this time. After a while, I realized that I had to tell her something more specific, so I told her that I was concerned about special trouble at work.

"I invented a big cock-and-bull story about clients and how I was upset that a certain company couldn't pay us a big sum because they were close to bankruptcy. She said that I shouldn't let it get me down, that we had more than enough money, and I told her that she didn't understand, that I was the one in the firm who had brought them in and backed them up when my partners doubted them. I told her it wasn't just money, but my reputation.

"Of course, I told her not to mention any of this to anyone—she's friendly with a few of the wives. And she promised that she wouldn't. I can always count on Louise's being absolutely confidential. I can truthfully say that she has never let me down that way. After a while she let it go, especially because I told her that the details were very technical.

"I said I realized that I'd been a terrible husband in recent times. Damn it, she was very reassuring—she would say no, that I hadn't been bad, that I was wonderful, and that made me feel even worse. Doctor, it's pretty obvious I guess—I am a terrible husband, let's face it, though to this day, Louise has no idea how."

He stopped and seemed to be cogitating something for a moment.

Then he said, "You know, now that I think about it, I guess I've always had a jealous nature. In retrospect, I think I even married Louise because another man was interested in her. That was a long time ago, when I was in law school and she was starting out as a high school teacher. We had never slept together—I mean, actually had intercourse—people didn't in those days, at least not people from good Catholic families. It's true we came close, but she had said that she was saving it for the man she was going to marry.

"Looking back, I obviously liked her a lot, but I actually made my decision because this other guy was starting to show serious interest in her.

He was taking her to football games, and she was beginning to like him. Anyhow, I proposed, she accepted, and we've been very happy. Louise has always been a wonderful wife and mother. I realize this whole thing with Karen is a hundred percent me—it's my problem."

"That's interesting, Timothy. I'd like to ask you a little about your life," I started to say.

"Certainly," he broke in. "I'll tell you, of course. But please, I'd better go on. There's a lot more to it. I really haven't told you the worst with Karen, what's been going on for the last three months. This is stuff I haven't even told Felix. When I tell you, you may even say that you don't want me as a patient."

"I'm sorry," I said. "Please go on."

By then, my curiosity was perhaps as keen as his own need to continue uninterrupted.

"It's very embarrassing," he said, and paused, gathering his thoughts.

I recalled a comment that F. Scott Fitzgerald had once made, that the perfect lead for a short story would be the narrator's saying, "Now I'm going to tell you something that I'm really ashamed of." In my practice I could often concur that this was, indeed, a peerless beginning. Of course, Timothy had told me a lot already, but his need to unburden himself of the rest seemed so great that I resolved to myself to help him in that mission, and if he did stray from his narrative, to bring him back to it.

In reality, that proved unnecessary.

"Anyhow, my jealousy wouldn't go away. I began to remember a lot of things about my relationship with Karen, and they started to look different. I mean, little things that I didn't care about while they were happening. I started to feel like a fool."

"Can you give me an example or two?"

"Sure. Of course. For instance, Karen used to say to me, quite often, 'Too bad you're married.' It would bother me, because I didn't like to disappoint her. But all of a sudden I realized that if she had another lover, she would naturally say this to explain to me, and maybe to herself, why she was doing such a thing. Also, she used to say, 'I couldn't wait till you got here.' I used to take that as a wonderful compliment, and maybe it was, in a way, but all of a sudden I saw it as something different."

"I don't follow you."

"Don't you see, Doctor. She was saying, 'I couldn't wait, so I took another lover.' She was letting me know in little ways, which in my naïveté I had overlooked. I mean, it was a kind of concealed confession that I could take any way I chose to take it.

"Oh yes, and another thing. I remembered that once or twice, when Louise had been out with friends, I had called Karen on a weekday evening, just to surprise her. This was during a period when Karen had said that she was spending all her evenings at home studying. Both times I called her, she wasn't there. When I spoke to her the next day, she would always say she had just stepped outside to buy something. I, like a fool, believed her. But then I remembered that this was the very lie she had told whoever had called that night. Before that, I had believed whatever she told me. But after all that came back to me, I didn't know what to believe.

"Naturally, I realized that because I was married, Karen had the right to do whatever she wanted to. But still I couldn't bear to think that she was lying to me and that there was someone else.

"I began calling her up to say hello, or on some pretext, on nights when she had said she'd be there. She was taking a few courses and she would stay home a lot studying. Obviously, I couldn't call her three times a night, so once in a while I would call, and as soon as she answered, I would hang up. I would feel very relieved when she did answer. I couldn't do this too often, of course, I realized that, so I picked my spots.

"I decided never to let on to Karen that I was jealous of her. I knew that she wouldn't like it, and if she had someone else, she would only take more precautions not to let me know.

"Whatever the situation was, I thought, she had accomplished one thing. I tried harder than ever to do exactly what she wanted. I stopped complaining about her legal questions. On the contrary, I actually welcomed them. I discussed the law at length with her, especially accident law. I even went to the books and boned up on it a little. Felix would kiddingly describe me as a model prisoner.

"But it was hard never to talk to Karen about something that was this important to me. After all, we would spend hours talking about her topics, and this one was in my mind all week. I began asking her very lightly, 'By the way, are you dating anyone else these days?' She usually said quite warmly, 'No. Of course not.' Just what I wanted to hear. But then one night, after she said, 'Of course not,' she added, 'Anyhow, I don't have the time.'

"I must have looked upset, because she beckoned me over right away, and we made love. It was good medicine, but it didn't last long, because after that, even though I tried not to ask her or look jealous, I did.

"I could see that my questions weren't going over, and I still hadn't learned anything. Sometimes she would seem really hurt, but at other times she would get very indignant, as if I was calling her a slut. All right, Doctor, I better tell you the truth: When I was making love to her and I had that picture of her having intercourse with another man, the sex was unbelievably wonderful; it just burned me up, and I couldn't control myself. But during the week, when I wasn't with her, I was starting to go crazier, because I still had no idea.

One Friday, I was distracted the whole day by Felix's line that I would never know. By the evening, when I was driving up to Karen's, it bothered me more and more. When I saw her, I did something very foolish. Without provocation, I actually accused her. I asked her very sarcastically if this other guy had to wear a tuxedo, too, when he was having sex with her. She was taken aback. She told me to get out and to never talk to her again.

"I instantly would have given anything not to have said that, and I begged her forgiveness. I told her how much she meant to me. How we got over that one, I don't know. But we did. We made love that night, and I promised never to mention another man again. I actually felt better.

"But, as you must have guessed, it didn't help. My jealousy got worse, much worse, and I still didn't know. I really couldn't sleep. For some reason, I pictured this other man as tall and slim, maybe a revolutionary type, somebody even younger than she was. I don't know why I got that picture of him, fucking her all night. I thought, how could I compete with that, even if I wasn't married? Well, I just couldn't.

"I cursed myself for my body, for being old—for my sparse hair. I know I should have exercised more in recent years. Even a little would have helped. I never went to gyms. Louise had always been after me to exercise for my health, but I never did. I said I never had the time. I hated the grooves in my face.

"Then one day I got the idea to do something completely against my nature. When I first thought of doing it, I saw it as ridiculous, as just a fantasy. It was so completely not me."

"What was that, Timothy?"

"I thought, I'm not really the wimp she thinks I am. She underestimates me completely. I'll tell you what: I'll find out. I'll go up there when she's not expecting me to, and see for myself. I thought, so what if her neighborhood has the elements of a horror movie, I have to know.

"When I first got this idea, I saw it as ridiculous—just a fantasy. But I was surprised that the concept kept coming back to me, and pretty soon it seemed almost reasonable. I thought, why shouldn't I have the information? Why shouldn't I find out once and for all? I can't stay in this state.

"The question was when and how. I began on a Saturday night when Louise and I had tickets to *Rigoletto* at the Met. We were going with the Knolls, some old friends. I begged out, saying that the big case I'd been talking about was coming to a head and that I had to look at some papers in my office. I told Louise that I would join everybody at eleven o'clock when the opera was over and we'd all go out together for a sandwich. Louise made my excuse.

"Saturday was a perfect night. I figured that if Karen was seeing anyone, she'd probably have a date with him on a Saturday evening. I put on some old clothes and a jacket that I always used when I did outdoor work at our house in the country, and I drove up there. I brought some Mace with me, which I had bought a long time ago. I was nervous, but it was exciting in a way.

"I parked directly across the street from Karen's building. I saw that her living room light was on. I waited, but I didn't see her go in or out of the building, and at ten thirty I had to leave. I was an old hand at changing clothes in the car, so that was no problem, and I got to the theater, dressed appropriately, just as the opera was ending. That was the first time, and I realized, 'Hey, this is easy. If there's anything going on, you'll find out soon enough.'

"My wife and our friends were very welcoming, and I was glad to be back with them. They said that it was a great production, and I was sorry I missed it, but then I couldn't be in two places at once.

"That night made a big difference to me. For the first time, I felt that Karen's neighborhood didn't defeat me. I felt stronger. After that, I started to pick some random times and I would run my car up there on a whim, and just wait. I always stayed inside the car with the doors locked for obvious reasons—I didn't want to be seen and, of course, I was still pretty nervous up there.

"Meanwhile, I felt much better when I saw Karen. It was as if my surveillance had put me on a par with her. I felt sure that if she was up to no good, I'd find out. I tried to learn more about her life, to figure out when the most likely times would be. As I said, she was taking some courses. At this point, she had two, at Fordham, one in English and the other in fine arts, and she was a very diligent student.

"She was what you guys call compulsive. She took hundreds of notes and copied them over neatly; she said she always sat in the same seat in the front row, and she was compulsively clean and orderly around the house, too. She nearly always got As, and if she didn't, she would talk to the professor either to find out why or to complain about the way he marked her paper. When I called her on a study night, she would often hang up fast to be sure that she got her work time in. Anyhow, she said she was home studying every weekday night, but I picked some of those weekday nights, just to make sure.

"Then, one Friday night when I was at Karen's, I noticed something interesting. I had just arrived, and Karen and I were sitting and talking in the living room. She suddenly seemed distracted, and I followed her gaze to a red book on her dressing table in the other room. She seemed jarred by the fact that she had left it out. While we were talking, she got up and she idly put it away, as if I shouldn't pay any attention to it. It looked like a daybook, and I realized at once that I wanted to see it. After a while, when she went to the bathroom I was tempted to look at it, but I was afraid that she'd come right back, and I didn't dare.

"Later that same evening the phone rang, and Karen picked it up in the other room and spoke a few sentences that I couldn't hear. She came back from the call seeming very happy, and she was unusually warm with me for the rest of the evening. I offered to take her out to dinner, but she said she'd rather stay home. I remember her exact words. She said, 'I don't have to go out and meet the world. I have everything right here.'

"It was a good evening, but in the car going home I suddenly felt jolted. It occurred to me that Karen might have been happy because that was her boyfriend on the phone and she didn't want to go out because she was afraid that we'd be seen together. That would have been ironic.

"That week I did another thing that I shouldn't have. On Wednesday night Louise and I were at her sister's house playing bridge. We had five people and we were rotating players. I suddenly got the idea that I could slip out and check on Karen for a while, so I begged off saying that I had some work to do in my office and that I'd be back in an hour or so. They tried to talk me out of it, of course, but I insisted, and I zipped up there and parked alongside the building in my usual spot, which is always vacant because there's a hydrant there.

"A few minutes after I got there, I saw Karen going into the building with an older man, someone about my age. He was well dressed and carrying what looked like a package of groceries. The lights stayed on in her kitchen and her living room. I was tempted to wait a lot longer to see when the man came out, but obviously I couldn't. I had to get back, and even then, when I did get back, everyone was wondering what happened to me.

"The following Friday I asked Karen how her week had gone. I told her that I had called her several times on that Wednesday because there was a great television show on that I know she would have loved, but she must have been out. 'Oh,' she said, 'my father dropped by and took me out to dinner.' It was either the truth or a brilliant explanation that covered the data perfectly—I didn't know which.

"That night I stole my first look at her date book when she went to the bathroom. There was nothing there for the previous Wednesday, but of course, if her father had dropped by unexpectedly, there wouldn't be. Over weeks of further surveillance, I never saw Karen with anyone else, but I did get the chance to study her daybook three or four times.

"As I said, she was very compulsive. She put everything in her day-book, the times of her classes, the hours she was to study, even her exercise periods. There were plenty of reminders to meet Nancy and to meet her parents on weekends. She had my name down there on Fridays, which was hardly necessary, since we seldom missed one. She wrote 'Timothy'—I would have liked it better if she had written 'Tim,' but I can hardly complain.

"The only other things I saw were a lot of asterisks, two together, on certain Saturdays and sometimes during the week. I wondered what they were for, but of course I couldn't ask her. Really, I found nothing out for sure, what those asterisks meant or even if that was really her father.

"Well, I kept going up there, and I waited in my car. I decided to take my very good opera glasses up there with me, so I could see up into the apartment, and see her from further away. I was watching her windows, sometimes twice a week for an hour or two, and I was seeing her another night, so I was really spending a lot of time with her." He laughed.

Observing that I didn't smile, he stopped sharply, and admitted sheepishly, "I guess it isn't funny, huh?"

I didn't comment.

"Really, it was very painful, those few months," he said. "I was driving my wife crazy, and I must admit that I was driving myself crazy, too. But I got quite an education."

I asked him what he meant.

"In two months, I saw just about everything that can happen—drug deals, men meeting prostitutes who would drive by with their pimps in big automobiles. One day I actually saw two guys waiting for a white-haired man to come down the street. I knew they were going to hold him up when he turned the corner, and I wanted to warn him. But I couldn't, they would have killed me. When he did come into their view, one of them yanked a gun from a leg holster and pointed it at him, and he handed them his wallet, and they left. They didn't even run away. They just strolled down the block, right toward me.

"I wanted to start the car and get out of there, but it was too late. I just ducked down behind the wheel, and fortunately they weren't looking.

"Another night I saw two guys go into a gutted tenement building and then come running out fast. A few moments later, it was on fire. First I could smell the smoke, and I could see a blaze. I was starting to drive away when a fire truck came right toward me, and I got terrified that if they stopped me I could never explain what I was doing in the neighborhood. I pictured my photograph in the *Daily News* coming down the steps of 100 Centre Street. My whole reputation flashed before me.

"I sank down in my seat that time, too, and watched them put out the fire. A crowd got there fast, and people were staring out of their windows. I was also scared that Karen would look down and see me, so the first chance I had, I drove out of there.

"But I did gather some information. I got to see Nancy, Karen's friend—a very plump woman with long, stringy hair; she was totally unlike Karen—and I watched a man go up to her apartment. But he was definitely her father."

"How can you be so sure?"

"I had looked at her date book and saw 'Daddy' down for a Thursday evening at seven, so I waited a block away. Karen came downstairs at about ten to, and waited. When that same man I had seen before came down the block, she greeted him and he kissed her on the cheek and they walked the other way. She didn't take his hand. I'm sure he was her father. I felt very relieved.

"I felt good all week, but then, the night before my date with her, I saw her come out of her apartment with a young, handsome man, about thirty-five. This guy looked like a gigolo. He wore one of those Italian raw silk suits that they buy in discount houses—no tie, you know, and his shirt was open at the collar. He took her hand. My heart was thumping. I had to leave. I almost threw up driving downtown. He was definitely a date, a very lowlife-looking guy. I wondered what she could possibly see in a character like that.

"I always took the West Side Highway home. It gets me out of that neighborhood as fast as possible and I shoot downtown. But that night I was so upset that I missed the entrance and nearly piled into a car on Broadway at a red light. I wondered how the hell I would have explained an accident up there to Louise. I damn near threw up. I asked myself, Why would she need a guy like that? I could imagine the answer. He was one of those great lovers who just keeps going and going. One thing I'll say for him—he looked in good shape.

"I couldn't sleep at all. I kept seeing them together, hand in hand. I hated myself for having been there and for caring what she did, and I could hear her saying, 'More, more' to him in bed, the way she did with me. He looked very sure of himself.

"In the office I was half dead from exhaustion. But that picture of him on top of her kept waking me up. I tried to get involved in my work, but I couldn't. I decided to call up Karen and say it was over, to bow out. I dialed her number. She was home. Instinctively I asked, 'Are you alone?' and she said, 'Certainly.' I was glad. I assumed she was. We spoke warmly, I don't even know about what. When I hung up, I felt worse.

"I remembered how my daughters when they were children would turn an opera glass around and say, 'Daddy, you look so far away.' Louise and I would do the same with them. Whoever was being looked at would make faces, stick his tongue out. I tried doing that with Karen. I would tell myself, 'She's just a part-time legal secretary living in a depressed neighborhood. She has no claim on me.' It worked sometimes for a few minutes, but then I felt sick again. The next day was just as bad."

"You and Louise were still having sex sometimes?" I asked Timothy.

"Yes, we were. I liked sex with Louise, but even then I would picture Karen up there with Mister Lover.

"The next Friday Karen was actually very nice to me. I'll tell you the difference between her and Louise. Karen liked to go naked. She would walk around the apartment, sometimes with only high-heeled shoes and black stockings on, nothing else. She would cup her breasts with her hands and look in the mirror and say, 'I really look pretty good.' Actually, Louise is better looking by far, but she doesn't think she is. She would never do that. Karen stands up tall and I never realized before what a difference that makes. We had sex and it was great. But then I got in trouble."

"Trouble. How?"

"That night I noticed that she had put some blond streaks in her hair. I said it looked great, and she said, 'I just wanted a little change.'

"All I could think of was him and the idea that she was adorning herself for her date with him, and that she saw me as just like another woman, there to chat with her. She wanted to talk about bonds and interest rates. I guess in retrospect I hated the subject. It certainly was the opposite of sexuality and romance, you'll grant that."

I did grant it, inwardly, but I didn't say anything.

"It seems to me," Timothy went on, "that the two least sexual words in the English language are 'fiscal year.' "

"I wouldn't be surprised," I said.

He didn't smile at his comment, and neither did I.

"She started talking about a sure twenty percent on her money every year, with no risk and no taxes. She even said it was liquid, that she could get her money out at two day's notice any time. I realized I must have been angry because I told her, 'That's ridiculous.' She said, 'It's not. It's true.' I didn't mean to, but we got into an argument. She looked incredibly hurt, but I was hurt, too. I told her, 'My God, if everyone has that option, the entire economy must be crazy. Why would anybody take less?

"I guess it was a good point, because she looked really stung. I even thought she was going to cry, and I told myself, 'Timothy, what's the point of winning the argument and crushing this poor girl. You've risked your life to come up here and it certainly wasn't to win an argument.' I was about to drop it, but just then she said, 'Actually, I'm planning to get forty-five percent on my money, absolutely guaranteed, with no risk.'

"Naturally, I didn't believe it, and I asked her how, and she just said, 'Real estate.' I asked her where, and all she said was, 'Overseas.' I asked her, 'Who the hell told you that?' She said, 'Don't yell at me, and it's none of your business.'

"I was appalled and I warned her to be careful and double-check what she was doing with an independent expert. Doctor, I would say that to any client, but when I said it to her, she got really nasty. She asked me, 'Who? You?'

"I couldn't believe my ears. I felt completely exasperated, but then I got control of myself and apologized. She refused to have sex with me that night. She said she just wasn't in the mood. But she did go to the bathroom long enough for me to get a good look at her daybook. I went right for Wednesday, the night I'd seen her with that creep. There was no name, just a couple of asterisks. It's funny, but I had a real urge to ask her what they meant. But that would have been like asking the Japanese what they meant by a few obscure words in that coded message we deciphered the week before Pearl Harbor." He smiled.

"I glanced over the rest of the week real fast. I saw my own name for Friday, and Nancy was down, and Dr. Durant—she had talked about him, he was her faculty adviser. I returned the book to her desk just in time. Those twin stars were down another day too. They're pretty confusing."

"Twin stars, huh?" I said. My mind reverted to the wonderful Sherlock Holmes story "The Dancing Men," in which symbols represented key words. All I said to Timothy was, "Well, they must mean something to her."

"I'd give five thousand dollars to find out," he said earnestly.

If there ever was a man ensnared, Timothy was him. His "romance" had given way to something quite different, I thought. But to what? To something spooky—and mysterious, not in a good way. I wondered if there had ever been any romance in the first place, on either side? I strongly doubted it. Rather, theirs was a complex game that made the primping and machinations of animal courtship seem trivial by comparison. And I also wondered which was greater—Timothy's attempt to deceive Karen or his own self-deception.

And what had Karen ever gotten out of the whole affair? Obviously, the legal advice, and possibly she was even attracted to this well-spoken, venerable man whose status might have been aphrodisiac to her. Perhaps she, being precariously adrift herself, felt somewhat anchored by Timothy's prestige. She had bestowed youth on Timothy, allowed him the illusion of being young himself, while he lent her interludes of the respectability that she craved.

That idea prompted me to see that Karen's demand for the tuxedo might be more than just a whim. Previously, I had conceived of her as insisting on it merely to torment Timothy and put him on trial—as if, for her own mirth, she were imposing a condition akin to those that fair maidens levied on medieval knights.

But now I realized that even if Karen herself thought this, the tuxedo, as the attire of the respectability that he bestowed upon her, would be something more real to Karen than to most other people. Her demand for it might actually have sprung from an unconscious desire on her part to have

Timothy pursue her in the garb of the respectable citizen that she wanted—and that he truly was. Of course I recognized that even if this were so, I would never know it for sure, and that, in fact, even Karen herself might never realize it consciously.

Timothy went on. "My mind was swirling. So I called Karen the next day. I asked her politely, 'How can your money be liquid if it's in real estate?' I just wanted to see what she'd say. She answered, 'Oh, that wouldn't be. I get the forty-five percent every January. The rents yield that. The twenty percent was something else.'

"I was stopped in my tracks. I didn't know why I cared so much. I changed the subject at once and told her I'd had a wonderful time with her. She didn't say anything. So I asked, 'Didn't you?' She said, 'I would, but you're so argumentative.' I realized she was right. I apologized again. But inside I was burning up.

"That night I drove up there just in time to see her going into the building with that oily character. When her light went on I looked into her window and I saw their shadows. But after a few minutes they moved away from the window, and I couldn't see what they were doing. I could wait only an hour. A police car was cruising the neighborhood. I realized the officers saw me and I figured that maybe I looked suspicious, so I left.

"I could hardly bear it. I drove about a mile away and I called her from a diner. It was still a bad neighborhood, but I figured the diner was safe because there were so many people in there eating and drinking. It was very friendly, as if most of them knew each other.

"I expected to get that brush-off that she gave other callers when I was there. I don't know what I would have done if she had. I guess I had planned to keep her talking so she'd have to make it obvious. But she acted normal. She just chatted and chatted. I felt very relieved. But then, when I resumed driving home and went over the conversation in my mind, it occurred to me that he might have been there and that they were mocking me. When she said, 'I really miss you tonight,' he might have had his hand on her breast and actually been listening. The whole idea was like a knife in my midsection.

"That night I was so tired that I slept well. The next day I woke up thinking, 'Timothy, you don't really know. Why don't you admit it.' I realized I had to find out the truth. Doctor, I realized that I just couldn't go on not knowing. I felt that if she wasn't sleeping with this guy, that would be great. And if she was, and I could be sure, at least I would be free that way too. Maybe hurt, but not like this. It's hard to explain, but I couldn't bear not knowing, being in the middle.

"I realized what I had to do. I would drive up there and wait in my car. Then when I saw her go into that apartment with him I would go inside the building and listen right at her door. That wouldn't be hard. In spite of the precautions they take with the buzzer and everything, people going in or out of the building aren't really so careful. I don't look like trouble—I knew that some generous soul would let me in. If I could get right outside her door I could hear if they were having sex; those doors are like the balsa wood I used to make model planes out of. I would find out once and for all.

"I broke down and told Felix everything about what I had done, and what I was planning to do. I asked him if he would go with me and wait in the car downstairs with the motor on, so that I could get out of there fast if there was trouble. He thought awhile, but then he refused. He said he couldn't explain his absence to his wife. I told him I understood, and that, okay, I'd go alone.

"That was when he said I was losing it, and he really got upset. He asked me a funny question.

"What was that?"

"He asked me, 'If there was a drug in existence that could annihilate all your interest in Karen if you took one gulp, would you take it?'

"I told him that last year I would have said definitely no. I would never have given up what I had, but now I'm not so sure. I told him that maybe I would. But damn it, there isn't such a drug and I wanted to find out the truth about Karen.

"He looked very serious, and he said maybe there is.

"I asked him what it was called, and he said, 'Therapy.' I asked him if he was serious, and he said he had never been more serious. He mentioned for the first time that he had gone to a therapist when he was getting his divorce and it was in all the newspapers. He said he had found the situation hard to handle, and that therapy really helped him, and that if there was ever a person who needed therapy, it was me.

"I told him I'd consider it. But meanwhile I was all set to go up there on Saturday night and find out for sure. Karen couldn't see me Friday because it was her mother's birthday and the family was going out. She was telling the truth—"

"How do you know?" I asked Timothy.

"It was in her daybook, even the sweater she was buying her mom and what she spent for it—sixty-nine ninety-five plus tax. She said that on Saturday she would be studying for her summer session end-term exam."

"Was that down in the book, too?"

"No. Just two stars, the usual. I was starting to figure maybe they represented, 'Stay home and study.' I left an office party myself to drive up there. One of the secretaries was getting married.

"It was nine o'clock and the light was on in her bedroom. I felt sick when I saw that light, but I figured maybe she was studying in bed. It was a muggy night and everybody was out in the street. I brought a big bouquet of flowers with me, mostly roses, her favorite—"

"I don't understand. Why?"

"I knew what I had to do, and just on the off chance I got caught, I wanted to make it look like a surprise visit, you know, as if I was up there just to bring them and leave.

"There was a big domino game in progress on the sidewalk, four tables, right in front of my hydrant. They all looked into the car, and I had to put away my opera glasses. The streets were really crowded and a lot of kids were playing and running around. They sure let those kids stay out late. Who knows, maybe it's good. We never did that when we were children.

"I had just gotten out of the car when a Spanish man with a mouthful of gold teeth looked at the flowers and smiled at me. I don't know much Spanish, but I understood what he said."

"What was that?"

" '*Linda, señor policia*'—that meant 'pretty, the flowers are pretty, Mister Policeman.' Everybody laughed as if they knew I was a cop, and a big fat Spanish lady came over to smell them. I felt like an idiot. I wanted to go back and leave them in the car, but then I realized, 'Well, that's good if they think I'm the law.' It actually gave me courage. I tried to play it like a policeman pretending he wasn't one.

"I went right up to the white building and waited and watched them. Mercifully, they lost interest in me fast. Inside, a teenage girl on her way out of the building stopped and looked mostly at the flowers and not at me. That was good, because I had seen her before. I held the door and I went in and walked upstairs. My heart was really thumping, believe me.

"I waited at the end of the hall on her floor for a while. But then I got afraid I'd look suspicious there and someone would call a real cop. It was dark and shadowy. There was only one bare light bulb hanging on a chain or else it would have been pitch black. I kept looking at Karen's door. I half expected her to come out, but if she did I was ready to present the flowers to her.

"After a while I inched over to her door and crouched down next to it. I heard some voices from inside. One was her voice and there was also a man's voice. That was it. Mission accomplished, I told myself. I wanted to leave, but I wouldn't let myself. I had to listen. They were laughing—I couldn't hear exactly at what, but I thought they were having sex. I thought I heard her say, 'Cosmo, please.'

"Then I suddenly felt that he might be hurting her, even raping her, and I had the impulse to kick in the door like in the movies—I had my Mace with me. Or at least ring the bell and put him on notice.

"But then I heard them both laughing. That was all I could stand. I stuck the flowers inside my raincoat so the people downstairs would think I gave them to someone. They didn't even look at me as I got into my car. I drove to the same diner, on 145th and Broadway. I gave the waitress the flowers, a very sweet black woman, and she loved them. She smiled at me and she said, 'My boyfriend's going to be jealous, but they're beautiful. Thank you, Mister.'

"I called Karen right away, and we chatted a little, but I could tell she didn't want to talk. I was afraid to ask her if she was alone, on the off chance that she had heard someone outside in the hall and would guess it was me. The whole round-trip took me only an hour and a half, and I felt like a free man. I said to myself, 'Okay, now at least you know.'

"But the next day I couldn't bear it, and I called her and asked her about the evening. She said she'd been studying last night with a friend and they got a lot done. 'Male or female?' I asked her. She laughed coyly and she said, 'Male. You're such a jealous boy.' That word 'boy' really turned me on. It was either true or a brilliant lie. I realized that I still didn't know anything for sure and that I'd have to go up there maybe a lot more if I ever wanted to be certain.

"When I told Felix, the blood rushed out of his face. He said, 'Tim, you're a smart man, but you're losing it. You've got to get help. I can't help you, I'm not a professional.' He said he asked around and got your name, Doctor. He had already written it down with your phone number. I thanked him a lot. He's right, I am losing it. So, anyhow, here I am. I guess I've got to get out of this, huh?"

"Do you want to?"

He winced. "I don't like to see her get away with this. I'd like to find out for sure. What's your professional opinion?"

"Timothy, I'm a psychotherapist. I help people with emotional problems. I'm not a detective—"

"But you can read her."

"Are you here because Felix said you should come or do you see anything wrong inside yourself?"

"It changes, Doctor. Sometimes I think there's something wrong with me. Seriously wrong. And there are other times I don't. I figure, hey I'm entitled to know. I'm taking big chances in this relationship. I really have a right to know where I stand."

"And suppose you simply don't know where you stand," I asked him. "What does that mean to you—the state of uncertainty about it? Why is it so awful?"

He seemed confused, as if the answer was so obvious that the question made no sense at all. For awhile he said nothing, and then he could muster only, "I don't know. It just is."

He smiled. That answer wasn't good enough for him or for me.

"That's interesting," I said. "You can't say why this information about Karen is so important. And yet you're risking your marriage, your reputation, in a sense your sanity, and maybe even your life to find it out."

I paused so that he would have time to ponder this seeming contradiction. It was as yet one to me too. But of course there are no contradictions in nature, only in an incomplete understanding.

I was content that in selecting this line of inquiry, my unconscious had guided me well, and I decided to pursue it. With our session coming to an end, I went after it again.

"Timothy, I said, "think about it. The next time, try to tell me why you need to *know* so badly."

But the next session Timothy launched right back into his speculations about Karen's relationship with "this fellow, Cosmo."

Timothy's Friday night date with Karen had ended in near catastrophe. After sex with her he had overslept—presumably, I imagined, because he was exhausted from his worrying and spying. Though Karen knew full well that if he didn't get home by eleven thirty, he would be in trouble, she had not deigned to wake him.

To his consternation, Timothy woke up at one thirty and hurled on his tuxedo, then raced through the neighborhood to his car. His garage was closed, so he'd had to scurry along Broadway looking for a cab. Fortunately, he got one soon. He gave the driver a ten-dollar bribe to go as fast as he could, and then he continued to goad the cabbie so that the fellow almost had an accident dodging in and out of the pillars of the elevated subway, skidding through every curve.

Timothy told me, "I never want to go through an experience like that again. I sure was glad to get back to my green canopy."

Only once inside the lobby did he realize that he was still in his tux. He sneaked into his apartment, stuffed the tux into a pillowcase, hid it in his desk file drawer, and then climbed into bed. When his wife half asleep asked him perfunctorily if he'd had a good time, he told her it was terrible, that he'd had some very tough long distance calls to field, but that he thought he did well. She had said, "I'm sure you did."

His whole adventure sounded like a sexual experience.

"Were you upset with Karen for not waking you up?" I asked him.

"Not really," he said.

The next day, still exhausted, he had gone up to Karen's neighborhood to spy on her some more. She was out. "It was a two-star day in her book, and I still don't know what that means," he said.

I could imagine that Timothy truly wasn't aware of any anger toward Karen for not waking him up—or for exactions that must have made him look preposterous, even to himself. He had projected a powerful psychological spotlight on her as the woman he had to possess, a light that left all the remaining world in darkness. Timothy, in the frenzy of his neurotic courtship, could ill afford misgivings, and certainly not anger, which could wipe the smile from his face, crimp his style, and divert him from his course. Instead, his program was to show only alacrity and compliance. I mused that these were two traits that poor Louise virtually never saw in him anymore. Nor would anyone else, except those who might assist him in his quest for the unholy grail.

How far would he bend? I wondered. How close to perfectly inside out would he turn himself in his effort to package himself properly? I could already sense the potential of a powerful implosion if he went on escalating his demands of himself.

It was an irony that he had to possess Karen at all, that he pursued her with such increasing blindness to repercussions. At first being in Karen's presence had made him feel young, or at least he'd imagined it had had this effect. However, as always when an older person seeks someone younger as a device to feel youthful, setbacks make the pursuer feel older than ever. Whereas Timothy might have endured rejection by someone his own age with some equanimity, the very possibility of Karen's rejection seemed unendurable.

To Timothy, I felt sure, Karen represented all pulchritude and youth in womankind, and her closing the door on him, even in prospect, seemed an era about to say, "Good-bye, shriveled old man. This was all in your imagination. You do not qualify."

As I had several times before, I wondered how aware Karen herself was of her impact on Timothy or her meaning to him. She might have had little idea how much he was forfeiting or how far from his "normal" shape he had transmuted. Conceivably, she was fully cognizant of his fall and was enjoying it, or rather the power that such a collapse on his part implied she must possess.

For the first time, I wondered if that initial meeting had truly been an accident at all. Had her litigious molecules attracted a legal mind like his, and in a man so unsure of his manliness? Possibly she had even staked him out, or posted herself outside that law building at a time when a party of eligibles was heading uptown? But more likely, I decided, she was less diabolical than he was prone to surrender all, and, unless I could intervene, come toppling down from the tower of his own making, like Henrik Ibsen's Master Builder.

In our next session, when Timothy began his usual speculations about Karen's fidelity, I interrupted him and insisted that I needed to know a lot more about his own life.

Nor was it easy to come by even the most cursory sketch of his childhood. Time and again he would break off his account by asking me what I thought about Karen, what those two stars meant, whether she might really love him, whether any woman could enjoy sex as much as she did with him and not love the man, and whether it was possible for a woman to really enjoy sex with two different men. Since I didn't want to engage him on the subject, I held myself back from pointing out that because he was doing a similar thing with his wife, he was really in the best position to answer this last question.

I kept bringing him back to the broad picture of his life by asking him very direct questions about it. Even so, I could secure only the most general outline, and that came in fragments.

He was born in the borough of Queens, in New York City. His father was a lawyer who had worked for a department store chain "handling suits and petty complaints, mostly, I think." Timothy, Sr., had died young but had left Timothy's mother well-provided for. Both parents had been devoutly religious and had imbued their children with a strong moral sense. Timothy, the oldest of four, made a lot of good decisions for his brother and two sisters, all of whom were now happily married and hardworking, God-fearing people. One of his sisters was also a lawyer, in California.

Timothy had lived a well-ordered life, and I could tell that he was considered by his family and friends to be kindly, good-tempered, accessible. He had been debating champion in his Catholic high school, and had made the all-city team. He was renowned for the clarity of his logic. But, I mused, he had brought that logic to bear on academic topics, one step removed from his real life. In a sense, he'd also been dealing with once-removed topics ever since in his law practice. I could see a huge dichotomy between where his brain operated at top level and where it hardly functioned at all—namely, in his relationships with women.

I also came to see that Timothy had spent an underprivileged adolescence and life, so far as his getting into mischief was concerned—that is, when it came to recognizing it and getting out of it. I had the impression that he idealized too many people too readily. He was, if anything, too lacking in the skepticism that trouble and redemption teach many of us. His rather limited palate of companions had left him a social adolescent, unprepared for this younger woman he had met by accident.

At the end of that session, Timothy confessed that he had given absolutely no thought to my question of why it was so important for him to know whether she was faithful.

I saw him only a few days later and brought up the question again. But I found it still almost impossible to pry him away from his ruminations about Karen's fidelity. As in the poems and songs in which one imagines seeing a former lover or a deceased one in the streets, in the clouds, and in the moon, Timothy was subject to illusions. He ran ahead of a woman who got out of the elevator in his office building and peeked at her face to verify that she wasn't Karen. On another occasion, while sitting in his car waiting for a traffic light, he saw a couple walking in the street, the woman with her arm around the man's waist. After a moment of horror, Timothy again verified that they were two other people.

"What went through your mind when you thought it was Karen and this man?" I asked him.

"I had the fantasy that if it was, I would run them over by accident," he told me.

"Would that relieve you of your horror at her betrayal?" I asked him.

He smiled. "No," he said. "That's not what I want."

However, no matter what Timothy actually said, I felt sure that his rage toward Karen was welling up. It seemed to me that he must have an unconscious desire to punish her for what she was doing to him, both knowingly and unknowingly. It had been Karen's own idea to have him run the gauntlet as with the tuxedo and by demanding legal advice as a condition for sex. And though she presumably had little or no idea of his jealous obsession, in Timothy's unconscious mind he must have been furious at her for having put him to such pains.

I wondered, How could great anger toward Karen not be the unseen vector in his equation? Timothy could hardly escape it after treading the measure so far, virtually turning his life inside out, and then imagining himself so betrayed.

Timothy's insistence on talking about Karen to the exclusion of nearly everything else would sometimes make me feel quite futile. I sought to console myself by remembering that, after all, his obsession was the very essence of the problem that had driven him to me for help. But I was making little dent. Indeed, Timothy was so dedicated to trying to dope out Karen's motives that he had virtually no interest in understanding his own—in particular, why it mattered to him so much what she thought or did.

I felt sure that Timothy was suffering from what modern psychoanalysts call a "wound to his infantile narcissism." Karen herself had merely assumed the role of the woman who had inflicted this wound. Where such a wound is struck, the details of who the other person is hardly matter. The sufferer sees only his own injury, which revives the very earliest injury from childhood, that of discovering that one is not everything to mother. Some children's failure to fully outgrow the earliest stage of what Freud called *infantile omnipotence* leaves them especially subject to suffer such wounds recurrently in adult life.

Of course, knowing as little as I did about Timothy's early life, I couldn't tell exactly what had left him with such a vulnerability. Typically, a doting or possessive mother may foster such a feeling. The child benefits in the sense of having an eternal and dauntless optimism. On the other hand, defeats come hard to the narcissist, and Timothy simply could not allow one in his life.

When I had once told Timothy that I doubted whether he loved Karen at all, it was only partly to shock him into thinking about himself. I really did question his "love."

The problem of narcissism has always been identified with the incapability of loving other people. When Freud first identified the narcissistic personality type, he maintained that the narcissist cannot love others because he has saved all his libido for himself. This theory supposed a given quantity of love, which was apportioned by the narcissist too much to the self and not enough to others.

Today, however, the more widely held thesis is that put forth by the psychoanalyst Erich Fromm: He believed that narcissists cannot truly love anyone, themselves or other people. Fromm, in disputing the notion that narcissists love themselves, attributed what passed as love to mere self-absorption in the absence of love. Fromm maintained that whoever cannot love himself cannot love others either, and this formulation seemed, at least so far, to apply to Timothy perfectly.

Whether Timothy had ever loved his wife was hard to tell, but judging by the way he treated her, he certainly didn't seem to love her these days, and he obviously did not love himself.

Timothy's preoccupation with Karen continued to devour not just his life outside but our time in the sessions. The very fact that I still knew so little about him considering how many words he had uttered in the time we had spent together was of course attributable to that.

"Unstaid and skittish in all motions else, save in the constant image of the creature that is beloved," wrote Shakespeare of a compulsive lover, whom the bard had clearly intended to portray as a narcissist. The character, Orsino, in *Twelfth Night,* is in fact often played looking into a mirror much of the time, even as he talks to his servants. I recalled that, as was my experience with Timothy, after two hours we know virtually nothing about

Orsino by the time the play is over, except of course all the details of his obsessive love.

In fact, it even struck me that as a consequence of Timothy's narcissism, in a sense he hardly knew I was there. Though he spoke to me respectfully, I believed that if I had substituted a colleague for myself, he wouldn't have cared. I imagined that he felt the same way about Karen; that if another woman her age and with the same seductive sexuality had come along, he might readily have accepted her as a replacement. It was what Karen represented to him, and not Karen herself, that made all the difference to Timothy.

Timothy came in with his usual eagerness to tell me about his most recent surveillance of Karen and his newest theory. He seemed astonished when I told him that I wanted him not to discuss her at all for the first half hour "so that I can get a broader picture of the rest of your life." He assured me that this would be fine.

He did his best to answer my questions—about his daughters, about Louise, and about his law practice. I think he was surprised to realize how hard it was for him to do even this. He would blank out at times, more than once forgetting a question I had just asked him. He reminded me of a computerized machine that would fizz and falter as the polite words came up on its screen, "Please wait."

I did wait, and I repeated my questions dutifully, but when the half hour was over I described what he himself had obviously witnessed. "I guess you see how obsessed you are, and the rest of your life hardly counts for anything. It's amazing that you can talk to people in this kind of state," I said, "and that you can conduct your work."

He nodded, as if he already recognized this, and then, doing the same thing, remarked that he'd gotten into a big fight with Karen "over that financial advisor of hers." Timothy's newest theory was that the man— she'd admitted that much, that it was a man—was promising her money benefits that he knew he couldn't deliver so that he could have sex with her: "She's a fool if she believes him."

He had restrained himself from saying this to Karen because he realized that she would think of him as indulging in jealous ravings. But more than once he had disparaged the man and his credentials, still not knowing anything about him. It tormented Timothy that Karen didn't bother to defend the fellow and that she even insisted on withholding his name. She declared that he'd insisted on secrecy so that there would be no competition. She would disclose only that he was an expert and that he once taught economics at Columbia.

I had seen Timothy just a handful of times, but I realized that I would have to take a more active role. He was in a rapid decline and it would continue unless I did. His behavior, which I now saw as originally a response to his narcissistic wound, was worsening by the day. Already he was as driven by his compulsion to investigate Karen as any gambler is by his need to make his next bet or to perfect his "system." Or as any addict is by his desire for his next "hit."

And just as drinking or overeating or gambling generates increasingly greater reliance on the activity, and makes life seem pallid and pointless without it, so Timothy's surveillance of Karen, his reading her daybook, and his very going up there to spy on her, was poisoning his outlook increasingly. Self-help organizations, such as Gambler's Anonymous, call the compulsion a "progressive illness," and Timothy's spying certainly was. Exactly like those people, Timothy was driving himself insane.

Moreover, like other compulsive people, Timothy had no real insight into what his real motives were. Almost surely, there was rage toward Karen—the impotent, infantile rage of the narcissist denied—along with Timothy's desire to justify himself. But even this I had to infer because, as always with compulsions, the person's very indulgence in the activity serves to repress any insight into why the person is doing the thing. One sees only the need to do it again.

My active intervention was to ask Timothy to quit his surveillance for at least a month. I felt that doing this would impede his decline into a totally delusional state. In addition, getting him to stop even that briefly seemed the only way to surface Timothy's real motives—to get him to spell them out for me and for himself. While he was starving for the activity, he would virtually tell me—and tell himself—what his real motives were, why he needed to find out all these facts about Karen, and what they meant to him.

When I pictured telling him to stop, I anticipated a struggle. But I could see no other way.

Requesting a person in so many words to stop a compulsive activity is not a traditional psychoanalytic procedure. However, in asking Timothy to do this, I would be following the precedent of those who specialize in dealing with compulsive behavior. They reason that since the behavior is not merely a symptom but also a cause—a source of reinfection—stopping even briefly relieves the problem a little and makes it easier to stop entirely later on.

At worst, if Timothy agreed to stop, I reasoned, and then found that he couldn't, he would gain in appreciating that he was out of control, that the impulse to spy on Karen was rampant within him. In other words, my request would help him see more clearly than he did that he was suffering from a psychological problem.

My own addition to the method would be my in-depth investigation of how he would feel during his abstinence. Years had taught me that what people feel when they desist from a compulsive (or even habitual) act provides the best and often the only information as to why they have been doing the thing all along.

I didn't see him again until after Labor Day, a break of about ten days. I was out of town, and he had rented a house in West Hampton, Long Island, for the end of August. To minimize his privation, he had made alibis for coming into the city on Fridays when he saw Karen. However, I could tell that Timothy was already feeling the pinch of being unable to do his Saturday spy work. He'd had to return to the bosom of his family on the second of the two Saturdays when Louise and his daughters were out there. "One Saturday in the city out of two is enough," she had said.

"She's right. I wouldn't have minded it so much, but she said she'd discussed it with her sister and they'd agreed on it together. I wish she had a mind of her own," Timothy said.

"Well, I guess that's Karen's greatness," I commented, only half whimsically. "She certainly has a mind of her own."

Timothy smiled and agreed. Apparently, he'd missed talking to me during the week I was gone, and I was surprised when he complimented me highly. "You know, you're really a smart guy. You know a lot about relationships. You could probably control Karen with no trouble at all . . ."

I didn't respond to his tribute to me. I said, "You know, Timothy, this isn't just a relationship problem. This is a problem you have with yourself."

I told him bluntly that I felt that he was undergoing a kind of delusion.

He broke in sharply to say that he had thought of that himself. "I know. Felix says the same thing. But what's the difference what it is? It means a lot to me?"

But there was a difference if he was no longer master of his own fate. "Actually, I'm not sure you have a real choice about this anymore."

"Why not?"

"Because maybe you really can't stop spying on her—"

"Oh, I can stop easily," he assured me.

"You mean just see her for your Friday dates and not go up there any other time?"

"Why? Do you think I should?"

My moment had come. I told him in no uncertain terms that he should, if only to prove to himself that he wasn't out of control. "In my opinion, you're driving yourself crazy with all this CIA work," I said.

He said he didn't agree with me, but that he would stop right away if I was convinced that he should.

It was almost too easy.

Afterward, I recalled his strange comment that "a guy like you could handle Karen with no trouble at all." It suggested that he wanted me to take over the controls—perhaps to punish Karen for what she was doing to him.

I felt sure that though Timothy didn't admit it, he himself vaguely sensed trouble, that he knew he was out of control. Indeed, I saw him more as a man plunging through space than as a lover. I wondered what would emerge when he kept his promise.

I thought of Timothy as an awkward early teenager, insecure but delighting in his furtive game of creeping up on Karen. The danger, even his staying out late while "mother" was waiting home, was reminiscent of the teen years—in his case, was an attempt to produce a teenage era that he had never known. His comment to me about handling Karen was the teenager's idealization of the older-boy Lothario, the lady tamer. Sex, love, friendship with Karen sank to nothingness in my estimation as I considered him in this light. Revenge and triumph over her, vindication of himself, were emerging as his dominant motives—I no longer even questioned them.

That week he didn't spy on Karen, "though my thoughts were with her, I can tell you that."

Another restraint had come into play unexpectedly. There was trouble on the home front, a potential insurrection which on its own would have made foreign deployment inadvisable. Louise had confronted him on his total indifference to her and the family. She hadn't mentioned his disappearances but had cited his forgetting appointments and paying no attention to family matters.

A client whom Louise had gotten to know had told her that Timothy was blundering at work, that he was forgetting things there and confusing appointments. The client had said that she was worried about Timothy. Louise had reported this after saying, "Everyone can see that something has gotten into you."

Timothy had confessed his distraction, once again attributing it entirely to the big case that was purportedly consuming him. He thanked Louise for telling him and promised to reform. He assured me, and himself, that things were back in order, and thanked me, too, for telling him not to spy that week or it would have been even worse.

I assumed from Louise's failure to censure him for being so disinterested in her that he had long been unresponsive. Presumably, they hadn't conversed freely for years, if ever, and Louise had pieced together whatever personal life she had in relationships with other people.

I finished the session by insisting even more vehemently that he do no more surveillance work.

He didn't protest.

But the next time I saw him it was as if he'd misheard me completely.

"I've been thinking about what you said—about the danger of hanging around up there. So I applied to the police precinct for a permit to get a gun. You're right. I shouldn't go up there unarmed."

I was horrified.

"What the hell good is a gun going to do you!" I said. "That wasn't the reason you shouldn't go up there, just your physical safety," I said.

What was my reason?, he demanded to know.

I gave him a full blast of explanation. I told him first of all that he was becoming delusional, that he was making Karen's fidelity to him the most important fact of his life. "You've given her a power over you that no human being should have."

When he still protested, I pointed out that his very pleading to continue spying on her should show him how out of control he was.

That slowed him down, but only momentarily. "Well, I sure hope you know what you're doing," he said, with a hint of truculence toward me that I had never seen in him before.

"I do," I said, meeting him head-on. "You're a smart guy, Timothy, but your judgment is really off on this one. You're losing your perspective altogether."

I had no idea whether he would heed me, whether he would desist for even another week. If he did, I felt sure that strong feelings would surface. It would take little sifting through his reactions to see into his motives and to learn a lot more about him. But I also realized that if he saw me as preventing him from gathering his precious information, then much more anger toward me might be in the offing.

"Look," he said the next time, "I did what you said. And Louise is watching me pretty closely, too. Okay, so I didn't go up there . . ." His voice trailed off.

Then, as if he'd just recognized the terrible penalty that he was paying for having given Karen her freedom, he said bitterly, "In other words, she's supposed to get away with this. Felix was right, she's a torturer."

"I wouldn't say that," I replied. "You're torturing yourself. She only left a self-torture device in the room and you started playing with it."

I asked what exactly he thought Karen was getting away with.

"She's getting the best of me, that's obvious. She's making a fool out of me. This just isn't fair. It has to be all straightened out."

" 'Straightened out?' "

"Evened out." That phrase seemed to capture the concept perfectly for Timothy, but I took it as mere narcissism masking as theology.

"Well, it's obviously unfair that I should be so much more taken up with her than she is with me. How *dare* she think I'm just *nothing.*" He sounded like a man exposing a cosmic injustice.

"I'll tell you what," he said, discovering what he considered an earth-shattering plan. "I want to make her more obsessed with me than I am with her. But to do that, I've got to find out what I'm up against. Important, you say? You're right, Doctor. This is a matter of honor."

"Why honor?"

"Why?" he shouted. "Because I've never been through such a bad period in my whole life, and she did this to me. I want her to appreciate that I'm not just here to satisfy her. Life's not as easy as she thinks it is."

It crossed my mind how fragile this thing called masculinity is—at least in some men—and how frail Timothy's sense of worth was if one woman toying with his masculinity could threaten him with extinction.

"You don't just leave me for *dead,*" Timothy went on. "I know what you think, Doctor. You think I'm just a middle-aged man who can't accept getting older. I know more about life. I've studied more and worked harder than any of these women." His eyes were luminescent.

"Which women?" I asked him.

"Louise, Karen—all of them."

"What's their role?"

"Their role? All I've ever done is work to please women ever since I was a child. I had a job after school and another one on weekends. I've always worked."

"But not for women," I started to say and then realized that Timothy was indeed surrounded by women. With the early death of his father there had been two sisters, and then Louise and two daughters. I knew nothing about his brother, but Timothy certainly had a private life almost exclusively with women, though his professional life must have been at least partially with men.

"So you've always wanted to please women, huh?" I said.

"Oh, I don't mind that, but I don't think that Karen or Louise or any of them really appreciate who I am. And Karen *will,* goddamn it. I'm going to find out what's happening up there and confront her. She'll appreciate me. Believe me, she'd better. You don't just play games with me."

At that moment I understood vividly that Timothy had spent a whole lifetime trying to look good to women, that this was his quest, more than actually enjoying them. I remembered his saying that he'd married Louise to quash competition, to prevent her from liking another man better.

He had never done what he'd really wanted, or gotten what he wanted, because of his narcissism. His need to be praised, esteemed, pursued, this surging demand from within, had driven him to sacrifice so much for esteem that he'd never had love or freedom. And now, facing what looked to him like the final verdict of old age with its disqualifications, he was becoming frantic.

Of course, it wasn't age at all, I thought. I'd had narcissistic kids in their twenties in my office despise themselves for being old or fat or attack themselves mercilessly for some physical trait that they thought did them in. The fact was that for Timothy, as for them, real fulfillment was impossible without inner change.

"She really isn't going to get away with this one," he was saying. "I'm not going to let her. You don't play with my love. You don't laugh at me."

Suddenly I remembered his application for the gun permit, and I was terrified. Taking stock, I could see that I'd found out a lot about him. In that sense, asking him to give up his surveillance, to return to Karen her rightful freedom of motion, had paid off—that is, in discovery. But the rush of anger brought about by this deprivation would not be worth it, I thought, if he was to go up there with that gun. Timothy, a furious man with a gun, hunting whoever had stolen his lost youth, was a very dangerous creature.

I hadn't the slightest doubt that he would revert to his spying—his pursuit of data to make his case. This time, I felt almost glad for it if the project could subdue his anger even for a while.

I settled for asking him not to get a gun, and tried to explain that this would be a bad time because his mind was playing tricks on him. He didn't agree, but I felt slightly relieved when he said that the permit would take another two weeks. Maybe I could talk him out of it in that time.

That weekend Timothy finally pried open his own narcissistic wound, putting the question of Karen's infidelity beyond all doubt.

"It's sexual all right," he said to me, smiling in obvious pain of discovery. He squeezed his eyes shut and momentarily looked like a little child, balding, sixtyish, in a blue pinstripe suit and wing-tipped shoes. "Doctor, I despise her for what she's done to me, and if it takes me a lifetime I'll find a way to get even. I may not even tell you."

He hadn't seen her that Friday because his wife's father was seriously ill. When Timothy had told Karen that the weekend was out, she had said, "Okay" casually, which filled him with suspicion.

On Saturday he had pulled up across the street from her apartment at about eight o'clock, just in time to see her entering the building "with that lizard." Timothy had watched her living room light go on and then the bedroom light almost at once. "I'm sure she dragged him in there. She couldn't wait."

He had lurked in his car only briefly and then gone upstairs and straight to her door. "I could smell some marijuana on the landing—I wasn't sure where it was coming from. Maybe there. Doctor, I could hear her crying out, 'Cosmo. Cosmo.' Then I knew it was over and they were laughing. I wanted to ring the bell to surprise her—to expose them, but I just waited. They were drinking. I could hear glasses and her cabinet opening, and then they had sex again.

"It had gotten dark. I needed to get back, but then I heard her say, 'Cosmo, you're the greatest lover.' 'Well, I'm Greek,' he said. 'We have a long history,' and then they were muttering. I couldn't hear what they said. He laughed a lot—he had an ugly, nervous laugh, probably at things that weren't funny.

"Some people came out of another apartment and I went around the corner. When they got on the elevator I went back. I swear they were having sex again.

"Doctor, I was a broken man. I went downstairs and I even had thoughts of waiting in my car and running him over. Then, out of nowhere a dirty-looking teenage kid appeared. I backed away. I thought he wanted money, but he asked me if I wanted a good time. He put his face right up to me. He repulsed me, and I pushed him back hard. I couldn't believe how violent I was. He looked startled. He asked me, 'What are you doing, man?'

"Driving downtown on the highway, I thought I had a fever. I looked at the Hudson River. It was black and shiny and I kept imagining myself drowning there. Nobody would care besides my family. Certainly not Karen. By the time I put the car in the garage I could hardly see. But I remembered something you said, 'Don't give her all that power.' That helped.

"Then I thought, 'After all, Timothy, she's still seeing you. She wants you in some way. The sex is there. Maybe there's more. You're not out of it. Maybe you can still beat this guy Cosmo.' But all I really wanted was to kill him—to blast his head open with a tire iron in front of that building and then drive off."

Timothy stopped talking, but from his changing countenance I could tell that thoughts were running through his mind and I asked him what they were.

"What was I just thinking? Nothing. It's silly."

"Maybe it isn't. What?"

"Well, I could see the whole thing as a Hitchcock film in black and white. They find the guy dead and Karen is crying and I'm gone, and now they're asking everyone in the neighborhood about that strange guy in the tuxedo who used to come around. I guess Karen would tell them. She has no loyalty at all.

"Doctor, do you think she just had sex with me for the legal advice because she likes to sue everybody?" Again he shut his eyes fast. "Oh no," he answered his own question. "That's impossible. She got into it too much. But it's the same with this guy. I'm sure he promised her all that interest on her money just to sleep with her. We're in the same boat, huh?"

Status and mastery for youth—that was an old equation, I thought; at least the constants were old, though the variables were ever-changing.

I told Timothy that I really didn't know what was going on in Karen's mind. I was about to add that I was worried about his own mind.

But then he said with evident resolution, "I *know* what I'm going to do. I'm going to ask her about the whole thing. I'll confront her about Cosmo—"

"And how will you say you know about him?" I asked.

"How? I won't actually mention his name. I'll just surprise her with evidence—with inference. She won't know how I know, that's part of it. She'll tell me. Columbia University didn't choose me to be their moot court judge last year for nothing. I'm no fool. I hate people who think I am. Especially naive people—like her and Louise, they're the two most naive people I ever met. Believe me, I know how to approach her. Don't worry, she'll tell me."

Before leaving, he addressed me as if I had deliberately misled him. "I know you asked me to stop," he said. "But I figured, one more time. Well, you were wrong. I found out everything, and now she's going to hear about it."

He smiled at me like a victor instead of a loser.

Later that smile scared me. I was afraid that he might get violent toward Karen in their confrontation. Suppose she gracelessly told him that it was over. Timothy's real life without Karen would look far worse to him than it had before he had ever met her. If he did get out of control it would not be the first time that a man suddenly faced with what seemed like his own decline had gone berserk against a lover who informed him, "You were living in a dream. Face it, fellow, you've had it."

I could see my task ahead of helping a narcissist make peace with what must appear to him like the unfairness of advancing age, of decline, of human limit.

Recent writers on narcissism, such as the psychiatrists Heinz Kohut and Otto Kernberg, have given us the symptom picture as we never possessed it before: the abusiveness of others, the view of other people merely as suppliers and reflectors of the narcissist's own greatness. But the changeability of the narcissist's own mind, his readiness to reinterpret events as in his favor, this defies all plausible thinking. I was unprepared for the next two developments. First, the reconciliation.

"It's all settled. We're going to Europe for a week," Timothy said, beaming, as soon as he sat down next time.

"How did that come about?" I asked him.

"I told her point-blank that I knew there was somebody. 'If he's a rival, I must know about it,' I told her. 'Listen,' I said, 'you've always demanded that I be honest. Now it's your turn.' At first she denied it. She looked hurt. But I pressed her. I said, 'Don't kid me. You've been spending time with someone.'

"Finally, she admitted, 'Well, I have been studying with someone. I told you that.' That wasn't good enough for me. I insisted that she tell me how long she had known him. What was his name? I held my breath so that I wouldn't look tense and I asked her, 'Tell me the truth. Are you sleeping with him?' When she acted shocked, I told her that I would understand it if the answer was yes, but she had to tell me.

"She kept insisting that it was no. Finally, she broke down and told me that the man's name was Cosmo—which of course I knew, but I didn't let on. She said that she spent time with him because he was helping her with her money. I asked her, 'Is he the guy who's going to get you forty-five percent on your money.' Of course I was very skeptical. I asked her how long she had known him. She started to cry and asked me why I was questioning her like this. She said he was a financial investor. 'A financial investor!' I said. 'Has he made a lot of money for himself?' She said that he had, that he owned a lot of property in Greece.

"Then she said something that was excruciating. She said, 'He's not as old as you, but he's a man of the world.' 'How old is he?' I asked her. She didn't answer. I told her I was only worried about her, about her money. I said I wanted her to have the best because I love her. She answered, 'I know you do, Timothy, but don't worry. He's tough, he's experienced.' I asked her, 'At what?' That got her furious and she shut her mouth hard to show me she wouldn't answer any more questions.

"But I kept after her. I asked her, 'You say he once taught at Columbia?' She wouldn't answer. 'What did he teach?' I asked her. She was very defensive of him. She repeated, 'He's tough. He's in great shape.' I shouted at her, 'What has that got to do with it if you're not sleeping with him? You only said that to hurt me, didn't you?'

"Then I went over to her to try to kiss her, but she pushed me away. I started to cry and I told her I loved her. Finally she let me put my arm around her and we sat down on her couch and didn't say anything for a while. I was sobbing. I guess I interrogated her some more, I couldn't help it, and she said to me, 'It's your own fault. You had the chance. You weren't available.' 'So you did sleep with him,' I said, and she finally admitted that maybe she had."

As Timothy went on, I realized that his sobbing was pure rage and nothing more. What seemed like a sudden change of face, of tactic, really wasn't. He was using trial and error like a baby.

"I was going mad," he said. "I told her, 'I guess this is it. We won't be seeing each other anymore, ever.' Of course I was bluffing. I wanted to see how she would react. But she just sat there and it was hard to tell and I felt desperate. I felt I was losing her. We were both quiet for a long time, and then she told me a few more facts. She said she had known him for about three months, but she wouldn't say how they met—"

I wondered if it was by accident in a cab.

"Anyhow," Timothy went on, "I told her how important she was to me, that she was what I lived for. We both softened. But she accused me of hating that guy Cosmo. I do hate him, but I denied it. Doctor, I hate him because he's a phony, promising to double her money just to have sex with her. I admitted that I wasn't available enough. She let me kiss her, but I wanted more, and she stopped me. I thought, you don't stop him. Suddenly on a whim, I said to her, 'Let's go to Europe for a week. We'll have a great time.'

"To my amazement she didn't react. Louise would die with happiness if I offered her that. I was worried that if Karen didn't jump at that I really lost her. But she just said she wasn't sure I meant it. That really hurt me. I told her, of course I did, and I would make plans.

"The instant she agreed, I realized that I had put myself in a terrible spot. But later I figured that I could do it when Louise would be in Florida. If I could cut my trip to five days with Karen, it would be perfect.

"It's complicated, but I can arrange it. Karen is excited. She's never been to Europe. It will go a long way to destroy that Cosmo. All I do is dream about being with Karen again. We've been talking on the phone every day. It's really marvelous."

But I observed that Timothy looked angry and tense as he said this. The last thing he looked like was a man in love. He looked more like one of those sailors after the sinking of the *Indiana* who had been in the water for four days and was about to be rescued.

The following week Timothy spent mapping out the details of what he not so kiddingly referred to as "the perfect crime." Every feature of his trip to Europe with Karen had to be planned in detail—when he would leave and return, what he would say to Louise before, during, and after the trip, and how he could cover his tracks. The one thing he didn't consider was the advisability of going.

He had already primed Louise by saying that he might have to go to Chicago on an important business trip. "I told her it was top secret, so if she talks to people from the firm, she won't mention it and they won't know about it." It galled Timothy that he had to pay almost double to a travel agent for the exact days he needed. Louise had long planned to go to Florida for four days and Timothy decided to leave a day before she was to go.

"Of course, I'll have to tell Louise that it will be hard to reach me. She'll accept that if I call her regularly. I won't tell her where I'm staying in Chicago, so she'll assume it's at the Drake, where I always stay."

He would call Louise regularly from Paris and London—not from his hotel because Karen would overhear him and because a desk clerk might give his location away. "Thank God for the time difference," he said. "I can call from restaurants during the day and that solves both problems."

"My God, I hope nothing happens to my family while I'm gone," he suddenly exclaimed.

I wondered if guilt over what he was about to do had prompted this fear, but he clarified, "Because then Louise would keep calling me and asking questions. The jig would be up."

A moment later he called it "a calculated risk."

When I asked him if he was looking forward to the trip, he began to say yes, that he couldn't wait for all that sex. However, he involuntarily glanced around the room like the hunted animal he was to be. He foresaw that he would be under continual pressure to conceal his tracks, but he had to do it for Karen.

Clearly Timothy was not a profound student of how he felt about anything. On the way out he asked me if he was really in love with Karen, and I commented that it was too big a question for us to answer at the door. Apropos of nothing that I could identify, he said nervously, "Doctor, I'm glad you're in my corner."

Later it struck me how incredibly alone he was, but of course his own secrecy and his subterfuge were responsible.

Timothy's inability to love anyone condemned him to his isolation, for it is loving—and not simply being loved—that joins us to others. He had no real commitment to anyone. Before us in therapy, if we could get past his Karen obsession, lay the prospect of an in-depth investigation of his terrible solitariness.

He had his travel agent bill the tickets to another name and paid cash for them. Of course he and Karen would have to produce passports and Timothy would need to declare his identity in hotels. He would still be easily traceable if anyone cared enough to try. It struck me that Timothy liked subterfuge for its own sake. Creating complications was a form of grandiosity, implying as it did that anyone would consider him worth the pain of pursuit like an international spy. In a curious sense, Louise must have disappointed his narcissism by her absolute trust. But then Timothy had a way of construing accessibility and trust as deficits while regarding loftiness in a woman as the supreme challenge.

With the great vacation still three weeks away, Timothy boasted to me that it would be an experience that Karen would never forget. The package included theater tickets for two nights in London and a three-star restaurant in Paris. How could she think about Cosmo after that? I could see that competition still riled him. He went up and saw Karen once more. "The sex was great. She kicked a table over," he bragged.

The following weekend his sister came in from California with her husband and two kids. They were to stay for only the weekend and Louise begged Timothy not to rush away. It was hard to tell which rankled him more, being deprived of his night with Karen or being unable to spy on her. He felt riddled by jealousy.

On the phone Karen seemed preoccupied and insufficiently apprecia-tive. Timothy was disappointed that she didn't sound as excited about the trip as he wanted her to. He worried that she was concerned about losing Cosmo or about explaining her absence.

Then Karen called him at the office near tears and said she had something very important to say to him, could he go up there that night. She wouldn't tell him what it was. Timothy told me that he planned to rush up there right after dinner. He felt furious, anticipating that she might cancel the trip. "What a terrible thing to do to me that would be," he said. It was hard to calm him down.

Timothy called me the next morning and said joyously, "It's over. The relationship is over."

"She reneged on the trip?" I guessed out loud.

"Not at all. I did. Doctor, you won't believe the story," he said exultantly. "It all came out."

Someone must have knocked on Timothy's office door, because I could hear him say, "This will take just a few minutes."

Then he whispered to me, "All the guy wanted was her money. Cosmo, I mean."

I told him that I didn't understand.

"He talked her into giving him twenty thousand to invest. And he apparently ran off with it." Timothy said this with unconcealed delight. "When I got there last night she was hysterical.

"She showed me a postcard from Cosmo. It was from Greece. I thought it was so funny, I read it about six times. I remember every word of it. 'Dear Karen,' it said. 'You won't be hearing from me any more. I'm spending the money wisely. On myself. I will remember you until it's gone. You really were very sweet.'

"Can you believe it? She wanted me to take her case, to be her knight in shining armor. She actually wanted me to pursue the guy in the Greek courts."

By then the person at Timothy's door seemed insistent and Timothy had to hang up. He said he'd tell me the rest when he came in later on.

★ ★ ★

Karen had spent the whole previous day, Timothy told me when he arrived, lying on her couch, sobbing and furious over the theft and the disaffection of Cosmo. "Maybe she was like that for two or three days, for all I know," Timothy remarked unsympathetically. The month before, when Karen had confessed to knowing Cosmo, she hadn't gone so far as to admit that she had actually put cash into his hand, but she had. After he got the cash, Cosmo had apparently seen Karen only one more time, and that in an attempt to get more. He had promised her a higher yield for more capital, but some remnant of discretion had kept Karen from parting with her last five thousand dollars.

"It was all that money she'd acquired by suing people," Timothy stated. Of course, Timothy felt justifiably outraged because she hadn't heeded him, and even more so because she hadn't given him the whole picture. Finally forlorn, she had gone to Timothy for vindication—for revenge. "Her whole body was limp. She wasn't the same person," Timothy said.

"Oh, by the way," he added with a twinkle in his eye, as if I were enjoying the outcome as much as he was. "Those two stars were Cosmos's trademark, his signature, you might say. I saw that his postcard from Greece wasn't signed and I asked her about it. She pointed to the asterisks and said, 'That's the way he signs his name. People know the stars are for the cosmos.'

"I asked Karen, 'Is that the way he signed his IOU?' She said no, and she showed it to me. Just a brief note, and it had the signature of Constantine something, it was illegible, and then the two stars underneath. To make it authentic," Timothy said, and winked at me.

He laughed. "From that moment on, I had nothing but contempt for her. I guess I always did—all that suing and opportunism. I wasn't even furious at Karen for lying to me about her real dealings with Cosmo. She told me that all of this happened a week ago. She said she'd tried to find Cosmo in the Bronx at some address he'd given her, but whoever was there had no information about him at all. I guess that since then she's been hoping to hear from him. She really is a fool."

I was starting to get it. Cosmo's violation of Karen was a pure enactment of the rage that Timothy himself had been feeling toward her but had been unable to express. In a sense, his was a rage toward all women. To

Timothy, women were a source of constant demands, and he saw no alternative but to comply, no matter how miserable he felt. Cosmo's destruction of Karen was Timothy's triumph. In Timothy's eyes, Cosmo had disqualified her as the messenger of any valid truth, and so the sharp rejection that Timothy had felt at Karen's hands was now rendered null and void. In consequence, Timothy's own status to himself had risen.

I had no doubt that Timothy was one of those men who secretly savored news reports of violent rapes, even as he deplored them in conversation. In Timothy's view, Cosmo had acted for him, for all men, against women, whom he saw as controlling. After Karen's fall, Timothy had instantly lined up with his young rival, in his own mind. As a result of Cosmo's violence toward Karen, Timothy himself finally felt expressed, delivered, and liberated from her.

While I was thinking about this and noting Timothy's adolescent glee, he remarked that Karen had pleadingly offered him half of whatever he could recover if he pursued Cosmo over there. Timothy had delightedly replied that he had no authority in the Athenian courts.

" 'I know,' " he said she had begged. " 'But can't you persuade some judge over there to give me a break?' " To which Timothy responded quite righteously, " 'Oh no, I must be ethical at all times. That wouldn't look good. You know, I have to be very careful. My God, if they ever found out that I was approaching some judge for you I could be disbarred.' " He had prolonged the conversation, relishing his newly resumed role as honest family man, and repeatedly contrasting his life to hers, which he implied was sordid and unredeemed.

Finally he had told her pedantically. " 'Actually, I must admit that all I know about those Greek law courts is that Athens had an influence on Roman law, which gave rise to our law. Just read Blackstone.' " He delighted in his sarcasm, as if saying by innuendo, "You should have trusted me. You should have thought about all this beforehand."

Of course Karen didn't hear him or understand any of this. But that didn't matter to Timothy. He didn't expect her to follow him and he didn't care. He was too busy savoring every minute of his victory as that of males in general over the adversary sex.

My mind evoked images of little boys pulling the wings off flies, and of a crowd at Madison Square Garden applauding joyously when an out-of-town basketball star broke his ankle near the end of a playoff game and was carried off the court.

I also remembered debates about the famous Profumo scandal in London, in which a few prostitutes became suddenly world famous and were ruined. There were several suicides. It was maintained that if some of their influential customers had said anything on their behalf, the women would not have suffered as they had. But the counterargument ran that their customers had paid for their anonymity and for the avoidance of risk and so had no obligation to the women they had made love to. Of course, Karen was no prostitute and there was real complexity in this relationship. But what struck me was the incredible rapidity with which Timothy became able to dissociate himself from someone who days before had meant the world to him.

I was hardly surprised when Timothy reported next saying to Karen that he didn't think Europe was a good idea under the circumstances and canceled the trip on the spot.

"I can't tell you how relieved I feel, not having to go," he said to me. "What would we say to each other for five days anyhow? And besides, the risk was tremendous. Every time I went up to that neighborhood I was taking my life in my hands, or at the very least I was risking being caught by someone or being recognized by someone in that neighborhood."

"You mean you're not going to see her anymore?" I asked, still digesting the outcome.

"No. Absolutely not."

I realized that Timothy was utterly unconflicted about this decision. He had not the slightest impulse ever to see Karen again. She had lost all allure, and the rage toward her which he so evidently had been suppressing, his contempt, was now in the foreground, governing his outlook and all of his intentions.

"You were right," he said to me. "The whole thing was preposterous."

"Who on earth would recognize you up there?" I asked, still stuck on a detail because the whole was more than I could yet absorb.

"Oh, a delivery boy. Or one of those Spanish messengers our office uses routinely. Or nearly anyone," he explained, with pseudoprecision. "Felix was right, that this was a good joke but nothing more and that I have a wonderful family I'm neglecting."

Felix, too, I realized more sharply than I had, was a cynical, sexist man, who had delighted in this war and what it represented.

"I told her we'd take a break and that if I felt like it I would call her," Timothy said. "It's definitely the thing to do."

"How did she react?"

"She looked upset, but she'll live with it. We met by coincidence, so she'll just have to imagine that I was never there. Believe me, the whole thing was preposterous. But you always knew that. The money she lost is money she didn't deserve, so it's not a real loss, I guess," he said, and pulled out a cigar.

When I darted a glance at him he recalled that he wasn't to smoke in my office and put it away.

"Oh, Doctor, I'm going to use those tickets. I transferred the date, which they did quite readily when I informed them that I was a senior partner in a big firm. I'm going to take Louise to London and Paris for five days. She was overjoyed when I told her."

Timothy did not even bring Karen up as a topic the next time; he spontaneously extolled his wife as "very extraordinary in her own way." Each time I mentioned Karen he took it as an intrusion. I asked him how come he had gone from such preoccupation with her to utter indifference. "Oh, that's over," he said, disinterested even in my question.

To Timothy it was as if the whole episode, which had lasted about a year and a half, the passion, the jealousy, the incredible risk of life and reputation, the folly of the tuxedo, the obsessional thoughts, had burst like a bubble.

In retrospect, it was as if the whole interlude were a dream or possibly a play that had just ended and now, with the rest of the audience, he was marching out of the theater. It was all gone in the wink of a moment. Such is the nature of the narcissistic compulsion. An utter stranger, Cosmo, had shorn Karen of her power over him, and Timothy, as if liberated under some statute that applied to all men, was freed of his compulsion to possess her.

I exhorted him several times to talk about Karen, the topic that he formerly could not put aside for a moment. But I could not get him to consider why he had been so obsessed with her. He seemed loath even to remember that she had once mattered so much to him. The most he would do when I brought her up was to list the benefits of having put her permanently out of his mind.

"She obviously wasn't good for me."

"I'll never have to wear a tux up there any more, that's for sure."

"Felix predicts that those characters on the street will talk about me for a long time." Timothy smiled.

I was hardly surprised when he thanked me courteously for my help and said he was cured. Even before he actually stated that he would not be coming back, I surmised that he had reached that decision. I, too, was part of a dream from which he had awakened, not a romantic one to him now, but a sordid one. Besides, he associated me with himself at his worst and he needed to forget me.

Of course I had no choice but to accept his decision. Perhaps in an attempt to assure me that he was truly cured, he told me that he would never again have an affair. At the door he said, "I really don't need one." His last words were some drivel about my being a very good man.

Although I still knew remarkably little about him considering how many hours he had spent in my office, it was obvious to me that Timothy's real problem had nothing to do with Karen personally, and indeed had nothing to do with romance or having affairs. He had suffered from a profound psychological imbalance for a long time, and finally chose someone to represent his struggle for self-esteem.

It made no real difference who the woman was personally—Timothy merely used her as an object. What he sought from Karen was a sense of himself as youthful and desirable, but in his heart Timothy was neither. Timothy felt elderly and lost, and probably always had, even when in his twenties he had married Louise. Who Louise was personally had even then mattered to Timothy far less than the fact that he was stealing a woman away from another man—for him that was the real proof of his virility.

I suspected that over the years Timothy had developed little real relationship with Louise, and naturally whatever glow he experienced after his success in capturing her soon wore off. He had gone back to feeling elderly and lost, and thus perhaps for years the stage had been set for serious trouble. The form that trouble finally took was Timothy's entering his obsessional state.

In this respect, Timothy's psychological state was like the physical condition of someone who in later life eventually succumbs to what medicine has recently identified as a "slow virus." This kind of virus is characterized by a long incubation period, during which the disease takes a protracted course, finally manifesting itself in symptoms. For instance, many specialists think that rheumatoid arthritis and multiple sclerosis undergo this process. Prolonged skirmishes between the virus and the immune system, which take place unseen, ultimately result in a decisive outcome one way or the other. The challenge for researchers is to detect the presence of slow viruses before they do their mischief.

By analogy, we might argue that Timothy was rife for an obsessional "romance." His emotional isolation (he took little delight in the people close to him), his contempt for women, and a growing feeling of personal unfulfillment had rendered him vulnerable.

Naturally, not everyone with Timothy's symptoms fixates on a potential lover and tries to redeem himself. A more usual outgrowth of such states is growing depression—at worst the condition described as *involutional melancholia,* in which the person feels that his life of hard work and of striving has all been pointless. "I have heard the mermaids singing, each to each," wrote the poet T.S. Eliot about J. Alfred Prufrock, who had endured such a state. "I do not think that they will sing to me."

Timothy of course had had his share of depression as well—of disappointment in himself and in the world. Like a certain fraction of people on the brink of involutional melancholia, he sought to escape by a last-ditch effort to create a brave new world. For him Karen was the mermaid who might yet sing to him and redeem him.

Paradoxically, the more he fixated on Karen the sorrier the rest of his life looked to him. Even as he pursued her, sensing his own dependency upon her, Timothy hated himself. And when Karen finally fell from grace he directed the full brunt of his own self-loathing toward her. No woman had the power to convince Timothy that he was truly a lover because he did not feel like one.

Perhaps the key marker to defeat in some form that lay in store for Timothy, however, was his idealization of people whom he could not touch and his inability to treasure anyone who was vulnerable and available to him. Those who cannot enjoy what they possess live a paradox of frustration and a sense of defeat. Just as Louise had come plummeting down when she gave up her rival and married Timothy, so would any woman who approached him with love or even genuineness.

Would Timothy succumb again, conceivably staking his marriage, his reputation, or even his physical safety on another obsessional relationship? It is tempting to imagine that he learned from his "near-death" experience and would not so extend himself again. But people who succumb to compulsions and escape for a time without truly discovering what the vectors were are very likely to fall prey again. The old need arises, more predictably if anything, as if the indulgence that cut grooves in the psyche disposes them to repeat the behavior. They may avoid exact repetition, as if learning from experience, but the new activity is only superficially different.

I thought about Timothy sometimes after that, especially one night the next winter when I could see my breath in the air, bouncing off the granite stones. I imagined him lurking in his car in front of some other woman's building, or even standing at her door. Or, I then thought, perhaps the scenario was enough different this time for him to imagine that he was not engaging in the same irrational behavior. Conceivably, this new woman had money and status. No matter. The dynamics would be the same. If Timothy were in hot pursuit once again, he would only be using the woman to prove to himself his own worth. She herself would be incidental. The instant she gave herself to him she would lose all value to him anyhow. For her sake, I hoped she wouldn't.

Epilogue: Defeating the Invisible Masters

Compulsions are always decoy acts—their intention is to hoodwink the self into thinking that an urgent problem is being dealt with. Proving his worth to a young woman was Timothy's repeated attempt to annihilate a gnawing sense that he was old and decaying. Martin's penury and sourness were attempts to placate his loneliness—to persuade himself that his mother had never really died and would return to him.

But compulsions, being modes of self-delusion, never really solve anything; they are like dreams of having solved a problem that the person refuses to look at in daily life. This is why, after experiencing temporary relief, the person soon feels the urge again. Every succumbing to a compulsion is like paying an extortionist, who will return.

Compulsions are invisible masters who inflict a variety of harms. Many drain away physical health and reputation; they steal away precious time. All are demoralizing. There are people who go a lifetime without letting anyone else discover their compulsive rituals. But inevitably these people see themselves engaging in those rituals, spilling life into pointless repetition.

And compulsions are more than mere symptoms of an underlying problem, as psychoanalysis originally thought. Consistent with what self-help organizations have been arguing about alcoholism and gambling, for instance, every compulsive activity is progressive. Engaging in the behavior worsens the underlying problem and reinfects the person with an even greater need to carry out the activity.

Compulsions must be thought of as more than activities—they come linked with their own special memories. While engaging in the behavior, the person is experiencing himself and his life as they were at the instant the behavior was adopted.

Martin had retained an unconscious cameo image of his mother returning—an image that maintained his compulsive sourness toward all would-be replacements.

Marianne's unconscious memory of herself as a needy child and her father's rejecting her—this "photo" drove her to keep men away emotionally. It made her an isolationist. And her isolationism kept that picture alive and vivid.

Every single compulsion comes equipped with an unconscious idea—and a memory. A woman still talks much too fast. As a child she had to. In the living room with her parents she would sometimes think, "They believe I'm not too bright. And I'm not. If I talk slow, they'll consider me a bore and won't like me."

The idea behind the compulsion, the memory, is still there right with the activity. But the only way to bring it back to consciousness is to stop the activity temporarily. As the urge intensifies, the idea will come to the person's mind in fragments. Usually it will appear in present-tense terms, not past. "I'm talking too slow. My husband must think I'm a moron. He's right."

Resisting the compulsive urge will bring back that early experience nearly every time. When Martin first trusted women, he was hit hard by the very feelings he had had when his mother died. When Marianne first opened herself emotionally to men, she expected the brutal betrayal that her father had shown her in her childhood.

Those thoughts that come when we first combat any compulsion give us glimpses into our own past—into the history and meaning of the compulsive behavior. It's as if we got into a car and drove back to our old neighborhood, made ourselves small, and resurrected our parents or others as we saw them back then. It's as if we reconstructed the predicament we were in long ago when we began the compulsive pattern. We can unseal the envelope and break the code—if only we stop the behavior for a while and ask the right questions.

This insight into the real meaning of our compulsive behavior is invaluable, though in itself it is not curative. We must then address the real problem, alone or, if necessary, with help.

But to recognize our fear is to see that it is out-of-date and unwarranted. And seeing this helps us stay on course. We no longer project the past into the present. With clear sight we can take further measures—real measures and not merely symbolic ones. We can weaken our invisible masters and ultimately starve them out of existence—liberate ourselves from the compulsion.

The study of compulsions proves that the psyche is not frozen, it does not harden as psychoanalysis originally believed. Rather a person, having "solved" problems early in life, repeats those same solutions. Compulsions are merely solutions once arrived at, perhaps quite reasonably. But they are ineffective activities now—and they have become self-destructive.

In respect to compulsions, we are all like those Japanese soldiers who, years after the war, still hid themselves in caves and crept out at night for food. If word that the war was over reached them, they could not believe it. Perhaps their fear was too great. To them, the risk of being killed if they emerged outweighed the possible benefits. Only by taking the big chance, by emerging sooner or later and trusting themselves to modern conditions, could they undeceive themselves. Little by little, they adjusted themselves to the daylight and to the safety that was there for them.

★ ★ ★

Beyond this truth about compulsion lies a broader truth.

Our actions—compulsions, habits, indeed our every choice—exert an effect on our subsequent outlook. Our past is critical because it engendered beliefs and patterns of behavior. But we are reproducing ourselves, sustaining our beliefs by acting on them, sending a steady flow of unconscious messages to our own brain. These messages convey full emotional pictures of ourselves and of others. If we give no thought at all to what we do—that is, run on automatic—we reproduce all the expectations and beliefs of our past lives. But we can change these expectations—the levers are in our own hands.